Reading the Novel in English 1

READING THE NOVEL

General Editor: **Daniel R. Schwarz**

The aim of this series is to provide practical introductions to reading the novel in both the British and Irish, and the American traditions.

Reading the Novel in English 1950–2000

Brian W. Shaffer

Blackwell
Publishing

© 2006 by Brian W. Shaffer

BLACKWELL PUBLISHING
350 Main Street, Malden, MA 02148-5020, USA
9600 Garsington Road, Oxford OX4 2DQ, UK
550 Swanston Street, Carlton, Victoria 3053, Australia

First published 2006 by Blackwell Publishing Ltd

1 2006

Library of Congress Cataloging-in-Publication Data

Shaffer, Brian W., 1960–
Reading the novel in English, 1950–2000 / Brian W. Shaffer.
p. cm.—(Reading the novel)
Includes bibliographical references and index.
ISBN-13: 978-1-4051-0113-4 (hardback : alk. paper)
ISBN-10: 1-4051-0113-X (hardback : alk. paper)
ISBN-13: 978-1-4051-0114-1 (pbk. : alk. paper)
ISBN-10: 1-4051-0114-8 (pbk. : alk. paper)
1. English fiction—20th century—History and criticism.   2. English fiction—Irish
authors—History and criticism.   3. Commonwealth fiction (English)—History
and criticism.   4. English-speaking countries—Intellectual life—20th
century. I. Title. II. Series.
PR881.S53 2006
823′.91409—dc22
2005006122A

A catalogue record for this title is available from the British Library.

Set in 10/12.5pt Minion
by Graphicraft Limited, Hong Kong
Printed and bound in the United Kingdom
by TJ International Ltd, Padstow, Cornwall

The publisher's policy is to use permanent paper from mills that operate a sustainable
forestry policy, and which has been manufactured from pulp processed using acid-free and
elementary chlorine-free practices. Furthermore, the publisher ensures that the text paper
and cover board used have met acceptable environmental accreditation standards.

For further information on
Blackwell Publishing, visit our website:
www.blackwellpublishing.com

To Rachel,
Hannah, and Ruthie

Contents

Acknowledgments

I wish to thank in particular two individuals who read early drafts of this study and offered invaluable feedback: my colleague and friend Jennifer Brady and my mother Dorothy Shaffer. While all of the volume's remaining flaws are of course my own, I cannot overestimate the positive impact each had on the finished product. Thanks are also due to my colleagues – in particular Michael Leslie, Cynthia Marshall, Anne Reef, and Lynn Zastoupil – and former students – Anna Teekell and the students in my spring 2003 Contemporary Anglophone Novel class – for their helpful feedback on various portions of this work. The volume benefited from the support I have received as holder of the Charles R. Glover Chair of English Studies since 2001. Dean Robert R. Llewellyn also deserves my sincerest thanks for his support of this work and faculty research and creative activity at Rhodes. Without the help of Mimi Atkinson and Margaret Handwerker of the Rhodes English Department and Academic Affairs Office, respectively, and Annette Cates and Kenan Padgett of the Rhodes Library, this volume could not have come to fruition. I would also like to thank several editors at Blackwell – Emma Bennett, Mary Dortch, Karen Wilson, and Astrid Wind – for their expert advice and tireless efforts on behalf of this volume; and Professor Daniel R. Schwarz of Cornell University for approaching me to contribute a volume to the present series. As always, I am deeply grateful to my wife Rachel and daughters Hannah and Ruth for making everything possible and worthwhile.

An earlier version of portions of Chapter 9 first appeared in Brian W. Shaffer, *Understanding Kazuo Ishiguro* (University of South Carolina Press, 1998).

Preface

Arthur Marwick opens his book *British Society since 1945* by observing: "Nobody has ever said precisely how many ways there are of skinning a cat. Probably there are about the same number of ways of writing a Social History of Britain since 1945."[1] The same might be said of the subject of the present volume, the novel in English, exclusive of the US novel, between the end of World War II and the turn of the millennium. This vast, rich, spectacularly heterogeneous field of the British and postcolonial Anglophone novel is only now, at the beginning of the twenty-first century, coming into focus. John Brannigan cautions in his book on literature in England between 1945 and 2000 that "the period since 1945 is too recent to see anything but its diversity and complexity, and is too diverse and complex to enable us to construct one coherent, meaningful narrative of its literary, cultural or historical events."[2] While the present volume is not meant to be a comprehensive literary history of the field or an exhaustive survey of the novel in English outside the US over the last half of the twentieth century, *Reading the Novel in English 1950–2000* seeks to map out and explore the variety and breadth of novel writing in English within the relevant period and geographical boundaries.

More significantly, the volume aims to be a practical introduction to the contemporary English-language novel, with an emphasis on important contexts and concepts for interpreting and understanding – for "reading" – this field. In an introductory chapter I address three important contexts within which the novel of the period takes shape: as a response to literary modernism and, later, "antimodernism"; as a response to the "crisis of civilization," in particular the rise of European fascism, the Second World War, and Hitler's death camps; and as a response to the end of the British Empire, the rise of formerly subject nations, and the phenomenon of reverse patterns of migration, with peoples from formerly colonized lands moving to the large, industrialized cities of England, Scotland, Wales, and Northern Ireland. Although few novels in the field respond to all three phenomena, all of them respond to at least one them.

The chapter closes with a discussion of the novel as a genre that is open-ended, socially engaged, and exploratory, one that challenges and stretches the prevailing canons of knowledge, perception, and literary representation in its bid to picture and probe an evolving contemporary reality. Along the way this introductory chapter also addresses important rubrics and categories – including the "modernist," "postmodernist," "postcolonial," and "black British" novel – under which the fictional texts of the period are commonly grouped and assessed. Each of these terms is a highly contested locus of meaning, a protean concept that shifts in sense over the course of the period under investigation. My goal here is to provide readers with a useful set of rubrics and terms with which to approach the contemporary British and postcolonial Anglophone novel.

This introductory chapter is followed by ten more focused chapters, each of which treats a critically acclaimed and influential, widely read and taught novel from the period. In each case I provide key contexts for interpreting, followed by a detailed reading of, the novel in question. There can be no question of selecting for more thoroughgoing analysis the ten "right" novels from among the hundreds of obvious, and thousands of possible, choices. What can be affirmed is that the ten works selected for fuller treatment here comprise a representative sampling of significant novels from the field, from a variety of decades, from the 1950s to the 1990s, and geographical locales: Canada, England, Ireland, Nigeria, Scotland, South Africa, and the West Indies.

Chapter 1

Introduction: Contexts and Concepts for Reading the Novel in English 1950–2000

The Modernist British Novel and After: "Antimodernist" and "Postmodernist" Reactions

Much of the debate about appropriate form in the English novel since the [Second World] war has been concerned with the acceptance or rejection of appropriate or inappropriate models.

A. S. Byatt, "People in paper houses"[1]

The response to literary modernism in the British novel of 1950–2000 took two divergent paths, resulting in the adoption of two conflicting novelistic "models": antimodernist realism and postmodernist experimentation. Literary modernism – a transatlantic cultural phenomenon that influenced the direction of the twentieth-century novel and that engaged with myriad extra-literary developments of its day – is explored in another volume in this series. It nevertheless deserves brief treatment here as a key context within which the post-1950 British novel took shape and to which it responded. Readily recognizable features of high-modernist novels, which predominated between the turn of the century (Conrad's 1900 *Lord Jim*) and the late 1940s (Malcolm Lowry's 1947 *Under the Volcano*), are easily catalogued: radical experiments with point of view and with the representation of time and space; the shattering of the illusion of a unified, omniscient narrator; linguistic pyrotechnics, textual self-referentiality, and literary allusiveness; and narrative fragmentation, replete with disorienting stream-of-consciousness and interior monologue

1

narration. It remains to explain why such features evolved, if only to provide the context within which the post-1950 novel came about.

The enthusiasm with which literary modernists engaged in such radical narrative experimentation is perhaps best expressed in the American poet Ezra Pound's famous charge to his literary contemporaries to "Make It New." Pound here meant more than that his fellow artists should break with tradition. After all, we may presume that all writers in all periods seek to be innovative in some way, even if it is only to tell a familiar story in a new or modern style. By "Make It New," as Malcolm Bradbury argues, Pound meant that "the modern arts have a special obligation, an advanced or *avant-garde* duty, to go ahead of their own age and transform it" – to break "free from the frozen structures of the past."[2] Pound also expressed this sentiment in a poem, "Commission," in which he exhorts his readers to "Be against all sorts of mortmain."[3] By this, Pound meant that we should wage war against the dead hand ("mort/main," in his French neologism) of the past. In this same vein, the Norwegian playwright Henrik Ibsen, who would come to exert a great influence on the young James Joyce and other literary modernists, remarked that "The great task of our time is to blow up all existing institutions – to destroy."[4] As the enlightened millionaire in George Bernard Shaw's 1905 play *Major Barbara* laments, the problem with the world today is that while "It scraps its obsolete steam engines and dynamos," it "won't scrap its old prejudices and its old moralities and its old religions and its old political constitutions."[5] Collectively, these passages suggest that George Orwell was misguided to associate literary modernism with "art-for-art's saking," with the "worship of the meaningless," with the mere "manipulation of words" for the sake of an art divorced from "the urgent [political] problems of the moment."[6] Orwell, who penned this accusation in 1940, was probably thinking of James Joyce, who a year earlier published *Finnegans Wake*, a supremely modernist work that parades, indeed fetishizes, its arcane linguistic and narrative dimensions.

Joyce's *sui generis* 1939 text notwithstanding, literary modernism was less about the joys of experimentation and iconoclasm for its own sake – what Orwell calls the "frivolous notion that art is merely technique"[7] – than it was about overthrowing literary forms and structures, and by extension social forms and structures, that were felt to be repressive, outmoded, or constraining. Novelty and innovation per se were less important than making the new literature faithful to contemporary social, technological, psychological, epistemological, and aesthetic realities. Put another way, modernists such as Conrad, Eliot, Joyce, Lawrence, Woolf, and Yeats were less interested in "art for art's sake" than they were in creating works of literature that comported with their new understanding of the world around them. As Eliot argued in 1921, modern poets (and we might add modern novelists) "must be *difficult*" because "Our civilization comprehends great variety and complexity, and this variety and complexity, playing upon a refined sensibility [that of the poet], must produce various and complex results."[8] In other words, modernist literature was not meant to be an autotelic or narcissistic *retreat* from modern life so much as an attempt to face and depict it unflinchingly.

Perhaps the most important influences on modernism in the novel, influences to which the novels of our period continued to respond, were a series of revolutionary ideas in European thought that contributed to a *Zeitgeist* within which these novelists wrote. The principal idea was a crisis lamented by Matthew Arnold in his mid-nineteenth-century poem, "Dover Beach": the retreat of the "Sea of Faith" and the seeming disappearance of God,[9] an anxiety that emerges full-blown in W. B. Yeats's celebrated 1919 poem "The Second Coming," with its theologically resonant title (and in which "Things fall apart; the center cannot hold;/ Mere anarchy is loosed upon the world").[10] Three seminal modern intellectuals – Karl Marx, Friedrich Nietzsche, and Sigmund Freud – all speculated that humans created God out of their need for a protecting father and to explain an otherwise inexplicable, threatening, chaotic world. Marx saw religion as the "sigh of the oppressed," the "*opium* of the people,"[11] as a means for the "haves" of society to keep the "have nots" mystified and downtrodden; Nietzsche famously asserted that "God is dead. God remains dead. And we have killed him";[12] and Freud likened our devotion to the "fairy-tale of religion" to a "childhood neurosis," and, following Marx, likened "the effects of religious consolations" to a "narcotic."[13] While some found the prospect of a God-less universe liberating, others found the absence of transcendental meaning and teleological human history to be frightening prospects. Unsurprisingly, this shift in thinking had important implications for the ways in which novels were written, as many novelists now took it for granted that the traditional view of the world – one subject to a single overarching interpretation, corresponding to God's intention – was obsolete. Objectivity was an illusion; subjectivity reigned. Many legitimate truths and perspectives replaced the notion of a single "Truth"; "Reality" was supplanted by a series of competing *realities*. In short, how one saw things now was determined by one's unique perspective, put in dialogue with other individuals and their unique perspectives. This notion informed many novels of the modernist period – for example, Conrad's *Lord Jim*, Joyce's *Ulysses*, Woolf's *Mrs Dalloway*, Faulkner's *As I Lay Dying*, and Lowry's *Under the Volcano* – in which multiple narrators and shifting perspectives force readers to reconstruct events by negotiating among the various possible ways in which those events can be understood. Put another way, the multiple points of view in each of these modernist texts are offered not to impede our grasp of the novel's meaning but are the very point of it. As Orwell argues, in seeming contradiction of his indictment of the modernists for their escapist avoidance of politics,

> *Ulysses* could not have been written by someone who was merely dabbling with word-patterns; it is the product of a special vision of life, the vision of a Catholic who has lost his faith. What Joyce is saying is "Here is life without God. Just look at it!" and his technical innovations, important though they are, are there primarily to serve this purpose.[14]

Another development that influenced the modernist novel – and that which followed – was the late-nineteenth-century emergence of the discipline of psychology, which further eroded traditional faith in objective norms of perception, knowledge, and certainty. The year 1890 marked the appearance of William James's *Principles of Psychology*, a work that reoriented our take on "reality." Rather than being something objectively given, reality was to be understood as something subjectively perceived through the "stream" of human consciousness. If James's terrain was consciousness and perception, Freud's, more radically, was the *unconscious*, which he defined as that area of the mind that remains inaccessible to conscious scrutiny, the refuge of repressed wishes too dangerous, subversive, and conflicted for us to acknowledge consciously.[15] Freud's impact upon the modernist novel was considerable and obvious. One critic even went as far as to attribute the "shift in the basis of characterization in fiction after about 1900" largely to the "revolutionary impact of Freudian concepts of the unconscious."[16]

It is against this background that the British novel of our period took shape. In the 1950s and early 1960s, the novel tended to reject literary modernist innovations, reacting *against* the modernist novel's conspicuous complexity. Kingsley Amis, Iris Murdoch, Angus Wilson, and many others countered in their novels with an antimodernist, anti-*avant-garde* "neorealism." As Bradbury characterizes the mood between 1945 and 1960,

> Modernism was over, even tainted; the deaths of Joyce, Woolf, Yeats and Freud had reinforced the feeling. In critical circles, it was already being historicized, defined, monumentalized, given its name and structure; it was no longer *avant* . . . but *arrière*.[17]

While realistic novels continued to be written over the next few decades and prevail today (consider, for example, the works of Anita Brookner, Margaret Drabble, John McGahern, Iris Murdoch, and Muriel Spark), a second and divergent response to modernism and its antimodernist wake in the

British novel – the "postmodernist" novel – began to evolve in the early 1970s. Indeed, as divergent in their formal, linguistic, and thematic dimensions as the novels of Martin Amis, Julian Barnes, A. S. Byatt, Angela Carter, John Fowles, Ian McEwan, Salman Rushdie, and Graham Swift may be, it is reasonable to group their fictions under the banner of the postmodern novel. This novel rejects the antimodernist backlash; indeed, it internalizes many of the attitudes and perspectives of modernism, yet also takes further and revises a number of modernism's tenets. As Gerald Graff argues, "postmodernism should be seen not as breaking with romantic and modernist assumptions but rather as a logical culmination of the premises of these earlier movements."[18] The American novelist John Barth puts the relationship between modernism and postmodernism similarly: the "ideal postmodernist author" has "the first half of the [twentieth] century under his belt [even if] not on his back."[19]

It is thus fair to say that the response to literary modernism in the British novel of 1950–2000 took two divergent paths. The first reaction was blazed in England in the 1950s by the prickly, antimodernist backlash of traditionalist novelists such as Kingsley Amis, John Braine, Iris Murdoch (early in her career), C. P. Snow, John Wain, and Angus Wilson, who rejected both the narrative and stylistic experiments associated with Joyce and the refined literary aesthetics associated with Virginia Woolf, either on the grounds that these were arcane and mystifying or that they had been worthwhile experiments in a now-exhausted vein. For example, John Wain, writing in 1963, insisted that the "experimental" novel "died with Joyce." Since *Ulysses*, Wain argued, "there has been very little experimental-writing that strikes one as serious, or motivated by anything more than faddishness or the irritable search for new gimmicks."[20] According to C. P. Snow, "Joyce's way" was "at best a cul-de-sac,"[21] and the literary "doctrine" of Virginia Woolf and others culminated in the novel becoming "totally meaningless in a very short time."[22]

If there was an antimodernist *movement* in the English novel of the time it was to be found in the so called "Angry Young Men" – comprised of Wain, Braine, Kingsley Amis, and others – whom Amis deemed "reactionaries rather than rebels" because they sought a return "to the pre-Joycean tradition"[23] of broadly accessible and relevant literary works. Amis was at his most strident and outspoken in this regard in a 1958 piece in the *Spectator*. There, he famously declared:

> The idea about experiment being the life-blood of the English novel is one that dies hard. "Experiment," in this context, boils down pretty regularly to "obtruded oddity," whether in construction – multiple viewpoints and such – or in style . . . Shift from one scene to the next in midsentence, cut down on

However differently Amis's *Lucky Jim*, Murdoch's *Under the Net*, and Wilson's *Hemlock and After* (all from the early 1950s) respond to literary modernism, each of these works represents a desire to return the novel to an earlier, more realistic and linear model.

The antimodernist reaction to modernism in the English novel was followed by another reaction, beginning in the early 1970s. Born of what David Lodge characterized as "the pressure of skepticism on the aesthetic and epistemological premises of literary realism,"[25] the postmodern novel of the final three decades of the twentieth century continued and furthered "the modernist critique of traditional realism."[26]

Just as Amis and other traditionalists of the 1950s and 1960s registered their frustration with the modernist novel's lack of accessibility and relevance, so the early postmodernists, in an anti-antimodernist backlash, registered their frustration with the realistic, linear novel's lack of artistic courage and innovation. The English avant-garde novelist B. S. Johnson, for example, writing ten years after John Wain had said that the experimental novel died with Joyce, lamented that while Joyce was "the Einstein of the novel,"[27] very few novelists in Britain now followed his lead. For Johnson,

It is not a question of influence, of writing like Joyce. It is a matter of realizing that the novel is an evolving form, not a static one, of accepting that for practical purposes where Joyce left off should ever since have been regarded as the starting point.[28]

"Why then," Johnson demanded, "do so many novelists still write as though the revolution that was *Ulysses* had never happened?"[29] Johnson concluded by quoting the French author Nathalie Sarraute's description of literature "as a relay race, the baton of innovation passing from one generation to another," and then by accusing the "vast majority of British novelists" today with having "dropped the baton."[30] Johnson's reference to Sarraute here is telling, as many avant-garde English novelists of the 1970s gained their inspiration from French writers and intellectuals, specifically from Sarraute, Samuel Beckett (born in Ireland but living in Paris and writing in French and English), and Alain Robbe-Grillet (theorist of *le nouveau roman*) – rather than from British ones. John Fowles, for example, the author of one of the earliest important English postmodernist novels, the 1969 *French Lieutenant's Woman*, admits to finding himself "much more at home in French than in English literature."[31]

Be this "French connection" as it may, British postmodernist novels – among them Fowles's *French Lieutenant's Woman* (1969), Golding's *Darkness Visible* (1979), Gray's *Lanark* (1981), Swift's *Waterland* (1983), Barnes's *Flaubert's Parrot* (1984), Martin Amis's *Money* (1984), A. S. Byatt's *Possession* (1990), McCabe's *Butcher Boy* (1992), and Angela Carter's *Nights at the Circus* (1994) – built upon many modernist novelistic innovations. While "postmodernism" as a theoretical construct defies easy definition – Malcolm Bradbury has called the term a "moveable feast,"[32] and Hans Bertens has characterized it as "exasperating" for being "several things at once"[33] – it is clear that postmodern novels, in practice, deliberately blur categories that were formerly thought to be antithetical. That is, they blur elite and demotic narrative forms, the author and the reader, fiction and fact, and they attack realistic conventions of representation, notions of generic purity, and the feasibility of a unified subject.

In his exhaustive *The Idea of the Postmodern: A History* Hans Bertens observes that postmodernism

> has meant different things to different people at different conceptual levels, rising from humble literary-critical origins in the 1950s to a level of global conceptualization in the 1980s. The result was, and still is, a massive but also exhilarating confusion that has given important new impulses to and opened new territories for intellectual exploration. If there is a common denominator to all these postmodernisms, it is that of a crisis in representation: a deeply felt loss of faith in our ability to represent the real, in the widest sense. No matter whether they are aesthetic, epistemological, moral, or political in nature, the representations that we used to rely on can no longer be taken for granted.[34]

This "crisis" of representation – that representations create more than they reflect reality – is discernible in the work of the most important French theorizers of the postmodern, Jean-François Lyotard and Jean Baudrillard.

To sketch an immensely complex thesis, Lyotard in *The Postmodern Condition* (1979; trans. 1984) argues that the condition of postmodernity is one of "incredulity towards metanarratives":[35] toward those grand, universal, or master narratives upon which modernity stands, but which have now come to be seen as "stories that we tell ourselves to convince ourselves of their truth" rather than as empirically verifiable conceptual foundations that possess the power to "hold things together."[36] In the postmodern world, universal, overarching explanatory systems and ideologies – for example, Enlightenment scientific rationality, capitalist or Marxist economic theory, the Christian or Freudian view of the human psyche/soul – have come to be seen as narratives that lack credibility and adequacy. These all-encompassing systems have been replaced with a plurality of more credible if limited *petit recits*, discrete micronarratives of only local and particular applicability. In an equally involved argument that I will only sketch here, Baudrillard defines postmodernity as an "age of simulation" and "hyperreality," in which the "actual" and its "representation" are impossible to distinguish, and in which representations therefore can only be understood to refer to other representations and not to any underlying "reality." In his *Simulacra and Simulation* (1981; trans. 1994) Baudrillard holds that the postmodern world – unlike the modern one, which is "organized around the production and consumption of commodities" – is "organized around simulation and the play of images and signs,"[37] and in it "hyperreality," constructed in the virtual world of free-floating images and mediatized events, has become the only knowable reality. Baudrillard sees the hyperreal as providing "experiences more intense and involving than the scenes of banal everyday life,"[38] what he calls the "desert of the real."[39] Although these French theories of the postmodern had little direct influence on the British novels of the period, they nevertheless contributed to a postmodernist intellectual and artistic climate out of which the novels evolved.

In *The Postmodern Turn*, Steven Best and Douglas Kellner explore post-modernist literature within the context of this wider postmodernist climate forged by Lyotard, Baudrillard, and many others. Although Best and Kellner view postmodernism as less of an outgrowth of modernism than I do here, they nevertheless concede that "some of the stylistic techniques of postmodern literature were defining features of modernism itself," motivated by its revolt against "realism, mimesis, and linear forms of narrative."[40] That said, Best and Kellner make useful distinctions between modernist and postmodernist works of literature.

> [W]hile high modernists defended the autonomy of art and excoriated mass culture, postmodernists spurned elitism and combined "high" and "low" cultural forms in an aesthetic pluralism and populism. Against the drive toward militant innovation and originality, postmodernists embraced tradition and techniques of quotation and pastiche. While the modernist artist aspired to create monumental works and a unique style . . . postmodernists were more ironic and playful, eschewing concepts like "genius," "creativity," and even "author." While modernist art works were signification machines that produced a wealth of meanings and interpretations, postmodern art was more surface-oriented, renouncing depth and grand philosophical or moral visions.[41]

Indeed, for Best and Kellner, postmodernists "abandon the idea that any language – scientific, political, or aesthetic – has a privileged vantage point on reality; instead, they insist on the intertextual nature and social construction of all meaning."[42] The postmodernist novel's "self-reflexive and nonlinear writing" counters both "realist theories of mimesis, depth psychology and character development" and notions of "the author as a sovereign subject in full command of the process of creation."[43] Finally, "postmodern writers implode oppositions between high and low art, fantasy and reality, fiction and fact. Spurning 'originality,' postmodern writers draw on past forms, which are ironically quoted and eclectically combined."[44] As the poet and critic Andrei Codrescu puts this last point, "where the modernist Pound had commanded 'Make It New,' the postmodernist imperative is 'Get It Used'."[45]

It is also worth emphasizing that postmodernist narrative experimentation in the novel, like that of modernist experimentation before it, was undertaken *not* in the spirit of absurdist *anti*realism, as many assumed, but in the spirit of *hyper*realism, one which accounts for the new theories of perception, knowledge, and consciousness alluded to above. What Virginia Woolf argued of the modernist Joyce and other novelists of his ilk is also true of the postmodernist Fowles and other authors of his ilk: they all attempt, in their fictions,

> to come closer to life, and to preserve more sincerely and exactly what interests and moves them, even if to do so they must discard most of the conventions which are commonly observed by the [realist] novelist. Let us record the atoms as they fall upon the mind in the order in which they fall, let us trace the pattern, however disconnected and incoherent in appearance, which each sight or incident scores upon the consciousness.[46]

Woolf's point is clear: Joyce and other modernists wrote out of a sense of fidelity to things as they are subjectively and fragmentarily experienced and known rather than out of an unfeasible stance of objectivity and omniscience. As Woolf hints here, Joyce's use of interior monologue narration worked as a means of plumbing the depths and shallows of character as never before, a device allowing for the direct representation of the psyche in action. However, one important difference between the modernism of Joyce and Woolf and the postmodernism of Fowles and Swift is that, as one critic argues, whereas "the Modernist aimed at providing a valid, authentic, though strictly personal view of the world in which he lived, the Postmodernist appears to have abandoned the attempt towards a representation of the world that is justified by the convictions and sensibility"[47] of any single individual consciousness or historical account. Indeed, such observably "postmodern" novels as Fowles's *French Lieutenant's Woman*, Rushdie's *Midnight's Children*, Swift's *Waterland*, and Byatt's *Possession* deconstruct traditional notions of subjectivity and history, and problematize the distinction between fact and fiction, in ways that go beyond what Joyce and other modernists envisioned. Another clear difference is that postmodernist novels tend to be far more demotic and less elitist in orientation than their modernist forerunners. John Carey's observation that the literary intelligentsia in the years leading up to 1939 was distinctly elitist and anti-democratic – hostile to the "large reading public" that came into being after "nineteenth-century educational reforms"[48] – no longer holds sway in our period, as the postmodernist novel's abundant use of popular cultural discourse suggests. It is difficult, given the postmodern novel's demotic orientation, to imagine its practitioners defining their art in the terms hazarded by D. H. Lawrence: "[B]eing a novelist, I consider myself superior to the saint, the scientist, the philosopher, and the poet . . . The novel is the one bright book of life."[49]

It *Can* Happen Here: The British Novel as a Response to the Crisis of Civilization

As I write, highly civilized human beings are flying overhead, trying to kill me.
George Orwell, "England your England"[50]

The novel, with its emphasis on the depiction of human societies and social interaction, is an inherently dialogic, richly social literary genre, one which necessarily represents and critiques the social world of its production and initial consumption. The novel of our period is of course no exception to this rule; it too engages with the socioeconomic and political, not only with the artistic, trends of its time. Numerous cataclysmic and revolutionary events were occurring in European as well as in world politics in the years leading up to and away from 1945: the rise of European fascism in Spain, Germany, and Italy; the horrific carnage of World War II and Hitler's genocidal "Final Solution" and death camps; the dropping of two nuclear bombs in Japan; Stalinism and the purges and gulags in the Soviet Union; and the Cold War between America and Russia, which held out the continuing threat of global nuclear obliteration. As Bradbury sums up the importance of World War II as an historical watershed, "There was no doubt that the Second World War was as terrible a fracture in the twentieth-century experience as the First had been," and that "its impact on world history, human consciousness, and artistic expression was ultimately far greater than that of the conflict of just twenty-five years before."[51] In a similar vein the novelist Iris Murdoch, as late as 1961, affirmed that "We have not [yet] recovered from two wars and the experience of Hitler."[52] Given the apocalyptic intensity and global reach of the above events, and the ever-present threat of totalitarian regimes and geno-cides, it is no surprise that sociopolitical trauma would make its way, in one form or another, into the British novel of the period. Specifically, the growing realization that the barbarity of mid-twentieth-century historical events emanated from within "civilized" Europe rather than from outside it, as cap-tured in Orwell's line above, soon became an unavoidable conclusion.

In his 1967 *Language and Silence*, for example, George Steiner observed that the "political bestiality" of our age was a barbarity of our own making and that we learned that one "can read Goethe or Rilke in the evening[,] can play Bach and Schubert, and [then] go to . . . work at Auschwitz in the morning."[53] Moreover, according to Steiner, the eruption of barbarism in mid-twentieth-century Europe

> did not spring up in the Gobi Desert or the rain forests of the Amazon. It rose from within, and from the core of European civilization. The cry of the murdered sounded in earshot of the universities; the sadism went on a street away from the theaters and museums. In the later eighteenth century Voltaire had looked confidently to the end of torture; ideological massacre was to be a banished shadow. In our own day the high places of literacy, of philosophy, of artistic expression, became the setting for Belsen.[54]

This insight concerning our involvement in the darkness that descended over Europe in the twentieth century – more than depicting the battlefields of World War II – became an obsession of the British and Anglophone novel of our period, from Lowry's *Under the Volcano* (1947) and Orwell's *Nineteen Eighty-Four* (1949), to Golding's *Lord of the Flies* (1954) and *The Inheritors* (1955), Robin Jenkins's *The Cone-Gatherers* (1955), Jean Rhys's *Wide Sargasso Sea* (1966), Coetzee's *Waiting for the Barbarians* (1980), Graham Swift's *Waterland* (1983), Kazuo Ishiguro's *The Remains of the Day* (1989), Pat Barker's *Regeneration* trilogy (1991, 1993, 1995), Ian McEwan's *Black Dogs* (1992), and Mark Behr's *The Smell of Apples* (1995), to name only a few examples. Put simply, the idea that "civilized" persons could abide – indeed, could conspire in and advance – apartheid and murder against dehumanized enemy "Others" became a recurring trope in the novel of the period.

This notion of "civilized barbarity" was not new; indeed, it was anticipated in H. Rider Haggard's 1887 novel *Allan Quatermain*, in which "Civilization" is said to be "only savagery silver-gilt",[55] and in Conrad's 1899 novella *Heart of Darkness*, in which the Company chief accountant helps make possible the plundering, enslaving, and murdering of the native Congolese yet remains apparently oblivious to his crimes and contentedly "devoted to his books [the company accounts], which were in apple-pie order."[56] The realization that "civilized" Europeans were capable of perpetrating the most atrocious barbarities underwent something of a renaissance in the British novel of our period. In particular, the Holocaust of European Jewry captured the imagination of much British writing after 1945; genocide could no longer be dismissed as the practice solely of "primitive" tribes but rather was to be understood as the deliberate policy of "civilized" European peoples.

In his provocative and penetrating study *Modernity and the Holocaust* (1989), the sociologist Zygmunt Bauman theorizes the relationship between modern civilized society and genocide. In contrast to the naïve belief that the two phenomena are antithetical, Bauman argues that modernity makes possible two parallel processes that enable genocide: the "division of labor" and the "substitution of technical for moral responsibility."[57] For Bauman, in the modern corporation "Technical responsibility differs from [and supplants] moral responsibility in that it forgets that the action is a means to something other than itself."[58] Morality now "boils down to the commandment to be a good, efficient and diligent expert and worker"[59] above all else. This leads to the "dehumanization of the objects of bureaucratic operation" because it is now possible "to express these objects in purely technical, ethically neutral terms."[60] The result of this moral distancing between the bureaucrat and the object of bureaucratic interest, which is now understood in abstractly "quantitative" terms, is the "dehumanization" of the latter.[61] "Reduced, like all other objects of bureaucratic management, to pure, quality-free measurements, human objects lose their distinctiveness" and become dehumanized.[62] For Bauman, this line of reasoning explains how "good" Germans could perpetrate genocide against Jews; but its implications are far broader. Whether one considers the relationship between the Coketown boss Mr Bounderby and the exploited, downtrodden industrial "hands" in Dickens's 1854 novel *Hard Times,* the Belgian Trading Company employees and the enslaved, murdered Congolese in Conrad's *Heart of Darkness*, the Third Bureau employees and the assaulted "barbarian" Others in Coetzee's *Waiting for the Barbarians*, or the Commanders and the sexually violated Handmaids in Atwood's *The Handmaid's Tale*, the victimized "Others" in these novels are persecuted as a result of a dehumanizing shift in the way they are represented and understood by those who define them. In each case "Dehumanization of the objects and positive moral self-evaluation [of the functionaries] reinforce each other. The functionaries may faithfully serve any goal while their moral conscience remains unimpaired."[63] Indeed, fully half of the novels that come in for greater scrutiny in the next section of this study – those by Atwood, Golding, Ishiguro, Coetzee, and Spark – deal in one way or another with the crucible of the mid-century years, in particular (in the case of *Lord of the Flies*, *The Remains of the Day*, and *The Prime of Miss Jean Brodie*) with Britain's indirect culpability in some of its most odious dimensions.

Spark's The *Prime of Miss Jean Brodie*, for example, explores the perceived allure of the charismatic, fascistic teacher or leader (consider both Miss Brodie's admiration for Mussolini during the war and the demands she makes on her students blindly to follow her lead ["Mussolini's fascisti," she lectures her students, "are doing splendid things"]).[64] Ishiguro's Booker Prize-winning *The Remains of the Day* treats emotional fascism, the willingness of individuals to subordinate not only their behavior but their critical faculties to their "betters," while rationalizing such self-enslavement as the price happily paid for serving a higher social order. (Consider both Lord Darlington's appeasement of his German guests in the 1930s and Stevens's subordination of his rational and moral faculties to those of his master, such as when he blindly follows Lord Darlington's orders to fire two Jewish maids "for the good of this house."[65]) Golding's *Lord of the Flies* uses a group of marooned British boys on an island during the Second World War to probe what Erich Fromm calls the "escape from freedom," the individual's desire to relinquish major decision-making capacities to someone outside the self, "in order to acquire the strength which the individual self is lacking."[66] As Golding puts the lessons of the mid-century, to which his early novels respond,

> Before the Second World War I believed in the perfectibility of social man; that a correct structure of society would produce goodwill; and that therefore you could remove all social ills by a reorganization of society . . . [B]ut after the war I did not because I was unable to. I had discovered what one man can do to another . . . There were things done during that period from which I still have to avert my mind less I should be physically sick. They were not done by the headhunters of New Guinea, or by some primitive tribe in the Amazon. They were done, skillfully, coldly, by educated men, doctors, lawyers, by men with a tradition of civilization behind them, to beings of their own kind.[67]

Lord of the Flies culminates in the "civilized" British boys, now divided into tribes, literally hunting each other down.

This fear that the moral gap between "civilized" Europeans and uncivilized barbarians may not exist at all is explored not only in mid-century British works such as Robin Jenkins's *The Cone-Gatherers* (1955), a novel set during the Second World War that interrogates the enigmatically malign, murderous behavior of a gamekeeper of an aristocratic Scottish estate toward an innocent if physically deformed laborer, but in late-twentieth-century works as well.

Witness, for example, Pat Barker's *Regeneration* trilogy of the early 1990s, an anti-war narrative that provocatively blurs the boundaries between history and fiction. In the first novel, *Regeneration* (1991), Barker problematizes the medical and legal category of "madness" and interrogates the psycho-social mechanisms by which the British government sent thousands of its psychologically traumatized soldiers back to the slaughter of the Great War trenches despite their mental unfitness to fight and the near certainty of their deaths. In the second novel, *The Eye in the Door* (1993), it is victimized pacifists and homosexuals who become pawns in the British government's war machine; while in the third novel, the Booker Prize-winning *The Ghost Road* (1995), the "civilized" British penchant for war is suggestively juxtaposed with a "primitive" Papua New Guinea tribe's cult of death. How "civilized," these works ask, can the warmongering British really claim to be?

The trauma of the mid-century years also accounts for the prevalence of dystopian elements, which are largely vehicles for social criticism, in so many novels of our period, from the late works of Orwell and the early works of Golding, to Anthony Burgess's *A Clockwork Orange* (1962), Alasdair Gray's *Lanark* (1981), and Atwood's *The Handmaid's Tale* (1986). In Atwood's feminist dystopia a puritanical, patriarchal, theocratic government effectively enslaves, sexually or otherwise, all females in the service of the state, the Republic of Gilead.

Shifting Literary–National Paradigms: From the "English Novel" to the "Novel in English"

Postwar Britain was an austere and insecure place. British people knew that their role in the world was shrinking, and the years between the handing over of India in 1947 and the Suez crisis of 1956 were years in which the reality of Britain's increasingly limited role in world affairs was becoming painfully evident.

Caryl Phillips, *A New World Order*[68]

[F]or a long, long time Britain thought of itself as the center of a huge empire. For a long time writers who wrote English literature felt they did not need to think consciously about whether they were international or not. They could write about the smallest details of English society and it was, by definition, of interest to people in the far corners of the world because English culture itself was . . . internationally important . . . But that finished [sometime after the Second World War]. And then suddenly . . . people came to this realization: We're not the center of the universe. We're just this little backwater in Europe. If we want to participate in the world, culturally speaking, we've got to find out what's happening in the rest of the world.

Kazuo Ishiguro, in interview[69]

The novel has never been a more international form . . .

Salman Rushdie, *Imaginary Homelands*[70]

The last half of the twentieth century witnessed a monumental shift in the character of both literary and national identity: the "novel in English" supplanted the "English novel" in significance and cogency. What was at one time on the margins of canonical literature – the English language but non-British (or "Commonwealth") novel – is at present squarely at its center: the English-language novel is now a genuinely international affair, with postcolonial Anglophone and "black British" works as widely read and critically esteemed as "British" ones. As important as the English novelists of this period have been and continue to be, it is non-English novelists who now arguably dictate the parameters of literary debate and attract the most interest. As the novelist Emma Tennant, as early as 1978, declared, the majority of the important "developments" in English language fiction are as "likely to have come out of Africa, or the West Indies, or India"[71] as out of Britain. Feroza Jussawalla and Reed Way Dasenbrock, in the Introduction to their illuminating volume of interviews with postcolonial writers, amplify this point:

> The single most important development in literature written in English over the past century has been its increasingly international – indeed, global – nature. Once the language of a few million people on a small island on the edge of Europe, English is now spoken and written on every continent and is an important language inside at least one-quarter of the world's one hundred sixty countries. As English has become an important international language, it has also become an important international literary language.[72]

It is no mystery why this shift occurred. World War II helped accelerate the breakup of the British Empire, and Britain's abortive intervention in the Suez Crisis of 1956, obliquely alluded to in Ishiguro's The *Remains of the Day*, marked the demise of British imperial prestige. If London dominated 25 percent of the earth's surface at the turn of the nineteenth century, with control of nearly 4 million square miles, this dominance, in the thirty years following the Second World War, would shrink to a tiny fraction of that figure. India and Pakistan gained independence from Britain in 1947 (Sri Lanka achieved independence one year later), with the African nations of Kenya, Nigeria, South Africa, and Uganda following in the years 1960–3, and the vast majority of British-held Caribbean countries – among them the Bahamas, Barbados, Dominica, and Jamaica – gaining independence between 1962 and 1983. Closer to England, the Irish Free State was internationally recognized in 1921 (the 1931 Statute of Westminster formalized the secession of the Irish Free State from the United Kingdom); Scotland, although remaining a part of the United Kingdom, moved in the direction of devolution, re-inaugurating its Parliament in 1999; and Wales inaugurated a Welsh Assembly in this same year. As one observer remarked, Britain's "major historical experience" in the twentieth century, other than the two world wars, was "the final flourishing, later decline and eventual loss of the Empire."[73]

Britain's political empire may be gone, but its "linguistic empire" is stronger than ever. As Jussawalla and Dasenbrock observe, "The sun may now have set on the British Empire, but that Empire, in establishing English as a language of trade, government, and education in that sizable part of the world ruled by the British, helped create what may be a more enduring 'empire' of the English language."[74] The Indian novelist Salman Rushdie casts this linguistic dominance in yet more favorable terms. While it is true that English is *the* global language as "a result of the physical colonization of a quarter of the globe by the British," Rushdie eschews viewing this language as an unwanted imposition on formerly colonized peoples, instead regarding it as "a gift of the British colonizers," a legacy that in any case "ceased to be the sole possession of the English some time ago."[75]

At this point a word on the distinction among three terms – "imperial," "colonial," and "postcolonial" – will be useful. In his *Keywords: A Vocabulary of Culture and Society*, Raymond Williams notes that "imperialism" is variously understood as "a political system in which colonies are governed from an imperial centre, for economic [and] other reasons," and as an "economic system of external investment and the penetration and control of markets and sources of raw materials."[76] Imperialism is thus both a set of practices wrought by an empire and an ideological "justification" of those practices. If imperialism emphasizes the conquering and exploitation of "foreign" territories for the purpose of securing political and economic hegemony, colonialism emphasizes the settling of those territories for the purpose of transforming the indigenous socioeconomic and cultural order. As this description of colonialism would suggest, "postcolonial" defines a political and cultural order following the departure of the colonizing power and the birth of the independent nation: a hybridized culture that mixes elements of the formerly invading power and that of the indigenous population. As Ashcroft, Griffiths, and Tiffin put it in their *The Empire Writes Back*, "Post-colonial culture is inevitably a hybridized phenomenon involving a dialectical relationship between the 'grafted' European cultural systems and an indigenous ontology, with its impulse to create or recreate an independent local identity."[77] It should come as little surprise, then, that decolonization would have a major impact on the English-language novel of the period.

We may consider English-language novels (as opposed to English novels in the narrowest sense) in three broad groups, taking into account the history of contact, including colonization, between the peoples producing them. In the first group are novels from countries in which the literature and culture are British or demonstrate a significant "degree of continuity with that of Britain."[78] Scotland, Wales, and Northern Ireland – British, yet maintaining discrete cultural traditions – are conveniently considered, as far as the novel is concerned, with Australia, New Zealand, and Canada, dominions in which the majority of the inhabitants were British (or in any case European) settlers. The Republic of Ireland, given the violent and protracted struggle through which it achieved independence from the UK, is exceptional among these nations, but the links through language and culture justify including the Irish novel in this group.

In the second group are "postcolonial Anglophone" novels, which emanated from formerly subject, British-held colonies in which the majority of the inhabitants had been living *in situ* for centuries (rather than being "transplants" of British or European origin). Such formerly colonized nations include, among others, present-day Kenya, Nigeria, South Africa, and Uganda; India, Pakistan, and Sri Lanka; and the many English-speaking nations of the West Indies.

In the third group are novels written by formerly colonized peoples who subsequently migrated to Britain, and whose works are frequently viewed within the context of multicultural British fiction. As Jussawalla and Dasenbrock remind us, after the end of colonial migration a sort of reverse migration occurred, "as a result of the political and economic problems the new states of the nonwestern world experienced after independence."[79] This reverse pattern of migration resulted in an influx into Britain of large populations of formerly colonized Asians, West Indians, and Africans. The novels of such formerly subject peoples who settled in Britain (usually in the larger, industrialized cities of the UK, such as London, Birmingham, Bradford, Liverpool, and Glasgow) brought a revitalizing multicultural, international dimension to English literature and are sometimes grouped under the banner of "black British" writing. Such novelists and novels also revitalized the accepted manner of studying and categorizing literature, which had been within the context of "a single, cohesive national literary tradition." As Jussawalla and Dasenbrock argue, the assumption that literature in a given language and the literature of a given nation are compatible and readily combinable ways of studying literature breaks down in the face of the multilinguality of so many countries in the world and the global reach of writing in a number of European languages, [including] English.[80]

The traditional model of literary classification makes little sense, for example, in the face of the "black British" novel, which problematizes as never before the "center/margin" political and cultural dichotomies inherent in the earlier, single-nation-centered taxonomic approach. As Simon Gikandi reminds us, it is in any case now difficult to maintain the earlier "organization of knowledge and literary culture, [which separated] the Great Tradition of English literature from the new body of writing that had been produced in the former colonies."[81]

Space does not allow for more than a brief overview of the three overlapping dimensions in the evolving metamorphosis of the "English novel" into the "novel in English" during 1950–2000. To explore part of the first group outlined above: closest to the heart of Empire are novels of the "Celtic fringe," from Ireland, Scotland, and Wales. While relations between these national literatures and English literature have been understandably close, there is no doubt that the former literatures also defined themselves *against* the more widely disseminated and hegemonic English literary mainstream of the time, and that they have long functioned as literatures of resistance. In Ireland the novel has been a vibrant literary form in our period, with many Irish novelists, in both the Republic and Northern Ireland, writing in the wake of James Joyce's seminal early-twentieth-century fictions, *Dubliners*, *A Portrait of the Artist as a Young Man*, and *Ulysses*. Such novelists as John McGahern and Edna O'Brien, both of whom wrote novels that were banned for a time in Ireland (O'Brien's *Country Girls* trilogy [1960, 1962, 1964] and McGahern's *The Dark* [1965], the latter of which might be said to rewrite and update Joyce's *Portrait*), are two such examples.[82] The Anglo-Irish novelist William Trevor, a Protestant from County Cork, and Brian Moore, a Catholic from Belfast (who subsequently emigrated to North America) are two other authors whose novels of the past decades have explored and interrogated an evolving Irish (as opposed to British) identity. Moore's first novel, *The Lonely Passion of Judith Hearne* (1955), which reads like a novel-length *Dubliners* story, added an urban dimension to McGahern's mid-century indictment of the Church's stranglehold over rural Irish life. Brendan Behan's autobiographical *Borstal Boy* (1958) was politically provocative and was banned in Ireland. In more recent decades the novelists John Banville, Dermot Bolger, Emma Donoghue, Roddy Doyle, Bernard MacLaverty (who was born and raised in Belfast but who spent much of his adult life in Scotland, and hence may be viewed as both culturally Irish and Scottish), Patrick McCabe, and Colm Tóibín have written novels that further probe and problematize Irish identity in the late twentieth century. Irish novels that have gained the attention of international readers (and Booker Prize committees) include William Trevor's *Mrs Eckdorf in O'Neill's Hotel* (1970), *The Children of Dynmouth* (1976), *Reading Turgenev* (1991), and *The Story of Lucy Gault* (2002); Molly Keane's *Good Behavior* (1981); John Banville's *The Book of Evidence* (1989); John McGahern's *Amongst Women* (1990); Roddy Doyle's *Barrytown* trilogy (1989–91) and *Paddy Clarke Ha Ha Ha* (Booker Prize winner, 1993); Patrick McCabe's *The Butcher Boy* (1992) and *Breakfast on Pluto* (1998); Seamus Deane's *Reading in the Dark* (1996); Bernard MacLaverty's *Grace Notes* (1997); and Colm Tóibín's *The Blackwater Lightship* (1999) and *The Master* (2004).

The contemporary Scottish novel likewise has striven to forge a cultural identity for a marginalized nation whose literature too often has existed in the shadow of England's. In Scotland, toward the beginning of our period, Muriel Spark and Robin Jenkins wrote novels that gained the attention not only of a Scots but of a wider English-speaking readership. In particular, Jenkins's *The Cone-Gatherers* (1955) and Spark's *The Prime of Miss Jean Brodie* (1961), the first set in a Lowland Scottish aristocratic estate, the second set in Edinburgh (and both during the Second World War), announced a new skeptical mood in postwar Scottish writing. A renaissance of sorts in the Scottish novel was heralded by Alasdair Gray's *sui generis Lanark: A Life in Four Books* (1981), widely regarded as one of the greatest Scottish novels ever written. Comprised of four books, printed out of order, in which two related life stories unfold – one centering on Lanark and set in the nightmare-fantasy city of Unthank, the other centering on the autobiographical Duncan Thaw and set in Glasgow – *Lanark* attempts for Glasgow and Scotland what Joyce's *Ulysses* does for Dublin and Ireland: to be an epic-encyclopedic novel that explores the ways in which the modern artist can help engender national renewal. After *Lanark* there appeared on the scene a number of novels sometimes grouped under the "Scottish New Wave" rubric – works that tended to be grittily demotic and proletarian in thrust – that further plumbed the depths of late-twentieth-century Scottish national and cultural identity and that functioned to dispel the sentimental image of Scotland cultivated in Robert Louis Stevenson's High-land adventure romances and in the work of the Kailyard school of a century earlier. Such Scottish "New Wave" novelists include James Kelman, Janice Galloway, A. L. Kennedy, Irvine Welsh (*Trainspotting* [1993]), and Alan Warner (*Morvern Callar* [1995]). Andrew O'Hagan's lyrical *Our Fathers* (1999) is an example of a contemporary Scottish novel that explores national identity by skirting both the rural sentimentality of the earlier twentieth-century Scottish novel and the urban despair of the later twentieth-century one. The most celebrated Welsh novel of the period, Bruce Chatwin's *On the Black Hill* (1982), depicts over many decades the insular lives of the identical Jones twins on a Welsh farm near the English border. Scottish novels to make the Booker Prize shortlist include Muriel Spark's *The Public Image* (1969) and *Loitering With Intent* (1981); James Kelman's *A Disaffection* (1989) and *How Late It Was, How Late* (winner, 1994); George Mackay Brown's *Beside the Ocean of Time* (1994); Andrew O'Hagan's *Our Fathers* (1999); and Ali Smith's *Hotel World* (2001).

Much further from the center of the former empire were novels written by members of sovereign countries once ruled from London that to this day remain members of the "Commonwealth of Nations": Canada, Australia, and New Zealand. All three of these nations (along with South Africa and the Irish Free State) gained their formal independence from Britain with the passage in the British Parliament of the 1931 Statute of Westminster. Like the novels of 1950–2000 in Ireland and Scotland, the English-language novels in these countries comprise discrete traditions that nevertheless also engage dialogically with the more globally mainstream English novel. In Canada a number of novelists gained a readership both in their own country and in the wider English-speaking world: Malcolm Lowry (a transplant from England and author of *Under the Volcano* [1947]), Robertson Davies, Mordecai Richler, Brian Moore (a transplant from Ireland), Michael Ondaatjee (originally from Sri Lanka and the author of *The English Patient* [1992]), Margaret Laurence (Canadian-born yet much of whose life was spent in Somaliland, Ghana, and England, and many of whose novels are set in Africa), and Margaret Atwood, the most celebrated of contemporary Canadian novelists (and an incisive critic of patriarchal forms of power).[83] Booker Prize shortlist novels from Canada include Mordecai Richler's *St Urbain's Horseman* (1971) and *Solomon Gursky Was Here* (1990); Margaret Atwood's *The Handmaid's Tale* (1986), *Cat's Eye* (1989), *Alias Grace* (1996), *The Blind Assassin* (winner, 2000), and *Oryx and Crake* (2003); Robertson Davies's *What's Bred in the Bone* (1986); and Michael Ondaatje's *The English Patient* (winner, 1992).

In Australia, toward the beginning of our period, the novels of Patrick White and Christina Stead received widespread interest. In more recent decades David Malouf, Thomas Keneally (*Schindler's Ark* [1982]), Clive James, and, in particular, Peter Carey (one of only two novelists to win more than one Booker Prize, the other being South African novelist J. M. Coetzee) have written novels that have received worldwide acclaim. In New Zealand Keri Hulme, of mixed English, Scottish, and Maori ancestry, authored *The Bone People* (1985), a remarkable and disturbing novel, twelve years in the making, in which prose and poetry, modernist European novelistic and traditional

Maori literary conventions and idioms are fused in the service of an enigmatic psychological mystery-thriller. Other significant New Zealand Maori novelists from the period include Patricia Grace and Witi Ihimaera (*The Whale Rider* [1987]). Booker Prize shortlist novels from Australia and New Zealand include Thomas Keneally's *The Chant of Jimmy Blacksmith* (1972), *Gossip from the Forest* (1975), *Confederates* (1979), and *Schindler's Ark* (winner, 1982); Keri Hulme's *The Bone People* (winner, 1985); Peter Carey's *Illywhacker* (1985), *Oscar and Lucinda* (winner, 1988) and *The True History of the Kelly Gang* (winner, 2001); and David Malouf's *Remembering Babylon* (1993).

A second instance of this evolving story of the impact of decolonization on the English-language novel of the period, the "postcolonial Anglophone" novel, is a body of work deriving from countries recently liberated from British imperial domination, whose populations are largely indigenous rather than British (or European) in origin. Postcolonial Anglophone novels tend to resist and interrogate the imperialist doctrines that sought to justify the unbalanced power relationship of the past (or still passing) colonial situation as well as to replace a national identity and history of the imperial power's making with a national identity and history of the newly liberated nation's making. In Salman Rushdie's now familiar formulation, such literature is an example of the "empire" writing back to the "center." Rushdie's model of postcolonial writing envisions a two-way rather than a one-way conversation: dialogue and cross-fertilization rather than the imposition of a single, controlling colonial-hegemonic voice. Instead of viewing the postcolonial author as a victim of the colonizer's language, Rushdie views "those peoples who were once colonized by" the English language as "now rapidly remaking" and "domesticating it," as "carving out large territories for themselves within its frontiers."[84] Jussawalla and Dasenbrock amplify this point by arguing that, while such literature "uses the language of the former colonial power," it also

> speaks in its own independent and quite original voice, often contesting the way it has been represented by earlier writers. The writing that emerges in this process issues from a remarkably complex combination of cultures, as the postcolonial writers draw on indigenous traditions and languages of their own as well as on the resources of the tradition of writing in English.[85]

It is my aim here to suggest the variety and richness of postcolonial Anglophone novelistic output.

One example of the postcolonial use of the colonizer's language *against* the empire – of the empire writing back to the center – is to be found in the Nigerian Chinua Achebe's novel *Things Fall Apart* (1958), easily the most famous and widely-read African novel in English. This work may be taken as a riposte to Joseph Conrad's *Heart of Darkness* (1899), Joyce Cary's *Mr Johnson* (1939), and other works of European literature that for Achebe constitute racist misrepresentations of Africa and Africans that attempt to rationalize colonization (Achebe accuses Conrad of this directly in his famous 1975 address, "An image of Africa: racism in Conrad's *Heart of Darkness*"). *Things Fall Apart* mounts a provocative challenge to the British imperial account of Igbo history and society, and reveals how British missionaries, traders, and government officials worked hand-in-glove to colonize Nigeria. Despite the novel's bold interrogation of colonization, Achebe's decision to write in English, the language of the colonizer, rather than in his native Igbo tongue, proved controversial. Achebe defended his choice on two grounds. On the one hand, Achebe states, "We chose English not because the British desired it but because . . . we needed its language to transact our business, including the business of overthrowing colonialism itself in the fullness of time."[86] On the other hand, Achebe employed English in order to extend this language's "frontiers" and accommodate African literary modes,[87] almost as if he sought to "colonize" the English language itself from within and thereby gain revenge against the British Empire.

A second example is to be found in Salman Rushdie's Booker Prize-winning *Midnight's Children* (1981), the postmodern, postcolonial novel *par excellence*. It uses the language of the British colonizer to write the epic history of the liberation of India and Pakistan from British control as well as the history of the intertwined, tortured relationship of these two warring, Indian subcontinental nations. Owing more to *The Arabian Nights*, to Günter Grass's *The Tin Drum*, and to Latin American magic realism than to the British novelistic tradition, *Midnight's Children*, with its myriad interweaving narratives and voices, stretched the English-language novel, linguistically and structurally; it altered the literary landscape in Britain by opening up the novelistic mainstream to Anglophone writing from outside Europe, North America, or the Antipodes. Responding to the controversy over his decision to write his novels in English rather than in an indigenous Indian language, Rushdie, similarly to Achebe, observed that Indian writers intend to use English to different ends than the British, to remake it "for our own purposes": "Those of us who do use English do so in spite of our ambiguity towards it, or perhaps because of that . . . To conquer English may be to complete the process of making ourselves free."[88]

In addition to using the English language in a new way and for new "purposes," some postcolonial novels "rewrote" canonical British works for the purpose of countering British imperial ideology. This is certainly the case in the novel by the ethnically British, West Indian-born Jean Rhys, *Wide*

Sargasso Sea (1966), which revises Charlotte Brontë's 1847 *Jane Eyre* in such a way that the British husband of Bertha Mason, and not the West Indian "madwoman in the attic," is to blame for the ensuing domestic tragedy. Rather than viewing Bertha's madness as the cause of Rochester's unhappiness and paranoia, Rhys's novel suggests that it is the imperial Rochester – both as a British colonizer in the West Indies and as a patriarchal colonizer of a powerless Caribbean woman – who is to blame for the marginalization, imprisonment, and downfall of Jane's dark, "diabolical" double. Crucially, the center of the novel's gravity, rather than being the British Jane Eyre, is the British-West Indian "Creole" Antoinette; this, as much as anything, advances the novel's subversive postcolonial strategy of deconstructing the "subject/object" dichotomy upon which colonialism stands.

The "postcolonial Anglophone" novel is a large and still burgeoning field. For purposes of convenience we may subdivide this field into three groups – novels from Africa, from the Indian subcontinent, and from the British West Indies – even if all such novels are united by their resistance to various forms of British political and cultural dominance (and in some cases also to post-independence governmental abuses). Space does not allow for more than a cursory list of some of the relevant figures and texts.

In Africa, the postcolonial Anglophone novel has been particularly vibrant in Nigeria, the most populous English-speaking country on the continent. Major Nigerian figures of the period include Chinua Achebe, Wole Soyinka, Buchi Emecheta, and Ben Okri. Achebe is best known for five novels – *Things Fall Apart* (1958), *No Longer at Ease* (1960), *Arrow of God* (1964), *A Man of the People* (1966), and *Anthills of the Savannah* (1987, Booker Prize finalist), of which the first four form a loose tetralogy depicting Nigerian history from just before colonization to just after independence. Soyinka, although best known as a Nobel Prize-winning playwright, is also the author of two novels, *The Interpreters* (1965) and *Season of Anomy* (1973), which owe a clear debt, in ways that Achebe's novels do not, to literary modernist narrative innovations. Emecheta, whose works portray the plight of African women in both Nigeria and England, is the author of numerous novels written between the mid-1970s and the present. Perhaps the best known of these are *The Bride Price* (1976), *The Slave Girl* (1977), and *The Joys of Motherhood* (1979); they collectively confront Nigeria's oppressive patriarchal culture in the first half of the twentieth century. Okri's first two works, *Flowers and Shadows* (1980) and *The Landscapes Within* (1981), are postcolonial coming-of-age novels that treat the process of modernization in urban, civil war-torn Nigeria. His next three novels – *The Famished Road* (1991, winner of the Booker Prize), *Songs of Enchantment* (1993), and *Infinite Riches* (1998) – form a trilogy that mixes indigenous Yoruba and foreign magic-realist narrative forms in the service of depicting a West African nation during the period of its transition from colonial to postcolonial state.

It is not only West Africa that has produced important postcolonial Anglophone novels. In East African Kenya the novelist Ngugi wa Thiong'o wrote a number of English-language novels that engaged British–Kenyan political and cultural tensions – *Weep Not, Child* (1964), *The River Between* (1965), *A Grain of Wheat* (1967, which echoes Conrad's *Heart of Darkness*), and *Petals of Blood* (1977) – before he decided, unlike Achebe, to write exclusively in his native African language, Gikuyu. Also from Kenya comes a writer of South Asian decent, M. G. Vassanji, whose novels *The Book of Secrets* (1996) and *The In-Between World of Vikram Lall* (2004) explore both the British imperial presence in and the large Indian diaspora of East Africa. In Somalia, which was granted independence from Britain and Italy in 1960, Nuruddin Farah produced English-language novels critical of both colonial and postcolonial Somali realities. Farah's first two novels, *From a Crooked Rib* (1970) and *A Naked Needle* (1976), critique aspects of this East African nation's patriarchal culture; while the three novels that form his trilogy, *Variations on a Theme of an African Dictatorship* (1980–3), tackle various abuses of governmental authority. From Tanzania comes Abdulrazak Gurnah, whose novel *Paradise* (1994, Booker Prize shortlist) depicts events in East Africa before the onset of the Great War.

In South Africa, two English-language novelists, J. M. Coetzee and Nadine Gordimer, have attracted worldwide attention for their anatomizations of racial apartheid, a legal code that prevailed there between 1913 (the British formally severed ties with South Africa in 1934) and the downfall of the South African Nationalist Party, in 1994. These Anglophone novelists, both of whom are white, the first from an Afrikaner background, the second from a Jewish immigrant background, are not normally thought of as "postcolonial." Nevertheless, both write from within a formerly colonized nation whose government and white minority in effect "colonized" from within the nation's majority black population. J. M. Coetzee is winner of the 2003 Nobel Prize for Literature and a Booker Prize each for *Life and Times of Michael K.* (1983) and *Disgrace* (1989), and the author of *Waiting for the Barbarians* (1980) and six other novels written between the late 1970s and the present; he interrogates the distorted power relations that stand behind apartheid racial policies. Nadine Gordimer, recipient of the 1991 Nobel Prize for Literature, uses realism in her novels, rather than Coetzee's more allegorical approach, to plumb the depths and shallows of apartheid life in South Africa. She is the author of thirteen novels, *The Conservationist* (1974, winner of the Booker Prize), *Burger's Daughter* (1979), and *July's People* (1981) among the most acclaimed. Mark Behr, another South African novelist of note, is the author of *The Smell of*

Apples (1995), a riveting and powerful first-person account of a white child's indoctrination into 1970s South Africa's racist, apartheid ideology, and the high price, morally and intellectually, to be paid for such indoctrination. Behr's *Embrace* (2000) deals with many of these same themes more expansively.

The postcolonial Anglophone novel from the Indian subcontinent has been similarly rich and various. In India, the third largest English-language book-producing nation in the world (after the US and the UK), the Anglophone novel has been a staple of literary life for many years. In the early part of our period R. K. Narayan dominated the field. Discovered by Graham Greene in the mid-1930s, Narayan set his many novels (published between 1935 and 1990) of the British–Indian encounter in the fictional South Indian town of Malgudi. Bombay-born Salman Rushdie, presently the most celebrated Indian Anglophone writer, is the author of *Midnight's Children* (1981, Booker Prize winner), *Shame* (1983, Booker shortlist), *Satanic Verses* (1988, Booker shortlist), and *The Moor's Last Sigh* (1995, Booker shortlist), among other novels. Of these works two in particular, *Midnight's Children* and *The Satanic Verses*, brought Rushdie international fame and notoriety. The first novel altered the landscape of Anglophone Indian writing, encouraging a new fabulist, post-modernist narrative approach to complement a more traditionally realist one. In 1993 this novel received the honor of being named the "Booker of Bookers": the best Booker Prize winner in the award's then quarter-century history. The second novel captured the attention of the world after Iran's Ayatollah Khomeini in 1989 issued a *fatwa* against the author, forcing him into hiding, on account of this novel's alleged blasphemy against Islam's Prophet Muhammad. *The Satanic Verses*, which problematizes subjectivity and history in ways similar to *Midnight's Children*, confirmed Rushdie's standing as the pre-eminent postmodernist, postcolonial Anglophone novelist.

Also from the west Indian city of Bombay (now Mumbai) and also employing linguistic hybridity in his fictional explorations of postcolonial sub-continental reality is the Zoroastrian Parsi novelist Rohinton Mistry (now resident in Canada), whose novels, *Such a Long Journey* (1991, Booker shortlist), *A Fine Balance* (1996, Booker shortlist), and *Family Matters* (2002, Booker shortlist), achieved international acclaim. Anita Desai, of mixed Bengali and German parentage and from a village in North India near Delhi, published a number of novels between 1963 and the present, among them three that were shortlisted for the Booker Prize: *Clear Light of Day* (1980), *In Custody* (1984), and *Fasting, Feasting* (1999). Less experimental in approach than Rushdie's novels, Desai's tend to be peopled by Anglicized members of the Indian middle class and to focus on feminist concerns or, as in the case of *Baumgartner's Bombay* (1988), on European–Indian encounters. Kamala Markandaya, originally from the southern Indian city of Bangalore, also focuses in her many novels on East–West tensions and on the plight of women in postcolonial India. She is best known for her first novel, *Nectar in a Sieve* (1954), which became one of the earliest Indian "best-sellers" in Britain.

Numerous other postcolonial Anglophone authors have contributed to what many regard as a renaissance in the contemporary Indian novel, among them Arundhati Roy, from the south-west Indian state of Kerala, whose novel *The God of Small Things* won the 1997 Booker Prize; and a number of writers originally from the east Indian city of Calcutta: Amit Chaudhuri, Amitav Ghosh, Sunetra Gupta, and Vikram Seth (author most notably of the 1993 *A Suitable Boy*, nearly ten years in the writing and nearly 1,500 pages in length), among others.

Acclaimed Pakistani practitioners of the postcolonial Anglophone novel include Zulfikar Ghose (from Sailkot, formerly India and now Pakistan) and Bapsi Sidhwa. Ghose, who at one point collaborated with the English experimental author B. S. Johnson (discussed above), is the author of many novels, one of which, *The Murder of Aziz Khan* (1967), is set in Pakistan and anticipates the work of Salman Rushdie. Sidhwa, a Zoroastrian Parsi from Lahore, is best known for her acclaimed novel *Ice-Candy Man* (1988; also published as *Cracking India*). This novel is narrated by a Parsi child, neither Hindu nor Muslim, who describes the events of the bloody partition of India and Pakistan during the time in which the British are exiting the subcontinent. From the South Asian island nation of Sri Lanka, formerly Ceylon, comes Michael Ondaatje (now resident in Canada), best known for *The English Patient* (1992, Booker Prize winner) and *Anil's Ghost* (2001), and Romesh Gunesekera, author of *Reef* (1994, Booker Prize shortlist), among other figures.

The island nations of the British West Indies – the Bahamas, Barbados, Dominica, Grenada, Jamaica, and Trinidad among them – also produced a great number of postcolonial Anglophone novels of high standing. The ethnically-British, Dominica-born Jean Rhys is something of an interstitial figure – being identified as a West Indian "Creole" in Britain and as a Briton in Dominica – but her masterpiece, *Wide Sargasso Sea* (1966), set in Dominica, Jamaica, and England, explores issues common to many postcolonial Anglophone novels of the Caribbean.

Certainly the towering contemporary figure from the region, and another writer with a strongly interstitial identity, is the Trinidad-born, ethnically Indian V. S. Naipaul, the author of numerous celebrated novels – among them *A House for Mr Biswas* (1961), *The Mimic Men* (1967), *In a Free State* (1971, winner of the Booker Prize), *A Bend in the River* (1979, Booker shortlist), and *The Enigma of Arrival* (1987) – and the recipient of the 2001 Nobel Prize for Literature. Naipaul's fiction, which treats life in postcolonial nations in various states of political and cultural transition, is reminiscent of Joseph Conrad's in its genuinely global reach (his works are variously situated in England, Africa, the West Indies, the Middle East, and the Indian subcontinent). Naipaul has been a controversial figure for what the West Indian born novelist Caryl Phillips deems the author's "undisguised contempt for the people of the Third World."[89]

Other significant postcolonial Anglophone West Indian novelists include Guyana-born Wilson Harris, whose pioneering, surreal *Palace of the Peacock* (1960), the first novel in his *Guyana* quartet, depicts the European search for El Dorado and the resulting disruption of the Indian and African communities that had settled there previously (this novel also clearly echoes *Heart of Darkness*). Roy Heath (Guyana; *Georgetown* trilogy [1981]), George Lamming (Barbados; *In the Castle of My Skin* [1953], a notable Caribbean *Bildungsroman*), and Earl Lovelace (Trinidad; *The Dragon Can't Dance* [1979]), to name only a few important figures (and texts), have written English-language novels that probe the myriad political and cultural conflicts that have arisen in the West Indies owing to the past (or passing) British imperial order. Caribbean literature, according to Caryl Phillips, may be characterized by "Its restlessness of form, its polyphonic structures, its yoking together of man and nature, of past and present, its linguistic dualities and its unwillingness to collapse into easy narrative closure."[90] Jean Rhys provocatively elaborates upon this vision of the interpenetration of "past and present" when she writes, in a letter of 1934, that "[T]he past exists – side by side with the present, not behind it; . . . what was – is."[91]

A third instance of this evolving story of the impact of decolonization on the English-language novel of 1950–2000 is those works by writers who originated (or whose parents originated) in the former British colonies but who have subsequently immigrated to Britain and wrote within, and contributed to, a new multicultural British literary milieu. These novels, sometimes grouped under the "black British" nomenclature, by authors of African, Asian, and Caribbean background, explore the predicament of émigrés who make their lives in a post-imperial Britain: the difficulty of bridging their birth and adopted cultures, and the difficulty of negotiating their interstitial identities as citizens of two places – and of nowhere. This "black British" novel, which has achieved critical and popular prominence only since the early 1980s, in turn has helped shape and energize contemporary "British" writing at large, perhaps, as Rushdie argues, because its authors possess a hybrid identity and therefore "are capable of writing from a kind of double perspective," as both "insiders and outsiders in [British] society."[92] This new type of novel, which for Caryl Phillips poses "a sustained challenge to the English literary tradition in both content and form,"[93] also stands as the ultimate foil to the standard national categories by which literary canons traditionally have been formed. Is the West Indian-born, ethnically Indian, British educated and resident V. S. Naipaul, for example, best understood as a Caribbean, Indian, or British author? Posing the very question reveals the severe limitations of the nation-centered literary categories themselves, but also the advantages of "stereoscopic vision"[94] that pertain to these authors of transnational identity. Rushdie seeks to get around the problem of national identity altogether by viewing these "migrant" authors as citizens not of one physical place or another but of "imaginary homelands," as people

> who root themselves in ideas rather than places, in memories as much as in material things; people who have been obliged to define themselves – because they are so defined by others – by their otherness; peoples in whose deepest selves strange fusions occur, unprecedented unions between what they were and where they find themselves.[95]

It goes without saying that the category "black British" novel significantly overlaps that of the "postcolonial Anglophone" novel discussed above; such figures as Buchi Emecheta, Zulfikar Ghose, Romesh Gunesekera, Sunetra Gupta, Abdulrazak Gurnah, Wilson Harris, V. S. Naipaul, Ben Okri, and Salman Rushdie, for example, write novels that belong equally to both categories. These authors, now (or recently) resident in Britain, have written works that explore the conflicted lives and interstitial identities of former colonial subjects in the post-imperial metropole, reflecting the new international, multicultural reality of Britain's industrial cities and university towns.

The "black British" novel dates from the "Windrush generation" of West Indian immigrant authors of the 1950s and 1960s; they were named for the ship *Empire Windrush,* which landed 492 Jamaican passengers on 22 June 1948 at a port near London, and which represented, in Dominic Head's phrasing, "metonymically, a new generation of Commonwealth migrants recruited to a labor market in need of workers."[96] Between 1948 and 1962 some quarter million West Indians migrants would follow. This group of émigrés included West Indians of African descent who were displaced by the slave trade, and of Indian descent (lumped together with Chinese workers as "coolie labor") who were displaced by the contract or indentured labor trade that flourished after the abolition of slavery in the British colonies (1833).

Major figures (and novels) of the "Windrush generation" include George Lamming (*The Emigrants* [1954] and *Water with Berries* [1971]); Sam Selvon (Trinidad-born and of Scottish and Indian parentage; *The Lonely Londoners* [1956], *Moses Ascending* [1975], and *Moses Migrating* [1983]); and V. S. Naipaul. In the generation that followed, Caryl Phillips (born in St Kitts; *The*

Final Passage [1985], *Crossing the River* [1993, Booker shortlist], and *A Distant Shore* [2003]); David Dabydeen (born in Guyana; *The Intended* [1991] and *Disappearance* [1993]); and Zadie Smith (born in London to a Jamaican mother and an English-Jewish father; *White Teeth* [2000]), among many others, continued to probe a sociohistorically and culturally complex Afro-Caribbean-British identity. Caryl Phillips gets at this complexity when he defines his relationship to the Africa and St Kitts of his background and to the Leeds and London of his adoption by using precisely the same words for each: "I recognize the place, I feel at home here, but I don't belong. I am of, and not of, this place."[97] Smith's wildly popular *White Teeth*, a novel at once Dickensian and Rushdiesque, deserves special mention here because it has come to be seen by many as the quintessential "black British" novel, one that probes what Caryl Phillips calls the "helpless heterogeneity" of Britain's present multiracial reality.[98] The story of three London families, the British and Jamaican Jones, the Bangladeshi Iqbals, and the Catholic-Jewish English Chalfens, *White Teeth* satirizes generational, ethnic, and class tensions in an internationalized contemporary London while humorously bashing racial stereotypes that arise in the post-imperial metropole. As Caryl Phillips puts it in his review of Smith's novel:

The "mongrel' nation that is Britain is still struggling to find a way to stare in the mirror and accept the ebb and flow of history which has produced this fortuitously diverse condition, and its concomitant pain. Zadie Smith's first novel is an audaciously assured contribution to this process of staring into the mirror.[99]

"Black British" writing from authors of Indian subcontinental and African backgrounds has been similarly vital. To provide one prominent example of each, Hanif Kureishi, born in England to a Pakistani father and an English mother, is best known (outside of his popular plays and film screenplays) for *The Buddha of Suburbia* (1990), a humorous coming-of-age novel, set largely in London, that features a semi-autobiographical protagonist of mixed Indian and English heritage; while Buchi Emecheta, the first major English-language African female writer (discussed above) is the author, among other novels, of *In the Ditch* (1972), which chronicles a female ex-Nigerian attempting to negotiate life in an inhospitable and alienating London.

Two writers of East Asian background who are frequently associated with "black British" writing are Timothy Mo, born to a Cantonese father and an English mother in Hong Kong (in British hands between 1841 and 1997), and Kazuo Ishiguro, born in Japan to Japanese parents. Mo is best known for the humorous novel *Sour Sweet* (1982, Booker shortlist), which concerns Chinese immigrants who settle in London and which uses food as a metaphor for the dislocation and anomie inherent in the migrant experience. Ishiguro is best known for his Booker Prize-winning third novel *The Remains of the Day* (1989), although his most germane novels in the present connection are his first, *A Pale View of Hills* (1982), and his fifth, *When We Were Orphans* (2000, Booker shortlist). Both of these novels deal with psychological traumas undergone by characters who have immigrated to England, whether from late-1940s post-bomb Nagasaki (as in the first novel) or from the war-torn Shanghai of a decade earlier (as in the fifth).

Inflaming the situation for immigrants to Britain was the fact that, more than 30 years after the *Empire Windrush* first docked near London, the question of who was "British" remained a contested issue. The British Nationality Act of 1981 – which built on the Commonwealth Immigrants Act of 1962 that discouraged immigration to Britain by former colonials – functioned, in Dominic Head's view,

> to erode the automatic right of British citizenship for people of the former British colonies: to be British one had to prove one's descent from an ancestor born in Britain (being born in Britain oneself was now insufficient). This attempt to shore up a national identity (for this was really about Englishness) on the basis of biology flew in the face of the migrant hybridity that the end of empire brought with it.[100]

For Rushdie, writing in 1982, this piece of legislation was "expressly designed to deprive black and Asian Britons of their citizenship rights,"[101] and its passage was emblematic of Britain's division into "two entirely different worlds," based on skin color, in which "White and black perceptions of everyday life" have become "incompatible."[102] Rushdie, who viewed this "gulf" as leading to the formation of a "New Empire within Britain," charged that "It sometimes seems that the British authorities, no longer capable of exporting governments, have chosen instead to import a new Empire, a new community of subject people."[103] Some "black British" novels have sought to depict and critique this new "internal" empire, while others have approached the problem the other way around: by attacking Britain's cherished myths of historical and cultural purity, its notion of itself, in Caryl Phillips's words, as a "country for whom a sense of continuity with an imagined past continues to be a major determinant of national identity."[104] To provide one example of the latter strategy, Ishiguro's *The Remains of the Day* takes aim, according to its author, at England's mythical sense of itself as a nation "with sleepy, beautiful villages with very polite people and butlers . . . taking tea on the lawn": a sanitized yet potent image that occasionally is "used as a political tool" to bash "anybody who tries to spoil this 'Garden of Eden'."[105] The reality of interwar England, *The Remains of the Day* suggests, is far less harmonious or innocent than its butler-protagonist would have us believe.

The foregoing three contexts for reading the novel in English between 1950 and 2000 – as a riposte to modernism and, later, antimodernism; as a response to the betrayal and crisis of civilization; and as a reaction to decolonization – are of course by no means the only important contexts within which the novel of our period might be considered. These frames of reference are nevertheless indispensable ones to an understanding of this still-evolving field.

A Note on the "Novel"

Remember the etymology of the word. A novel is something new. It must have relevance to the writer's now . . .

John Fowles, "Notes on an Unfinished Novel"[106]

[P]rose art presumes a deliberate feeling for the historical and social concreteness of living discourse . . . a feeling for its participation in historical becoming and in social struggle; it deals with discourse that is still warm from that struggle and hostility . . .

M. M. Bakhtin, "Discourse in the Novel"[107]

Having explored three contexts out of which the novel in English of 1950–2000 emerged, it remains to explore the nature and function of the genre itself. The novel, at its most generic, may be defined as an extended fictional prose narrative. The word derives from the Italian word *novella*, which translates as "little new thing." In many modern European languages, including French and German, "novel" goes by the term "roman," which is of course related to our word "romance" (and indeed, the roots of the modern realistic novel can be traced to this earlier, more fanciful prose tradition). The novel in English, in the form in which we recognize it today, came into its own in the eighteenth century, in works by such authors as Daniel Defoe, Henry Fielding, and Samuel Richardson.[108]

Key qualities of the novel, then as now, include its tendency to be "expansive" and to engage with its present, with the "new." In his *Aspects of the Novel*

(1927) E. M. Forster speaks to the first point by calling "expansion" an "idea the novelist must cling to." "Not completion," Forster adds; "Not rounding off but opening out."[109] The second point is advanced by another English novelist, John Fowles, who reminds us (above) of what might be called the novel's inherent *novelty*. T. S. Eliot makes a similar point, although more negatively, when he lauds James Joyce's then-controversial *Ulysses* for concerning itself with a gallingly chaotic present, for using myth to control, order, give shape and significance to "the immense panorama of futility and anarchy that is contemporary history."[110] The point to be made here is that it is always "contemporary history," construed in one way or another, with which the novel by its very nature engages.

The novelistic qualities of "expansiveness" and "newness" blur into a third and related quality, "open-endedness," an idea that Mikhail Bakhtin, perhaps the twentieth-century's most important theorist of the novel, explores in his influential writings. According to Bakhtin, the novel – because it is oriented toward the here and now and is characterized by an "evolutionary nature," by "spontaneity, incompleteness and inconclusiveness," and by an "ability and commitment to rethink and reevaluate" – is "the quintessential register of society's attitudes toward itself and the world."[111] Unlike the language of other literary genres, that of the novel is not "unitary" but polyphonic, "a *system* of languages that mutually and ideologically interanimate each other."[112] Categorically-speaking, the novel is not a literary genre that ever places itself above and beyond contemporary history and quotidian discourse (epics do this, according to Bakhtin); it is always made up of "living discourse" that is "still warm" from its "participation in historical becoming" and "social struggle." In contrast to the epic, which presents itself as "completed, conclusive and immutable," the novel for Bakhtin "is a genre that is ever questing, ever examining itself and subjecting its established forms to review"; it is the genre with the most "contact with the present (with contemporary reality) in all its openendedness."[113] One might conceive of Bakhtin's perhaps overly schematic "epic/novel" distinction in terms of a series of dichotomies – "centrifugal" versus "centripetal," "becoming" versus "being," and "dialogic" versus "monologic" – that collectively make the case for the anti-hegemonic energies of prose fiction.

Akin to Bakhtin's distinction between "epic" and "novel" is Frank Kermode's distinction between "myth" and "fiction." In *The Sense of an Ending* (1967) Kermode argues that while "myths" presuppose definitive answers and "total and adequate explanations of things" as they are and were, "fictions" exist for the purpose of "finding things out, and they change as the needs of sense-making change." For Kermode,

> Myths are the agents of stability, fictions the agents of change. Myths call for absolute, fictions for conditional assent. Myths make sense in terms of a lost order of time . . . fictions, if successful, make sense of the here and now . . .[114]

Salman Rushdie puts the novel's distinctive interaction with the social world of its time and place in yet another way. Rather than pitting novels against epics or myths, Rushdie pits them against political discourses, viewing novelists and politicians as "natural rivals." Although both novelists and politicians "try to make the world in their own images" and "fight for the same territory," novels tend to counter "the official, politicians' version of truth."[115] While Rushdie would agree with George Orwell's point that an "atmosphere of orthodoxy is always damaging to prose" and "completely ruinous to the novel, the most anarchical of all forms of literature,"[116] he nevertheless insists that novels must in some fashion enter the sociopolitical fray,

> because what is being disputed is nothing less than *what is the case*, what is truth and what untruth. If writers leave the business of making pictures of the world to politicians, it will be one of history's great and most abject abdications.[117]

For Rushdie, literature is in "the business of finding new angles at which to enter reality,"[118] and the novel, although a vehicle for exploration and discovery, for questing and questioning, is also a vehicle for taking sides in the sociohistorical and political controversies of its day.

In the spirit of Forster, Bakhtin, Kermode, and Rushdie, then, the present study approaches the novel of the period as an open-ended, socially engaged, exploratory genre, one that challenges and stretches the canons of knowledge (the "conventional wisdom") as well as the prevailing standards of perception, subjectivity, and literary representation in its bid to picture and probe an evolving contemporary reality.

To say that the novel engages in an exploratory way with the historical realities and social and artistic conventions of its time is not to say that the novel is "most true" (or "best understood") in relation to its own time or that it is tethered, interpretively-speaking, to the era of its production and initial consumption. As the American novelist John Barth reminds us, "no single literary text can ever be exhausted – its 'meaning' residing as it does in its transactions with individual readers over time, space, and language."[119] Bakhtin takes this idea a step further in making a virtue of necessity and regarding the reader's temporal, geographic, and cultural distance from the text under scrutiny as requirements of meaningful interpretation. For Bakhtin, "In order to understand [any text], it is immensely important for the person who understands to be *located outside* the object of his or her creative understanding – in time, in space, in culture."[120] Texts live "only by coming into contact with" other texts (with contexts), against the backdrop of which they take on meaning. "Only at the point of this contact between texts does a light flash, illuminating both the posterior and anterior, joining a given text to a dialogue."[121] Distances of time, space, and language between texts and readers – ever-evolving new "contexts" – influence both the meaning and interpretation of texts and what texts reveal about their interpreters' (present and evolving) circumstances. Literary interpretation is thus best understood as a dialogic enterprise: we read novels and they "read" us. The following chapters, which explore ten novels published between 1954 and 1996 from seven different countries, take this conception of literary interpretation as their point of departure.

Chapter 2

Kingsley Amis's *Lucky Jim* (1954)

It was luck you needed all along; with just a little more luck [Jim would] have been able to switch his life on to a momentarily adjoining track, a track destined to swing aside at once away from his own.

Kingsley Amis, *Lucky Jim*[1]

The real revolution represented by *Lucky Jim* was primarily a cultural one; it represented a significant alteration in the register of fiction, a paradigm shift of clear importance.

Malcolm Bradbury, *The Modern British Novel*[2]

I

A major work of fiction associated with the "Angry Young Men" of the 1950s, Kingsley Amis's *Lucky Jim* signaled a new direction for the English novel. Deemed "a classic comic novel," the "seminal campus novel,"[3] and "one of the key books of the English 1950s,"[4] Amis's debut work, set in the years following the Second World War, "captured a powerful contemporary mood" and came "to seem the exemplary Fifties" novel.[5] As Malcolm Bradbury puts it, *Lucky Jim* "became a summative work of the new spirit in fiction much as John Osborne's *Look Back in Anger* did in drama"; and its author's "impact on the 1950s came to rival that of [Evelyn] Waugh on the 1920s."[6]

Over a nearly forty-year career Amis produced more than twenty novels, two volumes of poetry, a study of Rudyard Kipling, and two edited collections on science fiction. He also wrote hundreds of critical articles and reviews

– most famously and frequently in the *Spectator* – on subjects ranging from education and politics to literature and film, in which the author demonstrated his acerbic wit and attacked "pretentiousness in any form."[7] As the above sketch suggests, it is fair to regard Amis, like Orwell, as a journalist and man of letters as much as a novelist. As Amis himself affirmed,

> I'm not exactly an entertainer pure and simple, not exactly an artist pure and simple, certainly not an incisive critic of society, and certainly not a political figure though I'm interested in politics. . . . I'm just a combination of some of those things.[8]

To say that Amis was a successful writer with a wide following is not to suggest that he was uncontroversial. The controversy stems from the fact that his works attacked individuals from across Britain's cultural, social, and political spectrums. Indeed, Amis, who was sharply critical of both the Left and the Right, has "been described as a proletarian boor and an elitist dandy, both Philistine and University Wit."[9] In this same vein, *Lucky Jim* is both uproariously funny and deadly serious, both academic satire and comic romance; it directs its spleen both at what remained of England's traditional class structure and at the new Welfare State and the educational reforms that followed in the wake of the Second World War.

Lucky Jim was anti-modernist to the extent that it challenged, at least implicitly, the legitimacy and worth of the "experimental novel" of a literary generation earlier. Yet the novel represented far more than a conservative or traditional backlash; it was also innovative in many ways. As David Lodge observes, "*Lucky Jim* was the first British campus novel . . . to take as its central character a lecturer at a provincial university, and to find a rich seam of comic and narrative material in that small world."[10] *Lucky Jim*, Lodge continues, was a

> distinctly British version of a kind of novel that had hitherto been a peculiarly American phenomenon. My own novels of university life, and those of Malcolm Bradbury, Howard Jacobson, Andrew Davies et al., are deeply indebted to its example. Jim Dixon's anxiety about his professional future, his dependence on the patronage of a senior colleague whom he despises, is a recurrent feature of the genre.[11]

Put simply, *Lucky Jim* almost single-handedly launched an important British novelistic subgenre of the second half of the twentieth century.

II

Kingsley Amis was born in London in 1922. He was educated at the City of London School and then at St John's College, Oxford, where in 1947 he gained a BA in English. Amis's Oxford years were interrupted by his wartime army service, between 1942 and 1945, in the Royal Corps of Signals. Between 1949 and 1961 he was a lecturer in English at University College, Swansea, Wales; from 1961 to 1963 he was a Fellow of Peterhouse College, Cambridge. Displeased with academic life in general and with his Cambridge post in particular, Amis in 1963 left academia for good (not counting a couple of short stints as a visiting lecturer at American universities) and settled in the greater London area. By this time Amis had published three novels in addition to *Lucky Jim* – *That Uncertain Feeling* (1955), *I Like It Here* (1958), and *Take a Girl Like You* (1960) – which together solidified his literary reputation in the English-speaking world ("Looking forward to seeing you at the premiere of *Lucky Jim* on ice," Amis wrote to his publisher on the success of his first novel).[12] His novels of the sixties – *One Fat Englishman* (1963), *The Anti-Death League* (1966), and *The Green Man* (1969) – tended to be darker than his earlier works, though he never altered his view of himself as an entertainer writing for a popular audience. Amis continued to write novels and criticism during the seventies, yet it was in the eighties that his career experienced a renaissance. The author was made a CBE (Commander of the British Empire) in 1981, was awarded the Booker Prize for his novel *The Old Devils* in 1986, and was knighted in 1990. His *Memoirs* emerged in 1991 and Amis died in 1995. Kingsley's son (by a first marriage), Martin Amis, best known for such novels as *Money* (1984), *London Fields* (1989), and *The Information* (1995), has become an important writer in his own right.

   Lucky Jim as we know it would not have come about without the help Amis received from his St John's friend, the poet Philip Larkin. As one critic observes, Amis's first novel "was dedicated to Larkin," who "helped to inspire and to edit it," and who "has been seen as the original model for its main character."[13] According to Amis, the original inspiration for *Lucky Jim* was not, as many assume, the author's experience at Swansea, where he was then teaching; rather, it was a visit he paid to Larkin, in the mid-1940s, when the latter was employed at the university in Leicester. In his *Memoirs* Amis remembers looking around the Senior Common Room of that institution "a couple of times and [thinking] to myself, 'Christ, somebody ought to do something with this'. Not that it was awful – well, only a bit; it was . . . a whole mode of existence no one had got on to from outside . . . I would do something with it."[14] Amis also notes in his *Memoirs* that Jim Dixon's name derived from

"Dixon Drive," Larkin's address in Leicester; and that his poet-friend helped him thoroughly revise an early draft of the manuscript.[15]

Amis in general and *Lucky Jim* in particular are commonly associated with the "Angry Young Men" of the British 1950s, a politico-literary "movement" that was understood to embrace a political and artistic agenda. As David Lodge sums up this cultural phenomenon, "'The Angry Young Men' was a journalistic term, originally put into circulation by a leading article in the *Spectator*, to group together a number of authors and/or their fictional heroes, who appeared on the literary and theoretical scenes in the mid-to-late 1950s, vigorously expressing their discontent with life in contemporary Britain."[16] The roster of angry young male protagonists of the time includes Jimmy Porter in John Osborne's play *Look Back in Anger* (1956), Arthur Seaton in Alan Sillitoe's novel *Saturday Night and Sunday Morning* (1958), Joe Lampton in John Braine's novel *Room at the Top* (1957), Charles Lumley in John Wain's novel *Hurry on Down* (1953), and of course Dixon in Amis's debut novel. As disparate in disposition and situation as these male protagonists may be, they represent an emergent meritocracy, share an anti-establishment agenda, and "fulminate against the society in which they find themselves, criticizing its politics, morality, jobs, women, and the widespread complacency they perceive."[17] The new Welfare State and the democratized educational system are targeted by many of these lower-middle-class or working-class protagonists, who combine progressive social protest with cultural conservatism, a skepticism about the emergent Welfare State (which followed in the wake of the 1942 "Beveridge Report") with a concern about "the continuing impregnability of the ostensibly rich."[18]

Despite the social and intellectual common ground shared by these works and authors (indeed, Amis, Wain, and Larkin all overlapped at St John's College during the 1940s), Amis from the start questioned the very existence of such a "movement." While the above works collectively seemed to signal a trend – "people could be forgiven," Amis wrote, "for mistaking this for a sort of minor revolution or turning point in English writing"[19] – the author was nevertheless displeased with being "lumped together with some very strange people" in a "non-existent movement,"[20] and viewed this school as little more than "a phantom creation of literary journalists."[21] As Bradbury explains, many of the authors in this movement "were not angry, many were not young, and a lot of them were women."[22]

Like their fiction, the politics of the "Angries" incorporated both reactionary and forward-looking elements. In addition to expressing the general "feeling of exhaustion after the war"[23] – Jimmy Porter in Osborne's *Look Back in Anger* famously expresses the mid-1950s sense that there were no "good, brave causes left"[24] – Amis and the others associated with this group rebelled against what Lodge calls the "received wisdom" of the 1940s:

that the Second World War . . . the landslide victory of the Labour Party in the General Election of 1945, and the establishment of the Welfare State, with free secondary and tertiary education, had genuinely democratized British society, and got rid of its class divisions and inequalities for good.[25]

By the time *Lucky Jim* emerged, however,

Six costly years of war had been followed by seven or eight costly years of peace. The Labour Party's burst of postwar idealism was spent; an empire had been lost; the bill for it all lay on [Britain] like a blight. Cities were still bomb-shattered, landlords rapacious, railways and transport grimly run-down, commuting an expensive horror, rationing still in effect.[26]

Amis's first novel registers – explicitly or implicitly, humorously or not – many of these discontents.

Politically, Amis moved from the Left to the Right over the course of his long career (Amis likens his move to that undertaken by Wordsworth and many other authors).[27] In the early 1950s, for example, at the time of writing *Lucky Jim*, Amis was avowedly left-wing in orientation (earlier, at St John's, he even joined the Communist Party, albeit half-heartedly). Indeed, during the 1950s Amis "was announcing himself a probable lifetime Labour voter, and explored his Fabian allegiances" in a 1957 pamphlet, *Socialism and the Intellectuals*.[28] By the 1960s, however, Amis's rightward drift became noticeable; and by the 1980s Amis viewed himself a thoroughgoing Tory with a few "liberal" holdovers in the areas of "hanging, homosexuality, [and] abortion."[29]

Amis's drift to the right represents a less dramatic political shift than meets the eye, however. After all, as one critic explains, "In reality, Amis was only very hesitantly committed to the left," even in the 1950s.

His allegiance to the Labour Party was weak; Labour, to Amis, was only the lesser of two evils. Before the 1959 election he wrote, "My vote will be anti-Tory, not pro-Labour." As for his pamphlet, despite the fact that it was published by the Fabian society, it had very little to say in favor of Socialism. Rather, it [expressed Amis's] lack of political commitment.[30]

Indeed, Amis's professed apathy in this pamphlet for politics in general and for Labour in particular, and his attack on intellectuals for not knowing much about politics and for caring too much about general principles, "roused a furor" even "in liberal journals."[31]

Amis was particularly skeptical about the democratization of education – "more will mean worse," he famously wrote[32] – that was occurring in the British university system after World War II. He even penned some "Black Papers" on education, "manifestos designed to counter the official government 'White Papers' by pointing up a general decline in educational standards."[33] Interestingly, the author's worries regarding this system came to light in novelist W. Somerset Maugham's praise for *Lucky Jim*. Maugham noted the novel's "significance as a social document" yet regarded this significance as "ominous":

> I am told that today ... more than sixty per cent of the men who go to the universities [in Britain] go on a Government grant. This is a new class that has entered upon the scene. It is the white-collar proletariat.... They do not go to the university to acquire culture, but to get a job, and when they have got one, scamp it. They have no manners ... Their idea of a celebration is to go to a public house and drink six beers. They are mean, malicious and envious ... They are scum. They will in due course leave the university. Some will doubtless sink back, perhaps with relief, into the modest class from which they emerged ...[34]

Although different in tone from the critique of the educational system leveled by *Lucky Jim*, Maugham's words capture the novel's sense that academic standards after the war were much diminished from what they had been in the days prior to the push to bring university education to the masses.

An anti-modernist, anti-Romantic, anti-elitist aesthetic agenda accompanied the postwar sociopolitical agenda of many "Angries." As Bradbury observes, the new tone seemed determined "to dispense with the experimentalism of the 1920s and 1930s, with the romanticism and apocalypticism of the 1940s" (particularly that of the Welsh poet Dylan Thomas), and with "the Beckettian despairs emanating from Paris."[35] Speaking of such "so-called Angries" as Wain, Braine, and himself, Amis affirms that they wrote their fiction in a traditional style, that they were "reactionaries rather than rebels. We were trying to get back, let's say, to the pre-Joycean tradition."[36] Indeed, this fiction "offered to return the literary arts to the accessible ways that prevailed before the coming of modernism."[37] As one critic writes, "In their concern not to be associated in any way with genteel Bloomsbury traditions of fine writing," many of "these writers cultivated a deliberately slapdash, honest Jack style of writing, while the loose, picaresque structure often adopted was symptomatic of an emphatic rejection of the ... Jamesian concept of form in the novel."[38] Amis's antipathy to experimental prose, which he deemed arcane, obscure, precious, and rarified, was openly expressed and thoroughgoing: "I can't bear it. I dislike, as I think most readers dislike, being in the slightest doubt about what is taking place, what is meant [in fiction]. I dislike mystification."[39] Amis attacks another idea that is often associated with Bloomsbury literary culture: that "style is a self-sufficient entity to be separated at will from qualities of subject matter and capable of exhibiting a 'charm' or 'iridescence' of its own."[40]

Amis is at his most strident and outspoken in taking on modernist literary aesthetics in a 1958 piece in the *Spectator*. There he writes:

> The idea about experiment being the life-blood of the English novel is one that dies hard. "Experiment," in this context, boils down pretty regularly to "obtruded oddity," whether in construction – multiple viewpoints and such – or in style . . . Shift from one scene to the next in midsentence, cut down on verbs or definite articles, and you are putting yourself right up in the forefront, at any rate in the eyes of those who were reared on Joyce and Virginia Woolf . . .[41]

What Bradbury says of Jim Dixon, then – that he is an intellectual rebel "against genteel high culture, aestheticism and bohemianism, the hangover of Bloomsbury"[42] – is equally true of Jim's creator.[43]

Lodge is correct to place Amis's fiction within the tradition of British comic writing that stretches back from "Waugh, Wodehouse, Dickens and Fielding to Restoration and Elizabethan comedy";[44] and Bradbury is right to speak of Amis as having inherited "the role of the Comic Bad Man of English Letters which Waugh had so powerfully sustained a generation earlier."[45] Indeed, Amis describes himself as "writing novels within the main English-language tradition" about "understandable characters in a straight-forward style."[46] His novels borrow from the comic satire devices of the eighteenth-century British novel in general and of the works of Henry Fielding, the author of *Tom Jones* and *Joseph Andrews*, in particular.[47] As Walter Allen observes, "the Amis hero can be described as Fielding does Tom Jones: 'Though he did not always act rightly, yet he never did otherwise without feeling and suffering for it'; and like Tom Jones's, his life is 'a constant struggle between honour and inclination'."[48] One imagines that Amis agrees with the protagonist of his third novel, *I Like it Here*, who lauds Fielding as "the only non-contemporary novelist who could be read with unaffected and whole-hearted interest, the only one who never had to be apologized for or excused on the grounds of changing taste."[49] And Amis in a 1957 essay praises Fielding for his "wit," "irony," and concern "not to bore the reader, to keep the narrative going along,"[50] and affirms that, even after two hundred years, Fielding's realism has "not dimmed" and his humor "is closer to our own than that of any writer before the present century."[51]

III

Amis refers to himself as "a writer of serio-comedies,"[52] and *Lucky Jim*, a romantic comedy with picaresque elements, fits this mold. A "curious mixture of realism and fairy tale,"[53] *Lucky Jim* retells the Cinderella story, this time with a deserving male (rather than female) protagonist, who eventually triumphs over characters in superior positions of power who conspire against him. Jim is "unjustly doomed to low status and to enduring his own servility towards unworthy and even evil people,"[54] until such time, that is, that "luck," his inherent goodness, and poetic justice together secure his reversal of fortune.[55]

The deceptively simple plot of *Lucky Jim* is easily summarized. When we first encounter Jim Dixon, the novel's protagonist, he is a recently hired Medievalist in the history department of a provincial British University. His head of department, Professor Welch, is a pretentious and ineffectual bore that Jim must impress in order to keep his job and who holds his superior rank over Jim's head in an attempt to get Jim to do his bidding. Also contributing to Jim's misery is Margaret Peel, a neurotic, controlling female colleague of his with whom he is repeatedly thrown together and with whom he appears destined unhappily to be romantically involved. In contrast to Margaret is the novel's other major female character, the 19-year-old Christine Callaghan, the girlfriend of one of Welch's two sons, Bertrand, a painter. Jim skirmishes, verbally or physically, with this arrogant and pretentious artist at many points. The crisis of the plot occurs at Jim's public lecture, on "Merrie England," which Welch coerces him into delivering and which he delivers drunk and as a means of protest. After the lecture Jim "departs for comedy's literary reward of a good job and the nicest girl, out there in the ordinary commonsense working world."[56] That is to say, being fired for his disastrous lecture enables Jim to shake off Margaret, his low-paying academic job, and the provinces in one fell swoop. Thanks to a dream-job offer from Christine's Scottish uncle, the philanthropist Julius Gore-Urquhart, Jim leaves for London with Christine, who at last has seen through Bertrand. In structure, then, this third-person perspective novel is comic, with the promise of happiness, financial success, and marriage arising out of the ashes of the protagonist's self-doubt, humiliation, and bad luck.

One of the major tensions upon which the novel and Jim's fortune hinge is that between Margaret Peel and Christine Callaghan, two female characters who are not as they first appear (Margaret initially appears to be sympathetic and down-to-earth but is not; Christine appears to be snobby and duplicitous, but is later revealed to be admirable). We first encounter the "small, thin, and bespectacled" (18) Margaret convalescing at the Welchs, having recently "cracked up" (10) and attempted suicide by sleeping pills as a result of being jilted by her boyfriend Catchpole. (We later learn that this jilting is completely fabricated by Margaret in order to gain sympathy. Although Catchpole, who is in any case her acquaintance not her boyfriend, does leave town for Wales, he does so on purposes of business, not romance. He is correct to deem Margaret one of those people "who feed on emotional tension" [235].) Catchpole's departure leaves Jim, by default, in charge of this "neurotic who'd recently taken a bad beating" (77).[57] Carol, the wife of Jim's history colleague Cecil Goldsmith, concludes of Margaret to Jim: "Throw her a lifebelt and she'll pull you under" (121).[58]

Christine is everything that Margaret is not. In contrast to Margaret's "minimal prettiness" (195), false refinement, "decidedly ill-judged . . . royal-blue taffeta" gown (106), and "bright make-up" (18), Christine sports "fair hair . . . brown eyes and no lipstick . . . the premeditated simplicity of the . . . unornamented white linen blouse" (39). Just as the beautiful Christine's "plain" dress shows up Margaret's failed attempts at beauty, so Margaret's "silver-bells" (that is, affected female) laugh is shown up by Christine's more genuine if cacophonous "non-silver-bells sort" (95) of laugh. While the delicate and indirect Margaret embraces social conventions, the bolder and less formal Christine flouts them.[59] Unlike the socially correct yet artificial Margaret, Christine stands in an "awkward," "uncomfortable," and "ungraceful" fashion. For Jim, however, "there could be no more beautiful way for a woman to stand" (219). Also in contrast to Margaret, Christine's "absence of conventional [female] sensitivity" (198) strikes Jim as refreshing. At one point Margaret is even depicted as an "actress" playing a role rather than as a woman feeling an emotion (111). The contrast between Margaret's and Christine's treatment of Jim is also of relevance. Not only does Christine pay her own way when she goes out with Jim while Margaret lets the ill-paid and impecunious Jim pick up the tab, but Christine's unselfconscious sexuality contrasts sharply with Margaret's attempt to make Jim feel guilty for his advances, which in any case she has encouraged.[60]

If Margaret proves to be an imprisoning force in Jim's life, Christine sets him free. She gives Jim both the confidence to tell Margaret to "stop depending" on him "emotionally" (158) and the necessary help in overcoming his adolescent sexual anxiety and repression.[61] Moreover, Jim and Christine operate on a similar moral level. In contrast to Bertrand's and to Margaret's duplicity (Margaret fabricates a relationship with Catchpole and feigns a suicide attempt; Bertrand conceals an adulterous affair with Carol Goldsmith), Jim (even in his clownish shenanigans) and Christine act honorably and with integrity, even when it costs them. For example, as expedient as it would be for Jim, in the midst of his "Bertrand-war" (142), to divulge to Christine the fact that Bertrand is betraying her in his affair with Carol, he remains quiet. Neither does Christine betray Bertrand when she has an easy opportunity to do so.

Through Christine Jim also meets Gore-Urquhart, Christine's uncle and Jim's "eventual savior and benefactor."[62] A comic-grotesque character who is described as middle aged and oddly shaped, with the look "of a drunken sage trying to collect his wits, a look intensified by slightly protruding lips and a single black eyebrow running from temple to temple" (109), Gore-Urquhart is "a rich devotee of the arts who made occasional contributions to the arts sections of the weekly reviews" (47) and who shares Jim's antipathy for academic and artistic cant or pretension of any kind. Although Bertrand wishes to be the one to fill Gore-Urquhart's vacant "private secretaryship" (48) in London, assuming that the position will enhance his career as a painter, it is Jim, appropriately, who ultimately gets the job. Gore-Urquhart, Jim's "fairy godfather"[63] and "fellow sufferer" (215),[64] is something of a Prospero figure who both sees what will happen and brings it about. The novel's *deus ex machina*, Gore-Urquhart manages to make things end comically when otherwise they would not.

Lucky Jim is a well-made novel; there is a careful rhythm and intricate structure to the work and to the individual chapters therein, which are "tightly self-contained."[65] As one critic observes, "The twenty-five chapters are structured around three major events . . . the evening musicale at [Welch's] house, the Summer Ball, and the disastrous public lecture"[66] on the theme of "Merrie England."[67] Another indication of the novel's deliberate structuring is the fact that the first chapter ends with a reference to this lecture (17), the event that precipitates the crisis that in turn alters the course of Jim's life from a self-destructive and pathetic to a comic and redemptive one. Appropriately, this carefully structured comic novel ends with "laughter" (251) and with the union of hero and heroine. For Jim Dixon, at least, the world has been put in order and justice prevails.

One other example of *Lucky Jim*'s solid architecture is the analogy the novel constructs between the Jim–Margaret and the Jim–university relationships. Just as being freed from academic life gives Jim a new sense of energy (when he is fired Jim feels "almost free of care" [232] and thinks "how nice it was to have nothing he must do" [233]), so looking at Margaret causes "an intolerable weight" to fall "upon him" (185), and being free of her gives Jim a sense of newfound euphoria. As Lodge observes of Jim, "Just as he goes through the motions of being a university teacher, knowing he is in bad faith, but unable to do anything about it, so he feels bound to go through the motions of being Margaret's partner, even though he has no desire, and hardly any affection, for her."[68] Jim is freed from this prison-house of his own making by two interrelated developments in the novel: he is "liberated from an unsatisfying career in education" by Gore-Urquhart's offer of a post in London and he is "redeemed from his emotional thralldom to Margaret."[69]

To assert that *Lucky Jim* is a comic, and indeed sublimely funny, work is not to rule out its serious side, however. Put differently, although Amis "had something serious to say" in writing *Lucky Jim*, he "also thought the poor old reader had had a pretty thin time of it recently, with so many dead serious writers around, and that he could do with something funny."[70] The novel's comic and farcical dimensions work well with its psychological and social criticism to the extent that the novel is a satire, a literary genre, according to a standard definition, that "blends a critical attitude with humor and wit to the end that human institutions or humanity may be improved." The satirist "is conscious of the frailty" of the institutions of human "devising and attempts through laughter" less to tear such institutions down than "to inspire a remodeling."[71] In a similar vein, Amis comments that Dixon "certainly didn't want to *destroy* the system" and should not be thought of as a "rebel."[72] And in a 1957 essay on the post-war satiric novel, "Laughter's to be taken seriously," Amis affirms the importance of the satiric mode to the Britain of his day:

> We are in for a golden age of satire, in my opinion, and if this is so we will be fortunate indeed. Satire offers a social and moral contribution. A culture without satire is a culture without self-criticism and thus, ultimately, without humanity. A society such as ours, in which the forms of power are changing and multiplying, needs above all the restraining influences of savage laughter.[73]

Significantly, *Lucky Jim* ends on a note of healing and cathartic (if not actually "savage") laughter.

The particular butt of the novel's satire, of course, is academic life. Although academic satire, in which scholars are mocked and learning is called into question, is as old as Plato's *Republic* (Book IV) and *Symposium*,[74] Amis's university setting functions somewhat more widely, "as the epitome of a stuffy, provincial bourgeois world"[75] and as a focus for his "wider satire of contemporary life and society."[76]

A look at the way in which *Lucky Jim* exposes "the academic racket, and the pseudo-culture and social pretensions that so often accompany it,"[77] is of course essential in any reading of the novel.[78] Amis's most thoroughgoing assault on the academic personality – and certainly one of the most devastating satiric portraits of an academic in any novel – is found in his portrait of Professor "Neddy" Welch. Upon first meeting Welch we learn that "No other Professor" in all of Britain "set such store by being called Professor" (7).

Depicted as pretentious and pedantic, slow-witted and inarticulate (frequently not finishing sentences at all, many of which trail off in ellipses), solipsistic and boring, exploitative and eccentric, Welch is the stuff of academic caricature. At one point, touching upon Welch's self-absorption, Jim imagines that even if he went on a drunken rampage in the Common Room in Welch's presence, "screeching obscenities, punching out the window-panes, fouling the periodicals, [this] would escape Welch's notice altogether, provided his own person remained inviolate" (63). At another point we learn of Dixon's pleasure in seeing "evidence that Welch's mind could still be reached from the outside" (86). At still another, Jim, when driving with Welch, addresses his Professor's dullness by thinking, "Welch's driving seemed to have improved slightly; at any rate, the only death Dixon felt himself threatened by was death from exposure to boredom" (178). Merely being spoken to by Welch, as by Margaret, makes Dixon "feel heavy and immovable" (218).

Welch's exploitative attitude toward Jim stems from the "decisive power" the former has over the latter's academic future (8). Welch employs his "evasion technique" (86) in order to keep Jim guessing about where he stands, professionally speaking. By keeping Jim in the dark as to whether his teaching contract will be renewed in the coming academic year, Welch keeps Jim beholden to him, and therefore willing to do his bidding. None of this is lost on Jim, who correctly views Welch's requests of him to do his superior's research and to deliver the public lecture as forms of blackmail (82). That Welch frequently calls Dixon "Faulkner," Jim's doomed predecessor, underscores both the Professor's encroaching senility and his implicit threat not to rehire his underling. Surely Amis intended for readers to see a significance in the Professor's name: to "welch" (sometimes spelled "welsh") means to fail to fulfill a promised obligation. In any case, in Welch, as Lodge concludes, Amis drew "an immortal portrait of the absent-mindedness, vanity, eccentricity and practical incompetence that academic institutions seem to tolerate and even to encourage."[79]

Welch may be the primary target of Amis's academic satire, but Jim himself is a close second. Jim is depicted as far more interested in the trappings of academic life than in the work – the teaching and scholarship – of such a life. When walking with Welch one day on campus, for example,

> Dixon realized that their progress, deliberate and to all appearances thoughtful, must seem rather donnish to passing students. He and Welch might well be talking about history, and in the way history might be talked about in Oxford and Cambridge quadrangles. At moments like this Dixon came near to wishing that they really were. (8)

Threatened by what his better students know about his subject (do they know and care more about his field than he does?), Jim competes with his male students for the attention of the attractive female students rather than attempting to improve his own inadequate grasp of medieval history. At one point, for example, we read that "Dixon's efforts on behalf of his special [academic] subject, apart from thinking how much he hated it, had been confined to aiming to secure for it the three prettiest girls in the class" (28). At another, Jim sums up his relationship with his history students at large: "They waste my time and I waste theirs" (214).

If Jim has little real interest in teaching his academic field (the sight of the departmental timetable listing teaching assignments, for example, leads him to feel "over-mastering, orgiastic boredom, and its companion, real hatred" [85]), he has still less interest in researching it. His sole (and as yet unpublished) scholarly essay, "The economic influence of the developments in shipbuilding techniques, 1450 to 1485," is a case in point. To the extent that writing the article involved much "frenzied fact-grubbing and fanatical boredom" (15), Jim's title for the essay is "perfect":

[I]t crystallized the article's niggling mindlessness, its funereal parade of yawn-enforcing facts, the pseudo-light it threw upon non-problems. Dixon had read, or begun to read, dozens like it, but his own seemed worse than most in its air of being convinced of its own usefulness and significance . . . His thinking all this without having defiled and set fire to the typescript only made him appear to himself as more of a hypocrite and fool. (14–15)

Under pressure from Welch to make sure that his article is published if he wishes to be re-employed in the coming academic year, Dixon endeavors, at many points in the novel, to secure a home for it. When Dixon learns that the article will be published after all, he can only think, "Welch would find it harder to sack him now" (30). Jim's luck runs out once more, however, when he learns that the editor of the journal in which his essay was to appear has translated his piece into Italian and has published it under the editor's own name. He also learns that the thieving editor is shortly to become the "Chair of History of Commerce" in a regional university in Argentina (171) and that the journal in which his essay was to appear will likely fold. Like university teaching, then, academic scholarship in the world of *Lucky Jim* is both intellectually insubstantial and professionally corrupt.

Jim's reason for becoming a medievalist – he has no particular interest in the Middle Ages – is also revealing. As he explains to a colleague in the English Department, "the medieval papers were a soft option in the Leicester course, so I specialized in them. Then when I applied for the job here, I naturally made a big point of that, because it looked better to seem interested in something specific" (33). This explains why Jim has such a difficult time writing his one-hour "Merrie England" lecture, which is wholly derivative (he hopes to "construct" his lecture largely "out of others' efforts" [169]), toadying (he plans to play up to Professor Welch in a bid to have his contract renewed), and vacuous (he desperately searches for a way to fill his hour-long talk and can only reach for platitude after platitude). Jim likens the experience of writing this lecture to that of traveling "along the knife-edge dividing the conceivably-just-about-relevant from the irreducibly, immitigably irrelevant" (195). After adding "a presumably rather extensive conclusion" of fifteen minutes' duration, Dixon flirts with (but then abandons) the idea of closing his talk with the line, "Finally, thank God for the twentieth century" (195).

The lecture scene itself, one of the funniest episodes in modern fiction, is the riotous climax of *Lucky Jim*. Upon entering the lecture arena Jim notes that it appears "to contain everybody he knew or had ever known, apart from his parents" (213). This leads him to feel "like going round and notifying each person individually of his preference that they should leave" (213). So alienated is Jim from his own speech and so out of control does he become owing to severe intoxication that at one point, before his outright collapse that comprises his lecture's grand finale, he imagines himself to sound "like an unusually fanatical Nazi trooper in charge of a book-burning reading out to the crowd excerpts from a pamphlet written by a pacifist, Jewish, literate Communist" (226). Needless to say, for "wrecking a public lecture" (228) Jim is dropped from the staff of the university.

Amis's academic satire, then, cuts in two directions. On the one hand, Jim is "ill-at-ease and out of place in the university because he does not at heart subscribe to its social and cultural values, preferring pop music to Mozart, pubs to drawing rooms, non-academic company to academic."[80] On the other hand, Jim's academic pretence, indolence, and fraudulence, while perhaps more pronounced than those of his colleagues, is revealed to be endemic to the academic culture at large. The academy, *Lucky Jim* suggests, by no means lives up to its own professed ideal of itself.

The novel satirizes the artistic life as much as it is does the academic one, however. In *Lucky Jim* both the academic and artistic worlds – linked here by Welch blood – are stocked with elitist and pretentious phonies who are eager to victimize Jim. Early in the novel Welch invites Jim to his "arty get-together" (23) in order (Jim imagines) to test his "reactions to culture" and to determine whether he is "a fit person to teach in a university" (24).[81] Later in the novel Jim is greeted by a painting in the hall of the Welch home that appears to be "The work of some kindergarten oaf," recalling "in its technique the sort of drawing found in male lavatories, though its subject, an assortment of barrel-bodied animals debouching from the Ark, was of narrower appeal" (180).

Worse still than Welch himself in this regard are his two sons – "the effeminate writing Michel and the bearded pacifist painting Bertrand" (13) – whose political sensitivities and French names suggest a certain aesthetic pretension. Even Bertrand's diction and style of speech, with its double negatives and convoluted syntax, further this suggestion. For example, Bertrand at one point says, "Upon consideration I feel it incumbent upon me to doubt it" (40), and at another remarks, "I remember being not unentertained" (48). Bertrand's speech and demeanor inspire Dixon to fantasize devoting "the next ten years to working his way to a position as art critic on purpose to review Bertrand's work unfavourably" (50). Carol Goldsmith's assessment of Bertrand's thinking – that "Great artists always have a lot of women, so if he can have a lot of women that makes him a great artist, never mind what his pictures are like" (120–1) – underscores the novel's linking of artistic phoniness and romantic duplicity. As with academic life, Jim finds the trappings of artistic life, if not art itself, to be of some appeal: "Dixon himself had sometimes wished he wrote poetry or something as a claim to developed character" (140). That the Welch family is implicated in both academic and artistic pretentiousness and narcissism – "Bertrand's a bore, he's like his dad, the only thing that interests him is him" (143), Jim observes – further links the two institutions that are the special targets of the novel's satire.

Bradbury holds that Amis's novel turns from "political matters to commonsense moral vision,"[82] but this should not be taken to suggest that the novel lacks a politics. Amis has made clear his affinity for "the tradition of Tory satire,"[83] yet *Lucky Jim*, for all of its attacks on progressive educational reforms, also attacks the stubbornly class-bound, conservative orientation of English society. In other words, the politics of *Lucky Jim*, like the politics of the "Angries," is a curious mixture of right-wing and left-wing proclivities.[84]

That said, the novel more often than not associates conservatism and elitism with the scoundrels (Margaret, the Welchs), and progressive and democratic ideas with the heroes (Gore-Urquhart, Christine, Jim). Just as Amis remarked, "Let's . . . face the obvious truth that you're probably a better person and nicer to your fellows if you are reasonably contented, reasonably well off, and have a reasonably comfortable time,"[85] so Jim argues, in a socialist vein, "If one man's got ten buns and another's got two, and a bun has got to be given up by one of them, then surely you take it from the man with ten buns" (51). That is to say, commonsense justice rather than ideological principle drives *Lucky Jim*'s political orientation. As Lodge puts it, the left-wing stance of *Lucky Jim* "is an emotional, intuitive matter, more concerned with class and manners than with politics as such."[86]

Unsurprisingly, Jim argues the above point to his rival, the artist Bertrand, who takes up the elitist (and self-serving) position that "the rich play an essential role in modern society," having "kept the arts going" (51). Bertrand admires the rich, he continues somewhat circularly, "Because they're charming, because they're generous, because they've learnt to appreciate the things I happen to like myself, because their houses are full of beautiful things" (52). It is also implied that Mrs Welch, Bertrand's mother, possesses political views that incline to the right. Believing that the "Welfare State" and "so-called freedom in education" will lead to increased dependence on the government, her attitude toward the two is said to be negative (176). Margaret's political sympathies are more subtly suggested: she "turns out to sing for a local Conservative club."[87]

Essential to an understanding of *Lucky Jim* is an understanding of the mechanics of the novel's comic satire: the novel's humorous descriptions and wordplay, verbal jokes, and ironic or incongruous images. Much of the novel's humor rests on its situation and style, both of which rely on "Amis's flawless sense of timing: the way he controls the development of an action, or a sentence, to create that combination of surprise and logicality that is the heart of comedy."[88]

Humorous and apposite similes abound in Amis's novel: in response to a question from Dixon, for example, Welch's "clay-like features changed indefinably as his attention, like a squadron of slow old battleships, began wheeling to face this new phenomenon" (9). Later, "Welch's head lifted slowly, like the muzzle of some obsolete howitzer" (84). Figurative language is also employed at Jim's expense. For example, at one point we read that "Fury flared up in [Jim's] mind like forgotten toast under a grill" (28); at another we learn that "A sudden douche of terror . . . squirted itself all over Dixon" (127); at yet another, upon his awakening one morning, we understand that Jim's "mouth had been used as a latrine by some small creature of the night, and then as its mausoleum" (61).

In addition to its ingenious use of figurative language for descriptive purposes, the novel also generates its humor by detailing a series of absurd yet familiar events in Jim's life. In particular Amis focuses on Jim's elaborate yet futile attempts to limit his smoking (Dixon lit "the cigarette which, according to his schedule, he ought to be lighting after breakfast on the next day but one" [128]) and on his equally elaborate and futile attempts to conserve money, largely by cutting down on his beer consumption ("he'd spent more than he could afford and drunk more than he ought, and yet he felt nothing but satisfaction and peace" [54]). Dixon even vows to "review his financial position" to see "if he could somehow restore it from complete impossibility to its usual level of merely imminent disaster" (153).

Dixon's honest self-criticism and keen powers of observation also help power the novel's comedy. For example, we read that "As soon as Dixon recognized the mental envelope containing this [uncomfortable] question he thrust it away from him unopened" (60). At another point we view Jim's thoughts of Bertrand and Christine (before he comes to know the latter): "He disliked this girl and her boy-friend so much that he couldn't understand why they didn't dislike each other" (69). At still another Jim thinks, "Bertrand must not be a good painter; he, Dixon, would not permit it" (112).

As important to the novel's comedy as such moments of Jim's awareness may be, the main source of humor in the novel, as Lodge observes, is "the contrast between Jim's outer world and his inner world." While Jim tries, not very successfully, "to show the outer world the image of an industrious, respectable well-mannered young man, his mind seethes with caustic sarcasm directed against himself and others, with fantasies of violence done to enemies, of triumph for himself."[89] Examples of this contrast abound. At one point, for example, as Welch speaks, Jim's face becomes "the perfect audience for his talk, laughing at its jokes, reflecting its puzzlement or earnestness" (178). At another, when speaking with Welch, Jim maintains a perfectly collected demeanor but pretends to himself "that he'd pick up his professor around the waist, squeeze the furry . . . waistcoat against him to expel the breath, run heavily with him up the steps, along the corridor to the Staff Cloak-room, and plunge the too-small feet . . . into a lavatory basin, pulling the plug once, twice, and again, stuffing the mouth with toilet-paper" (9–10). Slightly later Jim catches "sight of his own face in the wall-mirror and was surprised to see that it wore an expression of eager friendliness" (12).

Two more examples of this comic contrast between Jim's inner and outer worlds merit our attention. In one, when forced to speak with Welch during a car voyage, Jim must control his face "with the strain of making it smile and show interest and speak its few permitted words, of steering it between a collapse into helpless fatigue and a tautening with anarchic fury" (13). In the second, while at Neddy's musicale, "Dixon kept his head down" and "moved his mouth as little as possible consistent with being unmistakably seen to move it" (37).

That said, Jim is "aware of the hypocrisy involved in preserving the discrepancy" between his inner and outer worlds;[90] indeed, his frequent glances at himself in mirrors[91] underscore this point. Seen in this light, Jim's "face-pulling, rude gesturing, and practical joking" are attempts "to give some physical expression to his inner life of protest."[92] Jim's menagerie of faces – these include his "tragic-mask face" (55), "crazy-peasant face" (74), "Martian-invader face" (91), "Eskimo face" (97), "lemon-sucking face" (141), "Evelyn Waugh face" (220), and "Sex Life in Ancient Rome face" (250) – are made in such a way that other characters cannot see them; they enable Jim to mock and vent his anger at those around him without causing offence.

Lodge is also correct to note that "The issues of the novel can only be resolved when Jim wills his inner life to coincide with his outer life";[93] this, more than securing a London job or the love of Christine, constitutes the real victory that he must achieve if he hopes to escape from the imprisoning situation in which he finds himself. The closing of this gap occurs, tellingly, after Jim's fist-fight with Bertrand. Immediately after flooring Bertrand Jim thinks, "The bloody old towser-faced boot-faced totem-pole on a crap reservation." He then tells Bertrand directly, "'You bloody old towser-faced boot-faced totem-pole on a crap reservation'" (209). This is the first of a series of events, which includes his drunken lecture and his escape to London with Christine, that anticipates Jim's mental (and also physical) liberation. At last "thought and speech, the inner and the outer worlds coincide," Lodge argues; "Jim ceases to be a guilty hypocrite and reaps his reward."[94]

Lucky Jim sews up neatly and comically: Jim must race the clock, on a public bus, to meet up with Christine at her London-bound train if he hopes to set things right between them. Unluckily, the bus he is on seems to crawl with comically absurd slowness; the very cosmos seems to be conspiring against his attempt to reach the station and Christine in time. When the bus at one point inexplicably stops altogether Jim imagines that the driver was perhaps "slumped in his seat, the victim of syncope," or had suddenly "got an idea for a poem" (243). Soon another vehicle on the road slows the bus down once again, and

> Dixon thought he really would have to run downstairs and knife the drivers of both vehicles; what next? what next? What actually would be next: a masked holdup, a smash, floods, a burst tyre, an electric storm with falling trees and meteorites, a diversion, a low-level attack by Communist aircraft . . . ? (245)

When Jim finally makes it to the station and meets Christine he learns that she has "finished with Bertrand" (248) and knows about the artist's affair with Carol, who also has dumped him. Jim informs Christine that he has broken off with Margaret for good and that he has gotten the job, from her "Uncle Julius" (250), that Bertrand had sought. The novel thus ends comically, pointing toward the union of two deserving people.

Importantly, Amis ends his work with laughter that is neither savage nor splenetic but cathartic and healing. Amis's debut novel, like his essay on postwar British satire, might well have been titled "Laughter's to be taken seriously." In the novel's closing scene at the train station, Jim and Christine run into the entire Welch family. Jim approaches Neddy and Bertrand to have it out. Rather than spewing verbal violence, however, Jim can only laugh: "Dixon drew in breath to denounce them both, then blew it all out again in a howl of laughter" (251). Amis leaves Jim an angry young man no longer and ends his scrupulous satire on a note of forgiveness and reconciliation.

Chapter 3

William Golding's
Lord of the Flies (1954)

Before the Second World War I believed in the perfectibility of social man; that a correct structure of society would produce goodwill; and that therefore you could remove all social ills by a reorganization of society . . . [B]ut after the war I did not because I was unable to. I had discovered what one man can do to another . . . [T]here were things done during that period from which I still have to avert my mind less I should be physically sick. They were not done by the headhunters of New Guinea, or by some primitive tribe in the Amazon. They were done, skillfully, coldly, by educated men, doctors, lawyers, by men with a tradition of civilization behind them, to beings of their own kind.

William Golding, "Fable"[1]

Lord of the Flies was simply what it seemed sensible for me to write after the war, when everybody was thanking God they weren't Nazis. And I'd seen enough and thought enough to realize that every single one of us could be Nazis . . .

William Golding, in an interview[2]

I

Hailed by novelist E. M. Forster at the time of its publication as a "remarkable book,"[3] William Golding's *Lord of the Flies* remains, half a century later, one of the most penetrating and provocative literary responses to the events of World War II. At once an "anthropological passion play"[4] and a riposte to R. M. Ballantyne's 1857 novel *The Coral Island*, in which a group of un-supervised British boys who are stranded on an uninhabited island behave responsibly and maturely, Golding's debut novel concerns British boys in a similar situation who quickly abandon "civilized reason" and embrace "savagery." *Lord of the Flies* embodies a hard-learnt lesson of the Second World War: that "civilized" groups can succumb to the temptations of fascism – to what Erich Fromm calls the "escape from freedom" – and fashion new societies that rationalize abhorrent acts of oppression, violence, and murder.[5] Deemed by Malcolm Bradbury one of Britain's "greatest postwar novelists,"[6] Golding received the Nobel Prize for Literature in 1983.

Despite some initial controversy, *Lord of the Flies* came to be regarded as a "modern classic," particularly on American college campuses (*Time* magazine in 1962 deemed the novel "Lord of the Campus"[7]) within a decade of its publication. This popularity, however, did not translate into critical consensus about the novel's meaning and significance. Many competing and even mutually exclusive explications of the novel – Freudian, neo-Freudian, Jungian, Roman Catholic, Protestant, Nonconformist, Scientific Humanist, Marxist, and Hegelian, by Golding's own count[8] – were generated in short order.[9] *Lord of the Flies* seemed to be something of a Rorschach blot, in which readers traced their own critical preoccupations. Christian readings in particular were influential at first, seemingly with Golding's encouragement; yet such readings, many felt, threatened to obscure the novel's more penetrating – and certainly more contextually immediate – implications. As early as 1965 James R. Baker stated:

> [C]ritics have concentrated all too much on Golding's debts to Christian sources, with the result that he is now popularly regarded as a rigid Christian moralist. This is a false image. The emphasis of the critics has obscured Golding's fundamental realism and made it difficult to recognize that he satirizes both the Christian and the rationalist point of view.[10]

Moreover, for Baker, the "traditional comforts of Christian orthodoxy" are absent from the novel's controversial final chapter, where it would be most likely to appear.[11] E. M. Forster arrives at a similar insight: Golding's novel, for him, depicts sin but not "the idea of a Redeemer."[12] For these and other critics it is not so much that biblical metaphor is unimportant in Golding's novel as that, in Baker's words, "it forms only a part of the larger mythic frame in which Golding sees the nature and destiny of man."[13]

II

Lord of the Flies must be read with the cataclysm of the Second World War in mind. As different as Golding's response to the war (and indeed to the fifties thereafter) was from that of the "Angries,"[14] Golding shared with these writers the soul-shattering experience of the war, which exploded, seemingly forever, the idea of progress and human perfectibility. As Randall Stevenson observes, "Any 'anger' in Golding's fiction arises not from social conditions in the fifties" but "from dark conclusions about human nature in general based on the experience of the Second World War."[15] Indeed, as James R. Baker opens his important, early study of Golding,

> It would be difficult to overestimate the impact of World War II on the life and art of William Golding. He entered the Royal Navy at the age of twenty-nine in December, 1940, and after a period of service on mine sweepers, destroyers, and cruisers, he became a lieutenant in command of his own rocket ship. He saw action against the *Bismarck*, in the Atlantic convoys, in the D-day landings in Normandy, and the attack on Walcheren [Island].[16]

It should therefore come as no surprise that these wartime experiences would significantly influence Golding's worldview and therefore both the subject matter and the vision of his work.[17] E. M. Forster saw in the "tragic trend" of Golding's first novel "the tragedy of our inter-war world";[18] Malcolm Bradbury deemed Golding's vision "dark and troubling, a challenge to the liberal or progressive spirit" in the wake of the holocaust;[19] and Walter Allen went as far as to claim that the events depicted in *Lord of the Flies* are reminiscent of "the vilest manifestations of Nazi regression."[20]

William Golding was born in the Cornish village of St Columb Minor in 1911. He attended Marlborough Grammar School, where his father taught science, and then Brasenose College, Oxford, where he graduated, in 1935, with a degree in English literature. The Anglo-Saxon period was of particular interest to him during his Oxford years. Like Kingsley Amis and so many others attending British universities between the wars, Golding initially flirted with socialist and other left-wing political movements, only later to reject them in favor of less revolutionary worldviews. Golding published a volume of poetry in 1934 but thereafter, also like Amis, turned his artistic attention almost exclusively to the composition of prose fiction. Shortly before the outbreak of World War II, in 1939, Golding took a position teaching English and philosophy at Bishop Wordsworth's School in Salisbury. Between 1940 and 1945, as outlined above, Golding served in the Royal Navy. After the war he returned to his teaching post in Salisbury, where he taught for more than a decade. As novelist Ian McEwan concludes of Golding's use of his grammar school experiences in *Lord of the Flies*, "The din of the lower school common room at the Bishop Wordsworth School was not wasted on Golding."[21] Golding then returned to Brasenose and, in 1960, gained an MA degree. After a one-year stint (1961–2) as writer-in-residence at Hollins College (Virginia, USA), Golding pursued a writing career full-time. He died in Cornwall in 1993.

Although Golding published three plays, three volumes of nonfiction, and numerous reviews (again, like Amis, in the *Spectator*), in addition to a volume of poetry, the author's reputation hinges mainly on the novels published between *Lord of the Flies* (1954) and the posthumous draft of *The Double Tongue* (1995), a dozen in all.

Astonishingly, *Lord of the Flies*, before being accepted for publication, was rejected by twenty-one publishers. Ironically, given the initial difficulty Golding had in placing it, the novel since that time has been filmed twice, in 1963 and 1990, and has been translated into more than twenty languages, attracting a worldwide following. *Lord of the Flies*, Golding's "attempt to trace the defects of society back to the defects of the individual,"[22] was quickly followed by another novel, *The Inheritors* (1955), which concerns the violent encounter of Neanderthal man and *Homo sapiens*. Narrated from the perspective of the Neanderthals, who are on the brink of extinction at the hands of their more advanced humanoid foe, the novel bears an obvious similarity to its predecessor, particularly in its questioning of more "advanced" cultures. Golding's third novel, *Pincher Martin* (1956), concerns a sailor wounded in a Second World War naval accident who is marooned on a desolate rock in the North Atlantic and whose life is presented in flashback. The novel's very outline suggests a parallel with the author's first. The work that followed, *Free Fall* (1959), also narrated in flashback, concerns a painter who joins the army and who has become a prisoner of war. As the artist is interrogated by the Nazis, Golding's by now familiar interest in the morally questionable behavior of humans under pressure is explored from yet another angle of vision. During the 1960s Golding published a number of poorly received novellas and only one novel, *The Spire* (1964). Set in fourteenth-century Salisbury and concerning the building of a cathedral spire on shaky foundations, this allegorical novel explores "the ambiguous nature of human art and aspiration."[23]

After a hiatus in literary productivity, Golding published a novel about a crazed Pentecostal prophet, *Darkness Visible* (1979), this time to critical acclaim. This work, his most technically complex and allusive thus far, also helped renew interest in Golding's earlier novels. In addition to *The Paper Men* (1984), which examines the troubled relationship between a novelist and his biographer, Golding in the 1980s composed a trilogy of novels: *Rites of Passage* (1980), *Close Quarters* (1987), and *Fire Down Below* (1989). The trilogy is set on a sailing ship en route to colonial Australia during the Napoleonic Wars of the early nineteenth century. As Malcolm Bradbury observes, even in these late novels Golding remains interested in exploring "the ambiguity of human nature, the tug of primitivism, the presence of evil, the formlessness of experience, [and] the uncertainty of progress."[24] Put this way, one sees that Golding's literary preoccupations remain remarkably consistent over his four-decade-long career. As one critic sums up the author's novelistic "fables," they "invariably show a protagonist moving toward a psychological crisis which ends with the shattering of his preconceptions and a belated recognition of the folly and damage [he has] caused." "In every book," the critic continues, "the larger universe is finally revealed to the distressed mind as a complex and ambiguous mystery beyond rational grasp."[25]

Golding's reputation steadily heightened between the mid 1960s and the late 1980s. He was made a CBE (Commander of the British Empire) and an honorary fellow of Brasenose College in 1966; won Britain's top literary award, the Booker Prize, in 1980 (for *Rites of Passage*); won the Nobel Prize for literature in 1983; and was knighted in 1988.

III

Critics have debated extensively the question of whether or not Golding's first work of fiction is best understood as a fable, an allegory, or a novel. L. L. Dickson, for example, has devoted a book-length study to the treatment of Golding's works as "moral allegories,"[26] while James R. Baker deems *Lord of the Flies* a "vital fable for our time."[27] Another taxonomic question that has interested readers is whether or not Golding's first novel is a dystopia. To be sure, *Lord of the Flies* frequently has been grouped with such works as Aldous Huxley's *Brave New World* and George Orwell's *Animal Farm* and *1984*.[28] And if, as Kathleen Woodward argues, utopian and dystopian literature is "primarily a vehicle for social criticism," a means of making critical statements "about our social values, practices, and institutions,"[29] then *Lord of the Flies* would appear to fit this mold as well.

However one answers such generic and taxonomic questions about *Lord of the Flies*, the novel's allegorical, fable-like, and dystopic dimensions must be taken into account. As novelist Ian McEwan puts it, "The boys set fire to their island paradise while their elders and betters have all but destroyed the planet."[30] In whatever category Golding's novel falls, it is clear that the author is more concerned, as he himself admits, with ideas than with characters,[31] with questions of human social behavior and interaction than with the rendering of three-dimensional psychological portraits.

The adventure romance tradition – a tradition that Golding "both participates in and criticizes"[32] – provides the most important literary backdrop for an understanding of *Lord of the Flies*. Of particular relevance is the strain of this tradition originated by Daniel Defoe in *Robinson Crusoe* (1719), and then extended by R. M. Ballantyne in *Coral Island* (1857) and Robert Louis Stevenson in *Treasure Island* (1883). Not only are the latter two works noted directly by the boys in *Lord of the Flies*, but Ballantyne's Victorian work, "one of the earliest such stories to have boys, in the absence of adults, for its main characters,"[33] is frequently cited by Golding as a major backdrop for his first novel.

It is difficult to overstate what Golding himself calls his "pretty big connection" with Ballantyne.[34] In Golding's words, "Ballantyne's island was a nineteenth-century island inhabited by English boys; mine was to be a twentieth-century island inhabited by English boys."[35] As in Ballantyne's novel, the tropical island setting in Golding's is something of a "natural paradise, an uncorrupted Eden offering all the lush abundance of the primal earth,"[36] replete with fresh water to drink, fruit, and (pig) meat to eat, and beautiful vistas for the eye to feast on. Like Ballantyne's schoolboy characters, Golding's are marooned – though not by shipwreck but by plane crash (are the boys in the process of being evacuated from England?) – presumably following a nuclear war.[37] And British imperialism, which was in its heyday during Ballantyne's time, figures prominently in both novels (in Golding's work, for example, the boys savor "the right of domination": "This [island] belongs to us," one of them boasts [29]). Even the names of two of the four major Golding characters, Ralph and Jack, derive directly from Ballantyne's narrative.[38]

The thrusts of the two adventure narratives quickly diverge, however. As Malcolm Bradbury observes, "Golding's late modern story is not a tale of young resourcefulness but a deeply pessimistic vision of human evil."[39] That the island becomes something of a fallen Eden after the arrival of the boys, who "scar" and burn the previously uninhabited paradise, also clearly signals Golding's departure from Ballantyne's "sentimental fable."[40] As one critic puts it, "The crash of the passenger capsule in the jungle growth of the island is like an injection of vermin into a healthy natural organism; the seemingly innocent lads are maggots who shortly evolve into flies."[41]

The connection between *Lord of the Flies* and *Coral Island*, then, is at bottom ironic: Golding's "*enfants terribles*" are "ironically juxtaposed with the spectacular success" of Ballantyne's God-fearing "Victorian darlings."[42] *Lord of the Flies* also has been called an "inversion,"[43] "parodic rewriting,"[44] and, by its author, "realistic" treatment of the "Ballantyne situation."[45] Minnie Singh, however, puts this relationship best:

....

Rhetorically and ideologically, the claim of *Lord of the Flies* over *The Coral Island* is the claim of experience over innocence, realism over romance, truth over illusion, maturity over naivete, and hardship over ease. [Golding's novel] makes childhood itself as archaic as the colonial metaphor of enthusiastic exploration.[46]

While *Coral Island* locates the potential for evil in the external world of savage cannibals and pirates, *Lord of the Flies*, by contrast, locates this potential in the boys' (and by extension in their parents' and civilization's) own makeup.[47] Golding, it might be said, "corrects" Ballantyne.

Kathleen Woodward observes that *Lord of the Flies* was constructed with "the perfection of a miniature,"[48] a comment that pertains as well to the novel's intricately plotted major characters (Ralph, Jack, Piggy, and Simon) and symbolic objects (the conch, the spectacles, pigs, and fire).

The 12-year-old Ralph, the first major character the reader encounters, is introduced as a "fair boy" (8) with the physique of a future "boxer" but also with "a mildness about the mouth and eyes that proclaimed no devil" (10). Almost immediately after the plane crash on the island, which occurs before the novel opens, he is elected "leader" by a vote of the boys, suggesting their unselfconscious attempt to mirror the democratic ways of British politics. In addition to representing a form of British democracy, however, Ralph represents a form of British imperialism. For one thing, the island, in Ralph's early image of it, is a "coral island" (in the Ballantyne mold), on which British boys, who are sure to triumph over nature as well as any heathen foe they may encounter, will pass the time in profitable adventure, an emblem of empire building, until their rescue. For another, Ralph's "Daddy," who is a "commander in the Navy," will rescue the boys when he gets his "leave" (13). Ralph brags:

> My father's in the Navy. He said there aren't any unknown islands left. He says the Queen has a big room full of maps and all the islands in the world are drawn there. So the Queen's got a picture of this island. (37)

Implicit in this boast, of course, is Ralph's uncritical acceptance of authority – his own, his father's, the Queen's – and of the legitimacy of imperial adventure.

The token of Ralph's significance as a democratic force is the conch, discovered by Piggy on the beach, which is used to call assemblies at which anyone who holds the shell is allowed to have his say. Described as "the white, magic shell" and "the talisman" (180), the conch also symbolizes the rule of law (Ralph is said to feel "a kind of affectionate reverence for the conch" [78]) and is imagined to separate the boys from the "animals" on the island (92).

Despite his respect for Piggy's "rational," democratic social formulas, Ralph at points succumbs to the lust for blood and violent aggression symbolized by the hunt[49] and to the allure of savagery.[50] Ralph undergoes a major change of heart, however, when his authority is threatened and finally stolen by Jack, head of the choirboys and hunters. Ralph eventually becomes pessimistic about what can be accomplished on the island, and gains a sense of responsibility for those in need of protection (Piggy and the "littluns" in particular [117]), and an appreciation of the value to the cause of democracy represented by Piggy and the danger to that cause represented by Jack. This change is suggested not only in Ralph's ever-weakening position in relation to the majority of the boys, who increasingly follow Jack's leadership, but in Ralph's increasing discomfort with the "dirt and decay" on his body and the long "tangled hair" that hangs in his eyes (77). It is also suggested in his frequent bouts of nostalgia, during which he remembers scenes – in which everything is "all right . . . good-humored and friendly" (112) – from his innocent English youth. Predictably, Ralph ends up not the leader but the hunted Other of the "tribe," and is only saved by the deus ex machina of the British naval officer, off the "trim cruiser," who at the last minute discovers the marooned boys (200–2).

Jack Merridew, the "tall, red-haired" (68) head of the choirboys-cum-hunters (his red hair gives him demonic associations), is Ralph's chief rival for the position of leader. This most straightforward of characters initially asserts his authority as head of the choir, with its implicit church authority, and then by seeking fun and adventure and by leading hunts. Jack loves shedding blood, which strikes a powerful chord in the "civilized" British boys, who after the plane crash are dressed in their school sweaters (7) or black cloaks with "a long silver cross on the left breast" (19), but who eventually wear only war paint and loincloths. If Ralph is the closest thing to a protagonist in the novel, Jack is the closest thing to an antagonist. If Ralph represents the will to democratic order, Jack, who is described in animalistic terms as "ape-like" (49) and "dog-like" (48), represents the will to chaos or, better yet, to a tribal, non-democratic order in which he is the all-powerful "chief" of a bloodthirsty "tribe." If Ralph, at first hesitantly and then with growing conviction, seeks to protect the asthmatic, physically feeble (if intellectually potent) Piggy from the rest of the boys, Jack is threatened by and therefore antagonistic to Piggy, and the "difference" he represents, from first to last. If Ralph comes to despise the "savage" trappings of island life, Jack embraces them, enjoys running naked and masked, and comes to wear "the damp darkness of the forest like his old clothes" (134). The mask of "dazzle paint" (63) that Jack initially uses for camouflage during the hunt becomes a "thing on its own, behind which Jack hid, liberated from shame and self-consciousness" (64). Indeed, Jack is in his element during the hunts, when the boys take up the chorus, "Kill the pig.

Cut her throat. Spill her blood" (69, 114, 152, 186), which the reader must assume is the antithesis of those songs of sanctity and peace normally sung by the choir.

Central to the novel's plot development is the ever-growing "antagonism" (51) and "tension" (72) between these two leaders, who at first seem on almost brotherly terms.[51] While Ralph encourages the boys to tend a rescue fire and build huts against the rain,[52] Jack encourages them to hunt pigs, both as a blood sport and for purpose of obtaining meat. The two also frequently clash over whether or not the rules initially established by the boys should be followed. When Ralph insists that "the rules are the only thing we've got," Jack replies, "Bollocks to the rules! We're strong – we hunt! If there's a beast, we'll hunt it down! Close in and beat and beat and beat – !" (91) Ralph and Jack are even characterized as "two continents of experience and feeling, unable to communicate" (55); at another their conflict is described as the "fresh rub of two spirits in the dark" (119).

Piggy, the third of the novel's four major characters, is marginalized by the other boys because of his weight, asthma, lack of physical stamina, "thick spectacles" (7), and lower-class background. He is also ostracized by the others because of his "intellectual daring" (129), which sharply contrasts with their more emotional, visceral reactions to the fearful situation in which they find themselves. For E. M. Forster Piggy is "the brains of the party," which is reinforced by the fact that, when he is killed, his "skull cracks and his brains spill out."[53] Piggy possesses an optimistic streak and scientific orientation; he predicts that "In a year or two when the war's over they'll be traveling to Mars and back" (84). As one critic remarks, Piggy is "the voice of reason"; he appears to believe that human problems can be solved if only our irrational urges can be contained.[54]

An admirable feature of Piggy's rationalistic and democratic orientation is his sense of responsibility for all in the community and his resistance to forfeiting "civilized" standards in favor of "savage" ones. At one point, for example, he displays the "martyred expression of a parent who has to keep up with the senseless ebullience of the children" (38). Piggy's difference from the others is suggested by the fact that "He was the only boy on the island whose hair never seemed to grow" (64). Importantly, he resists succumbing to the same irrational fear as the others over what he regards as a chimeric "beast" in the jungle. The novel proves Piggy to be both right (there is no external beast) and wrong (the beast lurks within) when it comes to the threat posed by the "beastie" on the island, which turns out to be a deceased soldier still attached to his fluttering parachute.

An unfortunate byproduct of Piggy's rationalism and respect for order is his naïve faith in the appeal of these things for the majority of boys and his naïve faith in adult authority, which he invokes time and again in failed attempts to reform his peers. Ironically, of course, it is the warring adults who have gotten the boys into their mess to begin with; the adult world at large seems incapable of teaching these boys much of anything about civilized interaction. Piggy's statement that "Grownups know things . . . They'd meet and have tea and discuss. Then things 'ud be all right" (94) has to be one of the novel's most ironic lines in that it is the warring grown-ups who appear to have taught the boys how to foul their own nest. Piggy's respect for authority is so profound that, early on, he even accedes to choir-leader Jack's authority: Piggy "was intimidated by this uniformed superiority and the offhand authority in Merridew's voice" (21). Piggy's naïve faith in reason and law reaches its lethal climax when he conveys "his passionate willingness to carry the conch against all odds" by confronting Jack and demanding that his stolen glasses be returned, simply "because what's right's right" (171). Golding betrays the intentions he had for this character when he says that Piggy is "a complete innocent": "naïve, short-sighted, and rationalist."[55] It is no wonder that he is powerless in the face of the hunters, the novel's "Demoniac figures" (140), who have no patience with Piggy's appeals to human reason and justice.

Piggy plays a symbolic function in the novel as well: he represents the hunted, violated, and ultimately murdered Other: a victimized Other that is used to bind together the tribe. As Freud reminds us in *Civilization and Its Discontents*, another work that worries the growth of fascistic group dynamics in the twentieth century, "It is always possible to bind together a considerable number of people in love, so long as there are other people left over to receive the manifestations of their aggressiveness."[56] At many points in the novel Piggy's role in maintaining the tribe's social cohesion is made clear. For example, the boys are described as "a closed circuit of sympathy with Piggy outside" (21); at another point we learn that "There had grown up tacitly among the biguns the opinion that Piggy was an outsider, not only by accent" but "by fat, and ass-mar, and specs, and a certain disinclination for manual labor" (65). At yet another point we read that the boys

> bumped Piggy, who was burnt, and yelled and danced. Immediately, Ralph and the crowd of boys were united and relieved by a storm of laughter. Piggy once more was the center of social derision so that everyone felt cheerful and normal. (149)

This "othering" does not apply exclusively to Piggy, however; at another point "the painted group felt the otherness of Samneric, felt the power in their own hands [and] felled the twins clumsily and excitedly" (179).

Piggy is also linked to the female (or feminized) hunted Others of the island, the pigs. And Golding connects the male rape of females with the violation of the Other by figuring the pig hunts, with their violence and blood-lust, in sexual terms, with "overtones of rape."[57] In the most graphic of the novel's hunt scenes, for example, we read that a wounded

> sow staggered her way ahead of [the boys], bleeding and mad, and the hunters followed, wedded to her in lust, excited by the long chase and the dropped blood . . . [T]he sow fell and the hunters hurled themselves at her . . . The spear moved forward inch by inch and the terrified squealing became a high-pitched scream. Then Jack found the throat and the hot blood spouted over his hands. The sow collapsed under them and they were heavy and fulfilled upon her . . . (135)

This hunt ends with the pig being "sodomized with a pointed stick"[58] ("Right up her ass!" one boy boasts [135]), a gratuitously violent act that highlights the pleasure the boys take in scapegoating defenseless creatures who become outlets for "desires previously repressed but now unleashed."[59] Figuratively, this pig-hunt is a dry run for the murder of Piggy and Simon and the would-be murder of Ralph: the boys move easily from hunting pigs to hunting humans over the course of their sojourn on the island. Ralph is correct to reason that "These painted savages would go further and further" (184). When Piggy is killed by a falling boulder, which is intentionally released by a member of Jack's tribe, it is appropriate both that "Piggy's arms and legs twitched a bit, like a pig's after it has been killed" (181), and that the conch, a vestige of democratic order, perishes with him, exploding and fragmenting, "smashed to powder" (186), by the tumbling boulder.

Piggy's spectacles, a leitmotif for this character, also have a symbolic function in the novel. The spectacles, without which Piggy is virtually blind, figure his physical inferiority yet intellectual superiority to the other boys. Like Tiresias, the blind Theban seer, Piggy later in the novel, after Jack breaks one of his lenses and then steals the other, becomes something of a blind prophet: his lack of vision is inversely proportional to his insightfulness and prescience. This is suggested both when Piggy "found that he saw more clearly if he removed his glasses and shifted the one lens to the other eye" (155) and when he sits "expressionless behind the luminous wall of his myopia" (169) – yet has a clearer view of their collective situation than any of the sighted boys. Nevertheless, that Piggy is a visionary does not prevent him, along with Ralph and Simon, from being a powerless, hunted victim of Jack's tribe – one of "three blind mice" (93).

Piggy's spectacles attract the attention of the other boys because of their use as "burning glasses" (40) to start fires. In an ironic Promethean echo, Jack and his tribe "raid" Piggy and Ralph "and take fire" (136) by stealing the glasses. (With characteristic naivete, Piggy, who is now virtually blinded [169], wrongly assumes that Jack attacks in order to steal the conch [168]). Importantly, the fire has two competing productive functions – as a rescue fire and a pig-roasting fire – and one destructive one: the boys at two points set wildfires that threaten to consume much of the island, including the boys themselves (a few already may have perished) and their sources of food (the pigs and fruit trees). Of course, this ultimately self-destructive act echoes that undertaken in the world at large by the adults, who are presumably in the process of destroying themselves atomically, rendering the earth unlivable.

Simon, the final and most enigmatic of the novel's four major characters, is also the most debated by critics and readers. And he is the least understood by the other boys on the island. Ralph, for example, finds Simon "queer" and "funny" (55), and Golding himself insists that Simon is "understood by nobody."[60] A "skinny, vivid little" (24) choirboy who first makes our acquaintance by fainting (apparently, he is susceptible to such spells), Simon is a kind-hearted character who at many points stands up for Piggy and the "littluns," even when this proves to be unpopular. Simon is also a solitary figure who prefers being "utterly alone" (56) and discovering his own path to coexistsing with others.[61]

This "inarticulate seer"[62] establishes his own jungle hideaway and later learns, as a result of his independence, two things that remain unknown to the other boys. First, he learns that the dreaded "beast" who haunts the island is actually a dead and decaying parachutist from the war. Second, he learns, in a hallucinated interview with the fly-covered sow's head on a stake – a head that speaks in the "voice of a schoolmaster" (143) and that is meant by Jack and his tribe to be an offering to the beast – that the beast is "only us" (89) and a "part" of all of the boys, "Close, close, close," and that there is no escaping it (143–4). The sow's head seems to lecture Simon:

Fancy thinking the Beast was something you could hunt and kill [that is, something external to yourselves]. I'm part of you . . . the reason why it's no go . . . why things are what they are . . . You know perfectly well you'll only meet me down there [where the other boys are] – so don't try to escape. (143)

As Golding elsewhere comments, the boys "don't understand what beasts there are in the human psyche which have to be curbed."[63]

Simon's discoveries lead to his tragic end as a hunted "pig" at the hands of the other boys, in a horrific scene that begins with a war dance and the familiar chant, "Kill the beast! Cut his throat! Spill his blood!" (152), and ends with "Simon's dead body" moving "out toward the open sea" (154). As with Ralph and Piggy, who also recognize that the beast may be inherent in the boys themselves,[64] Simon's difference from the others in the tribe means that he must be hunted and eliminated.[65]

The major debate surrounding the enigmatic Simon concerns his status as the novel's Christ figure. Golding himself asserts that "I included" this "Christ-figure in my fable," who is

> solitary, stammering, a lover of mankind, a visionary, who reaches commonsense attitudes not by reason but by intuition. Of all the boys, [Simon] is the only one who feels the need to be alone and goes every now and then into the bushes . . . He is really turning a part of the jungle into a church, not a physical . . . but a spiritual one.[66]

Elsewhere Golding remarks that when Simon attempts to take the good news about the parachutist back to "ordinary human society, he's crucified for it."[67]

Although it is true that he is something of a "sacrificial victim,"[68] that "in his martyrdom" he "meets the fate of all saints,"[69] Simon – in seeking his own world because he recognizes, with Jean-Paul Sartre, that "Hell" is "other people"[70] – flirts as much with escapism and solipsism as with sainthood or the life of a solitary. Despite Golding's comments, then, it seems unwise to read this enigmatic character exclusively in religious terms.[71]

The "beastie" itself is first mentioned shortly after the boys land on the island and takes many imagined forms thereafter. Initially, in what appears to be an Edenic allusion, the boys fear a serpent, a "snake-thing" in "the woods" (35, 36), which later becomes "a thing, a dark thing, a beast, some sort of animal" (83). Still later the beast is said to come "out of the sea" (88), or the "dark," or the "trees" (125, 126). That the boys do not understand the nature or meaning of the chimeric beast is precisely the point. That readers come to understand, as one critic concludes, that "the beast is *other*" is equally important. "Whatever one fears," this critic continues, "whether it is mythic like ogres and bogeymen, or real like countries and ideologies, it is not-I, beast, and ultimately evil."[72]

The idea that the beast inheres in us supports the idea that "civilization" is something of a veneer, and that what separates the English from those whom they would "civilize" is the finest of lines, a boundary that vanishes entirely during the boys' stay on the island. This vanishing line – the idea that civilization is at bottom an attempt to deny a universal human will-to-power – is imaged at many points in the novel, most ironically for the reader when Piggy asks the boys, "What are we? Humans? Or animals? Or savages?" (91).[73]

The novel's critique of civilization is best understood as an attack on British colonialism and hubris regarding Nazism, as imaged in Jack's nationalistic formulation: "We've got to have rules and obey them. After all, we're not savages. We're English, and the English are best at everything" (42).[74] As Golding puts it of British moral complacency,

> One of our faults is to believe that evil is somewhere else and inherent in another nation. My book was to say: you think that . . . you are safe because you are naturally kind and decent. But I know why the thing rose in Germany. I know it could happen in any country. It could happen here . . .
>
> The overall picture was to be the tragic lesson that the English have had to learn over a period of one hundred years; that one lot of people is inherently like any other lot of people; and that the only enemy of man is inside him.[75]

Even the "civilized" Piggy, in an echo of the German denial of responsibility, rationalizes his participation in the murder of Simon thus: "It was an accident . . . I was only on the outside . . . We never done nothing, we never seen nothing . . . We left early" (157–8).

The novel's title is relevant in this connection. "Lord of the Flies" is a translation of *Beelzebub*, the Greek transliteration of the Hebrew *Ba'alzevuv*, which denotes evil incarnate (the Devil, Satan, Mephistopheles). As one critic observes, "Golding equates the Lord of the Flies with the demonic force latent in humankind, a force so hideous" that "fly-covered excrement would best represent it."[76] The title also relates to the novel's feces and corruption motifs,[77] as excrement and decay function as metaphors for the perceived threat of evil, whether embodied in the decaying, "stinking" (147) body of the dead parachutist, who is mistaken for the beast, or in the fly-covered and corrupting pig's head on a stake, a gift to appease the forces of darkness.

Erich Fromm's 1941 exploration of the social psychology of fascism, *Escape from Freedom*, another response to and critique of the events that culminated in the death camps of World War II, sheds considerable light on Golding's *Lord of the Flies*.[78] Fromm's thesis, contrary to the "conventional belief" that "modern democracy" leads to "true individualism," is that although the "principles of economic liberalism, political democracy, religious autonomy, and individualism in personal life" have brought modern Europeans and Americans closer than ever before to achieving "freedom from the political, economic, and spiritual shackles that have bound" us, it is nevertheless the case that "in our own society we are faced with the same phenomenon that is fertile soil for the rise of Fascism anywhere: the insignificance and powerlessness of the individual."[79] Specifically, *Escape from Freedom* analyzes "those dynamic factors in the character structure of modern man" that make "him want to give up freedom in Fascist countries" and that so widely prevail "in our own people."[80] Like the late works of Freud, Fromm here "stresses the role of psychological factors" in the "social process" at large.[81]

For Fromm, the crux of the problem stems from the human "tendency to give up the independence of one's own individual self and to fuse one's self with somebody or something outside of oneself in order to acquire the strength which the individual self is lacking,"[82] thereby overcoming the feeling of "individual insignificance."[83] For Fromm this explains the allure of nationalism or any other "custom" or "belief," however otherwise "absurd" or "degrading":[84] it connects the individual with others and therefore functions as a refuge from what humans dread the most, isolation. The individual, for Fromm, paradoxically seeks "a kind of security by such ties with the world as destroy his freedom and the integrity of his individual self."[85] I take the following passage to be the kernel of Fromm's argument and of particular relevance to Golding's novel:

> The annihilation of the individual self and the attempt to overcome thereby the unbearable feeling of powerlessness are only one side of the [equation]. The other side is the attempt to become a part of a bigger and more powerful whole outside of oneself, to submerge and participate in it. This power can be a person, an institution, God, the nation . . . By becoming part of a power which is felt as unshakably strong, eternal, and glamorous, one participates in its strength and glory. One surrenders one's own . . . freedom; but one gains a new security and a new pride in the participation in the power in which one submerges. One gains also security against the torture of doubt. [Such a person] is saved from making decisions, saved from the final responsibility for the fate of his self, and thereby saved from the doubt of what decision to make. He is also saved from the doubt of what the meaning of his life is or who "he" is. These questions are answered by the relationship to the power to which he has attached himself.[86]

Although the price to be paid by anyone who takes this road is high – the very loss of the "self" – at least this automaton, "identical with millions of other automatons around him, need not feel alone and anxious any more."[87] That is to say, in blindly submitting to a "leader" the insecure individual "gains some security by finding himself united with" so many others who share the same fears of "weakness" and "isolation."[88]

The implications of Fromm's study of fascistic social psychology for an understanding of *Lord of the Flies* are surely clear. It is noted in Golding's novel, for example, that "The assembly [of boys] was lifted toward safety by [Ralph's] words" (37), and that the boys, who find themselves in an inherently insecure situation and who possess "tormented private lives" (133), savor "the comfort of safety" represented by the hierarchy of Jack's tribe (186). We also hear Piggy explain that all of the boys who join in the "bloody dance" that culminates in the murder of Simon do so because they are "scared" (156), and learn that even Piggy and Ralph find "themselves eager to take a place in this demented but partly secure society," and are willing, at least for a time, to forfeit freedom and individuality in order to gain the security that comes with being part of a group, part of the "throb and stamp of a single organism" (152). As Golding, sounding like Fromm, puts it in an essay, the war-dance episodes allow the boys to "fortify their own sense of power and togetherness. It is dark."[89]

Another example in *Lord of the Flies* of the human desire to escape from freedom and individuality is found in the seemingly interchangeable twins Sam and Eric, whose "substantial unity" comes to be taken for granted by all (100) and who come to share the same name, "Samneric." The two do everything together and respond to everything in the same way; they even nod "like one boy" (115) and appear as "four unwinking eyes aimed and two mouths open" (98). The two, the narrator adds, "could never manage to do things sensibly if that meant acting independently" (96).

The masks of war paint the boys wear also function in this way: they enable the boys to gain security and belonging in exchange for their sense of individual identity and freedom. The "concealing paint," however, brings a different sort of liberation: the "liberation into savagery" (172). In this way the boys are "Freed by the paint" (175); they can escape from freedom behind "the painted anonymity of the group" (178). For example, when Jack plans his face,

> He looked in astonishment, no longer at himself but at an awesome stranger . . . The mask was a thing on its own, behind which Jack hid, liberated from shame and self-consciousness. (63–4)

Even the destructive (and ultimately self-destructive) wild-fires set by the boys are explained by *Escape from Freedom*. Fromm would interpret such acts of self-destruction, which mirror the self-destructive acts of the warring adults at large, in terms of the attempt to "escape the feeling" of "powerlessness in comparison with the world outside" by "destroying" this world. "The destruction of the world," Fromm argues, "is the last, almost desperate attempt to save" those who would escape from freedom "from being crushed by" the world.[90] Revealingly, after they set the first fire, the boys are said to feel "the beginnings of awe at the power set free below them" (44). (Even Simon the recluse would be explained by *Escape from Freedom* as employing a mechanism of escape in which one withdraws "from the world so completely that it loses its threat" [Fromm, p. 208].)

Although critics have noted that Jack "is clearly drawn from contemporary alarms about the totalitarian personality,"[91] the extent to which Fromm's study illuminates the motivations of this sadistic tyrant has not been adequately appreciated. For Fromm, sadism is rooted in the desire of the "individual to escape his unbearable feeling of aloneness and powerlessness," to dispel "the burden of freedom" and "the self."[92] And the "sadist needs the person over whom he rules" very badly, "since his own feeling of strength is rooted in the fact that he is the master over someone."[93] Jack perfectly epitomizes the sadistic personality, as evidenced in his gloating remembrance "of the knowledge that had come to [the boys] when they had closed in on the struggling pig, knowledge that they had outwitted a living thing, imposed their will upon it, taken away its life like a long satisfying drink" (70).

Jack even rationalizes his sadistic power-mongering in a way anticipated by Fromm, who observes the tyrant arguing, "I have done so much for you, and [therefore] now I am entitled to take from you what I want."[94] The refrain Jack takes up with the boys, "I got you meat" (74), is meant to justify his wanton cruelty and acts of "irresponsible authority" (160) toward them, such as when he ties up and beats various of the boys for no apparent reason and when he establishes himself as "an idol" among them (149). And Fromm would explain Jack's particular hostility for Piggy – and for the defenseless sow – thus: "The very sight of a powerless person" makes an authoritarian one "want to attack, dominate, humiliate him." The more "helpless his object," the "more aroused" the "authoritarian character feels" to attack.[95]

Fromm also would explain Jack's exploitation of the boys' innate fear of the beast to consolidate his power by appealing to a "higher power outside the individual, toward which the individual can do nothing but submit."[96] Jack's idea of appeasing the fictitious beast with a "gift" of a pig's head on a stake (137) – "When we kill we'll leave some of the kill for it. Then it won't bother us, maybe" (133) – is a part of his strategy to maintain both the cohesion of the tribe and his power over it. Later, Jack warns the boys to remember that "the beast might try to come . . . again even though we gave him the head of our kill to eat . . . We'd better keep on the right side of him, anyhow. You can't tell what he might do" (161). Here, Jack implicitly promises to protect the boys from the beast as long as he remains chief. The chimeric beast is thus invoked both to create and to dispel fear – fear that is used in turn for purposes of political manipulation. This is suggested when we read that Jack's boys were "Half-relieved, half-daunted" at the implication of "further terrors" (161) at the hands of the mysterious beast.

Literally seconds before the hunted Ralph is to be killed by the boys in Jack's tribe, he is rescued by a "naval officer" (200) who suddenly appears on the island from "the trim cruiser in the distance" (202). Numerous ironies unfold in the novel's final pages, which Bernard F. Dick characterizes as not so much a moral as a literary "resolution" to the novel, a sort of "deus ex machina."[97] The officer, who wears a revolver and stands against the backdrop of his sub-machine gun-equipped cutter, asks Ralph if there are "any adults – any grownups with you?" He then notices the fuller beach scene: a "semicircle of little boys" whose "bodies" are "streaked with colored clay" and who hold "sharp sticks in their hands." The officer, unaware of his own irony given the exploits of the "civilized" adults at war, dismisses the boys' behavior as so much "Fun and games" (200) and wonders if they are having "a war or something?" (201). He then remarks, in the context of an allusion to Ballantyne's *Coral Island*, "I should have thought that a pack of British boys" would "have been able to put up a better show than that" (202). The boys at last begin to weep, and Ralph "wept for the end of innocence, the darkness of man's heart, and the fall through the air of the true, wise friend called Piggy" (202). As Samuel Hynes writes of this moment in the novel, the naval officer "may save Ralph's life, but he will not understand. And once he has gathered up the castaways, he will return to his ship, and the grown-up business of hunting men (just as the boys have been hunting Ralph). 'And who,' asks Golding, 'will rescue the adult and his cruiser?'."[98]

Lord of the Flies thus ultimately "offers no politics but shows instead the failure of politics,"[99] a fact that does not trouble its author. As Golding has commented, the novelist "should be free enough of society to be able to see it" clearly and should possess "an intransigence in the face of accepted belief – political, religious, moral."[100] An anatomy of the problem, and not any solution, is all we can ask of the novelist. And indeed our relief (and the boys' relief) at the close of *Lord of the Flies* is only temporary and partial: the equilibrium to which we are returned at novel's end is an equilibrium in which world war rages, tribalism reigns, and democracies fail.

Chapter 4

Chinua Achebe's
Things Fall Apart (1958)

I would be quite satisfied if my novels . . . did no more than teach my readers that their past – with all its imperfections – was not one long night of savagery from which the first Europeans acting on God's behalf delivered them.

Chinua Achebe, "The novelist as teacher"[1]

I

Things Fall Apart, by Nigerian novelist Chinua Achebe, is easily the most famous and widely read African novel in English. Translated into fifty different languages, with more than 8 million copies in print worldwide, this celebrated author's first novel is often compared to Greek tragedy for its straightforward, searing power, acute family dynamics, and potent sense of inevitability. Deemed "perhaps the most memorable account in English of an African culture and the impact upon it of white European encroachment,"[2] *Things Fall Apart* explores the traumatizing effects of British colonialism on a small Nigerian village at the turn of the nineteenth century. However, Achebe resists the temptation to portray his tribal past in romantic or sentimental terms;[3] rather, he adopts a "realistic" approach in the hope of countering the stereotypical representations of indigenous Nigerians and other Africans made familiar to western – and indeed to many African – readers in such works as Joyce Cary's *Mr Johnson* (1939). Cary was a colonial officer who served in Nigeria between 1910 and 1920. His once popular novel depicted traditional tribal society in patronizing and sentimental terms and served as an "ideological justification of the [colonial] status quo."[4] In addition to countering the view of African tribal life portrayed in Cary's novel, in Conrad's novella *Heart of Darkness*

(1899),[5] and in other works of literature familiar to British audiences, *Things Fall Apart* played a major role in African self-understanding; it became "the first novel by an African writer to be included in the required syllabus for African secondary schools, not only in Nigeria but (excluding South Africa) throughout the English-speaking parts of the African continent."[6] Published two years before Nigeria declared independence from Great Britain (Nigeria was under British control from 1906 until 1960), Achebe's first novel also explores what might be called the "politics of point of view" and the problem of alterity or "otherness": the difficulty, if not impossibility, "of completely imagining one individual or culture in terms of another."[7]

II

Many western readers of *Things Fall Apart* will have difficulty approaching the work given their dearth of knowledge about African history in general and the history of southeastern Nigeria, the setting of Achebe's novel, in particular. While a detailed treatment of this history is outside the scope of this study, a few relevant facts of historical context for the novel are essential. *Things Fall Apart* is set at the beginning of the twentieth century, soon after the European "scramble for Africa," when "British authorities, missions, and trade penetrated the Igbo hinterland east of the Niger river"[8] and traditional Igbo society began to undergo the cultural disintegration that followed colonialism. Nigeria, which "never had any integrity save one imposed by the colonial powers," was in fact an agglomeration of "hundreds of different ethnic and linguistic communities."[9] Achebe came from the third most populous of these Nigerian communities, the Igbo, who reside in the southeastern part of the country. Yet the Igbo themselves were not entirely homogeneous: Igbo villages only a few miles apart spoke languages, all of which were called "Igbo," that differed significantly from each other. Indeed, "the dialects, cultures, and political systems" of the various Igbo villages varied widely.[10] Despite these differences, according to Achebe in his recent memoir *Home and Exile*, the "more than ten million strong" Igbo people, one "of the major peoples of Africa," felt a strong sense of solidarity and national belonging:

> The Igbo nation in precolonial times was not quite like any nation people are familiar with. It did not have the apparatus of centralized government but was a conglomeration of hundreds of independent towns and villages . . . which were in reality ministates that cherished their individual identity but also . . . perceived themselves as Igbo . . .[11]

This sense of nationhood and cultural integrity led the Igbo, for all of their differences, to attempt, between 1967 and 1970, to secede from the artificial, colonial construction Nigeria in order to form their own nation, to be called The Republic of Biafra. This revolt was decisively crushed in 1970, and the "Biafran experience served as a warning for the rest of Africa not to try to undo the map-making of the colonial powers."[12]

Chinua Achebe was born in 1930 in Ogidi, an Igbo-speaking community in eastern Nigeria that was a center of Anglican missionary work. The son of a Christian convert who began proselytizing for the Anglican church in 1904, Achebe was baptized Albert Chinualumogu and only dropped "the tribute to Victorian England" (Victoria's consort was named Albert) when he enrolled at university.[13] Achebe received his formal education in English, first in church schools and then at University College, Ibadan (then affiliated with the University of London), where he graduated, in 1953, with a degree in English literature. At about this time, Achebe recalls, the "nationalist movement in British West Africa" sparked a "mental revolution": "It suddenly seemed that we too might have a story to tell. 'Rule Britannia!' to which we had marched so unselfconsciously on Empire Day now stuck in our throat."[14]

Achebe, who has received his nation's highest award for intellectual achievement, the Nigerian National Merit Award, is often mentioned as a leading candidate for the Nobel Prize in Literature and holds honorary doctorates from more than twenty universities in Canada, England, Nigeria, Scotland, and the United States. He is best known as the author of five novels – *Things Fall Apart* (1958), *No Longer at Ease* (1960), *Arrow of God* (1964), *A Man of the People* (1966), and *Anthills of the Savannah* (1987) – of which the first four form a loose tetralogy "covering the history of Nigeria from colonization until the first military coup."[15] He is also a respected essayist, advocate of African letters, and editor. In addition to editing important African literary journals, Achebe was the founding editor of the Heinemann Books African Writers Series, the first series to bring English language African writing to a wider audience. Since 1990 he has been the Charles P. Stevenson Jr. Professor of Languages and Literature at Bard College, in New York state.

Achebe, who is "perfectly bilingual," having grown up at what he calls a "crossroads of cultures,"[16] has been criticized by some for writing novels in English rather than in his indigenous Igbo tongue. Abdul R. JanMohamed poses this contentious issue as a question: "[C]an African experience be adequately represented through the alien media . . . of the colonizer's language and literary forms or will these media inevitably alter the nature of African experience in significant ways?"[17] In other words, should English be excluded "as a language of African fiction on purely ideological grounds"?[18] To be sure, as JanMohamed explains,

> The African writer's very decision to use English as his medium is engulfed by ironies, paradoxes, and contradictions. He writes in English because he was born in a British colony and can receive formal education only in English. More significantly, however, he is compelled to master and use English because of the prevailing ideological pressures within the colonial system . . .[19]

Another critic puts the problem even more baldly: "Achebe uses the written word brought by the colonizers in order to record and recreate the oral world obliterated or denied by them."[20] Some have questioned Achebe's commitment to African literary traditions in view of his choice of literary genre, the novel, in which to work. Since the novel is originally a European genre, this argument runs, no novel, not even an African one, can avoid exhibiting a "Eurocentric" worldview.[21]

Achebe's defense of his linguistic and artistic choices is surprisingly practical, his goal being to reach as wide an audience as possible, both inside and outside Nigeria. In an essay Achebe articulates the problem and explains his reasoning:

> Does my writing in the language of my colonizer not amount to acquiescing in the ultimate dispossession? . . . Let me simply say that when at the age of thirteen I went to [a] school modeled after British public schools, it was not only English literature that I encountered there. I came in contact also for the first time in my life with a large number of other boys of my own age who did not speak my Igbo language. And they were not foreigners but fellow Nigerian youth . . . [W]e had to put away our different mother tongues and communicate in the language of the colonizers . . . We chose English not because the British desired it but because having tacitly accepted the new nationalities into which colonialism had grouped us, we needed its language to transact our business, including the business of overthrowing colonialism itself in the fullness of time. Now, that does not mean that our indigenous languages should now be neglected. It does mean that these languages must co-exist and interact with the newcomer . . . For me it is not *either* English or Igbo, it is *both*.[22]

As one critic puts this problem, of the approximately 1,000 different languages and dialects to be found in Africa, "250 of them are to be found in Nigeria, and Nigerian writers quickly realized that if they wished to communicate not only with the English-speaking world at large, but also with considerable numbers of their fellow-countrymen," they would have to do so in English.[23] Achebe elsewhere adds "that the story we [Africans] had to tell could not be told for us by anyone else, no matter how gifted or well intentioned."[24] Not to write in English, then, would leave the definition and representation of Achebe's society to the discretion of colonial, and possibly even racist, literary authors.

The charge that Achebe's use of European novelistic forms compromises the Igbo integrity of his literary art is also easily countered, for *Things Fall Apart*, which in places reads like a folktale, is in fact a hybrid form, one which takes into account both European novelistic conventions and African oral forms. In any case, as Mikhail Bakhtin, the twentieth century's foremost theorist of the novel, reminds us, the novel, rather than being a univocal or monological entity, is necessarily polyphonic, the repository of the "diverse and dialogically opposed social voices of an era."[25] As one critic, following Bakhtin, observes, "African writers who use English are aware that their language is already populated with the political, social, and literary intentions of their colonial teachers, but they compel it 'to serve [their] own new intentions, to serve a second master'."[26] Indeed, Achebe sees himself as "extending the frontiers of English" so as to accommodate African literary modes.[27] The result is Achebe's successful adaptation of "a western literary genre into something that [is] authentically African in content, mode and pattern".[28] It is surely for this reason that Achebe can bridge the gap, as few authors have, between western and African readers and literary forms.[29]

Achebe has characterized *Things Fall Apart* as "an act of atonement with my past, the ritual return and homage of a prodigal son."[30] The novel is far more than this, however. For in addition to seeking to recover and celebrate the author's receding Igbo past, the work mounts a provocative challenge to western modes of understanding and to the British imperial account of African history. At the same time, it interrogates certain dimensions of patriarchal Igbo culture that are revealed to be compromised by their own biases and burdened by their own contradictions. Achebe's "nostalgia," ultimately, is anything but simple, straightforward, or smugly self-congratulatory.

III

Things Fall Apart treats the rise and fall of an Igbo man, Okonkwo; indeed, this three-part novel is structured around the three distinct phases of the protagonist's life, with the middle phase detailing his years of exile from Umuofia, his native village. Superficially, the novel follows the tradition of the European *Bildungsroman*, or novel of education, in which the novelist traces the protagonist's (usually) triumphal development against the backdrop of antagonistic social and familial forces.[31] The arc of Okonkwo's life conforms as well to Aristotle's conception of the tragic hero, "tragic flaw" and all.[32] Yet *Things Fall Apart* also concerns the triumphs and tragic demise of Okonkwo's Igbo (or "Ibo," as it is designated in the novel) village, Umuofia; Okonkwo's community, like the protagonist himself, is assaulted, and ultimately undone, by British colonial and modernizing influences. In this sense Achebe's colonial novel shares a goal of postcolonial criticism generally: to draw "attention to questions of identity in relation to broader national histories and destinies."[33]

"Okonkwo was well known throughout the nine villages and even beyond," the novel begins; "His fame rested on solid personal achievements."[34] Respected for his physical and military prowess and feared for his "very severe look" (3–4),

> Okonkwo was clearly cut out for great things. He was still young but he had won fame as the greatest wrestler in the nine villages. He was a wealthy farmer and had two barns full of yams, and had just married his third wife. To crown it all he had taken titles and had shown incredible prowess in two inter-tribal wars. (8)

Moreover, Okonkwo, "[A] man of action, a man of war," is "the first to bring home a human head" in "Umuofia's latest war" (10).

As the above passage suggests, male success in Umuofia is measured in martial ability and farming prowess – expressed in the number of titles, wives, and barns of yams one possesses – and not in cowries (a form a currency), or in family status alone. The novel repeatedly emphasizes the Igbo's meritocratic, rather than hereditary, social system; in Umuofia "a man was judged according to his worth and not according to the worth of his father" (8). This is fortunate for Okonkwo, who inherits nothing from his profligate and title-less father (8) and who achieves financial success only because of his tireless efforts as a share-cropper for another farmer. "With a father like Unoka, Okonkwo did not have the start in life which many young men had," we learn; "He neither inherited a barn nor a title, nor even a young wife" (18). Indeed,

> Anyone who knew [Okonkwo's] grim struggle against poverty and misfortune could not say he had been lucky. If ever a man deserved his success, that man was Okonkwo. At an early age he had achieved fame as the greatest wrestler in all the land. That was not luck. At the most one could say that his *chi* or personal god was good. But the Ibo people have a proverb that when a man says yes his *chi* says yes also. Okonkwo said yes very strongly; so his *chi* agreed. (27)[35]

Clearly, one dimension of Okonkwo's "heroism" is his ability to better his lot against all odds.

Things Fall Apart brings profound psychological depth, replete with Oedipal undertones, to the exploration of Okonkwo's personality formation. Above all, Okonkwo seeks to choose a path that deviates as much as possible from his father's "contemptible life and shameful death" (18). By Okonkwo's standards, and indeed by the traditional standards of the tribe, Unoka, his father, is an embarrassing "failure" (5): a "lazy and improvident" debtor who cannot properly feed his wife and children, a "loafer" who becomes a village laughing-stock, a "coward" who cannot "bear the sight of blood" (5, 6). Unoka is even called "*agbala*" – a title-less man but also a woman – by one of Oknonkwo's childhood friends, which highlights the patriarchal nature of Igbo society, in which demonstrated "manliness" was privileged (66). Okonkwo's determination to define himself against his father is noted repeatedly in the novel: Okonkwo's "whole life was dominated by fear, the fear of failure and weakness," a fear that "he should be found to resemble his father." Thus, Okonkwo is "ruled by one passion: to hate everything his father Unoka had loved" (13). Indeed, "Whenever the thought of his father's weakness and failure troubled him he expelled it by thinking about his own strength and success" (66).

Paradoxically, as successful as Okonkwo soon becomes, the seeds of his tragic fall are sown in the very making of his triumph. Okonkwo is best understood as a male version of an Antigone figure who, however nobly he stands up for traditional values, destroys himself – literally, in his case, by suicide – owing to his inflexibility and lack of compromise. In particular, the rigidity of Okonkwo's "masculine, martial values" is frequently noted in the novel. As Abdul R. JanMohamed puts it, however much the novel lauds his "pride, courage, and diligence," Okonkwo ultimately comes across as an "inflexible, calcified monomaniac."[36] Okonkwo's alarming inflexibility is first hinted at on the novel's second page, where we learn of Okonkwo's "slight stammer" and his propensity to "use his fists" whenever "he was angry and could not get his words out quickly enough" (4). "Okonkwo never showed any emotion openly, unless it be the emotion of anger," we learn shortly afterwards; "To show affection was a sign of weakness [and] the only thing worth demonstrating was strength" (28). Okonkwo possesses an "inflexible will" (24) and a "heavy hand" with his kin, yet his repressive behavior is not limited to family members – to the vicious beating of his wives or the cruel intimidation of his children – but extends to the "less successful" men of the tribe as well: "Okonkwo knew how to kill a man's spirit" (26). Thus, although *Things Fall Apart* celebrates Okonkwo's traditionalism and resistance to British colonialism – his commitment to doing things in "the grand, old way" (166) – the novel also questions his obsession with "masculine" values and his lack of tolerance and flexibility generally.[37]

The incident that most decisively reveals Okonkwo's tragic flaw is that involving Ikemefuna, a boy from the neighboring community of Mbaino whose father kills a "daughter of Umuofia" when she is visiting Mbaino's market (11). Umuofia being much feared, Mbaino accepts Umuofia's ultimatum to hand over a young man, Ikemefuna, and a virgin girl as compensation for the wrongful death. Ikemefuna, needing a place to reside in Umuofia, is taken in by Okonkwo and soon becomes an accepted member of Okonkwo's household. Okonkwo comes to treat him like a son and Ikemefuna, appropriately, takes to calling Okonkwo "father" (28, 57). A few years later the "Oracle of the Hills and Caves" decrees that Ikemefuna must be sacrificed by the elder males of Umuofia. Okonkwo, however, is advised not to have a "hand" in the death of anyone who calls him "father" (57). The tribesmen take Ikemefuna out of the village to kill him. The first blow that is delivered fails to do the job, however; and as the wounded boy runs toward Okonkwo for help, a "dazed" Okonkwo, who "was afraid of being thought weak," draws out his machete and cuts the boy down (61). As Jeffrey Meyers puts it of this revealing episode, "Though Ikemefuna's cry, 'My father, they have killed me!,' recalls the last words of the crucified Christ, the sacrifice is a re-enactment of the trial of Abraham and Isaac . . . but without the intervention of a harsh but just God."[38] In Achebe's novel, by contrast, Abraham follows through with the slaying of Isaac. Okonkwo's feelings of guilt for this act of infanticide – after all, he has killed an adopted son with his own hands – leads him to drink heavily yet at the same time to rebuke himself for becoming "a shivering old woman" (65) for feeling such guilt at all. Okonkwo yet again equates compassion with females and the lack of emotion with males. To the extent that Ikemefuna is, as one critic argues, an "ideal type" for the clan given his successful balancing of "masculine and feminine attributes," Okonkwo's murder of him

> is not only a tragic destruction of a promising and guiltless individual [but] connotes the murder of the clan's potential; Ikemefuna's sacrifice is both a symbol of what the clan lacks and a realistic dramatisation of the clan's inability to maintain a harmonious balance between male and female principles . . .[39]

That is to say, the killing of Ikemefuna can be read in gendered terms as embodying a critique of Okonkwo and his tribe.

As critical as the novel is of Okonkwo's complicity in the killing of Ikemefuna, however, Okonkwo is only punished by Umuofia when he accidentally kills the 16-year-old son of a titled man of the village during his father's funeral (124). Okonkwo's punishment is twofold: all of his property is destroyed by the tribe, in order to cleanse "the land which Okonkwo had polluted with the blood of a clansman" (125), and he is temporarily exiled from Umuofia to his mother's kinsmen in Mbanta. Okonkwo's goal of becoming "one of the lords of the clan" (131) and of remaining among "the nine masked spirits who administered justice in the clan" (171) is irreparably compromised by his being "condemned for seven years to live in a strange land" (133).

It is the "death" of a third son, however, his own, Nwoye, with whom he has strained relations, that most devastates Okonkwo. Nwoye's death is not literal but figurative: it involves his conversion to Anglicanism, the "new religion" that has gained ground in Umuofia during Okonkwo's seven-year exile (171). Indeed, "The clan had undergone such profound change during [Okonkwo's] exile that it was barely recognizable" (182): a church has been built, a handful of converts won, one of whom is Nwoye, and a number of evangelists now operate in the "surrounding towns and villages" (143). As Okonkwo sees it, "To abandon the gods of one's father [as Nwoye has done] and go about with a lot of effeminate men clucking like old hens was the very depth of abomination" (153). Okonkwo comes to view Nwoye as "degenerate and effeminate," and wonders, "How could he have begotten such a woman for a son?" (153) Okonkwo's greatest fear is here revealed: that his son, in addition to his now-deceased father, has become a "woman," and that these two tragedies reflect negatively on him – both in his own eyes and in the eyes of his fellow clansmen.

Okonkwo's eventual suicide, a figuration of the entire tribe's demise, stems in part from his conviction that he has no true heirs. It is also a result of his inability to adapt to changing circumstances: Okonkwo would rather end his life than deal with the British. Like other Achebe heroes, Okonkwo fails because his character becomes "ossified around certain traditional values."[40] Yet, as one critic observes, Oknokwo's suicide is not altogether explicable. Rather, it is best viewed as "ambiguous": a recognition of his own failure and a condemnation of his people and of the colonizers. In any case, Okonkwo's suicide "ironically brings on himself a shameful death like his father's, a fate he expended tremendous energy all his life to avoid."[41]

Raymond Williams is correct to note that Okonkwo "is destroyed in a very complicated process of internal contradictions and external invasion."[42] The protagonist's "internal contradictions" having been considered, it remains to explore the "external invasion" of British colonizers in Nigeria that Okonkwo relentlessly yet unsuccessfully battles. In another context Achebe observes that, "In the last four hundred years, Africa has been menaced by Europe." He then breaks these four centuries into three important periods: the slave trade, colonization, and decolonization.[43] Obviously, *Things Fall Apart* centers on the second of these three phases; references to the first – "stories about white men" who "took slaves away across the seas"(140–1) – are few and fleeting here. And the third phase is taken up in Achebe's *No Longer at Ease*, a novel about Obi, the son of Nwoye and grandson of Okonwko.[44]

Things Fall Apart interrogates what Achebe elsewhere calls the "psychology of religious imperialism":[45] the mentality that seeks to justify the replacing of the Igbo's "false gods, gods of wood and stone," with "this new God, the creator of all the world and all men and women" (145). Revealingly, religious imperialism is followed by other forms of British imperialism. Indeed, colonization is represented in the novel as beginning with the arrival of Anglican missionaries and as ending with a more obviously political and economic agenda. Even without this economic and political dimension, however, the missionaries appear to threaten the tribe's very existence. Okonkwo, for example, is prescient in viewing the rise of Anglicanism and the death of Igbo culture as coterminous:

> Suppose when he died all his male children decided to follow Nwoye's steps and abandon their ancestors? Okonkwo felt a cold shudder run through him at the terrible prospect, like the prospect of annihilation. He saw himself and his fathers crowding round their ancestral shrine waiting in vain for worship and sacrifice and finding nothing but ashes of bygone days, and his children the while praying to the white man's god. (153)

At numerous points Achebe's novel even associates the arrival of the Anglicans with the "death" of the clan and the massacre of Africans (138–9).

Things Fall Apart reveals the great extent to which religious missionaries were part of a comprehensive strategy of colonization, in which the Church functioned as a beachhead for political and economic imperialism. As one Umuofian tells Okonkwo, echoing the novel's title,

> The white man is very clever. He came quietly and peaceably with his religion. We were amused at his foolishness and allowed him to stay. Now he has won our brothers . . . And we have fallen apart. (176)

At countless other points in the novel it is made clear that "the white man had not only brought a religion but also a government" (155);[46] that British "religion and trade and government" (174) (what one critic calls "the colonial trinity"[47]) were inseparable from one another; that "The new religion and government and the trading stores were very much in the people's eyes and minds" (182–3). The novel cements the structural connection between religious and economic imperialism by reminding readers that, formally speaking, the titular head of the Church of England is the reigning monarch, Queen Victoria, herself, "the most powerful ruler in the world" (194). The head of the English Church and the British Empire, revealingly, are one and the same woman.

Paradoxically, the "imagined process of 'civilization' that the British believed they were giving to the savages"[48] is instead revealed in *Things Fall Apart* to lead to cultural disintegration and social chaos: the breakdown of Igbo society. As Frantz Fanon writes in his revolutionary *The Wretched of the Earth*, the goal of "colonial domination" was "to convince the natives that colonialism came to lighten their darkness," when in fact it functioned as a means of establishing control and mastery.[49] E. M. Forster points to the same duplicity in his 1924 novel *A Passage to India*, another study of British colonial ambitions, when he has Aziz think: "This pose of 'seeing India'," so popular with English visitors to the subcontinent, "was only a form of ruling India."[50] *Things Fall Apart* similarly represents the inseparability of knowing and conquering, of understanding and mastering the "Other." As Achebe concludes in his influential essay "Colonialist criticism," for the colonialist, "understanding [the native] and controlling him went hand in hand – understanding being a pre-condition for control and control constituting adequate proof of understanding."[51]

That the fledgling colonial entity is associated by Achebe with corruption, coercion, and hypocrisy only sharpens and deepens the novel's critique of British rule. The *kotma* or "court messengers, African agents of empire who in effect functioned as the 'colonial police',"[52] are depicted in *Things Fall Apart* as violent, cruel, bribe-taking enemies of Igbo tradition (197), as implants who come from an entirely different region of Nigeria. Even the fledgling imperial justice system, it is suggested, is corrupt; in a property dispute, for example, the "white man's court" finds in favor of a family that has "given much money to the white man's messengers and interpreter" (176). Put simply, Igbo culture is depicted as more "republican and egalitarian"[53] than British culture, with its monarchy, empire, and centralized power structures.

Yet *Things Fall Apart* is more nuanced and complex in its treatment of encroaching colonialism in Nigeria than has so far been suggested, with significant implications for what Ashton Nichols calls Achebe's "subtle critique of the politics of point of view."[54] For in addition to reclaiming and rehabilitating Africa's "past" – a past, in Nigerian critic Chinweizu's words, which has been "vilified by imperialism" and "imperialist education"[55] – Achebe's novel seeks to understand why so many Africans *embraced* Anglicanism, an entirely foreign religious worldview. This surprising attraction is explored most directly in the allure of the British Church to Okonkwo's son Nwoye:

It was not the mad logic of the Trinity that captivated him. He did not understand it. It was the poetry of the new religion, something felt in the marrow.
The hymn about brothers who sat in darkness and in fear seemed to answer a
vague and persistent question that haunted his young soul – the question of the
twins crying in the bush [in Igboland twins were regarded as evil and were
abandoned at birth to die] and the question of Ikemefuna who was killed. (147)

In other words, certain arguably inhumane practices of the Igbo are successfully
addressed and redressed by this "new" religion. More influential than this
new theology, however, was the new economic opportunity brought by British trade. We read at one point, for example, that "The white man had indeed
brought a lunatic religion, but he had also built a trading store" and "much
money flowed into Umuofia" (178). As Achebe puts it elsewhere:

the bounties of the Christian God were not to be taken lightly – education, paid
jobs and many other advantages that nobody in his right senses could underrate. And in fairness we should add that there was more than naked opportunism
in the defection of many to the new religion. For in some ways and in certain
circumstances it stood firmly on the side of humane behavior. It said, for
instance, that twins were not evil and must no longer be abandoned in the
forest to die.[56]

Ultimately, *Things Fall Apart* is more ambivalent than many readers have
admitted when it comes to the comparative merits of Igbo and British modes
of understanding; neither culture is seen as possessing a monopoly on "truth"
and both are ironized in the light of the other. Indeed, Achebe's "problematic
nostalgia" is perhaps best understood as a by-product of what JanMohamed
calls the author's "ambivalent attitude toward his characters and their respective
societies."[57]

Achebe's ambivalence in this regard points to an important implication
of the novel: that "one's very perceptions are shaped by the social and cultural
context out of which one operates,"[58] and that one's perceptions, therefore,
are open to question and "correction." Despite his spirited defense of Igbo
religious integrity and dignity (179–81), his compelling portrait of a "poetic"
Igbo culture that possesses "a philosophy of great depth and beauty,"[59] and
his powerful denunciation of the hypocritical and hubristic British colonial
mentality, "the cultural ethnocentrism that denies the validity, and even the
existence, of African customs, law, and morality,"[60] the author, at a still deeper
level, eschews definitive cultural allegiances of any kind in this novel. Rather,
Things Fall Apart reveals the power and intrinsic logic of both worldviews:

for Christians the world is divided into believers and heathen (for the British, into the "civilized" and the "savage"); for the Igbo, into "free-born" tribesmen and taboo "*osu*," outcasts who live "in a special area of the village" and who carry with them the mark of their "forbidden caste – long, tangled and dirty hair" (156). Achebe's implication is clear: as different as these ways of dividing up the world may be, they nevertheless share a need to celebrate and legitimate the self at the expense of an undeserving other. Freud's observation, in his *Civilization and Its Discontents*, about this ineradicable human need is as applicable here as it is to Golding's novel: "It is always possible to bind together a considerable number of people in love, so long as there are other people left over to receive the manifestations of their aggressiveness."[61]

The challenge of imagining the "Other's" legitimacy is traced, and its failure lamented, everywhere in *Things Fall Apart*. On both sides of the British/ Igbo cultural divide we encounter characters – Okonkwo and Reverend Smith, most importantly – who see things as "black or white" (184), and those – Obierika and Mr Brown, for example – who are capable of seeing reality in shades of gray. Although the Igbo appear to be more willing to tolerate differ- ence than the British ("You can stay with us if you like our ways," a Umuofian at one point informs Reverend Smith; "You can worship your own god. It is good that a man should worship the gods and spirits of his fathers" [190]), the same cultural blindness and religious invidiousness are depicted as being potent forces in both camps. On the Igbo side, in contrast to Okonkwo's monological rigidity stands Obierika's willingness to question his culture's worldview. In response to Okonkwo's uncritical assertion that "the law of the land must be obeyed," for example, Obierika admits, "I don't know how we got that law" (69). Obierika is described as "a man who thought about things . . . But although he thought for a long time he found no answer. He was merely led into greater complexities" (125).[62] At one point Obierika's eldest brother speculates that "what is good in one place is bad in another place" (73–4), while at another Uchendu, a fellow tribesman, remarks, "There is no story that is not true . . . The world has no end, and what is good among one people is an abomination with others" (141). One Umuofian thematizes the novel's concern with the "politics of point of view"[63] when he observes that Reverend Smith "does not understand our customs, just as we do not understand his. We say he is foolish because he does not know our ways, and perhaps he says we are foolish because we do not know his" (191).

This same tension between dialogic and monologic modes of understanding exists on the British side as well. For example, in contrast to Mr Brown's re- spect for dialogue, his "compromise and accommodation" (184) ("Whenever Mr Brown went to [a certain] village he spent long hours with Akunna . . . talking through an interpreter about religion. Neither of them succeeded in converting the other but they learned more about their different beliefs" [179]), Reverend Smith, his successor, sees "things in black and white. And black was evil. He saw the world as a battlefield in which the children of light were locked in mortal conflict with the sons of darkness" (184). Conversely, "The over-zealous converts who had smarted under Mr Brown's restraining hand now [in Reverend Smith's day] flourished in full favor" (185). One of these "over-zealous" coverts, Enoch, even hopes to wage a "holy war" against his former tribesmen (188).

The cultural myopia if not blindness of most British colonists is most powerfully revealed in the novel's justly famous closing moments, when we learn of Okonkwo's suicide by hanging, which follows his murder of a court messenger, and of Umuofia's reluctance to bury him.[64] It therefore remains for the British to bury Okonkwo, which leads the District Commissioner, in the closing paragraph of the novel, to remark to himself:

> In the many years in which he had toiled to bring civilization to different parts of Africa he had learned a number of things. One of them was that a District Commissioner must never attend to such undignified details as cutting a hanged man from the tree. Such attention would give the natives a poor opinion of him. In the book which he planned to write he would stress that point. As he walked back to the court he thought about that book. Every day brought him some new material. The story of this man who had killed a messenger and hanged himself would make interesting reading. One could almost write a whole chapter on him. Perhaps not a whole chapter but a reasonable paragraph, at any rate. There was so much else to include, and one must be firm in cutting out details. He had already chosen the title of the book, after much thought: *The Pacification of the Primitive Tribes of the Lower Niger.* (208–9)[65]

Astounding ironies of perspective and diction proliferate and reverberate in this passage. Not only do the words "pacification" and "primitive" here strike the reader as hypocritical misnomers, but the novel's final paragraph juxtaposes a reductive understanding of Okonkwo with our psychologically and cultur-ally nuanced understanding of him, which the novel has treated in all of its complexity and subtlety for over 200 pages.[66] Yet it is Achebe, as one critic argues, who in writing *Things Fall Apart* "pre-empts an attempted white usurpa-tion" of Okonkwo's story and culture, "trapping the 'official version' within a more sympathetic history."[67] That is to say, the irony of the novel's closing paragraph backfires on the District Commissioner himself, and on the imperial mentality that seeks to rationalize his colonial ambitions. It is the British – and not the Igbo – view that is revealed here to be the more parochial, delimited, and backward one.

This brings us, at last, to Achebe's choice of a title for his provocative colonial novel. This choice is both resonant and apposite: not only does the title – taken from W. B. Yeats's prescient poem "The Second Coming" – literally make sense, as Umuofia does seem to "fall apart," but it figuratively makes sense as well, as it alludes to the (normally violent) clash of civilizations. The aptness of Achebe's choice of title, as one reader puts it, is

> indicative of a profound pondering on Yeats's vision of history as a succession of civilizations, each containing the seeds of its own destruction because no single enclosed social order has so far succeeded in containing the whole range of human impulses and aspirations.[68]

This insight perhaps best explains the novel's cultural pluralism and perspectival democracy: like languages, cultures, rather than being permanent, "pure," or complete, are mutable, partial, and open to external influence. Few in *Things Fall Apart* acknowledge the porous nature of culture, and the result, for many, is lethal.

In his essay "The truth of fiction" Achebe blames our "self-centeredness" and lack of "imagination" for our failure

> to recreate in ourselves the thoughts that must go on in the minds of others, especially those we dispossess. A person who is insensitive to the sufferings of his fellows is that way because he lacks the imaginative power to get under the skin of another human being and see the world through eyes other than its own.[69]

This visualizing of the other – this phenomenological exercise – may be a "truth" that "fiction" best affords. It is in any case an imaginative recreation that Achebe's *Things Fall Apart*, if not the novel's British or African characters, powerfully and poignantly achieves.

Chapter 5

Muriel Spark's *The Prime of Miss Jean Brodie* (1961)

All great genius attracts legend to itself . . . Such legend is the repository of a vital aspect of truth.
> Muriel Spark and Derek Stanford, *Emily Brontë: Her Life and Work*[1]

There was a mystery here to be worked out . . .
> *The Prime of Miss Jean Brodie*[2]

I

The Prime of Miss Jean Brodie is a masterpiece of irony and understatement in the vein of works by Jane Austen and Anton Chekhov. The sixth published novel of Muriel Spark, *Brodie* explores the influence – sometimes abiding, sometimes limited, always enigmatic, and finally indefinable – of a colorful and domineering schoolteacher on her impressionable students. It is also a study in obsession – Brodie's, her students', and the reader's – as well as a testament to the presence of paradox in human affairs. *The Prime of Miss Jean Brodie* initially appeared in *The New Yorker* in the fall of 1961; it was then reissued as a book, in 1962, and produced as a play and film, in 1966, with Vanessa Redgrave on the London stage and Maggie Smith on screen playing the role of the memorable, idiosyncratic schoolmistress. Although the Scottish author has written more than twenty novels over her four-decade-long career, it is the magnificently subtle *Brodie* for which she remains best known and most critically acclaimed.

Based on Spark's experiences in the 1920s and 1930s at James Gillespie's School for Girls in Edinburgh, and in particular on her teacher there, Miss

Christina Kay, Spark's enigmatic "comedy of errors"[3] is considerably more than the sum of its parts. Like most of her novels, *Brodie* is a work that provides pleasures, as Frank Kermode comments, that are commensurate with "our being willing to work harder than usual" to discover them.[4] Spark's novel is absorbing, finally, less because of its plot than because of the way it is told: with time-shifts, in particular flash-forwards, which recall the high modernist achievements of Conrad's *The Secret Agent* (1907) and Ford's *The Good Soldier* (1915). In all of these works the advantages of "suspense and uncertainty are partly sacrificed in the interests of a dramatic juxtaposition that compels the reader to relate causes to their distant effects."[5] Another quality that makes the novel so fascinating is the apparent gap between its dark "central purpose" – exploring the exploits of a spiritual tyrant – and its "lightness" of surface.[6] As Norman Page characterizes this gap, "Many of the ingredients of this novel – old fashioned girls' school for the daughters of the Edinburgh bourgeoisie, the suspicious headmistress, the one-armed art master, the middle-aged spinster schoolmistress – seem to belong to farce or comedy of manners," yet "these promises of undisturbing entertainment are not fulfilled and the story shades into a theological drama with tragic overtones."[7] Put another way, Spark's textured and nuanced narrative combines "realistic, precisely localized, even autobiographical, elements with the fantastic and the supernatural."[8] As David Lodge observes, *Brodie* is deceivingly simple. Although it is possible to read the novel "quickly and lightly as nothing more than a collection of wry anecdotes about an eccentric schoolmistress and her pupils," its involved "web of cross-reference, anticipation and retrospect" render the work much more complex and interpretively elusive than one might think.[9]

II

Muriel Sarah Camberg was born in Edinburgh in 1918. Her father was a Jew of Lithuanian ancestry, her mother an Anglican Englishwoman, and she was educated in a Presbyterian school. Even from this mix of religious influences, Spark reports developing no durable religious allegiances in the first 35 years of her life. It has nevertheless been argued that the author's "Jewish-Scottish inheritance and upbringing" made her the "moralist" that she is, and that this mixed heritage allowed her "to combine a sense of moral responsibility of action with the determinism which says that all your actions have unavoidably and unalterably fixed your life in a certain shape."[10] The momentous religious event of her life was undoubtedly her conversion to Roman Catholicism in

1954, which neatly preceded the commencement of her lengthy career as a novelist. However one interprets this chronology, it is tempting to conclude, with Allan Massie, that Spark's "acceptance of the Faith and the Church removed certain barriers which had deterred her from writing fiction, and gave her a point of view from which to regard experience in a way that made sense" to her.[11]

Muriel married Sydney Oswald Spark, a schoolteacher from Southern Rhodesia (present day Zimbabwe), in 1937. She followed him to Africa but later, in 1944, divorced him and returned to Britain. Spark then worked as a propagandist for the Political Intelligence Department of the British Foreign Office, in London. Her next port of call, also in London, was the office of *Poetry Review*, during which time (1947–9) she edited the journal and was General Secretary of the Poetry Society. Her major early publications, between 1950 and 1953, consisted of a volume of verse and a series of literary biographies: of Mary Shelley, of John Masefield, and (with Derek Stanford) of Emily Brontë.

Spark's first novel, *The Comforters*, was published in 1957 to critical acclaim. *Momento Mori*, which also received positive reviews, followed in 1959. It was *The Prime of Miss Jean Brodie*, however, Spark's sixth novel, which launched her international career. And it was on the strength of this novel that Spark was given an office, on the editorial premises of *The New Yorker*, in which to write. There she penned her two next novels, *The Girls of Slender Means* (1963) and *The Mandelbaum Gate* (1965; winner of the James Tate Black Memorial Prize), which solidified her reputation on both sides of the Atlantic as a novelist of great promise. In 1966 Spark left New York for Italy, where she has lived and written novels – among these *Loitering with Intent* (1981) and *A Far Cry from Kensington* (1988) – ever since. Her colorful autobiography, *Curriculum Vitae*, emerged in 1992, and her *Complete Short Stories* was published in 2001. Spark has received many honorary doctorates in Scotland and England. She was awarded the Order of the British Empire in 1967, was made a Dame of the British Empire in 1993, and became a Commandeur in the French Ordre des Arts et des Lettres in 1996. She presently lives and writes in Tuscany.

III

Spark's novels possess the linguistic compression and subtlety of poetry. Spark herself maintains that "I love economical prose, and would always try to find the briefest way to express a meaning," and that "the novel as an art form" is "essentially a variation of a poem": "I was convinced that any good novel, or indeed any composition which called for a constructional sense, was essentially an extension of poetry."[12] Alan Bold attributes to this conviction the "extreme compression of her language" and her "elusive attitude to plot."[13] It is difficult not to think of numerous sentences in *Brodie* in these terms. For example, in one sentence on the novel's first page – "The girls could not take off their panama hats because this was not far from the school gates and hatlessness was an offence" (1) – the school's sexually repressive dress code and bourgeois culture is mocked, but so subtly that it is easy to miss.

Set in Edinburgh in the 1930s, Spark's novel concerns six girls – Monica Douglas, Rose Stanley, Eunice Gardiner, Sandy Stranger, Jenny Gray, and Mary Macgregor – who make up the "Brodie set" at the Marcia Blaine School for Girls. All six of Brodie's acolytes are "famous for something" (3); respectively, for mathematical prowess and a bad temper, for sex, for athletics, for having "small, almost nonexistent, eyes" (3), for beauty, and for being "a silent lump, a nobody whom everybody could blame" (4). Moreover, the "Brodie set" is

> what they had been called even before the headmistress had given them the name, in scorn, when they had moved from the Junior to the Senior school at the age of twelve. At that time they had been immediately recognizable as Miss Brodie's pupils, being vastly informed on a lot of subjects irrelevant to the authorized curriculum, as the headmistress said, and useless to the school as a school. (1–2)

In the best single piece of criticism on this novel, David Lodge lays out the superficially simple yet immensely complex plot of the novel most economically. Miss Brodie dominates the lives and fantasies of the girls in many ways, Lodge writes,

> but they are particularly intrigued by the question of her relationships with the two men on the teaching staff: the art master, Mr. Lloyd, who is Catholic and married, and the singing master, Mr. Lowther, a bachelor and an Elder of the Church of Scotland. Mr. Lloyd, who lost his arm in the Great War (in which Miss Brodie's first love fell), is the more romantically dashing, [but Brodie] also appears to be deeply involved with Mr. Lowther. As the girls move up through the Senior School . . . it becomes evident that Miss Brodie is in love with Mr. Lloyd, but has "renounced" him because he is married. However, she continues the romance vicariously through Rose, who models for Mr. Lloyd (though his portraits always bear an eerie resemblance to Miss Brodie). Miss Brodie conducts an affair . . . with Mr. Lowther, but refuses to marry him . . . At about

this time ... a new girl called Joyce Emily Hammond, with a record of delinquency, joins the school, and tries unsuccessfully to join the set. Later, however, Miss Brodie befriends her. The Headmistress impotently plots Miss Brodie's removal. One day Joyce Emily disappears and it is learned that she has been killed in an attack on a train in Spain. It is assumed she was trying to join her brother who is fighting Franco in the Spanish Civil War. Miss Brodie continues to nourish the idea that Rose will have an affair with Lloyd, but it is in fact Sandy who does so, while Miss Brodie is enthusiastically touring Hitler's Germany, in the summer of 1938. Through Lloyd, Sandy gets interested in the Catholic faith. One day Miss Brodie reveals to Sandy that she knew of and encouraged Joyce Emily's escapade, though she persuaded her to switch her allegiance to Franco. [Sandy reveals Brodie's indiscretion to the Headmistress.] In the summer of 1939, Miss Brodie is forced to resign, by which time Sandy has been received into the Catholic Church.[14]

Brodie is proven to be wrong about many things, but the novel leaves us with a sense of her domineering influence over the girls nonetheless.

However "brilliantly woven" the novel's plot may be,[15] plot suspense itself is subverted by virtue of the fact that we are told in the middle of the novel both that Brodie is fired and that Sandy has betrayed her. Spark is clearly therefore less interested in plot, conventionally understood, than she is in character psychology and motivation, the real emphases of her novel. One of *Brodie*'s chief narrative devices is the punctuation of the novel's "present" time (mainly in the 1930s) with a series of flash-forwards (extending into the 1950s) and fantasies, both of which are used by Spark in order to "demonstrate the unforeseen ways in which" Brodie "influences her students, especially Sandy Stranger."[16] David Lodge adds another purpose to the novel's chronological complexity, in particular its flash-forwards and fantasy-digressions: such narrative methods constantly check "any inclination we may have to 'lose ourselves' in the story or to sink into [an unreflective] emotional identification with any of the characters; it detaches us from the experience presented and makes us think about its meaning, or meanings."[17] This, more than anything else, accounts for *Brodie*'s difference from other novels that eulogize influential teachers or the educational process.

One striking example of the novel's flash-forward device comes early in the text and is embellished often throughout it: "Mary Macgregor, although she lived into her twenty-fourth year, never quite realized that Jean Brodie's confidences were not shared with the rest of the staff" (13). In the middle of a sentence that follows we learn that Mary, "before she died while on leave in Cumberland in a fire in the hotel," ran "Back and forth along the corridors ... through the thickening smoke. She ran one way; then, turning, the other way; and at either end the blast furnace of the fire met her" (13–14). Still later in the novel, Mary's culpability in own her end is suggested when she takes fright when a fire erupts in the school science lab, and she "ran along a single lane between two benches, met with a white flame, and ran back to meet another brilliant tongue of fire. Hither and thither she ran in panic between the benches until she was caught and induced to calm down, and she was told not to be so stupid" by the science teacher (81). Here the novel connects Mary's evident indecision and lack of intelligence with her death years later in the hotel fire. In this same way Brodie's nature and fate are probed in Spark's work. What is said of Brodie at one point – "it was only in retrospect that they could see Miss Brodie's affair with Mr. Lowther for what it was, that is to say, in a factual light" (91) – is true more generally of all the characters in Spark's novel. Events in life cannot be understood at the moment of their occurrence, *The Prime of Miss Jean Brodie* seems to suggest, but only, if ever, in the fullness of time.

The girls' (and particularly Sandy's) flights of fantasy, which are heavily indebted to works of romantic literature, shed light on the meaning of their experience and allow them a temporary respite from the more puritanical and quotidian dimensions of school life. For example, Sandy and Jenny compose "'The Mountain Eyrie', the true love story of Miss Jean Brodie" (41), a romance about their teacher and her former fiancé, Hugh Carruthers, who was killed in the Great War. In this composition, Hugh, who is very much alive, is spurned by Brodie and has made his abode in a "mountain eyrie," where he is holding Sandy hostage (Jenny has successfully made her escape). Sandy and Jenny, who take turns composing lines of this romance (17–18), also craft "the love correspondence between Miss Brodie and the singing master" (72). When the facts of Brodie's romantic life fall short, the two embellish these facts and live through them vicariously (just as Brodie later does with Rose, whom she compares to a "heroine from a novel by D. H. Lawrence" [117]). Sandy not only escapes into romances by Charlotte Brontë, Robert Louis Stevenson, and Lord Tennyson; she even converses and interacts (in her imagination) with romantic heroes from their works, among these Mr Rochester from *Jane Eyre*, Alan Breck from *Kidnapped*, and the Lady of Shalott from Tennyson's eponymous poem.[18] While the schoolgirls' fantasies may be regarded as normal mental outlets that will diminish as they age, this process seems not to have occurred in the case of their teacher. As David Lodge observes, "Miss Brodie continues to inhabit her own fantasies, rewriting the history of her first love to fit the circumstances of her subsequent liaisons with Lloyd and Lowther."[19] Indeed, Brodie at times seems to go beyond the girlish fantasizing of her students, and is revealed to be incapable of distinguishing between fact and fancy.

Sandy Stranger, as suggested by her surname, is somewhat outside the Brodie set. That said, her view of things, and that of the novel's narrator, seem closely aligned. Although the novel's narrator is "god-like" – one who both "sees the future and looks back into the past," possessing an "omniscience" that is "wittily particularized by the use of a rather prim, Edinburgh voice"[20] – and therefore is not strictly speaking one of the novel's characters, Sandy is the character who nevertheless seems closest to the narrator's perspective of things. In fact, Sandy appears to be, in Lodge's words, "the principal point-of-view character in the novel. Not only do we see most of the action through her eyes, but many of the authorial comments are in effect comments upon Sandy and her perceptions."[21]

Allan Massie has most strongly argued for Sandy's centrality to the novel and holds that, "However peripherally or obliquely it is presented," Sandy's conversion to Catholicism is "the true center of the novel."[22] Although Massie may overstate the case, it is nevertheless clear that Sandy, alone of all the characters, understands Brodie "with a clear-eyed, dispassionate vision of the hidden and even unconscious springs of her actions."[23] Lodge argues that Sandy is "the shrewdest, most complex, and most interesting of the Brodie set," despite the small eyes that are her "distinguishing mark throughout the novel," and then adds: "She is the only character who is interiorized to any significant extent – the only character whose thoughts we share intimately."[24] Indeed, Sandy's irritable and ironic voice seems to stand behind many of the narrator's statements, from the mocking reference to Brodie as "the heroine she was" (100), to the explanation that "The Lloyds were Catholics and so were made to have a lot of children by force" (108).

David Lodge is correct to note that "middle-class life in Edinburgh between the Wars" is "beautifully caught and communicated" in Spark's novel;[25] but the connection between Jean Brodie and the city in which the novel takes place goes considerably beyond this observation. Although Spark's relationship to and experience growing up in Edinburgh are well documented (she has claimed that Edinburgh "has definitely had an effect on my mind, my prose style and my ways of thought"[26]), Jean Brodie's symbolic likeness to the city of her habitation requires further scrutiny.

Brodie is no less than an emblem of the *genus loci*, or spirit of place, of Edinburgh. The novel hints at this relationship in such passages as "Miss Brodie looked beautiful and fragile, just as dark heavy Edinburgh itself could suddenly be changed into a floating city when the light was a special pearly white and fell upon one of the gracefully fashioned streets" (118); or when Brodie's beauty, like Edinburgh's, is described as "a quality" that "came and went" (121). Brodie is shown as self-divided or doubled; she appears to lead "a double life" (19). In this she is like the famous Edinburgher who shares her surname, Deacon William Brodie, town councillor by day and burglar by night, who is the source for Stevenson's *The Strange Case of Dr Jekyll and Mr Hyde* (1886). She has a parallel also in Edinburgh itself, with its Gothic and squalid old town (with its "reeking network of slums" [32]), and its Georgian and bourgeois new town, with its middle-class aura of respectability. The city's divided character is suggested when Brodie takes her students from the bourgeois Marcia Blaine school on a tour of the uncouth and violent old town, which seems a "foreign" land to the girls. It is perhaps for the "double life" (19) that she appears to lead that one critic considers "The realization that Jean Brodie can be two people, radical teacher with the best interests of her pupils at heart, and immoral leader willing to sacrifice them in her own interests," to be the novel's "main theme."[27] Alan Bold deftly articulates Brodie's myriad contradictions: she "idolizes the fascists yet deplores the team spirit; she speaks of love and freedom yet sleeps with the dreary Mr. Lowther and denies herself to one-armed Mr. Lloyd because he is married; she loves Rome and the Italians yet opposes the Church of Rome."[28]

In *Curriculum Vitae*, Spark remarks, "I do not know exactly why I chose the name Miss Brodie."[29] As if in response, Jean Brodie, in her own novel, answers: "I am a descendant . . . of Willie Brodie, a man of substance"; his story is "the stuff I am made of" (93). The self-divided Deacon Brodie is regarded by many to be Edinburgh's quintessential personage; he was understood by Stevenson to express the very "character" of Edinburgh.[30] Philip E. Ray has noted that both Jean Brodie and Deacon Brodie, while "'Edinburgh-born,' respectable citizens of the town," are both "rebels against Edinburgh's elaborate social conventions and strict moral code."[31] Moreover, "That sense of duality within a fictional hero or heroine (the destroyer who both loves and hates the object of obliteration, the sinner who is justified") is a major theme in Scottish fiction.[32] It recurs in the William Brodie legend, in Stevenson's *Jekyll and Hyde*, in James Hogg's *Private Memoirs and Confessions of a Justified Sinner*, and, of course, in Spark's novel.[33] In all of these tales the hero's "come-uppance" is "due to over-reaching"; in all of them he or she nurtures a "sense of secret alienation from society while at the same time claiming public allegiance to its morality."[34]

The plot of Spark's novel hinges on the sharp and persistent conflict between Miss Brodie's charismatic and romantic pedagogy and that of the more pragmatic and Calvinistic Marcia Blaine school faculty at large. As David Lodge characterizes this schism, Brodie's stimulating teaching style "contrasts favorably with the dry-as-dust academic approach of the rest of the staff [one teacher, revealingly in this connection, is named "Miss Gaunt"], and we feel a good deal of sympathy with her in her struggle with the jealously disapproving headmistress" Miss MacKay.[35]

Miss Jean Brodie's roots are in Miss Christina Kay, Muriel Spark's teacher in Edinburgh when the author was 11 years old. For all of the differences between the real and the fictional teachers – had Miss Kay met her fictional counterpart, Spark speculates in *Curriculum Vitae*, she would have put Brodie "firmly in her place"[36] – there are many notable similarities. Kay, like Brodie, never married; she was one "of the generation of clever, academically trained women who had lost their sweethearts in the 1914–1918 war."[37] Like Brodie, Kay was dynamic and theatrical, an "exhilarating and impressive" teacher who admired "Il Duce" and who displayed in class "a newspaper cutting of Mussolini's Fascisti marching along the streets of Rome," as well as reproductions of "early Renaissance paintings, Leonardo da Vinci, Giotto, [and] Botticelli."[38] Moreover Kay, like Brodie, referred to her acolytes as the "crème de la crème" and took them to dance and other fine arts performances (including one by dance legend Anna Pavlova), sometimes funding the outing from her own pocket.[39]

The Marcia Blaine School is depicted as a "traditional" (43), Calvinist-leaning, dourly rationalistic girls' school that aims to prepare women to become eligible wives of middle-class Edinburghers. This agenda conflicts with that of Miss Brodie. Brodie's romantic individualism is "out of key with the rest of the school" staff (133), which instead privileges useful knowledge, social conformity, and "the team spirit" (82). (Brodie frequently implies that the "Girl Guides," the British equivalent of the American Girl Scouts, are guilty of mindless conformism.) This conflict between Jean Brodie's mindset and that of the Marcia Blaine school is figured as a conflict between high culture ("Miss Brodie was reciting poetry to the class at a quarter to four, to raise their minds before they went home" [19]) and "hard knowledge" (69); between "stories and opinions which had nothing to do with the ordinary world" (13) and the ordinary world; between "glamorous activity" (119) and the "unsoulful" expertise and "industrious learning" proffered by the other teachers (81, 59); between experimental teaching methods (49) and more traditional ones; and between Brodie's eroticized view of the world and "gaunt Miss Gaunt's" puritanical one. Brodie dismisses the senior school staff as "gross materialists," and the junior school staff as "narrow-minded" and "half-educated" (114), while the other teachers dismiss Brodie as eccentric and possibly even dangerous. In contrast, say, to Miss Gaunt's austerity, Miss Brodie is an "Edinburgh Festival all on her own" (26).

The first intimation of a feud (25) between Miss Brodie and the rest of the teaching staff (7) over "her educational system" is registered on the novel's first page and only intensifies throughout the work. Brodie refers to this conflict as a plot "to force me to resign" (5); and the headmistress comes to think of Brodie as her "prey" (99). Brodie brings this very conflict into her classroom in order to turn her girls against the administration, and remarks to her class:

> It has been suggested again that I should apply for a post at one of the progress-ive, that is to say, crank schools. I shall not apply for a post at a crank school. I shall remain at this education factory where my duty lies. There needs must be a leaven in the lump. Give me a girl at an impressionable age and she is mine for life. (119)

Brodie here reveals her dictatorial and rebellious pedagogy, which masquerades as philanthropic self-sacrifice.

Brodie (in a romantic vein and echoing a debate in Charles Dickens's novel *Hard Times*) elaborates on the conflict between the pedagogically more conventional headmistress and herself in this way:

> To me education is a leading out of what is already there in the pupil's soul. To Miss MacKay it is a putting in of something that is not there, and that is not what I call education, I call it intrusion ... Miss MacKay's method is to thrust a lot of information into the pupil's head; mine is a leading out of knowledge. (36)

Brodie later adds, "my methods cannot be condemned unless they can be proved to be in any part improper or subversive" (39). Eventually, of course, these very accusations are proved.

The narrator looks ironically at the school's absurd fear of "dangerous Miss Brodie" (7) (and the false allegation that Brodie likes "her wee drink" [124]) as much as it does her equally absurd bid to make her girls into "the crème de la crème" and "heroines" (30). In one example that cuts both ways, Brodie dismisses one of the girls' more difficult mathematical problems by explaining that the solution to such a problem "would be quite useless to Sybil Thorndike, Anna Pavlova and the late Helen of Troy" (87). This comment reveals both Brodie's shallow pedagogy and the school's exaggerated fears about the threat posed by it.

Miss Brodie's pupils are instantly recognizable in the school by virtue of knowing much about "seditious" (25) and academically irrelevant topics ("Mussolini, the Italian Renaissance painters," the "love lives of Charlotte Brontë and Miss Brodie herself" [2]). Brodie's girls, all of whom are "held in suspicion and not much liking," may know of "the existence of Einstein and the arguments of those who considered the Bible to be untrue," but they are woefully ignorant of "the date of the Battle of Flodden" and "the capital of

Finland" (2), the kind of practical knowledge that schoolgirls, according to the faculty at large, should possess.[40]

David Lodge is right to conclude that "Miss Brodie is a Romantic by taste and temperament, and exemplifies the defects of the uncontrolled romantic sensibility."[41] Chief among these defects is her narcissistic and domineering teaching style. At one point, for example, when she is supposed to be teaching prescribed material, she instead lectures her students "about my last summer holiday in Egypt," about "the care of the skin" and "the hands," and about "the Frenchman I met in the train to Biarritz" (7). "Get out your history books and prop them up in your hands," she later tells the girls, in case one of the other teachers happens by her classroom during the lesson (48). While the charismatic instructor promises to offer her charges a "life-enhancing freedom,"[42] then, she is in fact shown to offer them lessons that are "absurd in their egocentricity" and "inconsequentiality"[43] – and which are just plain authoritarian. The following exchange with her pupils makes this latter point. When Brodie asks her students in class, "Who is the greatest Italian painter?" and a student answers "Leonardo de Vinci," Brodie then responds: "That is incorrect. The answer is Giotto, he is my favorite" (7–8). Brodie also tells her students the order of importance of "the great subjects of life": "Art and religion first; then philosophy; lastly science" (24–5), as if such a ranking is beyond question simply because it is her preference.

Lodge argues that Spark's novel is "about education and religion" and that the assessment of its heroine is ultimately "an ethical and theological matter, not merely an educational one."[44] Central to his argument is the notion that Miss Brodie is ultimately understood through Sandy's eyes and that "Sandy's developing understanding of her teacher's character is formulated more and more precisely, as she grows up, in religious terms, and is inextricably connected with the growth of her own religious awareness, from the secular indifferentism of her family to her conversion to Roman Catholicism."[45] The upshot, for Lodge, is that Spark's novel suggests that "all groups, communions and institutions are false and more or less corrupting except the one that is founded on the truths of Christian orthodoxy – and even that one is not particularly attractive or virtuous."[46]

The nature and degree of Miss Brodie's Calvinism have been much debated by readers. For Lodge, "Miss Brodie, though superficially in reaction against the Calvinistic moral code, in fact lives by a personal, secularized version of it, 'electing herself to grace,' but fatally ignoring the possibility that her sense of justification may be erroneous."[47] According to Sandy, Brodie believes that "she is Providence"; she "thinks she is the God of Calvin, she sees the beginning and the end" (129). As Lodge articulates Sandy's understanding, Brodie

> has created her own secular religion of which she is simultaneously the God, Redeemer and minister to the elect. She tries to create the girls in her own image, and to direct their destinies according to her own divine plan. Like Christ she does not know she is going to be betrayed, and never discovers for certain the identity of her Judas.[48]

In the words of another reader, Brodie's relationship with her set "replicates the relationship of the Calvinist God to humanity."[49] Ironically, she discourages her students' religious impulses, as Church authority recognized by the girls would threaten and undercut her own.

The fullest treatment of Miss Brodie's religiosity comes midway through the novel, when it is explained that she "always went to church on Sunday mornings," attending a number of Protestant denominations and sects, yet that she always avoided Roman Catholic houses of worship.

> Her disapproval of the Church of Rome was based on her assertions that it was a church of superstition, and that only people who did not want to think for themselves were Roman Catholics. In some ways, her attitude was a strange one, because she was by temperament suited only to the Roman Catholic Church; possibly it could have embraced, even while it disciplined, her soaring and diving spirit, it might even have normalized her. But perhaps this was the reason that she shunned it, lover of Italy though she was, bringing to her support a rigid Edinburgh-born side of herself when the Catholic Church was in question . . . (90)

While rejecting Catholicism, then, Brodie's Calvinism is admixed with a liberal cosmopolitanism: though she adheres "to the strict Church of Scotland habits of her youth" and keeps "the Sabbath," she also attends "evening classes in comparative religion at the University" (36). That is to say, by comparison with Miss Gaunt and others on the staff who say "good morning" with "predestination in their smiles" (79), Brodie is a Calvinist of only moderate leanings.

Sandy, an unpleasant and duplicitous "schemer who becomes Miss Brodie's Judas,"[50] is a more extreme figure, religiously-speaking. She deems Miss Brodie's sense of omniscience to be due to her "defective sense of self-criticism" (91) and to her having "elected herself to grace" (116). Eventually believing that the "Brodie set, not to mention Miss Brodie herself, was getting out of hand" (108), Sandy betrays Brodie to MacKay, accusing her of teaching fascism. What really offends Sandy, however, is not Brodie's politics at all but her heretical view of her mortal self, as understood by the Catholic Church, which Sandy later joins.[51] Just as Brodie eventually expresses disappointment that

Sandy has joined a convent – thinking it a "waste" and wondering whether it was done simply to "annoy" her (one might argue that it was) (66) – so Sandy rejects

> Brodie as a false Christ-figure and converts to the real thing by becoming a Catholic nun . . . The shift from Calvinist predestination to the centrality of free will within Catholicism points to a blunt theological divide.[52]

On the other hand, as Bryan Cheyette observes, "while Catholicism and Calvinism are contrasted" in the novel "as Sandy Stranger and Jean Brodie, Rome and Edinburgh, they are not straightforward oppositions," as "both Brodie and Sandy have strong and competing elements of Calvinism and Catholicism within them."[53] Moreover, it is not clear whether Brodie, in the final analysis, was really playing at God or was merely attempting to counter middle-class conventions; whether she was the manipulator/victimizer or the manipulated/victim in the novel.[54]

Sandy's aversion to Calvinism is revealed to have roots in her childhood. When younger she recoiled instinctively from the Scottish Church, as incarnated in the austere and frightening "outsides of old Edinburgh churches," which "were of such dark stone" and "were built so warningly with their upraised fingers" (35). She would stand "outside St. Giles' Cathedral or the Tolbooth, and contemplate these emblems of a dark and terrible salvation which made the fires of the damned seem very merry to the imagination by contrast, and much preferable" (115). Eventually seeking out "the religion of Calvin" to "reject" and to define herself against, Sandy views it as a theology in which "God had planned for practically everybody before they were born a nasty surprise when they died" (115), a theology in which it is "God's pleasure to implant in certain people an erroneous sense of joy and salvation, so that their surprise at the end might be the nastier" (115–16). Later, Sandy associates this doctrine with "the excesses of Miss Brodie in her Prime" (116). For example, when the class is walking through Edinburgh, "Sandy looked back at her companions, and understood them as a body with Miss Brodie for the head." She perceived them all, "in a frightening little moment, in unified compliance to the destiny of Miss Brodie, as if God had willed them to birth for that purpose" (30). When Sandy later converts to Roman Catholicism she becomes "Sister Helena of the Transfiguration" (33), and writes a psychological treatise, "The transfiguration of the commonplace" (39), which gains notoriety. This conversion does not seem to bring her peace, however: whenever she is depicted in the convent she is imaged, like an animal in a cage, clutching "the bars of the grille as if she wanted to escape from the dim parlour beyond": she "always leaned forward and peered, clutching the bars with both hands" (35). Catholicism may be said to have saved Sandy from Brodie's grip, but it is nevertheless represented as a trap in its own right.

Related to the novel's treatment of Brodie's secularized form of Calvinism is its treatment of her politics, which inclines toward fascism and the cult of personality associated with it. As Anne L. Bower concludes of the 1930s setting of Spark's novel, "This historical period, in which European fascism developed, is a perfect backdrop against which to display Jean Brodie's eccentric authoritarianism."[55] For one critic Brodie is a tyrant "whose egoistic romanticism is the link between an obsessive Calvinist doctrine of the Elect, of Justification, and the fascism of Mussolini and Franco."[56] Whether one views Spark's novel in theological or political terms, it is in any case a "persuasive study of the closed mind" and the "elitist mentality."[57]

It is clear that Brodie worships the likes of Franco, Hitler, and Mussolini, and that like them she seeks to influence her subordinates through her charisma. As Lodge puts it, "Aspiring to be a charismatic leader herself, she naturally admires [those three] successful dictators . . . The combination of dedication, elitism, bravura style and heady rhetoric characteristic of fascist movements appeals to her."[58]

Brodie's elitism is unmistakable. It underlies her regard of the girls under her tutelage as "the crème de la crème" (5, 11, 21), and as "heroines in the making" (30), and her boast "Give me a girl at an impressionable age and she is mine for life" (6). Her worship of and identification with Mussolini is equally unmistakable.[59] Like Mussolini, Brodie plays to the emotions of her followers; like him, she revels in social ordering for its own sake. Just as Brodie lauds "Mussolini's marching troops," his dark *fascisti* who, in the picture she shows her class, are "all marching in the straightest of files, with their hands raised at the same angle" (31), so Brodie insists that her girls "walk tidily" (29) and comport themselves in the most disciplined of manners. And Brodie herself appears "a mighty woman with her dark Roman profile" (6) and, "in her brown dress," like "a gladiator with raised arm and eyes flashing like a sword" (47). Moreover, she identifies with the imperial Caesar (47) and, as the leader of a set, with a "Roman matron" and an "educational reformer" (118). This identification of Brodie with Mussolini is not lost on Sandy, who thinks: "the Brodie set was Miss Brodie's fascisti, not to the naked eye, marching along, but all knit together for her need and in another way, marching along" (31).

Although Brodie is perhaps less interested in Mussolini's politics than in his iconography, symbolism, and fascist aesthetics, she nevertheless admires his political agenda and assails the Fabian socialists and pacifists (114) with whom she works at the school. In contrast to Mussolini, who "had put an end to unemployment with his fascisti and there was no litter in the streets" (31), the British leadership, Brodie hints, is ineffectual. On the girls' walk with Brodie through Edinburgh, for example, the girls see unemployed Scots, of whom it is suggested by Brodie that they drink their dole money. Brodie comments that such a problem has been "solved" in Italy (40) because of the "splendid things" Mussolini's *fascisti* are doing (45). Sandy notes the "inconsistency" between Miss Brodie's disdain for the Girl Guides (and for the "team spirit," which cuts across "individualism, love and personal loyalties" [82]) and her admiration for Mussolini's *fascisti*.[60]

Brodie's affinity with the fascist dictators of Europe only grows over the course of the 1930s. By the middle of the decade Brodie has graduated from making summer trips to Italy to making such trips "to Germany, where Hitler was become Chancellor, a prophet-figure like Thomas Carlyle, and more reliable than Mussolini; the German brown-shirts, she said, were exactly the same as the Italian black, only more reliable" (103–4).[61] Brodie's remark to Sandy after the war, "Hitler *was* rather naughty" (131), hints at the extent of her unreconstructed attraction to fascist dictators, even after their genocidal agendas have been revealed.

Unsurprisingly, it is Brodie's "political ideas" (121) that allow MacKay finally to be rid of her. Specifically, it is Brodie's dealings with Joyce Emily Hammond – a would-be member of the Brodie set whose anti-Franco brother (studying at Oxford) has gone off to fight in the Spanish Civil War (126) – that leads to her dismissal from the school. Joyce Emily mysteriously disappears from school, and the girls only later learn her fate (126–7). Still later is it revealed that it is because of Brodie that the student had gone to Spain – to fight *for* Franco (133): "I made her see sense," Brodie explains of Joyce Emily; "However, she didn't have the chance to fight at all, poor girl" (133). Brodie reveals her role in Joyce Emily's death to Sandy (though without appearing to feel any guilt), and Sandy informs MacKay that Brodie is a "born Fascist" (134). Brodie is fired for "teaching fascism," and

> Sandy, when she heard of it, thought of the marching troops of black shirts in the pictures on the wall. By now she had entered the Catholic Church, in whose ranks she had found quite a number of Fascists much less agreeable than Miss Brodie. (134)

A final and unflattering connection between religious and political forms of coercion is here suggested.

No reading of Spark's novel is complete without a discussion of Brodie's love life (and sexual prime) and of the strange likeness the art master's female portraits bear to Miss Brodie, whoever his subject may be. Brodie finds herself in a love triangle with the only two men on the staff: the bachelor Gordon Lowther, the school's singing master, a small man with "a long body and short legs" (21), who falls for Brodie; and the married Teddy Lloyd, the senior girls' art master, who, despite having lost an arm in the Great War, is "by far the better-shaped, the better-featured and the more sophisticated" (50) of the two, for whom Brodie falls. The idea of the love triangle is reinforced when we read that "the singing master was in love with Miss Brodie" and that "Miss Brodie was in love with the art master" (64). Indeed, both male teachers "were already a little in love with Miss Brodie, for they found in her the only sex-bestirred object in their daily environment, and although they did not realize it, both were already beginning to act as rivals for her attention" (50). True to Brodie's romantic bent, artistic and sexual energies become metaphors for each other, and both teacher-artists come to have a sexual meaning for Brodie, and for her girls. (For example, Rose believes that Teddy Lloyd steals a kiss from Brodie because "Mr. Lloyd is an artist and Miss Brodie is artistic too" [54].) This is suggested when Mr Lowther supplies Miss Brodie with apples from his orchard (49), which she offers to her students, an Edenic symbol of her passing on of carnal knowledge to her girls; and when Mr Lloyd in class uses his phallic pointer "all round the draped private parts of one of Botticelli's female subjects" and "along the lines of their bottoms" (51), in order to explicate the painting in question.

One of the reasons that Brodie's love life seems enigmatic is that the facts surrounding it remain vague for much of the novel. For example, Monica claims to see "Mr. Lloyd in the act of kissing Miss Brodie" in the school art room (52), yet the novel does not set the record straight for some time as to whether this stolen kiss actually has occurred. Because "The question of whether Miss Brodie was actually capable of being kissed and of kissing occupied the Brodie set till Christmas" (55), the girls "kept an eye on Miss Brodie's stomach to see if it showed signs of swelling" (56). Later, Brodie admits to the stolen kiss (58), and calls the love between the two a "great love" despite the fact that they "never became lovers": "I renounced him . . . He was a married man. I renounced the great love of my prime. We have everything in common, the artistic nature" (58).[62] As if to help her renounce her love of Teddy Lloyd, Brodie enters "into a love affair, it was the only cure," with Gordon Lowther: "he was a bachelor and it was more becoming" (62). She offers Lowther her "bed-fellowship and her catering" (111), yet refuses his marriage proposal. Lowther, in other words, proves to be "useful" (120) to Brodie as she attempts to ward off her amorous feelings for Lloyd.

Because Brodie must renounce the already-married art master, she hatches a plot to interest him in Rose, and thereby have an affair with him by proxy, at least according to Sandy: "Sandy looked at [Brodie], and perceived that the woman was obsessed by the need for Rose to sleep with the man she herself was in love with" (128). Not only is Brodie "in a state of high excitement by very contact with these girls [in her set] who had lately breathed Lloyd air" (97), but she at one point, in Lloyd's presence, puts "her arm round Rose's shoulder," as if "she and Rose were one," in a bid to convince Lloyd to ask Rose to model for a portrait (74). Because she will not risk an affair with the art master herself, Brodie imagines Rose to be enacting the role of "a great lover, magnificently elevated above the ordinary run of lovers, above the moral laws, Venus incarnate, something set apart" (38). According to Sandy, Brodie even stops "sleeping with Gordon Lowther" because "her sexual feelings were satisfied by proxy; and Rose was predestined to be the lover of Teddy Lloyd" (120).

Such displaced, projected affection works in many directions at once in Spark's novel: just as Brodie uses Rose as her sexual proxy, so the girls use Brodie as theirs; just as Brodie uses Lowther in place of Lloyd, so Lloyd uses the Brodie set in lieu of their teacher, his "muse" (129). This is suggested in the following double-entendre spoken by Lloyd at one point to the visiting girls: "one day . . . I would like to do all you Brodie girls, one by one and then all together . . . It would be nice to do you all together" (108). How else explain the mystery of Lloyd's portraits of the girls, all of which resemble Miss Brodie herself: "Teddy Lloyd's passion for Jean Brodie was greatly in evidence in all the portraits he did of the various members of the Brodie set" (118). Yet the nature of the resemblance itself is difficult to articulate, adding another enigmatic dimension to the situation. As Sandy thinks of Lloyd's portrait of Rose:

> Where was the resemblance to Miss Brodie? It was the profile perhaps; it was the forehead, perhaps; it was the type of stare from Rose's blue eyes, perhaps, which was like the dominating stare from Miss Brodie's brown. The portrait was very like Miss Brodie. (105)

Later she thinks:

> The picture was like Miss Brodie, and this was the main thing about it and the main mystery. Rose had a large-boned pale face. Miss Brodie's bones were small, although her eyes, nose and mouth were large. It was difficult to see how Teddy Lloyd had imposed the dark and Roman face of Miss Brodie on that of pale Rose, but he had done so. (107)

However, Brodie proves not to have the influence over the situation between Lloyd and Rose that she believes she has: although "It was plain that Miss

Brodie wanted Rose with her instinct to start preparing to be Teddy Lloyd's lover, and Sandy with her insight to act as informant on the affair" (116), it is nevertheless "Sandy who slept with Teddy Lloyd and Rose who carried back the information" (117).[63]

It remains to treat the novel's enigmatic title. Although Brodie refers frequently to her "prime" (as in: "my educational policy" reached its "perfection in my prime" [135]; and "in this last year with me you [girls] will receive the fruits of my prime" [48]), it remains a vague, ambiguous, perhaps even misleading word in this usage, as it can be "both a noun and an adjective."[64] Brodie herself complains about the confusion of the word "social," an adjective, which is used as a noun (65), just as we might be confused by the different possible usages of "prime." Although "One's prime is the moment one was born for" (8), and also has connotations of spring and sexual fecundity (as in Botticelli's *Primavera*, a reproduction of which Brodie shows her girls) the "launching of Miss Brodie's prime" (45) seems to occur when the teacher is already in her forties and, as Lodge surmises, may even be menopausal.[65] That is to say, Brodie's "prime" is used ironically: she is associated not with spring but with autumn,[66] not with beginnings but with endings, not with her students' menarche but with her own menopause. Brodie insists that her prime has brought her "instinct and insight, both" (114), yet she imagines Rose will be Lloyd's lover and Sandy the informer when the reverse occurs (117); she thinks she will never "be betrayed" (39), yet she is; she insists that Rose is deservedly famous for sex when in fact Rose "did not really talk about sex, far less indulge in it. She did everything by instinct, she even listened to Miss Brodie as if she agreed with every word" (117).

For all of Spark's proliferating enigmas, then, none is greater than the enigma of Brodie's influence over her "set," which is paradoxically profound yet tenuous. Bryan Cheyette puts this paradox well: "*The Prime of Miss Jean Brodie* is a deliberately uncertain rendition of a figure who is defined *par excellence* by her astonishing, if misplaced, certainties."[67] Brodie may be a catalyst for "magical transfigurations" (118) of a kind she herself cannot foresee, yet, just when she thinks her influence most abiding, she is revealed to have an impact that is only skin deep. While on the one hand it is noted that Rose "shook off Miss Brodie's influence as a dog shakes pond-water from its coat" (127), on the other we read that, even after betraying Brodie and rejecting her teaching, Sandy admits that one of the main influences of her school days was "a Miss Jean Brodie in her prime" (137). These last, the novel's final, words point to an enigma that Spark's deceptively simple and slight work lets stand rather than resolves.

Chapter 6

Jean Rhys's
Wide Sargasso Sea (1966)

Re-vision – the act of looking back, of seeing with fresh eyes, of entering an old text from a new critical direction – is for women more than a chapter in cultural history: it is an act of survival. Until we can understand the assumptions in which we are drenched we cannot know ourselves . . . We need to know the writing of the past, and know it differently than we have ever known it; not to pass on a tradition but to break its hold over us.

> Adrienne Rich, "When we dead awaken: writing as re-vision"[1]

She seemed such a poor ghost, I thought I'd like to write her life.

> Jean Rhys, on Charlotte Brontë's Bertha Mason[2]

There is always the other side, always.

> Antoinette, in *Wide Sargasso Sea*[3]

I

It is no exaggeration to call Jean Rhys's *Wide Sargasso Sea* a literary masterpiece, one of the great novels of the last half of the twentieth century. *Wide Sargasso Sea* is also the most important twentieth-century novel to reimagine an earlier "classic" novel; Rhys's work reimagines Charlotte Brontë's 1847 novel *Jane Eyre*, viewing its events and meanings not through the prism of Jane's English Victorian consciousness, but through that, largely, of the anti-heroine, Bertha Mason, the "madwoman in the attic," a Creole from the West Indies who becomes the first Mrs Rochester. As Ellen G. Friedman puts it, "In an unprecedented and aggressive revisionary move, Rhys enters and reimagines Brontë's text – glossing and subverting, reversing and transforming it – writing it into her own time and into her own frame of reference."[4] In other words, having once read *Wide Sargasso Sea* we simply cannot read *Jane Eyre* in the same way again; the Victorian novel is now – the perspective and mode of its telling having been challenged – a different book. In Friedman's view Rhys, with her novel, "ruptures" Brontë's text,

> making holes and blank spaces through which a reader is compelled to look with a self-consciously twentieth-century vision that will necessarily transform what it sees. In a cunning and spectacular extension and reversal of intertextual relations, Rhys transverses Brontë's text with an otherness that postdates it, forcing Brontë's narrative to be measured by a set of assumptions outside those of the master quest narrative in complicity with which Brontë wrote her novel.[5]

Caroline Rody puts this new situation baldly: "We can no longer think of our cherished heroine Jane Eyre [or the 'mad' Bertha Mason] in the same way" again.[6] Jane must, in Friedman's formulation, be "reconsidered, reevaluated."[7]

While not completed until 1966, Rhys's work, which the author began twenty-one years earlier, in many ways harkens back to the heyday of the high modernist novel, with its allusive, elliptical prose, its multiple (and often fragmentary) narrative perspectives, its obsessive attention to literary form, and its radically "interior" (psychological) orientation.[8] Although *Wide Sargasso Sea* is rooted in literary modernism and, as already noted, looks further back in time, revising Brontë's Victorian romance, Rhys's "haunting and hallucinatory prose poem of a novel"[9] also looks forward, anticipating various feminist, postcolonial, and postmodern preoccupations of the late twentieth century. As V. S. Naipaul, another novelist who probes interstitial, postcolonial identity, attests, "Jean Rhys thirty to forty years ago identified many of the themes that engage us today."[10] *Wide Sargasso Sea* also challenged numerous British representations of the West Indies, including Brontë's, and opened "a space for Caribbean writers, especially Caribbean women writers, to speak in their own voice."[11]

II

Ella Gwendolen Rees Williams was born in Roseau, Dominica, in 1890, the daughter of a Welsh doctor father (who emigrated from Wales in 1881) and a Dominican Creole mother of Scottish ancestry (I use "Creole" in the way in which Rhys understood the term, to designate a person of Anglo-European descent who is born in the colonies).[12] At 16, after her education in a convent school in Dominica, she moved to England to attend the Perse School for Girls in Cambridge, which was followed by a stint, in 1909, in London's Academy of Dramatic Art. These experiences, given her interstitial identity, proved to be a strain on her late adolescence; while her British ethnicity made life in Dominica difficult, her West Indian accent and dialect made it difficult for her to integrate socially into the more homogeneous English schoolgirl scene. In the words of one critic, "As a white descendant of British colonists and slaveholders, she was both resented by the black population in Dominica and despised in Great Britain for her odd accent and her lack of wealth, family, or social position."[13]

Her father having died suddenly in 1910, she supported herself as a chorus girl, film-extra, and, later, model. It is at this point that the attractive young woman became involved with the first in a series of men – most of whom were older and far more affluent than she – and adopted a bohemian life-style that included hard drinking. After her affair as mistress to a British aristocrat twice her age came to an end, she married, in 1919, a Dutch journalist and poet, moving with him to Paris, Vienna, and, finally, Budapest. In 1924 her husband was incarcerated for trafficking in stolen art; Rhys then found herself on her own in Paris, where she turned to writing in an attempt to support herself.

An event of considerable importance to her future career then occurred: she met and became the lover of novelist Ford Madox Ford, who encouraged her literary ambitions and published her short fiction in his *Transatlantic Review*, where he was also publishing work by such literary modernists as Joyce, Hemingway, Gertrude Stein, and Djuna Barnes. It is at this point too that she changed her name, at Ford's suggestion, to Jean Rhys. Rhys's affair with Ford lasted until 1927, at which time she published her first book, a series of stories, and returned to London. *The Left Bank: Sketches and Studies of Present-Day Bohemian Paris* (with a Preface by Ford) featured female characters in situations similar to Rhys's own who endured difficult relationships with husbands or lovers. Four novels followed over the next decade: *Postures* (1928; published in the US in 1929 as *Quartet*), *After Leaving Mr MacKenzie* (1931), *Voyage in the Dark* (1934), and *Good Morning, Midnight* (1939). These novels were followed by a hiatus during which her works went out of print and were largely forgotten. During this period Rhys divorced her Dutch husband and married her British literary agent. A third marriage, in 1947, coincided with increased alcohol-dependency and domestic acrimony. In 1948 Rhys was arrested for assaulting neighbors and the police, for which she was incarcerated in Holloway prison hospital in order to undergo psychological evaluation, an experience that doubtless informs her understanding of her heroine's experience in her final novel.

Rhys worked haltingly on *Wide Sargasso Sea* between 1945 and 1966, when it was at last completed. Upon its publication the novel was immediately hailed as a masterpiece, garnering for its author a W. H. Smith Award for Writers and a Heinemann Award. In this same year Rhys was made a Fellow of the Royal Society of Literature. In 1967 her novels of the 1930s began to be reissued, bringing her earlier work to the attention of a new generation of readers. Rhys went on to publish two collections of stories (in 1968 and 1976) and, in 1978, was made a Commander of the British Empire. She died in 1979, after which her unfinished autobiographical memoir, *Smile Please*, was published. A film version of *Wide Sargasso Sea* was released in 1993. Not quite British and not precisely Caribbean, poised between the era of high literary modernism and the rise of postmodern fiction, Rhys's identity and career are best understood as interstitial. As Mary Lou Emery writes, Rhys possessed "plural and often conflicting outsider identities as West Indian writer, European modernist, and woman writer at the closing of the era of empire."[14]

Many readers of *Wide Sargasso Sea* may find it difficult to appreciate given their unfamiliarity with the history of the West Indies, and particularly that of Dominica and Jamaica, two islands on which the vast majority of *Wide Sargasso Sea* is set. While a detailed treatment of this history is outside the scope of this study, some historical context will be useful. *Wide Sargasso Sea* is set between 1834 and 1845, three decades later than the setting of *Jane Eyre* (the action of Brontë's novel takes place in 1798–1808). Rhys altered Brontë's time-frame in order to have the events of her story correspond to the years of the Emancipation Act of 1833, which outlawed slavery in Great Britain and in its colonies. Joyce Carol Oates describes the years just following this Act, the time of Rhys's novel, as ones in which white landowners and black former slaves "lived in a state of undeclared war," with the former "forced to employ" the latter "as servants and utterly helpless without them."[15]

The island nations of Dominica and Jamaica share a similar (though decidedly not identical) history. Dominica, located in the Windward Islands and with its capital in Roseau, is populated by people of Carib, African, and French descent. Named by Christopher Columbus after the day, a Sunday in 1493, on which he first spied the island from his ship, Dominica, like many Caribbean islands, was fought over by France and Britain (in order to secure control of its natural resources, sugarcane, cocoa, and coffee), during much of the seventeenth and eighteenth centuries. The British gained decisive control of the island in the early 1800s, purchasing Dominica from France for 12,000 pounds sterling. It is only comparatively recently that Dominica became its own republic, gaining independence from Britain in 1978.

Jamaica, a much larger island to the west of Dominica, experienced its first European settlement when the Spanish took control in 1510 (Columbus landed there in 1494) and introduced sugarcane and slaves (African slaves arrived by the boat-load between the middle of the 1600s and 1838). The Spanish controlled Jamaica until 1655, after which the British annexed the island, establishing it as a colony in 1670 (its capital, Kingston, was called Spanish Town at the time of *Wide Sargasso Sea*). Although moving toward autonomy from 1938 onwards, Jamaica did not achieve formal independence until 1962 (significantly, during the time in which Rhys was drafting her novel). It is important to keep in mind that while Britain ended its slave trade in 1807, slavery itself was not abolished until the Emancipation Act of the mid-1830s; and that after this Act working conditions for former slaves, under the new "apprenticeship" system, were little improved from the days of slavery itself. This latter point is made clear in Rhys's novel.

III

Not surprisingly, critics have debated how best to understand the relationship between *Jane Eyre* and *Wide Sargasso Sea*, the latter of which has often been called a "prequel" novel to its Victorian progenitor in that, as Joyce Carol Oates puts it, "Bertha Rochester's pathetic death will make Jane Eyre's life possible."[16] To be sure, Rhys's working title for the novel, "The First Mrs Rochester," invites questions as to the extent to which her novel stands on its own. At the forefront of one camp in this debate is Walter Allen who, in a 1967 review, questions whether Rhys's novel is parasitically dependent on Brontë's for its meaning and worth, and concludes that Rhys's novel does not "exist in its own right" but needs Brontë's to "complement it, to supply its full meaning."[17] The other side of the debate is led by Francis Wyndham who, in a 1966 Preface to the novel, argues that Rhys's work "is in no sense a pastiche of Charlotte Brontë and exists in its own right, quite independent of *Jane Eyre*," however much it takes its "initial inspiration" from Brontë's novel.[18] This debate continues into our own time, as evidenced by Thomas F. Staley's contention that *Wide Sargasso Sea* "is an independent creation of great subtlety and skill,"[19] and Sandra Drake's recent assertion that Rhys's "novel stands on its own" and "could have been written without the relationship of intertextual referentiality of *Jane Eyre*."[20]

Even those critics who agree that *Wide Sargasso Sea* stands on its own disagree about the precise nature of this "intertextual referentiality." Rhys's novel has been called everything from a "recentering" of Brontë's text,[21] to a daughter text to Brontë's "mother text" ("Rhys does not kill Brontë's mother text in an oedipal rivalry but instead treats it with gratitude and ambivalence"),[22] to a text that is not only antithetical to *Jane Eyre* but is its revisionist "counter-text":[23] "[I]t is against *Jane Eyre* that Rhys writes."[24] I believe that Judith Kegan Gardiner strikes the right balance when she concludes that *Wide Sargasso Sea* "can stand on its own as a modernist text, self-enclosed and consistent in its patterns of imagery," with its "psychologically-convincing portrait of a woman misunderstood, rejected, persecuted," yet that, in our experience of the novel, it does not. Instead, Gardiner holds, *Wide Sargasso Sea* is experienced as a "rereading" of *Jane Eyre*, "perhaps the most influential female novel of development," and a re-evaluation of that work's Victorian assumptions.[25]

Rhys herself, in a 1958 letter, explained that "It might be possible to unhitch the whole thing from Charlotte Brontë's novel, but I don't want to do that. It is that particular mad Creole I want to write about, not any of the other mad Creoles."[26] While Rhys waxed enthusiastic about the Brontë sisters, in particular admiring their literary "genius,"[27] she also confessed to feeling "vexed" at Charlotte's depiction of Bertha Mason, "the 'paper tiger' lunatic" who "shrieks, howls, laughs horribly, attacks all and sundry – *off stage*." In *Wide Sargasso Sea*, Rhys counters, she will be placed "right *on stage*."[28] Rhys's goal was no less than to invest in Brontë's Creole, with whom she clearly identifies, a compelling past; to flesh out "the *reason* why Mr Rochester treats her so abominably and feels justified, the *reason* why he thinks she is mad and why of course she goes mad, even the *reason* why she tries to set everything on fire, and eventually succeeds."[29]

Wide Sargasso Sea is comprised of three parts, each of which is subdivided into short sections. Part I is set near Spanish Town, Jamaica, at the Coulibri estate, which has gone to seed after the abolition of slavery and the collapse of the plantation system. This Part is narrated entirely by the young, isolated, increasingly paranoid Antoinette, who feels "abandoned, lied about, helpless" (12), and who possesses an interstitial identity as a "white nigger" (a Creole of a formerly high class that has become déclassé [39]). Antoinette's philandering father, Cosway, who is partly to blame for the condition of Coulibri, is now dead. Antoinette's neglectful mother, Annette ("My mother never asked me where I had been or what I had done," Antoinette revealingly observes [14]), is in the process of arranging a second marriage, to the English gentleman, Mason, who hopes to use his wealth to restore the crumbling plantation and who is cast in the role of rescuer of the family "from poverty and misery" (20). Annette must also cope with the loss of her apparently retarded son, Pierre, who dies as a result of an arson attack on Coulibri by former slaves, who burn the estate to the ground. Her mother being in no condition to care for her, Antoinette is sent to the convent in Spanish Town, for a period of eighteen months, during which time her mother dies. She turns, thereafter, to Christophine, her mother's Martinique-born servant, for maternal comfort.

Part II of the novel is set at Granbois, Dominica. It is narrated principally by an unnamed Englishman, the Rochester figure who marries Antoinette, during the course of their honeymoon. One section in the middle of Part II is narrated by Antoinette; the confusion over this abrupt change of perspective is surely intentional, as it highlights certain similarities of thinking and situation between Antoinette and her husband. Like Antoinette's stepfather, Mason, Antoinette's husband marries, among other reasons, to gain control of his wife's assets, which include a dowry of thirty thousand pounds (41). British law at this time dictated that when two people married, the wife's property became the husband's absolutely. This situation did not change until the passing of the Married Woman's Property Act of 1870. The Rochester figure's feeling of unease (he finds the West Indies threateningly foreign) is only intensified by a letter he receives from a disgruntled Daniel Cosway, a mulatto who claims to be a half-brother of Antoinette's and who alleges that Rochester has been duped into marrying a woman who is both a lunatic and a nympho-maniac. His paranoia increasing and his desire for revenge kindled, the Rochester figure proceeds to sleep with the "half-caste servant" girl (38) Amélie, in an act that recalls Cosway's alleged sexual exploitation of his mixed-race female servants. The power-struggle between Antoinette and her husband culminates in his banishing of Christophine, her most loyal ally, who is thought to practice obeah (a form of black magic), from the property. Antoinette's mental condition continues to worsen over the course of Part II, toward the end of which she even tells her husband that she wishes merely to remain "in the dark . . . where I belong" (81).

Part III, by far the shortest of the novel's three Parts, is narrated mainly by Antoinette, who is now a prisoner both in the attic of the Rochester figure's English estate (the Thornfield Hall of *Jane Eyre* fame) and in her own mind (Grace Poole, her attendant, describes her as "that girl who lives in her own darkness" [106]). Her husband justifies locking Antoinette away by her lunacy and abnormal sexual appetite. But unlike Brontë's text, in which Bertha Mason's lunacy is dismissed as congenital and due to her West Indian ethnicity, Rhys's text explores, explains, and justifies Antoinette's "madness." Antoinette's narrative in Part III follows a brief introductory section that is narrated by the Rochester figure's hired female servant, Grace Poole. The reference to her, as well as to the events of Antoinette's end (she anticipates setting fire to her husband's estate and leaping from its roof, in an echo of the demise of Coulibri), firmly ties Rhys's novel to Brontë's. Although Antoinette presumably suffers physical death just after the close of her narrative, her true life, she realizes, has ended long before: "There are always two deaths," she tells her husband in an observation that is germane both to her and to her mother's situation, "the real one and the one people know about" (77).

Wide Sargasso Sea is best read as a modernist, feminist, postcolonial revision of *Jane Eyre*'s Victorian, patriarchal, colonialist assumptions. The principal effect of this revision is to humanize Antoinette, to rescue her from Brontë's effaced character. While some critics claim that *Wide Sargasso Sea* is best understood as a postmodern novel,[30] I believe that it is more accurately viewed as a latter-day work of literary modernism.[31] As Sylvie Maurel concludes, "Jean Rhys's writing shares some of the characteristics of modernist prose," especially "where the emphasis on subjectivity and the attention paid to form are concerned."[32]

This literary modernist "emphasis on subjectivity" is manifested in Rhys's novel, in contrast to Brontë's, in its myriad credible (and competing) subjectivities. For example, Jane Eyre's single, privileged truth, as represented in the Brontë novel, is challenged and relativized in the Rhys novel not only by Antoinette's competing truth but by the plurality of competing perspectives represented therein (Antoinette's versus Rochester's, Daniel Cosway's versus Christophine's, Grace Poole's versus Antoinette's, and so on). Jane Eyre's "truths" in the Brontë text are further relativized in the Rhys one in that formerly marginalized characters in the earlier novel take center stage in the later one, and vice versa (compare, for example, the respective treatments of Bertha/Antoinette and Jane Eyre). The multiple points of view that comprise *Wide Sargasso Sea* even become an explicit theme in the novel, such as when Rhys has Antoinette observe that "There is always the other side, always" (77).

Brontë's focused narrative trajectory, in which major questions are answered and major problems are resolved, gives way in Rhys's novel to a "mosaic of narratives"[33] and to the privileging of alterity; no psychologically satisfying "narrative closure" is granted us in the latter work. Put differently, while "in Jane Eyre's imagination all things of significance are related to one another in a universe in which God means well, in Antoinette's experience nothing is predictably related,"[34] nor can it be meaningfully controlled. In Brontë's Victorian romance the "autonomous and self-defined" heroine frequently determines her own course, while in Rhys's modernist narrative things merely "happen to" Antoinette; unlike "Jane Eyre, who both knows her personal history and what she should think about it, Antoinette barely 'knows' her story at all."[35]

Rhys's modernist pessimism undercuts Brontë's Victorian optimism about the possibility of achieving a comprehensive and objective view of one's situation; the characters in *Wide Sargasso Sea* are trapped within their own, sometimes paranoid, subjectivities to an extent that would have been unthinkable to Brontë. Although *Jane Eyre* is a psychological novel, it does not plumb the depths and shallows of character psychology to the degree that Rhys's novel does. In "Modern fiction" Virginia Woolf defends Joyce and other authors of his ilk – and this would certainly include Rhys – for attempting in their work "to come closer to life, and to preserve more sincerely and exactly what interests and moves them," by recording "the atoms as they fall upon the mind in the order in which they fall," and by tracing "the pattern, however connected and incoherent in appearance, which each sight or incident scores upon the consciousness."[36] In a similar spirit of psychological realism Rhys comments of Antoinette's story, it has "to be implied, *never* told straight."[37]

If *Wide Sargasso Sea*'s modernist orientation serves as a riposte to *Jane Eyre*'s Victorian one, the later novel's postcolonial and feminist orientations challenge the former novel's colonialist and (comparatively) patriarchal ones. "Charlotte [Brontë] had a 'thing' about the West Indies being" a "rather sinister [place]," Rhys commented, and she only provided "one side," the "English side," of "the poor Creole lunatic['s]" story.[38] The colonial prejudice that she attributes to the author of *Jane Eyre* is countered by her interrogation of the Rochester figure, whose prejudice in this regard is blatant. Moreover, related to Rochester's view of the West Indies, *Wide Sargasso Sea* suggests, is his understanding and treatment of women. That is to say, both women (and particularly Antoinette) and the Caribbean landscape function for Rochester as enticing yet threatening Others: foreign forces to be conquered and subjugated, and from which considerable profit is to be derived.

Time and again *Wide Sargasso Sea* links Antoinette and the West Indies in the mind of the Rochester figure. As M. Keith Booker and Dubravka Juraga observe, "Rochester feels for Antoinette a mixture of fascination and repulsion that can be seen as representative of the European attitude toward the non-European world as a whole."[39] More specifically, "Rochester desires to master and dominate Antoinette, while at the same time fearing that she may be the bearer of mysterious powers. His feelings for her are thus not only representative of patriarchal attitudes toward women, but of European attitudes toward the colonial world."[40]

The Rochester figure's "reading" of the West Indian landscape reveals more about what he expects to see there (and about English fears and desires pertaining to its colonies) than about what is "actually" there. His views of the island on which he and Antoinette sojourn in Part II derive less from his experience of it than from then-current English myths and stereotypes about the Caribbean. What he says of Antoinette's preconception of England is ironically and tragically true of his own preconception of the West Indies: "Her mind was already made up [about the nature of England]. Some romantic novel, a stray remark never forgotten, a sketch, a picture, a song . . . and her ideas were fixed" (56). Specifically, he imbues the West Indian landscape, which he figures in sexual terms and to which he confers a malign agency, with a threatening intent that is congruent with his own rapacious and imperialistic designs upon his wife (and upon her assets). In this connection, O. Mannoni's provocative observation that colonizers "project upon the colonial peoples the obscurities of their own unconscious – obscurities they would rather not penetrate"[41] is also pertinent to the Rochester figure's reaction to the colonial landscape.[42]

The Rochester figure's view of the Caribbean landscape matches his view of Antoinette: each is a sensual, "intoxicating" (43) (the "scent of the river flowers" leads him to feel "giddy" [49]), superficially inviting entity that proves, ultimately, to be a dangerous (55) and existentially threatening one. ("[I]t seemed to me that everything round me was hostile," he thinks [90]; "I feel very much a stranger here . . . I feel that this place is my enemy" [78]). The man's initial enthusiasm for the West Indies gives way to "confused impressions" of the place (45) ("the feeling of security had left me" [44]) and to the disturbing feeling of being overwhelmed: "Everything is too much . . . Too much blue, too much purple, too much green. The flowers too red, the mountains too high, the hills too near. And the woman [his wife] is a stranger. Her pleading expression annoys me. I have not bought her, she has bought me, or so she thinks" (41). His description of a "bathing pool" he discovers on the island could equally well serve as his description of his wife: "It was a beautiful place – wild, untouched, above all untouched, with an alien, disturbing, secret loveliness. And it kept its secret" (51–2).

Although the Rochester figure admits to feeling "lost and afraid among these enemy trees, so certain of danger" (62), he nevertheless insists that the enigma of the West Indies (and of his wife) is one in need of being solved: "I did not love her [he thinks of Antoinette]. I was thirsty for her, but that is not love. I felt very little tenderness for her, she was a stranger to me, a stranger who did not think or feel as I did" (55). When he fails to dispel the mystery he resorts to hating that which he cannot understand: "I was tired of these people . . . And I hated the place. I hated the mountains and the hills, the rivers and the rain. I hated the sunsets of whatever colour, I hated its beauty and its magic and the secret which I would never know . . . Above all I hated her [Antoinette]" (103).[43]

Antoinette's parallel misunderstanding of England ("their world," she thinks in Part III, when she is a prisoner in her husband's English estate, "is, as I always knew, made of cardboard" [107]) points to a situation shared by her and her husband: both have become paranoid; both are duped and pimped by family members; both inhabit "hostile" environments in which they imagine themselves to be a laughingstock. This shared psychological condition, moreover, makes for dramatic irony: readers can appreciate the common ground between the two (despite the great difference of power between them); Antoinette and her husband, tragically, cannot. This cultural myopia leads each to see his or her place of origin as "real" and the other's place as a "dream" or, more exactly, a nightmare. Antoinette views England as "quite unreal and like a dream" (61) and "London" as "like a cold dark dream" (47); the Rochester figure views Antoinette's "beautiful island" in the same way, as "quite unreal and like a dream" (48). If he finds the West Indies too sensual – too colorful, too richly scented, too sultry – she finds the little corner of England in which she finds herself too "cold and dark" (108), a two-dimensional, black and white prison.[44]

The attic of Thornfield Hall, in which Antoinette is cared for yet imprisoned, is only the final station on her journey from childhood in the West Indies to adulthood in England. Indeed, there are numerous walled sites within which, as a female Creole of precarious class standing, she experiences the paradoxical condition of what might be called safety-in-imprisonment. And the fleshing out of this paradoxical condition constitutes the most incisive feminist critique staged by the novel. I use the term "paradoxical" to describe a situation in which Antoinette must choose either the "safety" of patriarchal confinement or the freedom from such confinement. Yet the freedom is coupled with the abject vulnerability that accompanies such "independence" for females. In other words, Antoinette can live within the cloistered walls of a "patriarchal" household (whether Coulibri estate, the Catholic Church convent at Spanish Town, or the attic of Thornfield Hall) and be "safe" and cared for yet deprived of her freedom and sense of self-determination; or she can reject such patronage and gain her freedom but risk violation and death at the hands of the harsh patriarchal world without – a world, as Grace Poole puts it late in the novel, that "can be a black and cruel world to a woman" (106). Either way, Antoinette must give up something of significance: self-determination or security. Molly Hite, in a provocative feminist analysis of Rhys's work, points to the necessity of this choice on the part of Antoinette (and her mother Annette): "The defining characteristic of the Rhys woman is her financial dependency on a man" or on men.[45] It is Antoinette's (and Annette's) financial dependence on men (fathers and husbands), coupled with the laws and attitudes that support such a state of affairs, that is a prime target of *Wide Sargasso Sea*.

Coulibri, the house of Antoinette's father, is the protagonist's first site of "safety-in-imprisonment." Her childhood is characterized by a feeling of vulnerability, leading her to wish for "a big Cuban dog to lie by my bed and protect me" (22). The walls of Coulibri are seen as providing that security she seeks: "When I was safely home," Antoinette thinks at one point, having returned to her house after temporarily leaving it, "I sat close to the old wall at the end of the garden" and "never wanted to move again" (13). Later, she remembers thinking, "I am safe. There is the corner of the bedroom door and the friendly furniture. There is the tree of life in the garden and the wall green with moss. The barrier of the cliffs and the high mountains. And the barrier of the sea. I am safe. I am safe from strangers" (16). The patriarchal dimension of this security is also suggested when Antoinette notes that her widowed mother's new husband, Mason, however unlikable he may be, at least will provide them with peace, contentment, *and protection* (21–2, my emphasis).

The safety provided to Antoinette by Coulibri proves to be illusory, however, as former slaves set the estate on fire (presaging Thornfield Hall's fiery end). Just before Coulibri burns to the ground, the family parrot, Coco, who is now on fire and whose wings, revealingly, have been clipped by Mason (25), plummets to its death from the flame-engulfed upper storey of the house ("He made an effort to fly down but his clipped wings failed him and he fell screeching. He was all on fire" [25]). This moment not only looks forward to Antoinette's death-leap from the flame-engulfed roof of her husband's English estate; it is a comment on Antoinette's status as a caged bird: a pet who is provided for yet imprisoned, one who is fed but denied its natural freedom of flight, a subject turned into an object. Given the connections Rhys forges between kept women and caged birds, it should come as no surprise that Antoinette's mother and the family's talking parrot – both of whom are figuratively if not literally done in by the family patriarch – are heard to utter the same words, "*Qui est la? Qui est la?*" (25, 28)

After the demise of Coulibri, Antoinette is sent, for a period of eighteen months, to the convent in Spanish Town. This convent, *Wide Sargasso Sea* suggests, provides another patriarchal safe-haven-cum-prison, a walled and gated (30) refuge that provides safety yet which delimits movement, thought, and self-determination ("This convent was my refuge, a place of sunshine *and of death*" [33, my emphasis], Antoinette thinks, apparently glimpsing the paradox of her situation). The trope of the convent as prison is established when Antoinette is teased by some neighborhood youths because her Aunt sent her "for the nuns to lock up" (29); and the sense of the convent as a paralyzing force is established when Rhys, in a moment out of Joyce's *Dubliners*, renders a nun's hands "crippled with rheumatism" (31). The paradox of "security in imprisonment" and "vulnerability in freedom" is further glossed when Antoinette stops praying in the convent and then reports feeling "bolder, happier, more free. But not so safe" (34). The nuns, by contrast, are depicted as imprisoned within the gates of the convent yet as being perfectly "safe. How can they know what it can be like *outside*?" (35)

The final site of Antoinette's "safety in imprisonment" is, of course, Thornfield Hall, another patriarchal refuge with "thick walls" (106). The caged bird is now literally "locked away" (103), a prisoner in the "cold and dark" (108) attic of her husband's estate, and in the cold and dark of her own mind. Antoinette's keeper, Grace Poole, calls the house "big and safe, a shelter from the world outside" (105–6); yet we also see it as a place in which Antoinette's husband can imprison her while wresting control of her assets and enjoying the company of other women (in Brontë's novel he courts Jane Eyre during this period). Rhys at one point even depicts Antoinette's husband as deliberately planning his wife's imprisonment and dehumanization; back in Dominica, for example, he draws a picture of a large house, on the "third floor" of which he places "a standing woman – a child's scribble, a dot for a head, a larger one for the body, a triangle for a skirt, slanting lines for arms and feet" (98). Turning his wife into a stick figure of a human being, turning her from a subject into an object, Antoinette's husband figuratively murders his wife, just as Annette's two husbands figuratively murder her. Indeed, Antoinette seems fated to repeat her mother's experience of victimization at the hands of her husband: in the financial and sexual exploitation, the identity-theft, the decline into madness and alcoholism. "Tied to a lunatic for life," the Rochester figure remarks of his wife, "a drunken lying lunatic – gone her mother's way" (99). While the novel treats this contention ironically there is no irony in Christophine's comment to the Rochester figure shortly before: "You want her [Antoinette's] money but you don't want her. It is in your mind to pretend she is mad . . . She will be like her mother" (96).

Antoinette's patriarchy-induced madness leaves her a mere "ghost" of herself by the novel's end (111). Another sign of Antoinette's loss of identity is that she becomes an object of another's subjectivity – an individual determined and defined by another – rather than remaining a subject capable of self-definition and self-determination. This is suggested not only when Rochester renders his wife a stick figure in his drawing but when he insists on calling her "Bertha" (68, 81, 82, 88) (because "Antoinette" reminds him too much of his wife's mother's name, Annette). It reveals his desire to control her: he is the subject who names and defines; she is the object who is named and defined. While Antoinette at first has the strength to resist her husband's attempt to rename her ("Bertha is not my name," she tells him; "You are trying to make me into someone else, calling me by another name" [88]), eventually, like her mother before her, she succumbs to the identity-theft that accompanies the theft of her assets and her decline into madness. The Rochester figure also revealingly likens his wife to a "marionette" and a "doll" (92, 93), to an agency-less object of another's subjectivity. "The doll had a doll's voice, a breathless but curiously indifferent voice" (102); a "doll's smile . . . nailed to her face" (103) is how he thinks of Antoinette. The Rochester figure here implicitly blames his wife for her disappointing lack of humanity – for being a mere marionette – yet it is he, ironically, who is guilty of pulling the strings.

Seen in this light, Antoinette's final, suicidal act of burning to the ground Thornfield Hall, the patriarchal prison-house, takes on a rebellious and even a heroic cast. Indeed, the novel links this incendiary act undertaken by an aggrieved female Creole to that undertaken against Coulibri earlier by the aggrieved Jamaican ex-slaves. This connection is also hinted at in one of Rhys's letters: "I want it [Antoinette's end] in a way triumphant!"[46] Thus, the closing pages of *Wide Sargasso Sea* squarely turn the tables on Brontë's *Jane Eyre*. Rochester's reference to Antoinette as an "Infamous daughter of an infamous mother" (110), for example, now rings ironically in the reader's ears. While in the Brontë novel Rochester is victimized by a crazy wife, in the Rhys novel he relegates his wife to madness. Whereas Brontë depicts Bertha Mason's congenital lunacy as the cause of her alienation from her husband and world, Rhys, by contrast, allies "madness with rebellion" and makes "it the effect, not the cause, of her female protagonist's outcast status."[47]

In addition to being a modernist, feminist, and postcolonial novel, it is fair to characterize *Wide Sargasso Sea* as a psychological novel, one that emphasizes perception and the ways in which the imagination makes meaning of that which the senses perceive. For all of its differences from Brontë's novel, Rhys's novel shares with it (and with Romantic thought at large) a paradoxical sense both of the imagination's salutary power (as a place of escape from a painful reality) and of its potential to pose a dangerous, potentially even lethal, threat to the well-being of the self. (Mental illness may be understood as a condition in which one lives one's life entirely within one's own mind, in which case the imagination becomes an imprisoning force rather than a catalyst for the self's liberation.) This prison-house of the imagination is explored in Rhys's novel in her major characters' penchant for paranoia – for discerning malign meaning, and finding nefarious patterns, wherever they look.

Indeed, Rhys's novel is among other things a keen study of paranoia: Antoinette's, her husband's, and the reader's. Antoinette's paranoia is revealed as early as her childhood dream of being in the forest with "Someone who hated me" hiding in the foliage but "coming closer" (15). This dream is succeeded by another one in which the threat becomes more concrete: it is a man who is looking at her, "his face black with hatred" (36). Tellingly, the threatening man of Antoinette's dreams eventually blurs into her husband. Even her mistake in thinking her "plait [of hair], tied with red ribbon," is "a snake" (27), contributes to our sense that it is a specifically male (phallic) menace that she rightly fears, and sees everywhere she looks.

Antoinette's husband too suffers from comparable bouts of paranoia. Early on in their marriage he fears that Antoinette's relatives view him with "Curiosity? Pity? Ridicule? But why should they pity me?" (46) He too frequently feels "uneasy as though someone were watching me" (50) and fears poisonous snakes (52). He too admits of his fears of persecution ("It seemed to me that everything round me was hostile," he reports in Dominica. "The trees were threatening and the shadows of the trees . . . menaced me" [90]), much as Antoinette admits to such a fear later in England. Finally, like Shakespeare's Othello, the Rochester figure becomes paranoid over the question of his wife's sexual constancy – with tragic consequences for her as for Desdemona.[48]

That we readers become figurative paranoids as we read Rhys's text, seeking to make connections and find patterns that may or may not exist, only heightens our sense of sympathy for Antoinette and, at times, even for her husband. Like the novel's two major characters, readers too must read between the lines in experiencing Rhys's complex narrative world; we too must interpret the landscape of the text, negotiate and make sense of the different versions of reality, of "truth," with which we are presented. Indeed, readers are often tempted to pose the same question of whatever account is being given that the Rochester figure poses: "I began to wonder how much all of this was true, how much imagined, distorted" (80). In this sense *Wide Sargasso Sea* provides a model of reading as a paranoid – as an interpretively suspicious, cripplingly self-conscious – enterprise.

This brings us, at last, to Rhys's choice of title for her psychological novel: a title, of course, that associates the geographical Sargasso Sea with the interior life of her characters (and readers). The choice of title is also intriguing in that the sea itself figures mainly off-stage; it is the island nations of Jamaica, Dominica, and Britain in which the action of the novel takes place. The sea, which separates these islands from each other, functions as an interstice; Rhys's title thus becomes one more way of emphasizing the interstitial. Specifically, the Sargasso Sea denotes an area of the North Atlantic, in the vicinity of the Bermuda Islands, that is characterized by "weak currents, very little wind, and a free-floating mass of seaweed called Sargassum."[49] Far more interesting – and more relevant to Rhys's novel – than the fact of this seaweed is the myth that surrounds it. As one authority comments, "The dense fields of weeds waiting to entrap a vessel never existed except in the imaginations of sailors, and the gloomy hulks of vessels doomed to endless drifting in the clinging weed are only the ghosts of things that never were."[50] For Rhys, then, the Sargasso Sea is a metaphor for the abyss of the imagination, for paranoia, for fears, founded and otherwise, that end in the loss of identity and in death

– yet also for the rich and creative possibilities of the psyche. Ezra Pound's 1916 poem "Portrait d'une femme" opens with the line, "Your mind and you are our Sargasso Sea."[51] In the case of the present novel, the wide Sargasso Sea of the title pertains to the heroine's interstitial identity as well as to the mental state not only of the heroine but of her husband, the other characters, and their readers: it is an emblem of the modern psyche.

Chapter 7

J. M. Coetzee's *Waiting for the Barbarians* (1980)

The barbarian is . . . not only at our gates; he is always within the walls of our civilization, inside our minds and our hearts. In times of storm and stress within any society, his appeal is very strong. He offers immediate satisfaction of the simple instincts, love, hatred, and anger. He offers to help us forget our own unhappiness by making other people still more unhappy . . . He gives us the simple satisfaction of violence and destruction, the destruction of society . . .

Leonard Woolf, Barbarians Within and Without[1]

We push on towards [the barbarians] for half an hour before we realize that we are getting no closer. As we move they move too . . . But when I call a halt the three specks seem to halt too; when we resume our march they begin to move. "Are they reflections of us, is this a trick of the light?" I wonder. We cannot close the gap. How long have they been dogging us? Or do they think we are dogging them?

the Magistrate, Waiting for the Barbarians[2]

I

Waiting for the Barbarians, by the South African author J. M. Coetzee, twice winner of the Booker Prize and a recipient of the Nobel Prize for Literature, is a novel of Kafkaesque allegorical power. A provocative interrogation of the idea of empire and civilization, *Waiting for the Barbarians* is also a profound exploration of self–other relations or alterity: of the ways in which groups and individuals define themselves and each other in national, religious, ethnic, gender, racial, and/or class terms for purposes of invidious comparison. Moreover, Coetzee's uncanny first-person novel of ideas explores the psychology behind such "tribal" identification and the ways in which such self/ other binary thinking can lead to prejudice, hostility, and violence. Coetzee here joins Emmanuel Levinas, Jean-Paul Sartre, Mikhail Bakhtin, and other modern thinkers in grappling with a problem articulated compellingly by Sigmund Freud: "It is always possible to bind together a considerable number of people in love, so long as there are people left over to receive the manifestation of their aggressiveness."[3] Simone de Beauvoir puts this idea still more baldly: "The category of the *Other* is as primordial as consciousness itself . . . Otherness is a fundamental category of human thought."[4] Coetzee's novel is among the most thoughtful literary explorations and treatments of this dire truth.

II

J. M. Coetzee was born in Cape Town, South Africa, in 1940, and grew up in a home in which both English and Afrikaans were spoken. He attended the University of Cape Town, graduating in 1961, after which he worked in London as a computer programmer. While in England he also wrote his master's thesis, on the work of novelist Ford Madox Ford, for the University of Cape Town. In 1965 Coetzee began doctoral work in linguistics and literature at the University of Texas at Austin. His doctoral thesis, a stylistic analysis of Beckett's English-language novels, was completed in 1969. After a teaching stint at the State University of New York in Buffalo, Coetzee, in 1972, returned to the University of Cape Town, this time to join the faculty. In 1984 he was named Professor of General Literature at this institution. In more recent years he has also been a member of the University of Chicago's "Committee on Social Thought" and a Fellow of the University of Adelaide.

The years following Coetzee's return to South Africa were politically turbulent ones for his country: racist apartheid policies, which had been in force since 1913 (the Union of South Africa, a semi-autonomous state under British colonial rule, was founded in 1910), were challenged as never before, leading the government to adopt repressive measures on a grand scale; and Nelson Mandela's African National Congress party gained political ground. The ANC swept to power in 1994, toppling F. W. de Klerk's Nationalist Party, after the first-ever democratic elections in South African history (in 1990 Mandela, after nearly thirty years in jail, was released from prison and his African National Party was legalized). The details of South Africa's civil strife are conspicuously absent from many of Coetzee's fictions, which instead treat history and politics in an oblique or allegorical fashion.

Coetzee is the author of nine highly acclaimed novels and four works of non-fiction (on subjects ranging from African literature to censorship to animal rights). He is also the author of *Boyhood: Scenes from Provincial Life* (1997), in which he explores his own coming-of-age, using an intriguing second-person narrator, and a sequel volume, *Youth: Scenes from Provincial Life II* (2002). In addition to being awarded the Booker Prize in 1983 and 1999, Coetzee received France's Prix Etranger Femina (1983) and Israel's Jerusalem Prize (1987). In 2003 he was awarded the Nobel Prize for Literature.

This sketch of the author reveals Coetzee's dual career path. Like John Barth, Saul Bellow, Umberto Eco, William Gass, and Milan Kundera, Coetzee is a novelist who is also a practicing academic. A literary artist as well as a linguist and "powerful critic and intellectual historian of colonialism and the history of racist thinking, apartheid, and censorship,"[5] Coetzee views his two vocations as interanimating, mutually reinforcing ones. "I don't see any disruption between my professional interest in language and my activities as a [creative] writer,"[6] he has commented. Indeed, it is Coetzee's "dual allegiance" that makes possible what one critic calls the author's "unique combination of intellectual power, stylistic poise, historical vision, and ethical penetration."[7] That is to say, Coetzee's familiarity with numerous intellectual and artistic arenas – among these, the history and development of the novel, literary modernism (in particular the fiction of Kafka, Beckett, Nabokov, Borges, Conrad, and Ford), modern linguistics, and poststructuralist and postcolonial theory – has shaped his erudite and intellectually demanding novels. It has also made Coetzee, as one critic writes, "the first South African writer to produce overtly self-conscious fictions drawing explicitly on international postmodernism."[8]

Although Coetzee's novels treat numerous problems and issues typically associated with postmodernism – the nature of power, both individual and institutional, subject–object relations, and the self's presentation to itself, for example – the author's brand of postmodernism does not take autotelic experimentation or aesthetic innovation as its goal. Rather, as David Attwell puts it, "reflexivity here is a mode of self-consciousness" that "is directed at understanding the conditions – linguistic, formal, historical, and political – governing the writing of fiction in contemporary South Africa."[9] Moreover, as Derek Attridge observes, the formal properties of Coetzee's novels enable them to "engage with – to stage, confront, apprehend, explore – *otherness*, and in this engagement" to broach "the most fundamental and widely significant issues involved in any consideration of ethics and politics."[10]

Coetzee's first novel (really two interrelated novellas), *Dusklands* (1974), announces the author's fictional agenda. The first of the novellas, "The Vietnam project," concerns the US Department of Defense during the Vietnam War; the second, "The narrative of Jacobus Coetzee," is set in eighteenth-century South Africa. The juxtaposition of these two seemingly disparate narratives reveals a surprising similarity between the respective colonial projects and mentalities. Coetzee's next work, *In the Heart of the Country* (1977), concerns the political mentality and social implications of "settler-colonialism" in rural South Africa. Narrated in diary form, this novel is indebted to the French *nouveau roman*, which is defined by its proponent Alain Robbe-Grillet as a novel concerned with "the problems of writing," in which "invention and imagination" themselves "become the subject of the book."[11] This work was followed by the allegorical and parable-like *Waiting for the Barbarians* (1980), a novel set in an invented "world out of place and time,"[12] which won the CNA Prize, the Geoffrey Faber Memorial Prize, and the James Tate Black Memorial Prize. Coetzee then published *Life and Times of Michael K.* (1983), which was awarded the Booker prize and which revisits the more "realistic" South African settings of the earlier novels. Despite this return to comparative realism (specifically, to an apartheid South Africa torn apart by civil war), the Kafkaesque echo in the novel's protagonist, "K," alerts us to this work's allegorical dimension.

Foe (1986), Coetzee's "most allegorical" and "most obviously metafictional" work,[13] retells *Robinson Crusoe* as an account of the relations between the literary establishment, Foe (based on Defoe), a colonial storyteller, Susan Barton, and the silenced voice of a colonized manservant, Friday. The 1720 narration is told largely by Barton, who seeks Foe's help in getting the story of Crusoe's island to readers; "but the true authority, indeed potency, of the tale," as David Attwell holds, "belongs to Friday, whose tongue has been severed in an unspecified act of mutilation and who therefore cannot speak or articulate that authority."[14] This novel was followed by *Age of Iron* (1990), the most historically concrete and specific novel that Coetzee had yet written. Narrated by the terminally ill Elizabeth Curren, formerly a lecturer in classics at the University of Cape Town, this work takes place against the backdrop of the Cape Town riots of 1986 and treats the social chaos and moral corruption of the apartheid regime. *The Master of Petersburg* (1994), a mystery set in Russia in 1869 and concerning Dostoyevsky, and *Disgrace* (1999), then followed. *Disgrace* won Coetzee a second Booker Prize and confirmed his standing as one of the foremost living Anglophone novelists. This work returns Coetzee to many of his earlier concerns: "the nature of literary realism and the solitary confinement of the self, the cathartic potential of art as set against brute actuality, [and] the interaction of parent and child as a microcosm of domination."[15] Set in post-apartheid South Africa, the novel centers on David Lurie, a 52-year old university professor who is fired for taking sexual advantage of a student, and his daughter Lucy, who inhabits a smallholding to which he retreats after losing his job. The controversial *Disgrace*, which first appears to be an academic satire, ends up an enigmatic meditation on alterity. Coetzee's ninth novel, *Elizabeth Costello* (2003), which concerns an aging, Australian novelist whose eight formal addresses comprise the backbone of the narrative, further probes and problematizes the boundary between fiction and nonfiction.

For all the geographical and chronological differences among Coetzee's novels – the works are set in the eighteenth, nineteenth, and twentieth centuries, in abstracted landscapes and in readily identifiable ones in the USA, Russia, and South Africa – they all share a concern, as Derek Attridge writes, with the political issues that have rent South Africa, "most obviously colonialism and its legacy of racial, sexual, and economic oppression."[16] Yet all of these novels do so by eschewing "loosened abundance for impacted allegory."[17] It is perhaps for this reason that Coetzee "remains the most elusive of writers, one whose fictions seem almost deliberately constructed to escape any single framework of interpretation."[18]

As well received as Coetzee's novels have been, the author's predilection for allegory has troubled many readers on political grounds. Some have charged Coetzee with "quietism and rarified aestheticism"[19] for writing novels that appear to be "insufficiently engaged with the contingencies of the South African situation."[20] Coetzee himself has admitted that his novels, unlike many others in South Africa, were never censored because they were "too indirect in their approach, too rarified, to be considered a threat to the order."[21] As one critic affirms, "There is no doubt that Coetzee's engagement with history *seems* oblique when his work is compared with the forms of gritty realism associated with black prose fiction [or] with the novels of [fellow South African] Nadine Gordimer".[22] However, Coetzee's "allegorical tales" can be defended as reflecting "the metaphysical ground and philosophical landscape in which the present historical controversies and political disputes of his country are rooted,"[23] even if the author himself has called the novel a "rival to history" that must resist "the discourse of history."[24]

In the light of this description, it would be a mistake to construe Coetzee's fictions as attempts to evade South African history and politics. In eschewing realism for allegory, Coetzee, as novelist Caryl Phillips puts it, can free "himself from being viewed as a mere commentator on the political situation in South Africa"; that is, his works can "isolate" and hence better "scrutinize the psychological traumas of his exposed characters."[25] As confirmed by another critic, in "steadfastly refusing to specify either the geographic or historical setting" of *Waiting for the Barbarians*, Coetzee can successfully dramatize "the moral dilemmas and political paradoxes of all imperial enterprises," including but not limited to those relevant to South African history.[26] It is perhaps for this reason, as Coetzee himself notes, that "The magistrate and the girl [in *Waiting for the Barbarians*] could as well be Russian and Kirghiz, or Han and Mongol, or Turk and Arab, or Arab and Berber,"[27] and that these characters inhabit "a landscape I have never seen"[28] rather than any readily identifiable locale. To the extent that Coetzee sees South African literature as "unnaturally preoccupied with power and the torsions of power, unable to move from elementary relations of contestation, domination, and subjugation to the vast and complex human world that lies beyond them,"[29] it is arguable that, paradoxically, Coetzee's abstracted worlds better challenge and subvert this political reality than any "realistic" portrait could.[30]

III

The six-chapter *Waiting for the Barbarians* takes place within about one year. The novel concerns an unnamed "civil magistrate," our first-person narrator, at a remote colonial outpost "on the roof of the world" (2). The magistrate possesses a liberal-humanist and even anthropological bent (his hobby is to excavate the antique ruins in the vicinity and attempt to decipher the "illegible" script he finds painted on numerous "wooden slips" [14–15]). He is the chief government figure in the town; that there has not been a "military com-mandant" there for years (21) suggests that this outpost is of little strategic importance to the Empire. At the beginning of the novel the magistrate is content with his comfortable, humdrum, bureaucratic existence (23). His life changes, however, with the arrival of an official, Colonel Joll, from the "Third Bureau," the "most important division of the civil guards nowadays" (2). If the magistrate is the novelist's sympathetic, tolerant, and kind protagonist, Joll is its unsympathetic, intolerant, and ruthless antagonist. Joll oversees the "interrogation" of captured "barbarians" who are said to be plotting an attack on the town and the Empire. "Interrogation" is the Bureau's euphemism for torture, and Joll, who is described as "worse than a bureaucrat with vicious tastes" (22), appears to take pleasure in his gruesome work. The sadistic practices that Joll and, when he is away from town hunting barbarians, Warrant Officer Mandel bring to the sleepy outpost remove the "joy" from the magistrate's life (22): "I curse Joll for all of the trouble he has brought me, and for the shame, too" (20).

Joll's description of his torture techniques, undertaken in order to compel captured "barbarians" to admit to and reveal their devious plans – "First, I get lies ... then pressure, then more lies, then more pressure, then the break, then more pressure, then the truth. That is how you get the truth" (5) – reveals the circular reasoning of the Bureau's interrogation procedures. Victims will confess to anything when the pain becomes sufficiently excruciating, and the confessions then "justify" the torture. As Barbara Eckstein observes, such interrogation sessions represent "an inversion of a trial. In a trial, evidence may lead to punishment but punishment is not used to produce 'evidence'."[31] Witnessing such interrogation sessions, the magistrate comes to recognize the extent to which the Third Bureau torturers "have inverted animal and angel, barbarity and civilization."[32]

The turning point in the magistrate's evolving relationship with the Empire, however, comes following his encounter with a girl, one with "the straight black eyebrows, the glossy black hair of the barbarians" (25), who is left behind after a group of "barbarians" is captured and tortured. The narrator's unusual relationship with this girl, which occasions his meditations on sexuality, power, and otherness, leads him, at great personal and political risk to himself, to voyage a considerable distance in order to return her to her people. Upon returning to the outpost he is accused by the Third Bureau of "consorting" with the barbarians, following which he becomes an "enemy" of his own people and is imprisoned and tortured. Rather than representing the law in the town he is now a victimized "other" of the community, on the losing end of the outpost's crude and unforgiving social hierarchies. Finally, when the outpost is all-but-abandoned by the Empire – its soldiers and Third Bureau representatives having fled in the belief that the town is now a lost cause – the narrator returns to his earlier "routine" as the magistrate of an overlooked backwater of Empire, and to his old hobby deciphering "the archaic writing on the poplar slips" (154).[33] His story may be simple but its implications are not. As James Phelan articulates this complexity, *Waiting for the Barbarians* is concerned with the magistrate's

complicity with torturers as well as his own experience of being tortured; [with] his attempts to expiate the pain of one tortured woman, attempts that actually perpetuate her pain and oppression; [and with] his humiliation by the forces of his Empire and his continued complicity with the Empire.[34]

Waiting for the Barbarians alludes to numerous canonical works of European literature: works by George Orwell, Henrik Ibsen, Samuel Beckett, Franz Kafka, Joseph Conrad, and Constantine Cavafy, among others. One critic speaks of the "Orwellian power" of *Waiting for the Barbarians*;[35] and, indeed, Orwell's *Nineteen Eighty-Four*, in which the government uses the threat, real or fabricated, of a foreign "Other" to maintain internal social control, informs

Coetzee's novel. So too does Ibsen's drama *An Enemy of the People*, in which the sole man willing to speak the truth about the corrupt society, in the hope of saving that society, ironically suffers the fate of an "enemy" of the people; and Beckett's play *Waiting for Godot*, with its resonant title. In both *Waiting for Godot* and *Waiting for the Barbarians* the subject of the title never arrives and may not even exist (Coetzee's townspeople wait in vain for the "barbarian" onslaught just as Beckett's characters apparently wait in vain for Godot).

Kafka is the most important literary influence on *Waiting for the Barbarians*, however. Not only do Coetzee's abstract and austere landscapes and his parable-like prose passages at many points resemble Kafka's (these descriptors equally suggest Coetzee's debt to Beckett), but the Empire's torture techniques – particularly its disfigurement of barbarian "criminals" – are reminiscent of events in Kafka's "In the penal colony." The barbarians in Coetzee's novel are punished by having the word "enemy," which is written on their backs, beaten off them until it is illegible (105), while the criminals in Kafka's story are tortured by a machine that inscribes on their bodies the lesson that they are condemned to learn.[36] In both works the "disturbing congruence of writing, torture, and the execution of the law" is explored.[37] However, one might best describe Coetzee's prose in *Waiting for the Barbarians* as combining elements of Kafka and Beckett, "his two great literary masters."[38] Whatever Coetzee's influences here, the author is clearly drawn to "spare prose and a spare, thrifty world;"[39] indeed, what one reviewer holds of *Disgrace* – that it is written with a "scapel-like economy of effect"[40] – is equally true of *Waiting for the Barbarians*.

Although Coetzee's title echoes Beckett's, it also echoes that of a well-known poem, "Waiting for the Barbarians," by the turn-of-the-nineteenth-century Greek poet C. P. Cavafy. This poem, which concludes with a couplet, "Now what's going to happen to us without barbarians? / Those people were a kind of solution,"[41] is highly germane to Coetzee's novel. The poem suggests that "civilized" imperialists need a threatening, external "Other" ("barbarians") – against whom to define themselves, to hold themselves together, and to rationalize aggressive impulses and violent activities that might otherwise be turned inward. Like Cavafy's poem and like Joseph Conrad's *Heart of Darkness*, another work critical of imperialism to which *Waiting for the Barbarians* alludes, Coetzee's novel, as one critic observes, is

> a meditation on the question of whether all civilizations are not necessarily founded upon some arbitrary distinction between the civilized and the barbarian, a . . . distinction that seems to require an element of force and compulsion, an act of discrimination that has no moral basis.[42]

Waiting for the Barbarians interrogates and subverts the barbarism/
civilization distinction, "the most salient binary opposition in the novel,"[43] in
order to "exorcise the ghost of colonial and imperial consciousness."[44] This
interrogation and subversion is achieved, first of all, by questioning the very
existence of the "lurking barbarians" (124) who are said to plan "a great war"
against "the Empire" (10–11). Although such barbarian hordes have never
been seen, they are nevertheless rumored to exist; indeed, all of the setbacks to
the homeland – as in Orwell's *Nineteen Eighty-Four* – are blamed on shadowy
foreigners bent on destroying the civilization. It is hinted, however, that these
"barbarians" merely provide an excuse for the state to maintain a fascistic
control over its own people. When a period of "emergency" is declared at
the outpost, "the administration of justice is out of the hands of civilians
and in the hands of the Bureau" (113). Early in the novel the magistrate
remembers that

> once in every generation, without fail, there is an episode of hysteria about the
> barbarians. There is no woman living along the frontier who has not dreamed
> of a dark barbarian hand coming from under the bed to grip her ankle, no man
> who has not frightened himself with visions of the barbarians . . . raping his
> daughters . . . (8)

Later in the novel the magistrate reports that, at night,

> the barbarians prowl about bent on murder and rapine. Children in their dreams
> see the shutters part and fierce barbarian faces leer through . . . Clothing dis-
> appears from washing-lines, food from the larders, however tightly locked. The
> barbarians have dug a tunnel under the walls, people say . . . no one is safe any
> longer . . . Three weeks ago a little girl was raped. (122)

It is implied that the barbarians are seen everywhere simply because they are
expected to be everywhere. For example, when a portion of an embankment
on the outskirts of town disappears, leading to the flooding of the fields, the
barbarians are immediately blamed, despite the lack of evidence. Although
"No one saw them," they nevertheless somehow "came in the night." Refusing
to "stand up and fight," their way "is to creep up behind you and stick a knife
in your back" (98–9). What may be the result of internal sabotage or natural
cycles, then, is blamed on nefarious "Others" who may not even exist.

Even if it were possible to determine that the barbarians exist, however,
it is doubtful that they are the rapacious and threatening savages that they
are imagined to be. Rather, it is hinted that these "barbarians" are merely

scapegoats for the society's failure to distribute its wealth fairly and to discipline its own members effectively. What W. J. B. Wood writes of the Cavafy poem applies equally well to Coetzee's outpost society: "the apparent threat from without is symptomatic of the source of the problem which lies within."[45] Wood continues: "[T]he barbarians serve to reveal not what is inimical to Empire so much as what ails it: in misconceiving the barbarians, [the] Empire misconceives its own nature and condition – which must doom it to the disaster course it so much dreads."[46] Put simply, the external barbarity that the townspeople fear is actually an expression of their own inherently aggressive and violent tendencies. It is no surprise, then, that the raping and thieving attributed to the barbarians are eventually revealed to be acts of the Empire's own soldiers.

Hints abound that the barbarians are merely a double of, or a mirror image of, members of the "civilized" outpost society, that they are an expression of this society's darkest fears and unspoken desires. O. Mannoni's observation that colonizers "project upon the colonial peoples the obscurities of their own unconscious – obscurities they would rather not penetrate"[47] is of particular relevance here. So is an observation made by the authors of *The Empire Writes Back*:

> In order to maintain authority over the Other in a colonial situation, imperial discourse strives to delineate the Other as radically different from the self, yet at the same time it must maintain sufficient identity with the Other to valorize control over it. The Other can, of course, only be constructed out of the archive of "the self," yet the self must also articulate the Other as inescapably different.[48]

When the magistrate seeks to bring "the girl" back to her people, for example, he wonders whether the barbarians are "reflections of us," and then reports, "As we move they move too . . . We cannot close the gap" (68).[49] Later in the novel, after an unsuccessful expedition to root out the scheming barbarians, a beleaguered assistant of Joll admits, "We froze in the mountains . . . [and] starved in the desert . . . We were not beaten – [the barbarians] led us out into the desert and they vanished . . . They lured us on and on, we could never catch them" (147). Ultimately, there is no evidence that such subversives exist at all. One thing nevertheless seems clear: whoever these "barbarians" are, they are far less threatening than they are imagined to be. Rather than being "thieves, bandits, invaders of Empire," they are in all probability impoverished "fishing people" (17), "destitute tribespeople with tiny flocks," who live "along the river" (4). "These river people are aboriginal, older even than the nomads," the magistrate muses, and then asks: "Living in fear of everyone, skulking in the reeds, what can they possibly know of a great barbarian enterprise against the Empire?" (18). The magistrate notes that while the habits of these "pastoralists" (15) may be "frank and filthy" (19), the people themselves in no way threaten the outpost.[50]

The opposite is not the case, however. Indeed, it becomes clear that the "civilized" are the real barbarians in Coetzee's novel; the more they insist upon their difference from the "barbarians," the more barbarian the "civilized" themselves become.[51] As David Attwell observes, the Empire depends "on the maintenance of absolute differences, and it employs men like Joll to sustain these differences through torture."[52] Barbarian prisoners are routinely treated like "animals," are accused of carrying disease (19, 20), are tortured behind closed doors, are the victims of "patriotic bloodlust" (104), and, when they are not murdered outright, are rendered "sick, famished, damaged, terrified" (24).

Coetzee's novel continually associates the "civilized," not the "barbarians," with savage and bloodthirsty activity in an effort to subvert the "civilized/ barbarian" binary opposition that rationalizes the victimization of the weaker group by the stronger. References to people "roasting whole sheep" (13), to hunting parties returning home "with huge catches" of "birds with their necks twisted" (57), describe not the barbarians but the civilized "expeditionary force against the barbarians"; this returns home not having encountered the foe but instead, in the magistrate's imagining, having roamed "the up-river country, hunting down unarmed sheep-herders, raping their women, pillaging their homes, scattering their flocks" (90).

That the "civilized" violence eventually turns inward underscores the identity of the true barbarians in the novel. During the "emergency" period there is increased "drunkenness," "arrogance towards the townspeople" (123), and stealing on the part of the soldiers, culminating in the breaking in and burning of houses, the smashing of furniture, and the fouling of floors (130– 1). When the soldiers eventually withdraw from the town, which is to be abandoned to barbarian hordes (hordes that never materialize), the narrator registers the Empire's final act of "betrayal" – the wholesale looting of the townspeople's possessions – by the departing soldiers (141). The magistrate asks, "Of what use is it for the shopkeeper to raise the alarm when the criminals and the civil guard are the same people?" (123). The idea that the "civilized" become victims not of the barbarians but of themselves is most clearly revealed when we recognize that the entire outpost has come to resemble a gigantic prison – its "jutting watchtowers" visible "against the sky" (75) – in which the citizenry itself is imprisoned and victimized. As the magistrate tells Joll late in the novel, when the outpost appears to be on the brink of collapse: "When some men suffer unjustly . . . it is the fate of those who witness their suffering to suffer the shame of it" (139). He later adds: "The crime that is latent in us we must inflict on ourselves" (146). Surely it is poetic justice that the outpost collapses under the weight of its abusive treatment of the Other.

In all of his novels Coetzee seeks to challenge "the authority of master-narrators"[53] and to explore the "self's presence to the self."[54] The first-person narrator of *Waiting for the Barbarians* is no exception to either rule. What makes the magistrate particularly interesting is that, like Marlow in *Heart of Darkness*, he actively resists the worst abuses of Empire yet also works for and therefore furthers the aims of Empire. That is to say, the magistrate, like Marlow before him, "is not a man apart from his socio-political context as he might suppose or his mode of life might suggest."[55]

It is clear that the magistrate wishes to assert his moral distance from the Third Bureau; he repeatedly declares his distaste at being "drawn into" (8) its work.

> I did not mean to get embroiled in this. I am a country magistrate, a responsible official in the service of the Empire, serving out my days on this lazy frontier, waiting to retire. I collect the tithes and taxes, administer the communal lands [and] preside over the law-court twice a week. (8)

The moral complexity of the magistrate's position is here revealed: he both breathes and seeks to evade the Empire's ideological atmosphere.[56]

There is a period during which the magistrate can boast being an outright "enemy" of Empire, however. This is when, after returning the "barbarian girl" to her native people, he is accused of "treasonously consorting" with the enemy (77) and of warning "the barbarians of the coming campaign" (83). He is stripped of his authority, imprisoned, and tortured ("I am now no more than a pile of blood, bone and meat that is unhappy" [85]). He becomes an "Other" and is reduced to the status of a "beast" (80, 124–5), "dog" (117), "scapegoat" (120), and, figuratively speaking, woman (he is forced to wear a dress-like "salt-bag" [118] during his mock-execution). Like Dr Stockmann in Ibsen's *An Enemy of the People*, the magistrate is branded an outcast by the community for telling the truth. For example, he tells Warrant Officer Mandel, "we have no enemies . . . unless we are the enemy" (77). He then declares that "the false friendship between myself and the bureau" is coming to an end (77), that "my alliance with the guardians of the Empire is over." "I have set myself in opposition, the bond is broken, I am a free man" (78), he insists. He even takes a public stand against Colonel Joll during one of the public torture and humiliation sessions of the "barbarian" captives, accusing him of "depraving these people!" (106) He tells Joll: "You are an obscene torturer [and] deserve to hang!" (114).

This period in the magistrate's saga, however, proves to be the exception; as much as he would like to distance himself from Joll's work and the Empire's aims, he ultimately is forced to acknowledge how much "he and Joll are merely two aspects of the same imperial system."[57] With characteristic insight the magistrate asks the question, "[W]ho am I to assert my distance from [Joll]? I drink with him, I eat with him, I show him the sights, I afford him every assistance as his letter of commission requests, and more" (5–6). He and Joll, though they have not become friendly, "have managed to behave towards each other like civilized people" (24). "I cannot pretend to be any better than a mother comforting a child between his father's spells of wrath," he thinks when he condemns the Third Bureau's practice of torture yet fails effectively to counter it: "It has not escaped me that an interrogator can wear two masks, speak with two voices, one harsh, one seductive" (7). At another point the magistrate registers "his own twinges of [self-]doubt" (108), which later blossoms into outright fear that he is no less "infected" with the "mad vision" of Empire than the "faithful Colonial Joll as he tracks the enemies of Empire through the boundless desert, sword unsheathed to cut down barbarian after barbarian" (133).[58]

In his study of South African literary culture, Coetzee insists upon the importance of "reading *the other*: gaps, inverses, undersides; the veiled; the dark, the buried, the feminine; alterities"[59] – an issue that is of course germane to the magistrate's moral and intellectual journey in *Waiting for the Barbarians*. His desire to "read" the Other is expressed both in his excavation of the nearby ruin of a former civilization – to discover a "special historical poignancy" in the "vacuousness of the desert" (17) by deciphering script painted on "wooden slips" (15) – and in his enigmatic washing and oiling "ritual" with the naked "barbarian girl":

> I wash her feet . . . her legs, her buttocks. My soapy hand travels between her thighs, incuriously, I find. She raises her arms while I wash her armpits. I wash her belly, her breasts. I push her hair aside and wash her neck, her throat . . . I feed her, shelter her, use her body, if that is what I am doing, in this foreign way. There used to be moments when she stiffened at certain intimacies; but now her body yields when I nuzzle my face into her belly or clasp her feet between my thighs. She yields to everything. (30)

Unlike Joll's crude binary envisioning of self–other relations, the magistrate's grasp of alterity is intersubjective: self and other are for him inseparable if distinct categories. As one critic observes, "inter-subjective relatedness and responsiveness" are things to which the magistrate aspires and that Colonel Joll avoids.[60]

Mikhail Bakhtin, one of the twentieth century's foremost theoreticians of the novel and philosophers of language, addresses alterity in ways that shed light on the magistrate's situation. In his "Toward a reworking of the Dostoevsky book," for example, Bakhtin articulates his vision of self–other interdependence and interanimation:

I am conscious of myself only while revealing myself to another, through another, and with the help of another. The most important acts constituting self-consciousness are determined by a relationship toward another consciousness . . . To be means to be for another, and through the other, for oneself. A person has no internal sovereign territory, he is wholly and always on the boundary; looking inside himself, he looks *into the eyes of another* or *with the eyes of another* . . . I cannot manage without another, I cannot become myself without another; I must find myself in another by finding another in myself (in mutual reflection and mutual acceptance).[61]

As Giles Gunn puts this Bakhtinian perspective, "Otherness is not alien to consciousness but instrumental to its experience. Consciousness is not inimical to otherness but dialectically related to it and essential to its understanding."[62] Bakhtin elaborates on the crucial importance of the other to the self, and one culture to another culture, in his essay, "Response to a question from the *Novy Mir* editorial staff," in which he writes:

In order to understand, it is immensely important for the person who understands to be *located outside* the object of his or her creative understanding – in time, in space, in culture. For one cannot really see one's own exterior and comprehend it as a whole . . . our real exterior can be seen and understood only by other people . . . In the realm of culture, outsideness is a most powerful factor in understanding. It is only in the eyes of *another* culture that foreign culture reveals itself fully and profoundly . . . We raise new questions for a foreign culture, ones that it did not raise itself; we seek answers to our own questions in it . . .[63]

Put simply, for Bakhtin, "Life is dialogical by its very nature. To live means to engage in dialogue, to question, to listen, to answer, to agree."[64] In other words, "Self" means nothing without "Other," and the "truth" of any matter lies somewhere in between.[65]

However should one understand the magistrate's "inexplicable attentions" (33) to the girl? He uses her variously for purposes of achieving sexual release, "rapture" (29), and "blissful giddiness" (28); ablution or absolution (for purposes of healing, mending, soothing, cleansing, assuaging his guilt, and obtaining "penance and reparation" [81]); and self-understanding ("I take her face between my hands and stare into the dead centres of her eyes, from which twin reflections of myself stare solemnly back" [41]). There can be no doubt that he seeks with her (even if he does not achieve it) a dialogue of self and other, culminating in what Bakhtin calls "mutual reflection and mutual acceptance."[66]

The magistrate feeds and shelters the girl yet also uses her body, he comes to understand, for purposes of violation, mastery, and possession. At numerous points he is aware of his "questionable motives" (81) and "questionable desires" (73) and eventually comes to learn that he has made her "very unhappy" (152). Indeed, the magistrate's relationship with the "barbarian girl," who is nearly crippled and blinded by the Third Bureau "interrogators," is linked by the magistrate himself to the Empire's treatment of its "barbarian" victims.[67] For example, the magistrate asks:

Is this how her torturers felt hunting their secret, whatever they thought it was? For the first time I feel a dry pity for them: how natural a mistake to believe that you can burn or tear or hack your way into the secret body of the other! The girl lies in my bed, but there is no good reason why it should be a bed. I behave in some ways like a lover – I undress her, I bathe her, I stroke her, I sleep beside her – but I might equally tie her to a chair and beat her, it would be no less intimate. (43)

Elsewhere he comments:

[I]t has not escaped me that in bed in the dark the marks her torturers have left upon her, the twisted feet, the half-blind eyes, are easily forgotten. Is it then the case that it is the whole woman I want, that my pleasure in her is spoiled until these marks on her are erased and she is restored to herself; or is it the case . . . that it is the marks on her which drew me to her but which, to my disappointment, I find, do not go deep enough?" (64)

At yet another point the magistrate asks himself "whether, when I lay head to foot with her, fondling and kissing those broken ankles, I was not in my heart of hearts regretting that I could not engrave myself on her as deeply" (135). The significant moral and intellectual distance between Joll and himself, which he works so hard to maintain, all but dissolves at such points. Indeed, the magistrate shudders to recognize that "The distance between myself and her torturers . . . is negligible" (27). As Barbara Eckstein observes, "To the degree that the magistrate recognizes that his civil rule allows for Joll's more extreme military rule and that his seduction and questioning of the girl is like Joll's questions and willful penetrations" of her body, "he begins to acknowledge his complicity."[68]

The magistrate's desire to "read" the barbarian girl (as he might a foreign text) involves his desire to know what the torturers did to her and know which soldiers demanded sex from her; his actions thus may be related to the Empire's torturing of barbarians to attain a different sort of information. After all, the "interpretation" and the "mastery" of the girl are closely allied here, as are entering and claiming "possession" of women for the magistrate generally (45).[69] Indeed, the word "pressing" is used within the context of both the rape and the interpretation of the Other. Just as the magistrate imagines that the girl "cannot but feel my gaze pressing upon her with the weight of a body" (56), so he later asks, "What have I been doing all this time, pressing myself upon such flowerlike soft-petalled children . . . ?(97).[70] Like Colonel Joll when he tortures his victims, the magistrate attempts to trespass "into the forbidden" (12) with the barbarian girl. As Barbara Eckstein argues, "When the silence and the scars of the tortured girl thwart his will – even his good will – he wants to penetrate, rape, possess her, so that from her body will arise a certain interpretation of her . . . soul."[71] When he returns the girl to her people he freely associates himself with her torturers, referring to her as "a body we have sucked dry" and to himself as "a jackal of Empire in sheep's clothing" (72).

If Bakhtinian thought helps explain the magistrate's (and the novel's) dialogic intention, postcolonial theory helps us grasp the limits of dialogism when the two parties engaged in a dialogue possess vastly different degrees of power. As much as the magistrate would like to challenge the subject–object model of relations and achieve a dialogue of equals, he cannot. Try as he might to overcome the social hierarchy, he is frozen, as are all individuals in imperial situations, "into a hierarchical relationship in which the oppressed is locked into position by the assumed moral superiority of the dominant group, a superiority which is reinforced when necessary by the use of physical force."[72] The magistrate for this reason eventually comes to question the possibility of dialogue; as one critic puts it, "the tension between Self and Other engenders in the magistrate profound doubt about both."[73] He sees no way to overcome the power relations inherent in dialogue, which "bears a certain tragic potential, borne out repeatedly in the linked realms of the personal and political, where violence as a response" represents "the negative correlative of dialogue."[74]

That the girl is ultimately indecipherable to the magistrate – that she remains stubbornly unreadable and obscure, "opaque" and "impermeable" (75), "blank" and "incomplete" (42) – is beyond question. Just as the "sand drifts back" (14), frustrating his attempts at excavation, just as the wooden slips of script from the former civilization remain stubbornly unreadable, so the girl yields little of her foreign meaning to him. Finally, the magistrate is not even sure what he seeks from her; the reasons for his interest in her "remain as obscure to me as ever" (64). Yet he is certain that "until the marks on this girl's body are deciphered and understood I cannot let go of her" (31). Eventually, his need for her even strikes him as a sort of reverse tyranny: he is "in a measure enslaved" to her (42) and comes to resent his "bondage to the ritual of oiling and rubbing" (41). "There is only a blankness," he concludes, "and desolation that there has to be such blankness" (73).[75]

Coetzee's ambivalent ending – the magistrate likens himself to a man who "lost his way long ago but presses on along a road that may lead nowhere" (156) – may be appropriate to a novel that suggests "the situation of the contemporary South African liberal, facing the fact of complicity in apartheid."[76] But it does not necessarily follow, as Abdul R. JanMohamed maintains, that *Waiting for the Barbarians* "epitomizes the dehistoricizing, desocializing tendency of colonialist fiction" or that it "refuses to acknowledge its [South African] historical sources or to make any allusions to the specific barbarism of the apartheid regime," thereby implying that "we are all somehow equally guilty and that fascism is endemic to all societies."[77] Rather, as this same critic shortly thereafter admits, the novel demonstrates "without any hesitation that the empire projects its own barbarism onto the Other beyond its borders."[78] However one assesses Coetzee's novelistic challenge to political, cultural, and sexual forms of imperialism, *Waiting for the Barbarians* powerfully anatomizes the difficulty faced by even the most well-intentioned Self in understanding and valuing the Other.

Chapter 8

Margaret Atwood's
The Handmaid's Tale (1985)

I am thirty-three years old. I have brown hair. I stand five seven without shoes. I have trouble remembering what I used to look like. I have viable ovaries. I have one more chance.

Offred, in *The Handmaid's Tale*[1]

Tota mulier in utero (Woman is nothing but a womb)

Old Latin saying

I

In equal measure social satire and feminist dystopia, *The Handmaid's Tale*, by Canadian author Margaret Atwood, is a tour de force in the tradition of Aldous Huxley's *Brave New World* and George Orwell's *Nineteen Eighty-Four*. *The Handmaid's Tale* is set in the late twentieth-century Republic of Gilead (formerly the US) that follows a right-wing religious-political coup. The chief goal of this theocratic government, which claims to base its laws on "biblical precedents" (305), is to increase the population in a society where man-made ecological disasters have reduced fertility rates to dangerously low levels. With the exception of three epigraphs and an epilogue, Atwood's novel is narrated in the first person by a 33-year-old "Handmaid," Offred.[2] Through her eyes we learn of her own past and present life and of the feats of social engineering achieved by the Gilead regime, which has its capitol in Cambridge, Massachusetts. Ironically, the headquarters of this totalitarian regime is what was once the campus of Harvard University, Offred's (and Atwood's) alma mater and a center for critical inquiry in the service of a once open and democratic society.

Although the novel depicts both futuristic technological developments and retrogressive puritanical practices, it is best regarded as addressing contemporary social reality. Despite having a narrative frame set in 2195, *The Handmaid's Tale* is not really "about the future but about the present";[3] like other dystopic satires it portrays an "exaggerated version of present evils" in the hope of bringing "about social and political change."[4] Indeed, like all political satires, dystopian novels possess a "social-political message, a didactic intent to address the Ideal Reader's moral sense and reason as it applies to the protagonist's – and our own – place in society and in history."[5] In this case the catalyst for Atwood's dystopia was the resurgence in the US of the vocal religious right of the early 1980s. As in Orwell's *Animal Farm* and *Nineteen Eighty-Four*, in *The Handmaid's Tale* "There's not a single detail in the book that does not have a corresponding reality, either in contemporary conditions or historical fact."[6] As Atwood herself admits, "I didn't invent a lot" in *The Handmaid's Tale*. "I transposed" material "to a different time and place, but the motifs are all historical motifs."[7] In this sense, Atwood's "genius," like that of the Gilead regime she constructs, lies in "synthesis" (307).

Although largely a dystopian satire, Atwood's novel also has the feel of an elegy, a nostalgic lament for an idealized past. At many points in the narrative Offred reminisces over her days as a college student, during which time quotidian freedoms, such as the right to question gender roles and the right to associate with people of her own choosing, could be taken for granted. These memories clash profoundly with her present, straitened circumstances, in which compulsory sex with her assigned Commander – a monthly rape of sorts – is the mandatory focus of her schedule. Handmaids such as Offred are directed to pray, as she puts it, for "emptiness, so we would be worthy to be filled: with grace, with love, with self-denial, semen and babies" (194). The novel proceeds by, and gains its eerie power from, Offred's ironic juxtaposition of her imprisoned present and comparatively self-determined past.

Offred's powerful yet understated narrative, told in sparse yet poetically evocative language (Atwood began her career as a poet), depicts a government that claims to take the Book of Genesis at its word, with devastating consequences for the women of Gilead. I say "claims" to follow the Bible because, in fact, "the men of Gilead appropriate the text of the Bible" merely "to fit their political, social, and sexual goals."[8] Moreover, "sexual relationships are regimented and supervised by the ruling elite, ostensibly in the interest of producing the maximum number of children for the state but actually . . . to eliminate chances of forming personal relationships and private loyalties"[9] that could counter the regime's authority. Sex in Gilead is understood to be for purposes of procreation only, as it was understood by the Puritans in Massachusetts centuries earlier. In Gilead "Anatomy is destiny";[10] Handmaids who do not become pregnant have no value to the society. "The handmaid's situation," writes one critic, "lucidly illustrates Simone de Beauvior's assertion in *The Second Sex* about man defining woman not as an autonomous being" but merely as of value "relative to him."[11] Offred's name in Gilead – a patronymic "composed of the possessive preposition and the first name [in her case, Fred]" of her Commander (305), but also suggesting "afraid," "offered," and "off-read" (misread)[12] – is a linguistic emblem of the regime's misogynistic social system. By contrast, the use of Offred's pre-Gilead name (her "real" name, which we never learn) is now "forbidden" and must remain "buried": "I keep the knowledge of this name like something hidden, some treasure I'll come back to dig up, one day" (84).

In Gilead it is not only sexual rights that are denied to women; most personal liberties, including the right to hold property (178), choose a mate (marriages are now arranged [219]), and read and write are banned to most females, insuring that wealth and knowledge – and therefore power – remain decisively out of their reach. The price to women of transgressing Gilead's rules (or of being infertile) is high: the ever-present threat of being declared "Unwoman" and sent to the Colonies beyond the pale (where Offred's mother has been sent), in effect to die while working in a toxic dump or radiation spill (248) clean-up squad. As Offred's friend Moira puts the regime's use of these squads,

They figure you've got three years maximum . . . before your nose falls off and your skin peels away like rubber gloves. They don't bother to feed you much, or give you protective clothing or anything, it's cheaper not to. Anyway [the people in the squads are] mostly people they want to get rid of. (248)

Gilead's toxic waste problem is the result of such ecological catastrophes as "nuclear-plant accidents," "leakages from chemical and biological-warfare stockpiles and toxic waste disposal sites," and "uncontrolled use of chemical insecticides, herbicides, and other sprays" (304), all of which explain the society's low birthrate and rationalize its sexual and social engineering (and the social hierarchy that supports such engineering). Although less commented on than the novel's status as a "feminist *Nineteen Eighty-Four*,"[13] the novel also functions as an "environmentalist *Nineteen Eighty-Four*."

II

Margaret Atwood was born in Ottawa, Canada in 1939. She attended Victoria College of the University of Toronto, graduating in 1961 with honors in

English. In this same year Atwood published a chapbook, *Double Persephone*, for which she won the prestigious E. J. Pratt Medal for Poetry, and entered a graduate program at Radcliffe College of Harvard University, graduating in 1962 with an MA in English. She then accepted a series of instructorships in English departments at various Canadian universities, during which time she started writing a novel and continued her work in verse; in 1967 she published *The Circle Game*, which won Canada's highest literary prize, the Governor General's Award. Her third volume of poems, *The Animals in that Country*, followed in 1969, as did her first novel, *The Edible Woman*. In a burst of artistic productivity, a volume of poetry, *Power Politics* (1970), a work of nonfiction, *Survival: A Thematic Guide to Canadian Literature* (1972), and a novel, *Surfacing* (1973), then followed, the latter two while Atwood was Writer-in-Residence at the University of Toronto. These works solidified her reputation as among the most prolific and intellectually wide-ranging of Canadian authors.

Numerous novels (eleven), poetry collections (fifteen), short fiction collections (five), non-fiction and edited volumes (nine), and children's books (four) emerged in the next three decades. In particular, her novels *Bodily Harm* (1981), *The Handmaid's Tale* (1985; filmed in 1990 by the German filmmaker Volker Schlondorff with a screenplay by Harold Pinter), *Cat's Eye* (1988), *The Robber Bride* (1993), *Alias Grace* (1996), *The Blind Assassin* (2000; winner of the Booker Prize), and *Oryx and Crake* (2003) assured Atwood's standing as the most celebrated late-twentieth-century Canadian poet-novelist (writer Alice Munro has this standing in the short story category). Collectively, her novels – which explore among other things the socially-constructed nature of gender, male–female and female–female power relations, and "the notorious victim positions Canadians have adopted to survive in the face of domination by imperial powers"[14] – have been translated into thirty-five languages. The author has received sixteen honorary degrees (from universities in Britain, Canada, and the US) and her work has been recognized by numerous awards in addition to the Booker Prize: two Canadian Governor General's Awards (the second for *The Handmaid's Tale*), the Norwegian Order of Merit, the French Chevalier dans l'Ordre des Arts at des Lettres, the Welsh Arts Council International Writer's Prize, and a Guggenheim Fellowship. The author presently resides in Toronto.

Just where to place *The Handmaid's Tale*, generically speaking – it has been called a "dystopia," a "political satire," and a "postmodern subversion"[15] – has been much debated. Indeed, one critic, electing not to choose among the various possible options, has called the work a "dystopian-science fiction-satirical-journal-epistolary-romance-palimpsest text."[16] The question of the novel's generic affiliations is all the more vexing when one notes that Offred's story, which is narrated on cassette tapes that have been discovered and transcribed in the year 2195 by a male scholar, is flanked by other texts. Beforehand are three prefatory epigraphs (one from Genesis, one from Swift's "A modest proposal," and one a Sufi proverb),[17] and after it are the "Historical notes" of scholars in 2195. These notes constitute "not just a history of patriarchy but a metahistory, an analysis of how patriarchal imperatives are encoded within the various intellectual methods we bring to bear on history."[18] Indeed, the novel's narrative strategy – which we encounter in various incarnations in novels by Coetzee, McCabe, Rhys, and Swift – is postmodern to the extent that it is "designed to call attention to the acts of reading and interpretation."[19]

Although the genetic emphasis of *The Handmaid's Tale* is reminiscent of Huxley's *Brave New World*,[20] it is largely Orwell's *Nineteen Eighty-Four* – with its emphasis on social engineering in the service of a nefarious totalitarian regime – that stands behind Atwood's dystopia. As Jocelyn Harris writes, *The Handmaid's Tale* is "recognizably Orwellian" in both "structure" and in "minute detail."[21] Specifically, in Atwood's novel, as in *Nineteen Eighty-Four*, spies, secret police agents, and crack troops – "Eyes," "Angels," and "Guardians" – penetrate all dimensions of the society. In Orwell's novel denizens of Oceania are constantly reminded that "Big Brother is Watching You,"[22] while in Atwood's a standard greeting between two Handmaids is "Under His Eye" (45). In both novels manipulative neologisms and slogans are deployed by the state in order to control not just the behavior but the thought of its citizens. In *Nineteen Eighty-Four* "The Principles of Newspeak"[23] and such party slogans as "War is Peace," "Freedom is Slavery," and "Ignorance is Strength" (examples of "doublethink") are everywhere to be found, while in *The Handmaid's Tale* such public events as "Prayvaganzas" and "Salvagings" and such expressions as "God is a natural resource" (213) are commonplace. "Unpersons" populate Orwell's novel, "Unwomen" Atwood's.

In both dystopias the regime in question places the population on a constant war-footing and on food rationing (in Atwood's novel we read that "the war seems to be going on in many places at once" [82] and that "They only show us victories, never defeats" [83]) and seeks to control the present by altering the past. In Orwell's novel, for example, the party recognizes that "Who controls the past . . . controls the future: who controls the present controls the past";[24] and in Atwood's novel the regime works to erase accurate recollections of the past (the "Aunts," armed with cattle prods, attempt to condition the Handmaids to believe that their lot is actually better now than in pre-Gilead days).

In both novels the state manipulates emotion and rouses "bloodlust" through public spectacles, and uses scapegoats and public violence as "steam valves" (307) to defuse hostility to state oppression. In *Nineteen Eighty-Four* this takes the form of "two minutes of hate" and "Hate Week"; in *The Handmaid's Tale*, in the "Prayvaganzas" and "Salvagings," Handmaids actually take part in the brutal murder of state "traitors" (who turn out to be subversives). Finally, and perhaps most importantly, in both novels "sexual repression assists" the government in maintaining "social control."[25]

Winston Smith's utter resignation at the end of Orwell's *Nineteen Eighty-Four*, when he realizes that he has "won the victory over himself" and at last loves "Big Brother,"[26] is the forerunner of Offred's startling realization near the end of her tale:

> I'll stop complaining. I'll accept my lot. I'll sacrifice. I'll repent. I'll abdicate. I'll renounce. I know this can't be right but I think it anyway . . . I don't want pain . . . I want to keep on living, in any form. I resign my body freely, to the use of others. They can do what they like with me. I am abject. I feel, for the first time, their true power. (286)

Both Orwell's and Atwood's originally free-thinking protagonists, then, are eventually coerced into submission by the state. Although they may do so for different reasons, both finally surrender themselves up to the state, in body, mind, and soul.

That said, as one reader remarks, "For all the parallels to that powerful precursor *Nineteen Eighty-Four*, *The Handmaid's Tale* is a work with an entirely different scope and feel."[27] Specifically, while the earlier text focuses on "the design" and mechanics of dystopian social engineering, the latter one focuses on "the experience of living under it," as such knowledge of the totalitarian society's ways and means can be taken for granted, having become "part of the readers' cultural and generic awareness."[28] Seen in this light, *The Handmaid's Tale* both "participates in and extends the dystopian genre"[29] that was pioneered by Orwell and others in the mid-twentieth-century.[30]

To the extent that it may be regarded as a feminist dystopia, *The Handmaid's Tale* is "a clever appropriation of a predominantly male literature for feminist purposes."[31] That said, a little-acknowledged feminist precursor to Atwood's novel can be identified: Charlotte Perkins Gilman's satire "The yellow wallpaper." Like the female protagonist of Gilman's 1892 novella, one whose situation harkens back in turn to that of Bertha Mason, the madwoman in the attic of Charlotte Brontë's 1847 *Jane Eyre*, Offred is a prisoner of a patriarchal domestic tyranny, and passes the time, like her predecessor in the Gilman story, who also keeps a secret journal, doing whatever she can in the straitened circumstances of her bedroom-prison. She recalls wishing to explore her bedroom slowly:

> I didn't want to do it all at once, I wanted to make it last. I divided the room into sections, in my head; I allowed myself one section a day. This one section I would examine with the greatest minuteness: the unevenness of the plaster under the wallpaper, the scratches in the paint of the baseboard and the windowsill, under the top coat of paint, the stains on the mattress . . . (51)

Another moment of Offred's life that is strongly reminiscent of Gilman's "The yellow wallpaper" occurs somewhat later, when she is lying on her bed:

> I would like to rest, go to sleep, but I'm too tired, at the same time too excited, my eyes won't close. I look up at the ceiling, tracing the foliage of the wreath [around the missing chandelier, which Offred's predecessor used to commit suicide]. In a minute the wreath will start to color and I will begin seeing things. That's how tired I am . . . (128)

Toward the end of her narrative Offred feels the "presence" of this predecessor, this "ancestress" and "double,"

> turning in midair under the chandelier . . . a bird stopped in flight, a woman made into an angel, waiting to be found . . . How could I have believed I was alone in here? There were always two of us. Get it over, she says . . . There's no one you can protect, your life has value to no one. I want it finished. (293)

Similarly to Gilman's protagonist (and for that matter Brontë's Bertha), then, Atwood's contemplates suicide and imagines her double in a domestic prison of her "husband's" making.[32]

III

Glenn Deer observes that *The Handmaid's Tale* faces a challenge that is typical of satiric dystopias: "to portray the mechanisms of oppression as credible enough, as sufficiently powerful and seductive, to represent a believable evil, not an irrelevant or farfetched one."[33] This is a challenge that the novel handily meets. Everything from Offred's sense of space (she wears "white wings" around her face, "blinkers" that are "prescribed issue" and keep her from "seeing" and "being seen" [8]), to time ("There's a grandfather clock in the hallway, which doles out time" [9]), to speech ("Blessed be the fruit," Ofglen greets Offred; "May the Lord open," Offred answers [19]), is controlled by the Gilead regime. It is no surprise that Offred succumbs to fatalism, admitting, "I try not to think too much" (8).

While the Gilead regime claims that its social system is designed to "protect women," this system's "actual purpose is to control them and reinforce the notion that their biology is their destiny."[34] Lucy M. Freibert lays out the many-tiered female hierarchy of Gilead:

> The blue-clad Wives of the Commanders preside over their homes and gardens, and attend public functions . . . Sexual duties fall to the red-clad Handmaids, drilled in self-denial and renunciation and reduced to fertility machines. The green-clad Marthas clean and cook. The Econowives, married to upper-level menials, combine the functions of the other groups and consequently wear striped blue/red/green dresses. At the Rachel and Leah Center, the Aunts use electric cattle prods to keep the Handmaids in line. The black-clad widows, a rapidly diminishing group, live in limbo. The gray-clad Unwomen, those who refuse to cooperate with the system, work in the Colonies . . .[35]

Despite the widespread acceptance of this social hierarchy, the Wives of husbands with Handmaids remain uncomfortable with the monthly coupling ceremony and therefore view Handmaids as necessary evils. "I am a reproach to her," Offred imagines of the childless Serena Joy, her Commander's wife, but also "a necessity" (13).

This monthly event is the centerpiece of the Handmaid's life; it is her chief "duty" (95) and the focus of her schedule:

> I lie on my back, fully clothed . . . Above me, toward the head of the bed, Serena Joy is arranged, outspread. Her legs are apart, I lie between them, my head on her stomach, her pubic bone under the base of my skull, her thighs on either side of me. She too is fully clothed. My arms are raised; she holds my hands, each of mine in each of hers. This is supposed to signify that we are one flesh, one being. What it really means is that she is in control, of the process and thus the product . . . My red skirt is hitched up to my waist, though no higher. Below the Commander is fucking. What he is fucking is the lower part of my body. I do not say making love, because this is not what he's doing. Copulating too would be inaccurate, because it would imply two people and only one is involved . . . What's going on in this room . . . is not exciting. It has nothing to do with passion or love or romance . . . It has nothing to do with sexual desire . . . (93–4)

It goes without saying that this most "serious business" of the Handmaid's monthly calendar dehumanizes her, so completely is she determined – like the "hands" in Dickens's *Hard Times* – by the service her body performs for her master (63). Her worth is wholly bound up with whether or not she is a "worthy vessel" (65) and can fulfill her promise as a "natural resource" (65). "We are containers," Offred observes of the role of Handmaids; "it's only the inside of our bodies that are important" (96). "We are for breeding purposes: we aren't concubines, geisha girls, courtesans," she later concludes. "We are two-legged wombs, that's all: sacred vessels, ambulatory chalices" (136). Success or failure hinges exclusively on whether pregnancy ensues. "Each month I watch for blood, fearfully, for when it comes it means failure. I have failed once again to fulfill the expectations of others, which have become my own" (63). Worse than even this, however, would be for Offred to become sick: Handmaids who succumb to illness and therefore cannot bear children are regarded as "terminal" cases (155). As one critic puts this state of affairs, Atwood's novel "gives a new and ominous meaning to the phrase 'the body politic'."[36]

The regime's assault on intellectual freedom and its bid to colonize the minds of its subjects ("The Republic of Gilead," said Aunt Lydia, "knows no bounds. Gilead is within you" [23]) is perhaps best symbolized in the regime's closing of the universities and in its use of Harvard's buildings as a center for "the Eyes" (166). Ironically, the wall around Harvard yard, which at one time delineated a place of intellectual freedom, now functions as a part of the state's prison apparatus.[37] This red-brick wall is "hundreds of years old," Offred muses, "and must once have been plain but handsome. Now the gates have sentries and there are ugly new floodlights mounted on metal posts above it; and barbed wire along the bottom and broken glass set in concrete along the top" (31). The past and present function of Harvard's buildings are in even starker contrast, in that the dead bodies of murdered enemies of Gilead are typically hung from the wall for all to see. "It's the bags over the heads that are the worst, worse than the faces themselves would be," Offred comments of the corpses; "It makes the men look like dolls on which the faces have not yet been painted; like scarecrows, which in a way is what they are, since they are meant to scare" (32). Needless to say, the educational glory of Harvard's former days is over, to be replaced, for the Handmaids in Gilead at any rate, with a curriculum of "Gyn Ed" (117) at the Rachel and Leah Re-education Center.

Linda Kauffman is correct to argue that "*The Handmaid's Tale* functions as an anatomy of ideology, exposing the process by which one constructs, psychologically and politically, subjects of the state, and then enlists their cooperation in their own subjection."[38] This is particularly true of Gilead's use of women to enforce their own victimhood, to help release pressure built up by their oppression, and to spy on each other (19). The Gilead regime understands that the "best and most cost-effective way to control women for reproductive and other purposes" is through the women themselves, and that no "empire imposed by force or otherwise" ever succeeded without the "control of the indigenous by members of their own group" (308).[39]

Take, for example, the "crack female control agency known as the 'Aunts'," who are motivated by the logic that, "When power is scarce, a little of it is tempting" (308). The Aunts help oppress the Handmaids by monitoring their behavior generally and by presiding over such events as "Salvagings," aimed at eliminating the regime's "political enemies" (307), and "Particicutions," "steam valve[s] for the female elements in Gilead" (307). Women's Salvagings (such ceremonies are always single-sex events) take place at what was once Harvard University, again highlighting the intellectual freedoms that have been lost. "We take our places in the standard order," Offred describes one such event, "Wives and daughters on the folding wooden chairs placed towards the back, Econowives and Marthas around the edges and on the library steps, and Handmaids at the front, where everyone can keep an eye on us" (273). Two Handmaids and one Wife are to be executed on this occasion. As always, the event involves the participation of the entire audience: when the women accused of committing crimes against the state are hung on the stage, the assembled women lean forward and touch the rope placed in front of them and then place their hands on their hearts to signify their "unity with the Salvagers," "consent" to the murder, and "complicity in the death" of the victim (276).

Particularly ingenious are "Particicutions," in which Handmaids en masse murder a Guardian or other male former regime functionary who is accused of rape or the like. In one such Particicution, the victim is supposedly a Guardian who has "disgraced his uniform." "He has abused his position of trust," Aunt Lydia charges, citing the Bible; and "The penalty for rape, as you know, is death. Deuteronomy 22: 23–9" (279). On this occasion even Offred is moved, against her better judgment, by the accusation: "It's true, there is a bloodlust; I want to tear, gouge, rend. We jostle forward . . . our nostrils flare, sniffing death" (279). Just when the man, who is reduced in this ceremony to an "*it*" (280), begins to contest the charge against him, the crazed and enraged Handmaids "surge forward"; in this moment they are "permitted anything and this is freedom." They violently assault their scapegoat-victim, kicking him, punching him, ripping out clumps of his hair (280). Although the women do not really know anything about their victim – and the reader knows that they would be wise to distrust the information furnished them by the Aunts – the abused women are eager to blame anyone they can get their hands on for their misery. Temporarily, at least, the Handmaids have the opportunity to violate a male in retaliation for being violated by one. Such male scapegoats are useful to the regime, then, in that the Handmaids, who are "so rigidly controlled at other times," at least have the opportunity "to tear a man apart with their bare hands every once in a while" (307–8). Only with such a safety valve could the risk of rebellion at some unexpected time be avoided. Later, we learn that their victim on this occasion was not a rapist at all but "a political," and that the Handmaids, ironically, butchered someone who was working on their behalf and against the state. After the event, like Lady Macbeth in Shakespeare's tragedy, Offred wants to wash her guilty hands of their complicity in the murder of this innocent victim: "I want to go back to the house and up to the bathroom and scrub and scrub, with the harsh soap of pumice, to get every trace of this smell [of the warm tar of the rope] off my skin. The smell makes me feel sick" (281).

A further example of the regime's use of individuals to further their own oppression can be found in the phenomenon of the "Soul Scrolls" (nicknamed "Holy Rollers"): five different pre-recorded prayers – "for health, wealth, a death, a birth, a sin" – that can be purchased from the state by the denizens of Gilead. "You pick the [prayer] you want, punch the number, then punch in your own number so your account will be debited, and punch in the number of times you want the prayer repeated" (167). The machines "run by themselves," and "Once the prayers have been printed out and said, the paper rolls back through another slot and is recycled into fresh paper again" (167). Ironically, then, citizen-purchasers of prayers subsidize the state's infringement of their choice, freedom, and power while being given precisely the illusion of choice, freedom, and power.

In another cruel and ironic twist, the Gilead regime claims to adhere to a feminist philosophy in its treatment of women and paints a picture of a utopian future in which female society will at last become the sorority it was formerly prevented from being. Aunt Lydia preaches to her Handmaids-in-training that sacrifices in the present will justify social achievements in the future, "Women united for a common end!" Eventually "women will live in harmony together, all in one family," and there will be "bonds of real affection" among them. "Your daughters will have greater freedom [than you]," Aunt Lydia continues, "But we can't be greedy pigs and demand too much before it's ready, now can we?" (162–3). As we have seen in Jean Rhys's *Wide Sargasso Sea*, the patriarchy in Gilead embraces the paradox of protection-in-imprisonment: the more imprisoned the woman is, the safer she is; the less imprisoned she is, the less safe she is. Unlike today, runs the official Gilead line, "Women were not protected" in the past (24). "There is more than one kind of freedom," Aunt Lydia explains, "Freedom to and freedom from. In the days of anarchy [before], it was freedom to. Now you are being given freedom from. Don't underrate it" (24). The Commander similarly justifies the ways of Gilead to Offred by claiming that in the new order of things women will be "protected" and will at last be able to "fulfill their biological destinies in peace." He then adds, in an appeal to nature that rings hollow in Offred's ears, that all that Gilead society has done between the sexes is to return "things to Nature's norm" (219–20).

The net effect of this oppression is that Handmaids are reduced to the agency-less level of children, dolls (16, 124, 182), and animals in a cage: to objects, in other words, of another's subjectivity. Offred interprets the anchorman on state-run television, for example, as encouraging viewers to "trust" the regime. "You must go to sleep, like good children" (83). She remembers, "They used to have dolls, for little girls, that would talk if you pulled a string at the back; I thought I was sounding like that, voice of a monotone, voice of a doll" (16). Another time, she likens one Handmaid she knows to "a puppy that's been kicked too often, by too many people, at random: she'd roll over for anyone, she'd tell anything, just for a moment of approbation" (129). And when considering the death of her predecessor in her Commander's house, Offred muses: "If your dog dies, get another" (187). "A rat in a maze is free to go anywhere, as long as it stays inside the maze" (165), she also observes. And Offred is tattooed (65) – like livestock, like a Holocaust victim – so that she can be identified and processed. Atwood's implication is clear: children, dolls, and domesticated animals share a lack of self-determination and agency that epitomizes the plight of Handmaids.

There is little escape from the state of affairs that Offred must endure save for that which memory can afford. In this way, memory, which is capable of assessing Gilead's social structure from a critical distance, is subversive of and threatening to that structure. It is for this reason, among others, that the regime seeks to suppress it. As one critic notes, time in Gilead "is carefully manipulated so that all remnants of the past, pre-Gilead reality are obliterated: there are no dates after the 1980s [and] all historical documents are destroyed."[40] Offred nevertheless remembers the days "before," commenting, "I'm a refugee from the past, and like other refugees I go over the customs and habits of being I've left or been forced to leave behind" (227). She reminisces over her earlier days with her mother, her college friend Moira (whom she later runs into in the "present" of the novel), her husband Luke ("We thought we had such problems. How were we to know we were happy?" [51]), and, most poignantly, her daughter whom she has not seen for three years (since the regime came to power) and who would now be 8 years old: "She fades, I can't keep her here with me, she's gone now" (64). "Sometimes," however, Offred's reminiscences are involuntary, and "these flashes of normality come at [her] from the side, like ambushes. The ordinary, the usual, a reminder, like a kick" (48). Such reminiscences, which also come to her at times in dreams, are especially painful.[41]

Although resistance to the Gilead regime mainly takes on such a mental and nostalgic dimension, there are indications that an organized resistance exists. The first hint of the existence of such resistance is the Latin inscription, *Nolite te bastardes carborundorum* (52) ("Don't let the bastards grind you down" [187]), which Offred discovers scratched lightly into the floor of her bedroom by her predecessor (apparently, this predecessor, an eventual suicide, could not keep the regime from grinding her down). Offred then comes to believe in the existence of an organized resistance on philosophical grounds: "Someone must be out there, taking care of things. I believe in the resistance as I believe there can be no light without shadow; or rather, no shadow unless there is also light" (105). She finally learns from another Handmaid, Ofglen, that there is in fact such a group, the members of which identify themselves with the distress signal "Mayday" (from the French *M'aidez*) (202). This Mayday underground is quasi-military and has a connection with another group, the "Underground Femaleroad" (246), a "rescue operation" (309) that helps Offred's friend Moira, then a Handmaid-in-training, to escape temporarily from the clutches of the regime. As one critic observes, the "underground Femaleroad" clearly alludes to "the Underground Railroad by means of which the runaway slaves of the American South" entered Canada.[42] Ofglen is finally found out by the regime and is forced to hang herself ("She saw the van coming for her" [285]), and Moira is recaptured and sent to work as a prostitute in an illicit sex-club for Commanders. But this does not diminish the likelihood that such organized resistance, comprised of both male and female members (even Nick, the chauffeur of Offred's Commander, was probably "a member of the shadowy Mayday underground" [309]), has a potentially negative impact on Gilead's hold on power.

On the other hand, Offred's belief that an organized resistance exists does not ensure that she can successfully resist the regime's hegemony. As Linda Kauffman observes, despite "Offred's efforts to remember her prior existence, she has begun to take on the perception the regime wants her to have of herself."[43] For example, toward the end of the novel, when Ofglen offers to help Offred escape if ever she is in immediate danger, Offred no longer wishes "to leave, escape, cross the border to freedom" and instead wishes to remain in Gilead with Nick (271), with whom she is having an affair (and by whom she may be pregnant). She justifies her change of heart in terms of both love and expedience: "I have made a life for myself, here, of a sort" (271). As Kauffman points out, Offred "repossesses her body by making love with Nick, an act for which she could be executed," and in telling Nick her real name, "she unburies the body, the voice, the self that the regime sought to annihilate."[44] It is nevertheless also the case that Offred feels relief when she hears about Ofglen. Ofglen, the only person outside of her household with the knowledge to betray her, has committed suicide, which means that Offred can maintain the status quo, at least for the time being:

> So she's dead, and I am safe, after all. She did it before they came [to get her]. I feel a great relief. I feel thankful to her. She has died that I may live. I will mourn later. (286)

That said, what is true about Winston Smith and Julia in Orwell's novel is true about Offred and Nick in Atwood's: their forbidden relationship (and illicit sex) constitutes "a political act."[45]

Despite the lack of immediate success for the resistance, a careful look at Gilead society does reveal cracks in its edifice. For example, illicit and deceptive activities committed by officials are rife. As Celia Floren observes of Gilead society, a "Lack of freedom and strong restrictions" encourage a "circle of deceit":

> [T]he Commander deceives his wife; he sees the handmaid in secret . . . and even smuggles her into an unofficial brothel for high-ranking officers; Serena Joy, the wife, deceives the Commander, as she helps the handmaid meet their chauffeur, Nick, in secret, hoping that he will make the latter pregnant; Nick cheats the Commander, when he complies with Serena's wishes and makes love to the handmaid, and his wife as he helps the Commander see the handmaid, and take her to the brothel. The handmaid deceives both the husband and the wife with Nick and the Commander, respectively; Nick and the handmaid deceive their masters. The handmaid, with the help of another handmaid Ofglen, deceives them all, trying to connect with the underground network.[46]

Offred's illicit relationship with her Commander, who is apparently at the very top of the Gilead power structure, is the most interesting of these deceptions. It is especially ironic, given their obligatory monthly sex, that Offred becomes her Commander's "mistress" at all (163). For another, their secret trysts in his office involve not sex but the playing of Scrabble, during which time Offred engages in the forbidden pleasure of forming words, an emblem of what one critic calls the novel's focus on the "political nature of language use" and on "the self-liberating potential of an individual's act of storytelling."[47] Their affair takes another strange turn when the Commander brings Offred to an illicit Bunny Club of sorts, where Commanders, other male senior officials, and trade delegations (237) are entertained and provided with sexual favors by former prostitutes, political prisoners, and a few women who prefer this sort of work to the alternatives (238). Although the activities that take place at the club are "strictly forbidden," the Commander hypocritically affirms, violating his own repressive sexual and social codes, that "everyone's human, after all" (237). Offred imagines that such a transgression of the rules is a power-trip for her Commander: "He's breaking the rules, under their noses, thumbing his nose at them, he's getting away with it" (236). Although Offred, when at the club, feels like "used glitz" (254) and "an evening rental" (233) – and is even purple-tagged around the wrist, "like the tags for airport luggage" – she at least takes pleasure in being "no longer in official existence" (233) as a Handmaid. Indeed, Offred justifies going along with the Commander out of her desire for "anything that breaks the monotony, subverts the perceived respectable order of things" (231). At the Club she runs into Moira, who earlier was caught trying to escape from Gilead, was sterilized, and was sent to serve a term in the club. In Moira's view, Commanders bring women to the club against the rules just for kicks: "It's like screwing on the altar or something" (243). The evening ends with the Commander and Offred retreating to a private room for sex, which the latter finds even more objectionable and depressing than the Commander's officially sanctioned monthly attempts at impregnating her (255).

When Serena Joy (an ironic name for one neither serene nor joyful) learns of Offred's and the Commander's affair, she accuses Offred of being like her predecessor, "A slut. You'll end up the same [a suicide]" (287). Just exactly what happens to Offred at the end of her narrative – the black van with a white eye painted on the side comes to pick her up, and Nick convinces her to go quietly (he claims that the van is staffed not by members of the regime but by members of "Mayday" ["Trust me," he tells her] [293–5]) – we cannot know for sure. Her narrative proper ends on a note of ambiguity: "Whether this is my end or a new beginning I have no way of knowing: I have given myself over into the hands of strangers, because it can't be helped. And so I step up, into the darkness within; or else the light" (295). It therefore lacks a telos or "closure."

Atwood's recent lecture collection, *Negotiating with the Dead*,[48] might well be the subtitle of the present novel, for this is precisely what the academics in 2195, in resurrecting her narrative, attempt to do with Offred. Indeed, the entire meaning of Offred's story is altered by the thirteen-page appendix "*Historical notes on* The Handmaid's Tale." As Atwood reminds us, the last chapter of Orwell's *Nineteen Eighty-Four* is in fact the eleven-page "Appendix: The principles of newspeak," which functions in the same way as the "Historical notes" to *The Handmaid's Tale*: it suggests a future in which the totalitarian regime in question is no more.[49] In both cases, then, the epilogue retrospectively influences our reception of the main body of the narrative.

In this connection, although Atwood may dismiss the classification "post-modernist," she is clearly problematizing the "modernist, open-ended narrative" by seeming to offer two "endings" while actually providing none.[50] Offred's narrative proper, which does not (and cannot) detail her fate, simply stops (rather than ends); and the "Historical notes," which suggest that she survived long enough to narrate her story (onto 30 cassette tapes), throws into doubt the degree to which the meaning of Offred's narrative has been grasped by the scholars.[51] After all, the narrative is a transcription and hence an interpretation of a spoken text arranged and titled by its editors, who resorted at points to "guesswork" (310). And the novel "resists closure," leaving readers "with disturbing questions rather than soothing answers."[52] "*The Handmaid's Tale*," one critic concludes, is thus a "highly daunting, ambitious, postmodernist metafictional novel," in which the "form" is very much "part of the content."[53] To be sure, the novel's epilogue embroils Atwood's readers "in complex author-narrator-reader interrelationships."[54]

The appended "Historical notes" – comprising "a partial transcript of the proceedings of the Twelfth Symposium on Gildean Studies" held in the year 2195, chaired by Maryann Crescent Moon, Professor of "Caucasian Anthropology" at the University of Denay, Nunavit, and keynoted by Professor James Darcy Pieixoto, Director of Cambridge University's "Twentieth- and Twenty-first-Century Archives" (299) – has a parodic feel yet establishes how Offred's "private record has become a public document."[55] The "Historical notes" are also a version of the eighteenth- and nineteenth-century preface rationalizing the discovery of a lost manuscript.

Although this transcript of Gildean Research Association proceedings provides "comic relief from the grotesque text of Gilead," it is at the same time "the most pessimistic part of the book":[56] the academics, who condescend to their object of study and take their job to be to "understand" rather than to "censure" Gildean society (302), seem bound to repeat many of Gilead's indiscretions. Debrah Raschke, in addressing the novel's three systems of language and representation, puts this problem well:

The first is the Gilead system, a fixed system dominated by empirical realism, rigid binary oppositions, and implacable boundaries. The second system of representation (the narrator's) threatens to disrupt Gilead's patriarchal power by a slippery poststructuralist refusal of fixity and truth. The third, the academic rhetoric of the closing "Historical Notes," poses an open, liberated discourse, but, in effect, in its insidious insistence on univocal representation, is a repetition of Gilead. Thus, the narrator's method of representation functions not only as a challenge to Gilead, but to the Academy as well.[57]

Put another way, while the "Historical Notes" provide a gloss on the "social, historical, and political origins of Gildean society," they also serve to satirize the academics as "trivializers of history" who have turned "Gilead into a matter of textual authentication"[58] and a means of securing professional advancement. Offred's politico-sexual victimage at the hands of the regime is reduced by the assembled "historians, archeologists, and anthropologists" to "a source of quaint curiosity."[59] As Amin Malak concludes, "The entire 'Historical Notes' at the end of the novel represents a satire on critics who spin out theories about literary or historical texts without genuinely recognizing or experiencing the pathos expressed in them: they circumvent issues, classify data, construct clever hypotheses garbed" in "jargon, but no spirited illumination ever comes out of their endeavors."[60] As such, these scholars, again ironically, furnish readers "with an example of how not to read Atwood's novel."[61] The keynote speaker of this academic conference acknowledges that

> [T]he past is a great darkness, and filled with echoes. Voices may reach us from it; but what they say to us is imbued with the obscurity of the matrix out of which they come; and, try as we may, we cannot decipher them properly in the clearer light of our own day. (311)

Yet his analysis of Gilead belies his own testament to the limitations of historical interpretation.

Offred, by contrast, is a sensitive and self-conscious narrator, who is aware of the inherently problematic and fictive nature of all narratives. She is keenly aware of the extent to which her fears, desires, and lapses of memory necessarily impinge upon her ability to paint a comprehensive picture of her experiences. Although she "will try" against all odds "to leave nothing out" of her story (268), she nevertheless acknowledges:

> This is a reconstruction. All of it is a reconstruction. It's a reconstruction, now, in my head . . . [I]f I'm ever able to set this down, in any form, even in the form of one voice to another, it will be a reconstruction then too, at yet another remove. It's impossible to say a thing exactly the way it was, because what you say can never be exact, you always have to leave something out, there are too many parts, sides, crosscurrents, nuances; too many gestures, which could mean this or that, too many shapes which can never be fully described . . . (134)

At times Offred fills out the details of a conversation herself because she cannot "remember exactly" what was said (243); at others she admits to wishing to be able to tell a different story than the version she offers us (250, 267,

273), but that her powers of imagination are not vivid enough to fabricate a more palatable version:

> I wish this story were different. I wish it were more civilized. I wish it showed me in a better light, if not happier, then at least more active, less hesitant, less distracted by trivia. I wish it had more shape . . . I'm sorry there is so much pain in this story. I'm sorry it's in fragments, like a body caught in crossfire or pulled apart by force. But there is nothing I can do to change it. (267)

At times she even takes to revising her story midstream, offering us a series of versions of what might have occurred, as when she describes her illicit sexual encounters with Nick: "I made that [last part] up. It didn't happen that way. Here is what [really] happened" (261). Lois Feuer concludes that while Offred's narrative strategy is an expression in part of the "now-familiar twentieth century obsession with the unreliability of language and narrative, part of the self-reflexivity of the novel in our time," it is also about the "distrust of certainty" and the "cherishing" of "ambiguity" – those "multiple meanings" and "alternate possibilities" – "that the regime is ultimately unable to control."[62]

With this in mind, the fact that Offred narrates her story at all is a challenge to the regime's authority. Although it is true that the yarn she narrates keeps her busy and gives her a sense of purpose, as the Wives' knitting of yarn for scarves for "Angels at the front lines" is designed to do, Offred's "story" also allows her to theorize a sympathetic audience and an alternate reality to the one Gilead forces upon her:

> I would like to believe this is a story I'm telling. I need to believe it. I must believe it. Those who can believe that such stories are only stories have a better chance. If it's a story I'm telling, then I have control over the ending. Then there will be an ending, to the story, and real life will come after it. I can pick up where I left off. (39)

She later adds: "By telling you anything at all I'm at least believing in you, I believe you're there, I believe you into being." "Because I'm telling you this story I will your existence," Offred continues in a tweaking of the foundation of Cartesian philosophy, "I tell, therefore you are" (268).

The novel's title also speaks to the misogynistic tenor of the scholars in 2195. This title was appended to Offred's tapes, Professor Pieixoto explains in the "Historical notes," by one of his colleagues, "partly in homage to the great Geoffrey Chaucer" but also as an intentional pun on "the archaic vulgar signification of the word *tail*; that being [the] bone, as it were, of contention, in that phase of Gildean society of which our saga treats" (301). As one critic explains, "The dual effect of the double-entendre in the pun on the word *tale*, as literary creation and anatomic part," combines "humor and denigration" and is an emblem of the "conflict between the protagonist and the society that regards her as a sexual object."[63] Similarly, Professor Pieixoto, in "bracketing" Offred's tale, "reiterates the tension between Offred's words and [the] patriarchal control of her story," which is the very crux of the novel's meaning.[64] Like Gilead's "computer prayers" that "fall upon deaf ears," Offred's "voice falls upon deaf ears, unheard [in her own time] or misheard [in Pieixoto's]."[65] As in Dickens's *Hard Times* – which ends with the narrator's entreaty to readers of the novel to alter the state of social affairs for the better – in Atwood's *The Handmaid's Tale* it falls to the novel's readers to "hear" what was apparently inaudible both to Offred's contemporaries and to Pieixoto's colleagues 200 years later.

Chapter 9

Kazuo Ishiguro's *The Remains of the Day* (1989)

The great butlers are great by virtue of their ability to inhabit their professional role and inhabit it to the utmost. . . . They wear their professionalism as a decent gentleman will wear his suit: he will not let ruffians or circumstance tear it off him in the public gaze.

Stevens, in The Remains of the Day[1]

People are in general not candid over sexual matters. They do not show their sexuality freely, but to conceal it they wear a heavy overcoat woven of a tissue of lies.

Sigmund Freud, Five Lectures on Psychoanalysis[2]

I

Kazuo Ishiguro's *The Remains of the Day* is a profound novelistic exploration of narrator and narrative repression and of emotional fascism. Ishiguro's third, best-known, Booker Prize-winning novel is also a provocative examination of England's nostalgic, sentimental myths about its past and a commentary on its presently burgeoning "heritage industry." Like all of Ishiguro's protagonists, Stevens the butler, despite his ostensible eagerness to divulge his life story, works hard to conceal the alarming significance and troubling consequences of his past. Indeed, all of Ishiguro's first-person protagonists – Etsuko in *A Pale View of Hills* (1982; Winifred Holtby Prize of the Royal Society of Literature), Ono in *An Artist of the Floating World* (1986; Whitbread Book of the Year Award), Stevens in the present novel, Ryder in *The Unconsoled* (1995; Cheltenham Prize), and Christopher Banks in *When We Were Orphans* (2000;

Booker Prize finalist) – tell stories that mask or distort rather than uncover the most revealing implications of their tales. In *The Remains of the Day*, as in all of these works, one must read between the lines of the narrative to grasp its subtle meanings and hidden intentions. As one critic writes, "Few writers dare to say so little of what they mean as Ishiguro."[3] Salman Rushdie puts the serene surface yet disturbing depths of *The Remains of the Day* this way: "Just below the understatement of the novel's surface is a turbulence as immense as it is slow."[4] Ishiguro is above all a novelist of the unspoken.

II

The five novels by Ishiguro published in the period up to 2000 are intricately crafted, psychologically absorbing, hauntingly evocative works that betray the author's grounding not only in the realist European novelistic tradition (Ishiguro speaks often of his debt to Charlotte Brontë, Dickens, Chekhov, and Dostoyevsky) but in the discourse of modern psychology (before beginning to write fiction, Ishiguro was a social worker with the homeless in various Glasgow and London shelters). In all of these novels – whether the protagonist is a bereaved mother, an aging artist, a professional butler, a world-famous pianist, or a celebrated detective – the narrative moves back and forth seamlessly across events spanning several decades of the protagonist's life to form a vast web of personal and historical traumas. Whether these events take place in postwar Nagasaki, in an interwar England flirting with rising fascism, or in the war-torn, besieged Shanghai of the 1930s, it is always the central character's quietly anguished interior landscape upon which the novel's most compelling drama is enacted.

Ishiguro was born in Nagasaki, Japan, in 1954 and was raised and educated in England, his family having moved to Guildford, Surrey, after his father, an oceanographer, was hired to work on a North Sea oil project. Brought up as English by Japanese parents in a Japanese-speaking home, and hence feeling neither English nor Japanese, Ishiguro came to identify himself as an "international" or a "homeless writer," one who lacks a natural constituency or audience: "I had no clear role, no society or country to speak for or write about. Nobody's history seemed to be my history."[5] Kazuo studied English and philosophy as an undergraduate at the University of Kent, graduating in 1978, and then creative writing as a postgraduate with novelist-critic Malcolm Bradbury at the University of East Anglia, graduating in 1980. Ishiguro is now one of Britain's most celebrated contemporary novelists, and the author's acclaim extends far beyond the world of Anglophone readers. His works have been translated into twenty-eight foreign languages, and *The Remains of the Day*, in addition to being awarded the Booker Prize, was produced as a feature film by Merchant-Ivory Productions, in an adaptation by novelist Ruth Prawer Jhabvala. The 1993 film, which co-starred Anthony Hopkins and Emma Thompson, was nominated for eight Academy Awards, assuring the author an even wider global following.[6]

Ishiguro's first novel, *A Pale View of Hills*, concerns the post-World War II remembrances of a middle-aged Japanese woman, Etsuko, who has made a permanent move to a house in the English countryside. It focuses in particular on Etsuko's relationship with her two daughters (from two different marriages), one of whom has recently visited from London and the other has recently committed suicide. In the background lurks the nuclear devastation of Nagasaki and Etsuko's painful personal history. Ishiguro's second novel, *An Artist of the Floating World*, centers on an aging Japanese painter, Masuji Ono, who reminisces and agonizes over his career as artist in Japan during the war years. Like Etsuko, he has two daughters as well as unacknowledged regrets and unarticulated feelings of guilt about his earlier wartime activities. He too must alter his personal history in order to make it more palatable – for himself as well as for his readers. Ishiguro deems *The Remains of the Day*, his next novel, "more English than English,"[7] and reports having felt "a great sense of liberation" when moving his novelistic terrain from the Japan of his first two works to the England of his third. "There was a part of me that wanted to find out if my acceptance was conditioned on the fact that I was acting as mediator to Japanese culture. I wanted to see if people could appreciate me purely as a novelist as opposed to a Japanese novelist."[8]

Ishiguro's fourth novel, *The Unconsoled*, marks another significant shift in direction for its author. The work centers on a world-famous English pianist, Ryder, who visits an unidentified central European city for a few days in order to give a recital and to help the city resolve its nagging artistic and identity crises. This shift in Ishiguro's focus is not merely one of terrain – from Japan and England to continental Europe – but one of tone and temperament as well: in *The Unconsoled* the elegant Jamesian prose of the earlier novels gives way to a disturbing Kafkaesque dreamscape, just as the short and tightly-structured novel form is abandoned for a "baggy monster" of epic proportions. Yet even here self-deceptive memory, as in the earlier novels, takes center stage. Ishiguro's fifth novel, *When We Were Orphans*, bears a superficial resemblance to its predecessor and revisits certain themes and narrative devices found in the earlier three novels. Otherwise, it breaks new ground for its author. Christopher Banks, the thirty-something, ethnically English protagonist, tells of his childhood in Shanghai between 1910 and 1920: first recalling it in 1930, from London, to which he moved after losing his parents and in which he has established himself as "the most brilliant investigative mind in England"; and then in 1937, from Shanghai, where he returns after twenty-two years in the hope of solving the mystery of his missing parents and undoing his status as an orphan – a status that both haunts and defines him. Like Ishiguro's first novel, his fifth one may be viewed as a meditation on cultural and linguistic displacement, a phenomenon that recalls the author's own life experiences.

Ishiguro has received the Order of the British Empire (OBE) for services to literature (1995) as well as honorary doctorates from the two English universities he attended. He also has received Italy's Premio Scanno for Literature (1995) and was named a Chevalier dans l'Ordre des Arts et des Lettres by the French government. At present Ishiguro, who lives in greater London, divides his time between novel-writing and original screenplay work.

III

In a series of interviews he granted after the publication of *The Remains of the Day* (1989), Ishiguro revealed his own understanding of Mr Stevens, the novel's first-person protagonist and aging butler of Darlington Hall, who narrates his 1956 "expedition" to the English West Country against the backdrop of an even more significant journey: a journey into his past life at Darlington Hall during the politically turbulent 1920s and 1930s. In these interviews, Ishiguro emphasizes repeatedly Stevens's "suppression of emotion,"[9] his use of "memory" to "trip" himself up or to "hide" from himself and his past.[10] Stevens, Ishiguro contends,

> ends up saying the sorts of things he does because somewhere deep down he knows which things he has to avoid. . . . Why he says certain things, why he brings up certain topics at certain moments, is not random. It's controlled by the things that he doesn't say. That's what motivates the narrative. He is in this painful condition where at some level he does know what's happening, but he hasn't quite brought it to the front.[11]

Ishiguro here describes what Freud would call "repression," a function of the unconscious "that censors, displaces, and condenses dangerous material, driving it from the conscious into the unconscious."[12] Stevens is repressed in his sexual and political life: in his relationship with his co-worker Miss Kenton, a woman to whom he is deeply attracted, though he never admits it; and in his relationship with his two "fathers," his natural father, also a butler, and his employer and father-substitute, Lord Darlington, behind whom he hides his "political conscience" and on whom he bestows his uncritical loyalty. But while it is difficult to miss Stevens's repression, it is easy to over-look the myriad ways in which Stevens *conceals* his striking sexual and political disengagement, by clothing it under a "heavy overcoat woven of a tissue of lies."[13]

This concealment is first hinted at in the novel's Prologue, where Stevens initially considers a "five or six day" round-trip expedition to the West Country to visit Miss Kenton (now Mrs Benn), whom he has not seen in two decades. Here, Stevens muses on the matter of his traveling "costumes" (20), the "question of what sorts of costume" would be "appropriate on such a journey, and whether or not" it would be worth while investing "in a new set of clothes." Noting that he already possesses "a number of splendid suits, kindly passed on to me over the years by Lord Darlington himself," Stevens nevertheless worries that "many of these suits" may be "too formal for the purposes of the proposed trip, or else rather old fashioned these days" (10). Interestingly, this early, seemingly insignificant, reference to Stevens's "traveling costume" announces one of the novel's chief concerns and controlling metaphors: the literal and figurative ways by which the butler clothes his private self from his own understanding and from the "public gaze." More specifically, literal and figurative forms of clothing function to conceal – yet also, paradoxically, to reveal – Stevens's sexual and political repression to the extent that it is cloaked in the garb of "professional dignity." It is precisely this "dignity," after all, which in his view "comes down to not removing one's clothing in public" (210). As Stevens also tellingly insists at one point, "A butler of any quality must be seen to *inhabit* his role, utterly and fully; he cannot be seen casting it aside one moment simply to don it again the next as though it were nothing more than a pantomime costume" (169).[14]

Stevens's clothes conceal yet also paradoxically reveal his identity; clothes disguise the true nature and shape of the body, but they also serve as vehicles of self-expression in that something about identity is divulged in one's choice of attire. Similarly, Stevens's narrative "thread," his "public" presentation of his "private" life, functions as an attempt to clothe his sexual and political repression, however much it finally reveals about both. Indeed, his narrative (the novel itself) obscures as much as it illuminates the true nature of his earlier life at Darlington Hall and his present voyage west. Although Stevens remains largely oblivious of the idea, this physical trip, as figured and prefigured in the novel, is a voyage not only out of the house but out of his mental routine and psychological paralysis in search of amatory and political engage-ment. The journey, however, fails to accomplish its purpose, culminating not comically, in his new-found ability to cast off his "professional suit," but pathetically, in his reaffirmation of the necessity of wearing it at all times. Indeed, the nearly (spatially and temporally) circular novel closes on a note of "sorry disappointment" (245), with Stevens's projected return to Darlington Hall (without Miss Kenton and without a thorough reassessment of his role in Darlington's political blunders) and to the "professional" status quo ante.

Ishiguro's use of clothing metaphors is not original. As Marshall Berman observes, in modern culture "Clothes become an emblem of the old, illusory mode of life; nakedness comes to signify the newly discovered and experienced truth; and the act of taking off one's clothes becomes an act of spiritual liberation, of becoming real."[15] What *is* original about Ishiguro's use of clothing tropes is that Stevens conceals his sexual and political disengagement beneath his "professional suit" – that he hides his avoidance of amatory and social intimacy beneath the garb of his "professional demeanour" and "emotional restraint" (43). In this sense, it is no surprise that Stevens is incapable of removing what Rousseau calls "the uniform and deceptive veil of politeness" and instead insists upon wearing "mythic draperies heavy enough to stifle" his own self-knowledge.[16] However, Ishiguro is also original in that he invokes but then transforms the traditional English novelistic treatment of the relationship between servants and their aristocratic masters. Rather than cutting his master down to size in the eyes of the reader, Stevens instead idealizes Lord Darlington despite his familiarity with his superior's many patent faults. As Frank E. Huggett notes in *Life Below Stairs*, a study of domestic servants in England in the modern period, although some "Victorian servants seem to have had a genuine respect for aristocratic masters,"[17] many others were their "constant and inflexible judges." "Behind the servants' mask of perfect politeness and consummate gentility, there were dark thoughts and hidden feelings."[18] Salman Rushdie rightly characterizes *Remains* as "a brilliant subversion of the fictional modes from which it at first seems to descend";[19] put differently, the novel both "perfects and subverts" its own literary tradition.[20]

Before exploring the ways in which Stevens clothes his repression, it will be useful to examine the precise contours of this disengagement, "repression" having become, in John Kucich's words, "such a buzzword in the post-Freudian world that we rarely reflect on what we mean by it."[21] Freud defines "repression" as a device protecting "the mental personality," by which "forgotten memories" or "intolerable wishes" are originally "pushed" out of "consciousness." He defines the attendant phenomenon of "resistance" as that "force" which prevents these "intolerable wishes" from "becoming conscious" and compels them "to remain unconscious."[22] Freud further argues that the "forgotten material" originates in a wishful impulse which was in sharp contrast to the subject's other wishes and which proved incompatible with the ethical and aesthetic standards of his personality. There had been a short conflict, and ... the idea which had appeared before consciousness as the vehicle of this irreconcilable wish fell a victim to repression, was pushed out of consciousness with all its attached memories, and was forgotten ... An acceptance of the incompatible wishful impulse ... would have produced a high degree of unpleasure; this unpleasure was avoided by means of repression ...[23]

Put simply, the essence of repression "lies in turning something away, and keeping it at a distance," from conscious scrutiny.[24]

This "device" for protecting the "ethical and aesthetic standards of personality" illustrates nicely Stevens's ingrained habit of self-deception and self-censorship. The butler clearly represses his sexual attraction to Miss Kenton, a woman with whom he works "at close quarters ... during her maiden years" (47); represses his disappointment upon learning that she is engaged to be married to another (218); represses his "political conscience" through a total identification with his "master," Lord Darlington; and represses his emotional turmoil on the evening of his father's death, which he conflates with his successful professional trial-by-fire during that same evening at Lord Darlington's first international political conference – an evening which he now recalls, "for all of its sad associations," with "a large sense of triumph" (110). He at one point even represses his "disappointment" in his entire past, concluding, "Perhaps ... I should cease looking back so much" and instead "should adopt a more positive outlook and try to make the best of what remains of my day" (244).

Stevens betrays his inability to acknowledge what he has done, many times throughout the novel.[25] One striking example occurs in 1956 when Stevens is caught "denying" having known Lord Darlington during the era in which his master was, in effect, aiding and abetting Hitler's war effort. Once caught in this lie, Stevens lies again, rationalizing his betrayal with the claim that although his original explanation was "woefully inadequate," it was not "entirely devoid of truth": "I have chosen to tell white lies ... as the *simplest means of avoiding unpleasantness*" (my emphasis).[26] But "when one has so much else to think about," the butler adds soon afterwards, "it is easy not to give such matters a great deal of attention," and so I "put the whole episode out of my mind for some time" (125–6). At other points Stevens is seen *deliberately* refusing to face that which causes him pain, such as when, having run out of fuel, he walks through some muddy fields on the third evening of his journey and dirties the "turn-ups" of his trousers: "I deliberately refrained from shining my lamp on to my shoes and turn-ups for fear of further disappointment" (163). In another example, Stevens has the opportunity to comfort Miss Kenton after a death in her family, just as she has sought to comfort him on the death of his father. Kenton loses an aunt who is, "to all intents and purposes, like a mother to her" (176). However, rather than offering Kenton his "condolences," as he at first intends, Stevens excuses himself from such activity for fear of intruding "upon her private grief." The belief that she may have been "crying" provokes "a strange feeling to rise within" him, and he is reduced to standing "there hovering in the corridor" (176–7). And when he later catches up with her, he can only engage her in a "little professional discussion" during which he upbraids her for being "complacent" as regards some new employees under her charge (177–8).

Ishiguro has Stevens unwittingly and obliquely refer to the unconscious, painful issues that his conscious mind will not let itself address. Comments such as "I had become blind to the obvious" (5) and "I could gain little idea of what was around me" (117) abound, as do various visual metaphors for Stevens's lack of self- and world-engagement. The numerous references to "a mist rolling across" his path (160), "a mist" starting "to set in," a "mist" "thickening" and "encroaching," a "Great expanse of fog" (151–2) describe not only local meteorological conditions but Stevens's self-censoring, self-deceptive psychological orientation. In another example, his perceptions from the vantage point of old age sum up a melancholy life lived in isolation: it "was not a happy feeling to be up there on a lonely hill, looking over a gate at the lights coming on in a distant village, the daylight all but faded, and the mist growing ever thicker" (162). What the protagonist of Ishiguro's short story "Getting poisoned" says at one point applies equally well to Stevens's psychological predicament: "I don't want to think about things too much."[27]

More significantly, Stevens's sexual and political repression is figured on nearly every page of the novel. Near the beginning he is embarrassed by the way the new American owner of Darlington Hall, Mr Farraday, refers to Miss Kenton as his "lady-friend" and jokes about Stevens's sex-life (14–15). Throughout, Stevens never addresses Kenton other than by her family name, despite their "close working relationship" (234) for nearly fifteen years. To be fair, Stevens's sexual inhibitions reflect those of the culture at large. This is apparent when Sir David Cardinal asks Lord Darlington, who then asks Stevens, to explain "the facts of life . . . birds, bees" (82) to his 23-year-old son Reginald Cardinal before he is to be married ("Sir David has been attempting to tell his son the facts of life for the last five years" [82]). Unsurprisingly, Stevens is only too happy to escape this responsibility when "professional" obligations prevent him from carrying it out (85, 90).

The most striking instances of sexual repression in the novel occur in the Stevens–Kenton relationship. Stevens's fear of his own sexuality is associated with his dislike of flowers in his pantry; indeed, it is associated with his dislike of "distractions" there of any kind (52), which Kenton persists in supplying (he remembers Kenton trying "to introduce flowers to my pantry on at least three occasions over the years" [164]). Other attractive women are viewed by him as unbearable "distractions." Kenton observes that Stevens does "not like pretty girls on the staff," and then asks, "Might it be that our Mr. Stevens fears distractions? Can it be that our Mr. Stevens is flesh and blood after all and cannot fully trust himself?" (156).

The "turning point" in their relationship comes in the mid-1930s, when Kenton makes an unmistakable sexual "advance" on Stevens in his pantry. Arriving there with flowers (Stevens believes he remembers), Kenton – who is described as "advancing," "invading," and "pursuing" (166), as if she were trying to break into Stevens's pantry and rip off his clothes – asks to see the book Stevens is reading. Stevens responds by "clutching" the book to his "person" and insisting that she respect his "privacy" (166). Charging him with hiding his book because it is "something rather racy" and "shocking," she promises to leave him to the "pleasures" of his reading after he shows her his book. When she finally pries the book from his hands, revealingly, he judges "it best to look away while she did so" (166–7). She discovers, of course, that he is merely reading "a sentimental love story." His claim that he reads these romances strictly "to maintain and develop" his "command of the English language" (167) does not allay but rather heightens the reader's suspicion of his fear of his own sexuality. Caroline Patey here accuses Stevens of "impotence,"[28] but the evidence instead suggests repressed sexuality. This would also explain Stevens's monk-like existence, his choice of quarters, in Kenton's words, "so stark and bereft of colour" (52). In this connection, it is not surprising that Stevens possesses voyeuristic rather than exhibitionistic tendencies. At many points he listens in on others (94, 122, 171, 217), yet he always justifies this spying as prompted by "professional" considerations.

The parallel example of Stevens's political blindness occurs in the early 1930s. It is when Reginald Cardinal attempts to explain to Stevens that Lord Darlington is being maneuvered by the Nazis "like a pawn" (222), "the single most useful pawn Herr Hitler has had in this country for his propaganda tricks" (224). Naturally, Stevens does not want to acknowledge this, for, if true, it would render Stevens no more than the pawn of a pawn. Insisting that he does not see or notice what is really going on between Lord Darlington and the Germans (223, 224, 225), Stevens disowns his own political views, reasoning, "it is not my position to display curiosity about such matters" (222): "I have every trust in his lordship's good judgment" (225). Cardinal's response to Stevens – "you never think to *look* at it for what it is!" (223, my emphasis) – further emphasizes the butler's willed political blindness.[29]

Yet the clearest and most compelling example of Stevens's political repression is his total identification not with his lower-class natural father, who suffers both a literal fall (on Darlington's property) and a figurative one (in vocational status), but with his upper-class "cultural" father and master, Lord Darlington. It is clear that Stevens prefers his "gentleman" to his lower-class father, the latter of whom is depicted at one point "pushing a trolley loaded with cleansing utensils, mops, [and] brushes" that "resembled a street hawker's barrow" (78). Although Stevens emulates his natural father's "expression balanced perfectly between dignity and readiness to oblige" (38), his renewed contact with him at Darlington Hall, which begins in 1922, the year of Miss Kenton's arrival, nevertheless precipitates awkwardness and "an atmosphere of mutual embarrassment" (64).

That Stevens "substitutes" his adopted father for his actual one is made clear the night of his actual father's death, which coincides with the climax of his master's international conference. At first responding to his dying father's final words to him, "I hope I've been a good father to you," by nervously laughing and repeatedly saying, "I'm so glad you're feeling better now" (97), Stevens then quickly returns downstairs to his conference duties for his master. When his father dies later that evening, Stevens still claims not to have time for him, remarking to Kenton, who offers to close the dead butler's eyes, "Please don't think me unduly improper in not ascending the stairs to see my father in his deceased condition just at the moment. You see, I know my father would have wished me to carry on just now." He then adds, "To do otherwise, I feel, would be to let him down" (196). But by this point the reader is unsure whether the "him" Stevens wishes not to disappoint is his birth or his class father.

David Gurewich is thus correct but does not go far enough when he notes that "it is only through his master that Stevens manages to establish his own worth."[30] Indeed, Stevens's willingness to be a pawn of a pawn of Hitler betokens not any fascistic political leanings on his part but rather an "emotional fascism": an extreme, even perverse identification with his father-substitute. Appropriately, Stevens inherits many of Lord Darlington's "splendid suits" over the years (10), just as he dons his master's political beliefs. Moreover, Stevens "becomes" an aristocrat merely by following orders. As he explains to Miss Kenton,

[M]y vocation will not be fulfilled until I have done all I can to see his lordship through the great tasks he has set himself. The Day his lordship's work is complete, the day *he* is able to rest on his laurels, content in the knowledge that

> he has done all anyone could ever reasonably ask of him, only on that day . . . will I be able to call myself . . . a well-contented man. (173)

Surprisingly, Stevens's identification with his employer reaches its culminating point *after* Lord Darlington's death, when Stevens allows others to take him for a gentleman rather than the servant of a gentleman (184–8). Reginald Cardinal at one point tells Stevens that Darlington has "been like a second father to me" (221), yet it is even more truly the case for the butler to whom he speaks.

Having observed Stevens's amatory and political disengagement, it remains to discover the means by which the butler attempts to clothe this disengagement – to cover it up or justify it to himself and to his audience – beneath his "professional suit." In an interview Ishiguro commented of *The Remains of the Day*, "It seemed to me appropriate to have somebody who wants to be this perfect butler because that seems to be a powerful metaphor for someone who is trying to actually erase the emotional part of him that may be dangerous and that could really hurt him in his professional area."[31] This remark is misleading. Rather than viewing Stevens's emotional life as a threat to his professional life, it is far more convincing to view his obsession with "professional dignity" as an excuse to remain sexually and politically disengaged; and the obsession with his "professional suit" as an emblem of his desire to keep this repression under wraps. Stevens sublimates his sexual and political instincts by directing them to a higher and consequently unobjectionable purpose: his professional life. Hence, it is no coincidence that Stevens likens one who cannot "maintain a professional demeanour" to "a man who will, at the slightest provocation, tear off his suit and his shirt and run about screaming" (43). Cynthia F. Wong writes that "Stevens's motor trip" is a "journey reflecting on his repressed love for Miss Kenton . . . which had resulted from his loyalty to Lord Darlington."[32] Rather, Stevens's "professionalism" is best understood as a means of defending himself against "the messiness of life: sex, marriage, personal interests";[33] it is the "wall" he "labors to construct" against "his regrets,"[34] and not the other way around.[35]

There is much evidence of Stevens "clothing" his sexual disengagement beneath his professional costume – his "professional viewpoint" (48), "professional matters" (165), or "professional ambition" (115). It is clear that he views romantic encounters, with their anarchic, emotionally intimate, informal natures – during which clothing, after all, is often removed – to be a grave threat to the "professional order" of the house. Nothing saddens him more, he admits, than his memory of a housekeeper and an under-butler on his staff deciding "to marry one another and leave the profession": "I have always found such liaisons a serious threat to the order in a house." In particular,

Stevens views as a "blight on good professionalism" those "persons – and housekeepers [that is to say, women] are particularly guilty here – who have no genuine commitment to their profession and who are essentially going from post to post looking for romance" (50–1). Kenton highlights the mutually exclusive nature of professional and romantic life when she asks exclaims (with some irony) to the unattached Stevens: "Here you are . . . at the top of your profession, every aspect of your domain well under control. I really cannot imagine what more you might wish for in life" (173).

Particularly notable is the way in which Stevens uses his professional identity as a means of masking his obvious attraction to Miss Kenton – obvious to readers even if not to himself. When she begins taking days off from Darlington Hall for the first time, for example, Stevens admits,

> I found it hard to keep out of my mind the possibility that the purpose of these mysterious outings of Miss Kenton was to meet a suitor. This was indeed a *disturbing notion*, for it was not hard to see that Miss Kenton's departure would constitute *a professional loss* of some magnitude. (171, my emphasis)

Stevens repeatedly and defensively justifies his and Kenton's evening cocoa sessions in the "privacy of Miss Kenton's parlour" as "overwhelmingly professional in tone" (147), as "essentially professional" in character (157), and as exclusively for purposes of "professional communication" (174). But when she enters *his* pantry uninvited – a pantry in which all things must be "ordered – and left ordered – in precisely the way I wish them to be" (165) – revealing her attraction to him, and forcing him to reveal that he reads romance novels there, he resolves "to set about reestablishing" their "professional relationship on a more proper basis" (169). And things have not changed twenty years later when Stevens hides his "growing excitement" (12) at the prospect of taking the car-trip to see her once again beneath the garb of "professional matters" (5), that is, the "professional motive" of re-staffing Darlington Hall: "I would expect our interview . . . to be largely professional in character" (180). Stevens even worries that he has exaggerated the evidence in her letter that she wishes to return to "service" at Darlington Hall, calling it "wishful thinking of a professional kind" (140).[36]

Ishiguro contends that his "butler is a good metaphor for the relationship of very ordinary, small people to power,"[37] which announces the other major item Stevens hides under the folds of his "professional suit": a repressed "political conscience." Insisting that a butler's "professional prestige" lies "most significantly in the moral worth" of his employer (114), and that, as a professional, he serves "humanity" (117) by serving "the great gentlemen of our times in whose hands civilization" has been "entrusted" (116), Stevens contends that "a butler's duty is to provide good service. It is not to meddle in the great affairs of the nation" (199). For "it is, in practice, simply not possible to adopt . . . a critical attitude towards an employer and at the same time provide good service"; a butler "who is forever attempting to formulate his own 'strong opinions' on his employer's affairs is bound to lack one quality essential in all good professionals: namely, loyalty" (200). Stevens's sacrifice of his "political conscience" to his "professional loyalty" is revealed no more clearly than when he remembers that Darlington alone made the decisions "while I simply confined myself, quite properly, to affairs within my own professional realm" (201).

Stevens's political capitulation might have remained insignificant, at least morally speaking, were it not for Lord Darlington's flirtation, in the early 1930s, with anti-Semitism, and his decision, "for the good of this house" (146), to dismiss two maids from his staff purely on the grounds that they are Jewish. Naturally, it falls to Stevens to do the firing, forcing him to "cross the fine line between the loyalty that is the essence of his professionalism and the blind obedience of 'just following orders'."[38] And while Stevens claims that "my every instinct opposed the idea of their dismissal," he nevertheless also reasons that "my duty in this instance was quite clear . . . there was nothing to be gained at all in irresponsibly displaying such personal doubts. It was a difficult task, but . . . one that demanded to be carried out with dignity" (148). Raising the matter with Miss Kenton in a "businesslike" way, Stevens counsels her, "we must not allow sentiment to creep into our judgment" (148): "our professional duty is not to our own foibles and sentiments, but to the wishes of our employer" (149).

As for Darlington himself, it is hinted that his "going to bed with Hitler" (politically speaking) is motivated by his homoerotic feelings for the aristocratic German Herr Bremann. Bremann, we read,

> first visited Darlington Hall very shortly after the [Great] war while still in his officer's uniform, and it was evident to any observer that he and Lord Darlington had struck up a close friendship. . . . He returned again . . . at fairly regular intervals. . . . It must have been towards the end of 1920 that Lord Darlington made the first of a number of trips to Berlin. (71)

Further, when Darlington talks about his German friend, his voice resounds "with intensity" (73). Although this German officer is apparently married, Darlington is never able "to discover the whereabouts of any of Herr Bremann's family" (74). And Stevens describes Darlington's international conferences by reference to the "unbroken lines of gentlemen in evening suits, so outnumbering representatives of the fairer sex" (98), and to the "rather feminine room crammed full with so many stern, dark-jacketed gentlemen, sometimes sitting three or four abreast upon a sofa" (92).[39]

Stevens also uses language and memory itself to clothe a painful reality – and wasted life – from scrutiny. Like Joseph Conrad, who associates "words" with "mist" and comments, "like mist, [words] serve only to obscure, to make vague the real shape of one's feelings,"[40] Ishiguro states of the language of his novel, "I'm interested in the way words hide meaning . . . The language I use tends to be the sort that actually suppresses meaning and tries to hide away meaning."[41] Elsewhere Ishiguro puts this even more baldly: *The Remains of the Day* "is written in the language of self-deception."[42]

Readers have noted that Stevens is "a great manipulator of language,"[43] that he uses "his words and his narrative to convey information to us of which he is unaware."[44] Most significantly, Stevens can talk about himself only when he talks about others; when he talks about himself directly, he is compelled to lie. As with the route of his meandering car-trip, his story itself might seem "unnecessarily circuitous" (67), but that is precisely the point: his narrative intentionally impedes his voyage of self-discovery. For example, when Stevens concludes that Lord Darlington's "life and work have turned out today to look, at best, a sad waste" (201), or that Kenton's life has come to be "dominated by a sense of waste" (48), he in fact describes his own "life and work"; when he addresses Kenton's "guilt" at helping to precipitate his father's decline in professional status at Darlington Hall (66–7), he addresses his own; when he speaks of Kenton's "nostalgia" for the Darlington Hall of the old days (49, 180), he accurately reveals his own nostalgia; when he refers to Kenton's "sadness" and "weariness" (233), he instead registers his own ("you do not seem to have been happy over the years," he tells her [238]). When Stevens remarks that Kenton undoubtedly "is pondering with regret decisions made in the far-off past that have now left her, deep in middle age, so alone and desolate," and that "the thought of returning to Darlington Hall" must therefore be "a great comfort to her" (48), it is clear of whom he really speaks.[45]

Stevens also uses what he calls the "hindsight colouring" his "memory" (87) as a means of clothing his disengagement. He often uses the present to escape a failed past; at others times he uses the past to escape a failed present.[46] In either case, Stevens's ability always to be somewhere that he is not allows him to live what might be called a vicarious existence during the 1920s, 1930s, and 1940s. It is only in 1956, after all, that he ventures forth from Darlington Hall to see England "at first hand" (28) rather than through "Mrs. Jane Symons's *The Wonder of England*" (11); it is only then that he actively seeks the company of a woman rather than reading "sentimental" love stories from Darlington's romance collection "about ladies and gentlemen who fall in love and express their feelings for each other" (167–8); and it is only at that time that he seeks to engage his "political conscience" rather than blindly follow Darlington's lead. In this way, Stevens's trip to the West Country promises to be an act of self-liberation following a life of self-imprisonment (Kenton tellingly likens Stevens's quarters to "a prison cell," a place "one could well imagine condemned men spending their last hours" [165]; and Farraday rebukes Stevens, "You fellows, you're always locked up in these big houses helping out" [4]). Stevens's present voyage to the West may even be understood as his first (semi-conscious) attempt to engage the muted erotic and political sides of his character.

Indeed, Stevens's journey is figured as an attempt to break out of the house, out of himself, and out of his physical and psychical routine – to overcome his amatory and political disengagement – in the guise of a "pleasure" trip with business implications, the "professional motive" of re-staffing Darlington Hall (13). In this sense, the entire novel, which begins with the sentence, "It seems increasingly likely that I really will undertake the expedition that has been preoccupying my imagination now for some days" (3), concerns Stevens's present attempt to change his life after years of unacknowledged unhappiness, to gain self- and world-knowledge to supplement his "house knowledge" (54). Veiled references to the deeper significance of his proposed trip to the West of England – like Gabriel Conroy's proposed trip to the West of Ireland in Joyce's "The dead," replete with sexual and political undertones – are in pro-fusion. In both fictions, a physical voyage is associated with the protagonist's increased understanding of himself and the world. As Stevens himself seems to detect of his own case, "it is perhaps in the nature of coming away on a trip such as this that one is prompted toward such surprising new perspectives on topics one imagined one had long ago thought through thoroughly" (117).

That the butler's physical departure from Darlington Hall is also a psycho-logical one is suggested early on in *Remains*. Stevens, we read, "motored further and further from the house" until the "surroundings grew strange" around him. "But then eventually the surroundings grew unrecognizable" and he knew that he had "gone beyond all previous boundaries." The psycho-logical dimension of this physical description soon becomes unmistakable: "The feeling swept over me that I had truly left Darlington Hall behind, and I must confess I did feel a *slight sense of alarm*" (23–4, my emphasis). Of course, Stevens would never have ventured forth from Darlington Hall during the time when Darlington himself lorded over the house; it is the new American owner, Farraday, who urges Stevens to "get out of the house for a few days" (4). That Stevens initially finds this proposal extravagant is underscored by the fact that he worries that such a "journey" may keep him away from Darlington Hall "for as much as five or six days" (3).[47]

Despite Stevens's half-acknowledged desire to throw off the yoke of his repression, however, he ultimately resists the temptation. In the novel's own metaphor, the butler is involved in a struggle between the side of him that wishes to cast off his clothing and the side that wishes to keep it securely wrapped about him. There is much evidence of this internal conflict. Not only does Stevens, during his journey, refrain from exploring some beautiful English countryside for fear of "sustaining damage" to his "traveling suit" (121), but he at first responds negatively to Farraday's proposal that he take the trip to see his own country, countering, "It has been my privilege to see the best of England over the years" right within the walls of Darlington Hall itself (4). He adds that he remains reluctant "to change too much of the old ways" (7) and that "strange beds have rarely agreed" with him (47).

Stevens does not ultimately succeed in overcoming his repression. On the political front, he does not gain true insight about his own political disengagement; there is no change in what David Gurewich calls "Stevens's lack of awareness of the world outside his master's estate."[48] Specifically, his encounter with the middle-class Harry Smith, who represents democratic "political conscience" (209), who has strong political "opinions," and who therefore stands in stark contrast to the politically disengaged Stevens, makes no impact on the butler whatsoever. While the "common" Smith remarks that "it's one of the privileges of being born English that no matter who you are, no matter if you're rich or poor, you're born free and you're born so that you can express your opinion freely, and vote in your member of Parliament or vote him out" (186), that "England's a democracy, and . . . it's up to us to exercise our rights, everyone of us" (189), Stevens stubbornly adheres to his earlier elitist and oligarchic perspective: "There is, after all, a real limit to how much ordinary people can learn and know, and to demand that each and every one of them contribute 'strong opinions' to the great debates of the nation cannot, surely, be wise" (194). Smith also contends that protecting democracy is "what we fought Hitler for": If "Hitler had had things his way, we'd just be slaves now" (186). This comment is more telling of Stevens's situation than either realizes: Stevens indirectly worked for Hitler and directly worked to maintain his status as a "slave," at least intellectually-speaking, of Lord Darlington.

That Stevens fails to overcome his sexual repression is equally clear. This failure is mirrored in the "ferocious downpour" of rain, the "ominous stormclouds," the "gloomy" light, and the subsequent "drizzle" (232, 238) that surround the present meeting between Stevens and Kenton. It is appropriate that rain falls when they meet, just as it does on Gabriel and Gretta in Joyce's "The dead," in which precipitation foreshadows a downpour of tears betokening a love affair that pales in comparison with what it might have been. The entire novel prepares its readers for the Stevens–Kenton encounter which, however "pleasant" he claims it to be, is a brief, uneventful disappointment: rather than returning to service at Darlington Hall, Kenton vows instead to return to her husband from whom she has been separated.

Ironically, given the expectations that the novel raises in its readers, the gap between Stevens's private belief and public expression – his inner feeling and outer demeanor – is never so wide as in this final chapter. There, Stevens consistently calls his former co-worker "Mrs. Benn" to her face but "Miss Kenton" to himself; and he literally "smiles" at her even though his "heart" is "breaking" (239). This duplicity helps the forlorn Stevens convince us (and himself) that, despite a clearly failed excursion and failed life, "there is plenty of daylight left" – that "the evening" may well be "the best part of the day" (240). Although he breaks down when speaking with a retired butler whom he encounters two days after his meeting with Kenton, lamenting that he "gave it all to Lord Darlington" who "at least" had "the privilege of being able to say at the end of his life that he made his own mistakes" (243), Stevens nevertheless insists that his tears are the result of the fatigue that follows traveling: "I'm so sorry, this is so unseemly. I suspect I'm over-tired. I've been traveling rather a lot, you see" (244). He then adds:

> Surely it is enough that the likes of you and I at least *try* to make our small contribution count for something true and worthy. And if some of us are prepared to sacrifice much in life in order to pursue such aspirations, surely that is in itself, whatever the outcome, cause for pride and contentment. (244)

Stevens's concluding thoughts may strike the reader as surprising. After all, he has voyaged such a long way to go nowhere at all (Stevens's car journey forms a giant circle across southwest England, suggesting in geographical terms that he is merely going around in circles or "spinning his wheels" in personal or psychological terms). His thoughts are surprising only until they are viewed within the context of his failure to overcome his disengagement, his failure to cast off the "professional suit" that is a metaphor for his repression.

However, Stevens does make one new resolution that might appear to be a viable way for him to gain necessary emotional intimacy with others: he will learn to "banter," to engage in conversations of "a light-hearted, humorous sort" (13). In "bantering," Stevens now contends, "lies the key to human warmth" (245). But while Stevens is not being ironic here, Ishiguro undoubtedly is. For Stevens's new resolution promises not to be a panacea for his sense of emptiness and loneliness. Like Stevens's first-person narrative style itself, which, as Ishiguro writes, is as much a "form of cowardice" as dignity, "a way of actually hiding from what is perhaps the scariest arena in life, which is the emotional arena,"[49] bantering actually precludes rather than enables the "human warmth" that Stevens now seeks. This is suggested by a standard ancillary definition of "bantering," "to delude or trick, especially by way of jest." For this secondary definition, bantering functions less to promote intimacy than to maintain distance. *The Remains of the Day* thus ends neither comically nor tragically (despite the deathly resonance of the novel's title)[50] but on a pathetic and ironic note, as "old habits" of Stevens's "mind reassert themselves in a new guise."[51]

The Remains of the Day is one of the most profound novelistic representations of repression masquerading as professionalism, yet it is also aimed at an entire nation's mythical self-identity. Indeed, the novel associates Stevens's deceptive self-conception with that of England's at large. Stevens equates the significance of events in Darlington Hall with those in England generally, confuses "house knowledge" with world knowledge, and moves freely between the subject of what makes a "great butler" great and what makes "Great Britain" great, arguing that both exhibit "calmness" and a "sense of restraint" (28–9). And Stevens clearly equates a decline in the status of Darlington Hall[52] with the decline of English prestige, with the postwar Americanization of England,[53] and with what David Gurewich calls "the disintegration of the good old world where Stevens and his ideals held value."[54] (It is surely no coincidence that the present of the novel is set in July of 1956, the time of the Suez crisis, "a turning point for the British Empire,"[55] which decisively marked the end of England's claim to world military supremacy.) Yet if Stevens exhibits nostalgia for this "good old world" of "grand old English houses," *The Remains of the Day* does not. Rather, Ishiguro's novel exhibits only a *mock* nostalgia, one that throws into question the "good old world" and the grandeur of Stevens's "professional dignity" as much as it does England's recently burgeoning heritage industry. As Ishiguro himself maintains,

> The kind of England that I create in *The Remains of the Day* is not an England that I believe ever existed. . . . What I'm trying to do there . . . is to actually rework a particular myth about a certain kind of mythical England. . . . an England with sleepy, beautiful villages with very polite people and butlers . . . taking tea on the lawn. . . . The mythical landscape of this sort of England, to a large degree, is harmless nostalgia for a time that didn't exist. The other side of this, however, is that it is used as a political tool. . . . It's used as a way of bashing anybody who tries to spoil this "Garden of Eden."[56]

Clearly, Ishiguro "undermines" this particular ideal of England by showing how the soil in this "Garden of Eden" could nourish the seeds of a destructive fascism, and how the protagonist's professionalism – which nurtures those same seeds – could mask a paralyzing emotional and political disengagement.

Chapter 10

Patrick McCabe's
The Butcher Boy (1992)

As to our city of *Dublin*; Shambles [slaughterhouses] may be appointed for this Purpose, in the most convenient Parts of it; and Butchers we may be assured will not be wanting; although I rather recommend buying the Children alive, and dressing them hot from the Knife, as we do *roasting Pigs* . . .
Jonathan Swift, "A modest proposal"[1]

Ireland is the old sow that eats her farrow.
James Joyce, *A Portrait of the Artist as a Young Man*[2]

It was a good song but I didn't know what was going on in it.
Francie, on the song "The Butcher Boy," in *The Butcher Boy*[3]

I

The Butcher Boy, by Irish novelist Patrick McCabe, is a tour-de-force of linguistic verve and black comedy. Winner of the *Irish Times* Literature Award in 1992 and shortlisted for the Booker Prize the same year, McCabe's novel was filmed by Neil Jordan in 1996, bringing *The Butcher Boy* and its author to the attention of a wider audience. McCabe's novel is at once a first-person Irish *Bildungsroman* – it has been called a sort of "Irish *Huckleberry Finn*"[4] – and a "chronicle of cultural and artistic responses to the clash between colonizer and colonized, tradition and modernity, sacred and secular, ancient Celtic tradition and American popular culture."[5] Set in 1962, the year of the Cuban Missile Crisis and of the introduction of Ireland's national television service, in an unnamed rural village that closely resembles the Irish border town of Clones, approximately 60 miles from Dublin and the place of McCabe's birth and upbringing, *The Butcher Boy* was the author's third and breakthrough novel.[6] This work is narrated retrospectively, from the perspective of many years later, by Francie Brady, who appears to be roughly 12 years old during the vast majority of the novel's action. The only child of a terminally alcoholic father and a suicidally depressed mother, both of whom die in the course of the novel, Francie is abandoned to an unchecked fantasy life that segues into outright hallucination, paranoia, and, eventually, a gruesome act of murder. *The Butcher Boy* is far more than a portrait of an unstable boy within an impoverished and dysfunctional family, however; it is also a searing portrait of a society that fails to address the well-being of its children when the parents in question are neglectful, abusive, or mentally ill. Indeed, Francie may be seen as an objective correlative for that society.[7]

II

McCabe was born in Clones, Co. Monaghan (in the Republic but near the Northern Irish border) in 1955. He was raised in this town, where his cultural diet, like Francie's, consisted of British comic books and Hollywood films. Although it would be inaccurate to view Francie as a narrowly autobiographical character, he does share certain attributes with his creator. Like Francie, McCabe lived in the vicinity of an abattoir,[8] had an accomplished trumpeter for a father, and characterized the family life of his youth as "outwardly quite normal" but "inwardly – fireworks, catastrophic domestic stuff and all that."[9] McCabe's childhood is an informing context for Francie's, then, much as James Joyce's youth can be said to inform Stephen Dedalus's in *A Portrait of the Artist as a Young Man*.

McCabe attended, successively, the local national school, the boarding school at St Macartan's College in Monaghan, and St Patrick's teacher Training College in Dublin. He then accepted a series of teaching positions (during which time he also played keyboards in local country-and-western pick-up bands). In 1985 McCabe moved to London, where, until 1993, he taught school during the day and wrote fiction at night. The success of *The Butcher Boy* allowed McCabe to move back to Ireland and devote himself to writing full time. McCabe is also the author of five other novels, most notably *The Dead School* (1995) and *Breakfast on Pluto* (1998; shortlisted for the Booker Prize), as well as a short story cycle, *Mondo Desperado* (1999). McCabe presently lives and works in the Irish west coast town of Sligo.

McCabe's fiction frequently invites comparisons with James Joyce's. Specifically, *The Butcher Boy*'s linguistic effervescence and penetrating critique of Irish society echo Joyce's in *Dubliners* and *A Portrait of the Artist as a Young Man*. Although McCabe claims never to have been "consciously aware of belonging to any [literary] tradition"[10] and eschews Joyce's "Parnassian disposition,"[11] it is obvious that he is writing in the wake of this giant of modernist Irish prose fiction. The numerous allusions to Joyce's works in *The Butcher Boy* only confirm this notion.[12]

McCabe does admit to being "attracted to Joyce"[13] and remembers "picking up a copy of *Dubliners*" and thinking, "[t]his could have been written yesterday" – a judgment that McCabe extends to no other canonical work of Irish fiction. Somehow, "the sheer brilliance, the art of Joyce made it seem so contemporary, it was absolutely mindblowing." McCabe also aspires in his work to achieve "the intellectual Joyce, the sheer vision of it, and combine that with the humanity and language."[14] To that end, McCabe in *The Butcher Boy*, like Joyce before him, eschews quotation marks to denote spoken dialogue and aims to keep punctuation to a bare minimum. Indeed, McCabe's goal in this novel might be regarded as quintessentially Joycean: to "reinvent the language" so that readers can "feel the white heat of it" and the "sheer intensity of the [underlying] feeling."[15]

McCabe's language, like Joyce's, combines vibrancy and precision. Francie's punctuation-less "cavalry charge of words coming out of my mouth I didn't know where they were all coming from" (196), for example, recalls Molly Bloom's soliloquy in *Ulysses*, which, for all its verbal pyrotechnics, never relinquishes verbal discipline. It is difficult not to think of Joyce's prose when reading Francie's, as the following example suggests:

> This is a grand house I says to myself. Black kettle on the hob and a settle bed in the corner and looking out from under it Mr Chinese Eyes the cat glaring what are you doing here who the hell asked you in . . . ! Here you are now she [the lady of the house] says man dear I said that's the best cut bread ever and sank my teeth into it, gurgle more tea into the cup. (183)

Like Joyce's, McCabe's prose does not merely describe a scene; it performs it.

As important as Joyce's linguistic influence on McCabe is his thematic one; Francie's situation resembles that of many of Joyce's protagonists in *Dubliners*, who are disappointed, betrayed, or abused in one or more ways by their family, church, or nation, and who make paralyzing promises to neglectful parents in order to assuage their paradoxiacal feelings of guilt. In McCabe's satires, as in Joyce's, individual foibles and flaws are invariably used to probe more broadly sociocultural ones.

III

One of the most engaging aspects of McCabe's *The Butcher Boy* is first-person protagonist Francie's humorous, perceptive, and penetrating – yet also frequently crazed, disturbing, and radically unreliable – narrative voice, which is filtered through Francie's movie and comic book-saturated mind. Francie's narration combines the naïve and innocent charm of Mark Twain's Huck Finn with the jaded, experienced voice of a hardened criminal. It is retrospective, told from the standpoint of decades later; and the double perspective this affords – Francie is implicitly both commenting on his youthful experience and living within the white hot moment of it – lends the narrative its peculiar resonance and power.

Despite Francie's questionable mental balance, his keen eye for observation and detail and his potent sense of humor squarely hit their targets. The statue of Daniel O'Connell in Dublin, for example, is described as "A big grey statue mouthing about something in the middle of the street and birds shitting all over his head" (40), while "a big picture of Our Lord hanging on the wall" of a television store is imagined to say *"Buy a television or else you bastard!* No it didn't it said Our Saviour looks after us all" (107). At another point we read, "Off I went down the fresh, crunchy lane" (106), which both describes and, aurally-speaking, performs the moment. Francie often views things in obviously cartoon terms, which leads him to adopt pithy names and descriptions. For example, he takes to calling a priest with a "big bubble head" with whom he deals – a "man made of bubbles in charge of a school for bad boys" – "Father Bubble" (71); and a police sergeant assigned to Francie reminds him of Sausage the Clown and so gains the alliterative epithet "Sergeant Sausage" (70). Not all of Francie's humorous descriptions are intentional, however; some appear to be the result of the normal confusions of childhood. In one such example – which echoes his own desire to aid his ailing, trumpet-playing father – Francie notices an RCA Victor advertisement in a music shop depicting a dog "staring into a trumpet, trying to find his master's voice. I'm in here get me out Fido says the master. How says Fido. How do I know says the master just do it will you my best little pet dog?" (194).

John Scaggs observes "the spectre of narrative unreliability" haunting McCabe's novel from start to finish;[16] and indeed Francie proves to be an "unreliable" narrator of colossal proportions. In Wayne Booth's influential definition of the term, an "unreliable narrator" is one who fails to speak for or act in accordance with the norms of the work and who therefore is ironized by the work.[17] More than is true of most (even "unreliable") narrators, the meaning of Francie's narrative is not what he understands it to be. We can gauge that many of his "most poignant personal memories and stories" are "fabrications"[18] by virtue of the response of others to Francie's actions, even if Francie fails to comprehend this. Put differently, although the novel is comprised of Francie's first-person narration, this is not to say that his story's meaning and implications are within his grasp. What Francie says about the song "The Butcher Boy" may be taken as an emblem of his limited grasp of his own narrative at large: "It was a good song but I didn't know what was going on in it" (20).

In a study of first-person narrators David Goldknopf writes that I-narrators tend either to "haul us immediately into the narrative situation" through a "direct appeal for our attention," or to "intervene *between* us and the narrative situation, forcing us always to evaluate the latter *through*" them, rendering the "operation" of their minds "the true subject matter of the story."[19] In Francie's case – unlike that of Stevens in Ishiguro's *The Remains of the Day* or of Dowell in Ford Madox Ford's *The Good Soldier*, for example – the narrative unreliability stems less from the protagonist's repression[20] than from the protagonist's abuse and neglect at the hands of his parents. It is this abuse and neglect that, with the help of stout, whiskey, or drugs, occasion his flights of fancy and fantasy. Francie may believe that it is "better to be straight with people" (126) than not, but "straight" is a far cry from what Francie is with his readers – and with himself – in his wildly humorous but deeply disturbing narrative.

One example of Francie's creative misreading of events is contained in his description of his drunk father, who apparently has spilt whiskey on himself. When the whiskey spills "down his trouser leg," Francie reports that his father watches it

> dribble until it reached the floor parting into twin rivers on the lino. It went right across as far as the bottom of the door. He kept looking at it as if there was some hidden meaning in the pattern it was making. Then he started crying, his whole body shuddering with each sob. (38)

What Francie here describes is in all likelihood his father urinating on himself rather than spilling whiskey on himself; this far more painful interpretation of the scene before him is not one that Francie will allow himself to grasp.

A portion of the narrative's unreliability stems from what Donna Potts calls Francie's "*post hoc, ergo propter hoc* logic,"[21] his logically-challenged explanations of events. For example, the breakdown of Francie's family harmony is traced to the breakdown of the family television ("It was all going well until the telly went" [10]); at another point, Francie comes to believe that one friend's gift of a goldfish to another, which in fact follows from their friendship, is the cause of this friendship. Francie obsesses over this gift of a fish, which keeps swimming into view – "The more I tried to get the goldfish out of my head the more it kept coming back" (100) – as if it has talismanic power and can single-handedly make or break a friendship. Another object that Francie imagines has talismanic power is the gift – a wooden plaque with the words, "A Mother's love's a blessing no matter where you roam" (44) – he buys for his mother during his short-lived escape to Dublin after the family's bitter Christmas argument. Upon arriving home he learns that his mother has committed suicide and that he is too late to give her the gift. Before this fully sinks in, however, Francie comforts himself by feeling "the present inside" his pocket and by thinking, "It's OK. Everything's OK now" (44).

Francie's narrative unreliability is also explained by his "out of sight, out of mind" logic: his sense that the mere passing of time, which allows for the forgetting of upsetting occurrences, can cure all ills. For example, on one occasion Francie knows "that in a couple of days everything would be all right again" (121), and, on another, explains, "I left it for a few days so that it would all be forgotten" (122). A similar form of denial is contained in his fantasy that he can "fix" his falling out with his friend Joe by fixing it in his head, and so he "blank[s] it out so that it hadn't happened" (113). A simple mental alteration, he seems to believe, will put things "back the way" they "used to be" (115) between the two of them, just as it will between Francie and his parents: "Everything was starting again and this time it was all going to work out right" (19). Like Gatsby in Fitzgerald's novel, Francie imagines that he can alter the past and rewrite his personal history simply by mental fiat.

More alarming even than Francie's logical lapses are his daydreams that segue into full-blown paranoid hallucinations and psychotic breaks. To add insult to injury, Francie at points is unaware where his waking life ends and his fantasy life begins, posing a particular challenge to the reader's desire to reconstruct what is really happening. While it is true that not everything Francie says should be discounted, it is also true that, more than in most first-person narratives, we are "denied an anchoring or validating other voice, a reality against which to compare Francie's narrative."[22] We know, for example, that his dialogue with snowflakes is imagined ("the first dusty flakes of snow were starting to fall. We're early this year they said" [18]); what we do not know is whether this imagining represents boyish whimsicality or mental pathology.

McCabe has characterized the culture of his youth as both impoverished and "brutalised"; "there's no question" that in the small town of his upbringing "there was a deep hurt at all levels of society."[23] This is certainly true of Francie's upbringing as well. In contrast to the middle-class ideal of home life that was promoted by Irish President Eamon de Valera in his 1943 radio address – an Ireland "bright with cosy homesteads . . . whose firesides would be forums for the wisdom of serene old age"[24] – home in *The Butcher Boy* is a "thoroughly pathologized site."[25] Francie's home, which lacks any sense of order or security, is a site of unending conflict between his father and mother, his father and uncle, and his father and himself. The myth of middle-class Irish domestic life, "de Valera's vision of near Edenic wholeness and simplicity"[26] – the ideal that Francie yearns for – clash profoundly with the reality of domestic life for the Bradys: abject poverty, female depression, male alcoholism, and domestic violence. Francie frequently overhears the fights between his parents and tries, unsuccessfully, to tune them out. One of his many strategies of defense against such conflict is to "listen to the cars going by on the Newton Road." Yet when Francie stops "listening to the cars I'd hear him: God's curse the fucking day I ever set eyes on you!" (7)

The fights between his parents, Benny and Annie Brady, are both frequent and brutal. Benny constantly reminds Annie of his own father's abandonment of his family when he was 7 years old and accuses her of not understanding him and of losing interest "in his music long ago." He then accuses his wife of being "mad" like everyone in her family and of "lying about the house from the day they married never did a hand's turn why wouldn't he go to the pubs she had never made a dinner for him in his life?" (6). Her likely truthful reply to him, "Don't blame me because you can't face the truth about yourself, any chances you had you drank them away!" (7), only further fuels the fire of his belligerence.

Though he never admits it, Francie reveals that his mother, who frequently appears drugged and manic, has been deeply disappointed and traumatized by his father, and may even have become suicidally depressed because of his misery and misfortune. Revealingly, she asks Francie to promise that, "if you ever have a sweetheart you'll tell her the truth and never let her down won't you?" and then adds, "you would never let me down would you?" (5). Francie paints a portrait of his mother as clinically depressed, as the kind of person who stares "into the firegrate," even though "there never was a fire [and] ma never bothered to light one." Francie's defensive response to this early scene in the novel – "I said what fire do we want its just as good sitting here staring into the ashes" (6) – becomes a harbinger of his ever-growing denial at large.[27] When his mother attempts to hang herself using "fuse wire belonging to da," Francie refuses to understand what he is witnessing. It is shortly after this that Francie runs away to Dublin, to escape family acrimony; this time her suicide attempt is successful and her body is dredged up from the bottom of a nearby lake.[28]

If Francie's mother is a suicidally depressed victim of Irish patriarchy, his father is a self-destructive alcoholic and washed-up musician who is haunted by his childhood in a Belfast orphanage, to which his own father abandoned him and his brother Alo. He is verbally abusive, and constantly blames his wife, son, brother, and others (Francie frequently hears his father curse "the town and everybody in it" [6]) for his own failures. He frequently returns home from the Tower Bar (a pub in which he once played the trumpet to acclaim) so drunk that he has "to be left home" by another (6). Most painfully for Francie, his father blames him for his mother's death (at one point he even asks Francie how he can call himself "a son after what" he "did" [91]), and then departs for the Tower Bar in a reenactment of his own father's abandonment of him: "I'm off up to the Tower I might be back and I might not" (46). Benny Brady's abdication of his paternal responsibility is illustrated in scene after scene, even if Francie refuses to see it. In one such scene, he describes his house as "littered with bottles" and his father as "asleep on the sofa with the trumpet beside him" (121). Francie is frequently reminded that his "father was a great man one time," one "of the best musicians [there] ever was in this town" (13), as if such nostalgia can justify his father's present lethargy and drinking. McCabe, like Joyce before him, portrays such nostalgia, lethargy, and drinking as interrelated Irish social pathologies of epidemic proportions.[29]

Francie alternately resists and accepts the blame his father attempts to place on him for the death of his mother. At one point Francie remarks that his mother is "in the lake, and it was me put her there" (69); at another he expresses his feelings of guilt for turning his "back on" his "own mother" (202). At other times Francie fantasizes that he has had nothing to do with her death. In the following imagined dialogue with his dead mother, for example, Francie sees his "ma smiling and saying to me over and over again don't worry Francie no matter what [Mrs Nugent] says about you I'll never believe it" (97–8).

Francie's Uncle Alo, his father's brother, is used by the other Bradys to dignify the family name. Alo apparently has made more of himself than Francie's father (we are frequently told that Alo has "ten men under him" at work), though, as Donna Potts puts it, he has most likely "sacrificed his personal and national identity – as well as his first love, a working class Irish woman significantly named Mary – for the sake of wealth, attained largely by his marriage to an English woman he does not love, and who does not love him."[30] Alo, who is visiting the Bradys for Christmas from his home in Camden Town, a neighborhood in London heavily populated by Irish émigrés, argues bitterly with his brother. Perhaps McCabe intends the two brothers, like Joyce's two alienated brothers in his *Dubliners* story "Clay," to be an emblem of an Ireland divided and at war with itself.[31] Francie's father attempts to take his more successful brother down a peg, accusing him of "shite-talk" (35), of

"Closing a gate in a backstreet factory" and of "tipping his cap to his betters in his wee blue porter's suit" (36). Francie's mother's rejoinder to his father – "Don't blame it on your brother that you were put in a home!" (36); "no shame should make you turn on your own brother like a dog!" (37) – elicits the usual red herring from his father: "at least" he was never taken "off to a madhouse to disgrace the whole family" (37).

The important other member of Francie's "family" is his friend and surrogate brother, Joe Purcell (the two even become "blood brothers" [53]). For some time Joe is the one positive human link in Francie's life; playing with Joe allows Francie at least a temporary respite from his dysfunctional home life. Yet Joe, like other members of Francie's family, finally rejects him; he cannot abide Francie's frequent acts of violence – breaking into and defecating in the Nugent home, attacking Philip Nugent in the chicken house, and accepting sexual abuse at the hands of Father Sullivan, for example – that increasingly define Francie's life. Joe is Francie's last human connection, and now "Joe was going to leave me and I'd be left with nobody no ma nothing" (52). So important is his link with Joe that, when Joe threatens to end his friendship with him, Francie feels as if he is "on a cliff edge" (53).

The hope of renewing the severed tie with Joe motivates Francie, when he is incarcerated in the industrial school, to study for what he calls the "Francie Brady Not a Bad Bastard Anymore Diploma" (75), his ticket to freedom. He becomes so desperate to win back Joe's friendship that he even contemplates buying it back: "Anything you want Joe I'd say to myself on the way to his house you can have it now because I'm going to buy it for you" (143). As in his fantasies that his parents love each other and love him, Francie pretends, despite the overwhelming evidence to the contrary, that he and Joe remain on the best of terms. Although the two have argued, although Francie has heard Joe say of him to another, "I'm not hanging around with him. I *used* to hang around with him!" (119), Francie nevertheless reasons that the two remain "blood brothers" and "always will. That's the way it was meant to be" (121). Long after Joe has rejected Francie for good, Francie thinks of Joe as his "friend for God's sake," his "best friend!" (173) Francie even bicycles to Joe's distant boarding school to reclaim him, just as he walked to Dublin in the attempt to escape family acrimony. Notably, both of these excursions end in bitter disappointment and failure for Francie.

Francie takes one other long-distance walk that ends in failure and dis-appointment: a walk to Bundoran, the seaside town on Donegal Bay that was the site of his parents' honeymoon and that therefore comes to represent his ideal of marital love and harmony. This walk, undertaken after the death of both parents, represents Francie's final, desperate attempt to regain the family unity and love that have been shattered by the time of the novel's setting.

McCabe remembers that when he was growing up in Clones, Bundoran had a "magical fairytale" feel to it. "It was the first place that people from an inland town like Clones would have seen the sea so it does have that kind of evanescent quality about it."[32] Bundoran is where McCabe's parents (as Francie's parents) were married, and is therefore linked in McCabe's, and in Francie's, mind "with the place where it all began."[33] Francie imagines a scene over and over again in which his parents, on their honeymoon in Bundoran, come to be known as "the two happiest people in the whole world" (142), "*The lovebirds! Benny and Annie Brady*" (90), and in which his father looks "longingly" into his mother's eyes (91). The reality of his parents' time together in Bundoran, Francie eventually learns from the proprietress of the Bundoran boardinghouse at which the couple stayed, was far from idyllic. This woman angrily remembers "a man who behaved" dishonorably "in front of his wife. No better than a pig, the way he disgraced himself here . . . God help the poor woman, she mustn't have seen him sober a day in their whole honeymoon!" (193–4).

James M. Smith maintains that "Francie's slide into madness emerges, surely, from his need to create a charade of familial respectability by suppressing the truths of his parental history."[34] The surest indication of this "slide into madness" is Francie's denial that his father has died – and is rapidly decomposing – in the living room of their home and that Francie is officially an orphan. In an emblem of the way in which this "repressed" narrative works, Francie appears to know that his father is dead, but cannot admit to this knowledge. Put differently, the story that Francie tells – like Stevens's in Ishiguro's *The Remains of the Day* – is not the story that he thinks he is telling. As his dead father decays Francie uses "perfume and air freshener and talcum powder" to mask the smell (150) and flypaper to deal with the flies, rather than face the fact of his father's death and decomposition. Francie reports giving his father's shoulder

> a bit of a shake and when the hankie fell out of his pocket I saw that it was all dried blood. Oh da, I said, I didn't know and I felt his forehead it was cold as ice. I said: Don't worry da. I'll look after you. I'll see that you're all right. I might have let you down before but not this time! Oh ho – not this time! Us Bradys – we'll show them . . . we stick together! I saw him smiling when I said that . . . Da looked at me and when I seen those eyes so sad and hurt I wanted to say: I love you da. They said to me: You won't leave me son. I said: I won't da. I'll never leave you. This time it's going to be all right – isn't it son? I said it was. (126–7)

Polishing his father's trumpet and then "laying it to rest like an infant after a long day," Francie assures his father that "Your worrying days are over" (127) and assures himself that "I wasn't going to let ma and da or anyone down ever again" (129–30). The guilt Francie here reveals for not taking better care of his parents is, of course, ironic: it is he who is the victim of neglect by his parents, not the other way around.

Francie also relies on whiskey and drugs to help him deny his father's death and corruption, and to escape his nightmarish abandonment and isolation. Francie's drug-induced hallucination of family harmony dissolves just as the police and Doctor Roche arrive at the house to discover Francie with his father's corpse, replete with "Maggots – they're right through him" (153). Like Emily in William Faulkner's blackly comic "A rose for Emily" (in which the communal narrator comments of Emily's refusal to relinquish the dead body of her father, "We knew that with nothing left, she would have to cling to that which had robbed her, as people will"[35]), Francie here refuses to let go of his abusive father's corpse until forced to do so by the community, in a show of communal concern for Francie, as for Emily, that is best defined as "too little, too late."

Not only does Francie exhibit "the psychic and moral disintegration of a child forced to suffer each stage of the collapsing parental relationship";[36] he also must face the systematic and tragic abandonment of each of his loved ones. Francie catalogues those loved ones – "Da . . . Ma . . . Alo . . . Joe" – who are "gone on me now" (174) and thereby catalogues the implosion of attendant myths of family worth and security.

The Butcher Boy depicts the process by which Francie, owing to familial as well as sociocultural pressures at large, takes on the pathological character-istics of his parents, even if he does not see this process at work himself. As James M. Smith puts it, Francie's "madness duplicates that of his parents in telling detail," and "the shared experiences of institutional confinement" connect "all three family members."[37] Repetitions of various kinds emerge: Francie becomes violent and abusive like his father, killing Mrs Nugent just as his father has "killed" his mother; Francie is incarcerated, like his father, in a "house of a hundred windows" for "bad boys," and projects his anger for parental abuse onto others; and Francie eventually attempts suicide, as his mother has, and is even institutionalized in the same mental hospital as she.

The connection between Francie and his father in this regard is particularly notable: like his father, Francie "turns increasingly to alcohol to cope with anger, punishing others for his own despair."[38] He takes to heavy drinking, to frequenting the Tower Bar and even to lying "in the doorway of the Tower singing into the neck of the beer bottle" (146), and to hanging around with other drunks. He becomes more like his destructive and self-destructive father with each passing day. At the end of the novel an incarcerated Francie even plays a trumpet and proudly remarks: "So now I have a trumpet and if you could see me I look just like da" (230).

Despite the novel's focus on the Brady family itself, *The Butcher Boy* also enacts a critique of Irish society at large and of its "institutions of containment" in particular. As James M. Smith argues, "In a landscape offering no shortage of institutional alternatives, Francie's community chooses to confine rather than provide treatment or support." Through Francie's progression from industrial school, to mental asylum, to prison for the criminally insane, McCabe "interrogates society's sequestering of those it deems socially aberrant."[39] Moreover, time and again "respectable society turns its back" on Francie, and "in so doing repeatedly fails to acknowledge the consequences attending childhood institutionalization."[40] As Tom Herron concludes, it is not merely the Brady family but the "notion of community" itself that is the target of *The Butcher Boy*.[41]

Francie's first experience of incarceration, in an industrial school, occurs after he has broken into, stolen from, and defecated in the Nugent home. Upon entering this "school for bad boys," Francie begins "a terrible repetition of his father's career as a terminally damaged borstal boy. Here, supposedly in the safe arms of the Catholic Church, the iniquities of the fathers are visited upon the son with dreadful force."[42] Specifically, Francie is sexually abused by Father Sullivan (whom he calls Father Tiddly), a "pederastic priest recently returned from the missions,"[43] who uses Francie's feigned "religious visions and his anecdotes of his homelife, which are actually fantasies of being at home with the Nugents," for purposes of self-gratification.[44] While the "juxtaposition of religious and sexual ecstasy" may be humorous,[45] the implications of this sexual abuse are serious and considerable: the industrial school, while ostensibly seeking to instill "a sense of moral conformity, religious faith, and individual responsibility" in Francie, instead encourages his "delusional tendencies"[46] and puts him in contact with yet another abusive "father." When school officials catch Father Sullivan professing love to Francie, Sullivan is transferred rather than punished, and Francie is rewarded for not speaking out: "after the Tiddly business" I "knew they were going to let me go the first chance they got I was like a fungus growing on the walls they wanted them washed clean again" (102). It is only the fear that Francie will blow the whistle on Father Sullivan's sexual advances that prompts school officials to offer Francie an exit visa.

While incarcerated at the industrial school Francie receives a visit from another abusive father, his own. Benny Brady arrives, revealingly, with bottle of whiskey in hand, and blames his son once again for what he "did" to his mother (91). Another neglectful father figure, Father Dom, the priest in Francie's village, furthers the novel's critique of Church blindness toward Francie's suffering. After his return home from the industrial school Francie runs into this priest, who says to the obviously troubled Francie, before going on his way, "you've got so tall! I'm glad things have worked out for you" (111). Still later Father Dom runs into Francie carrying home stout, and is too easily convinced that the stout is for Francie's "da" (it is really for himself, his father now being deceased) and that he therefore need not be concerned (129). Martin McLoone broadens this point to include Catholic society at large: Francie's psychosis is for him in part "the product of the narrow Catholic society" into which he is born, a culture "riven by poverty, complacency, hypocrisy and neglect."[47]

Francie's second experience of incarceration is in a mental hospital – a local asylum that was "previously the site of his mother's incarceration for mental illness"[48] – after the discovery of his father's decaying corpse in the family parlor. Francie's response to this incarceration is to reduce "the process of medication, rehabilitation, and recovery to a game."[49] This time it is not the Church but the medical community that is held up to scrutiny. Doctor Roche, who looks not at you but "right through you" (119), and the medical community at large are shown as failing to see Francie's problems for what they are and as proposing superficial bureaucratic solutions. The medicos in the asylum put Francie "in a big chair with this helmet on [his] head and wires coming out all over the place" in order to perform experiments. At another time Francie describes an army of "starchy bastards of students with clipboards gawking at you *I hope he doesn't leap up out of the chair and chop us up!*" (157), a description that both presages Francie's butchery of Mrs Nugent and reveals the extent to which the doctors, like Francie's neighbors, exploit his suffering and freakishness for the purposes of gossip and entertainment value. The medicos give Francie tablets, have him weave baskets, and show him Rorschach blots ("they'd take me down to the room and hand me bits of paper all blotted with ink. What do you think about that says the doc. You won't be writing any more messages on that paper I says . . . Its destroyed I says, look at it" [164–5]), as if such therapies can identify, much less solve, his myriad problems. Upon being released from the hospital Francie runs into the homeless "drunk lad" who frequents the Tower, but who now will have nothing to do with him (205) (both this drunk lad and the stray dog Grouse Armstrong function as versions of Francie, as means of commenting on his social standing). Such rejection – by his family and by society at large – only encourages Francie's violent feelings for Mrs Nugent.

It is for this murder that Francie is incarcerated a final time, in a prison for the criminally insane, "*another* house of a hundred windows" (229). Solitary confinement is an ironic treatment for one driven to violent acts by rejection and isolation ("How can your solitary [confinement ever] finish?" Francie asks; "That's the best laugh yet" [230]). It is from this prison hospital that Francie narrates, retrospectively, the novel we read.

Central to Francie's grasp of his place in society is his relationship with the Nugents, a middle-class Irish family recently returned from London, who are associated with the "trappings and aspirations of middle-class England" and who "represent everything unavailable to Francie."[50] They therefore come to represent a state of being he both covets and rejects. While the Nugents, "whose family name signifies both their colonial superiority and their modernizing impact,"[51] would in themselves have determined little of Francie's unfolding fate, they nevertheless come to loom large in his consciousness. Francie's obsessive paranoia over the Nugents is suggested as early as the novel's first sentence, which ends with Francie's reference to "what I done on Mrs Nugent" (1). Indeed, in Francie's mind all roads lead to the Nugent family conspiracy: it is not any shortcoming on the part of the Bradys but persecution at the hands of the Nugents that leads to the disintegration of Francie's world. "If only the Nugents hadn't come to the town, if only they had left us alone" (178), Francie thinks, echoing his father's blaming of him (and his mother) for his family's woes. Making matters worse in Francie's mind is the fact that the Nugents formerly were friends of the Bradys but then, after their English sojourn, betrayed them.

McCabe's novel establishes the Bradys and the Nugents as mirror images of each other. As Tom Herron puts it, "The Nugents possess everything Francie does not and embody everything he is not"; his life-style is the "antithesis" of theirs.[52] Both families consist of a father, mother, and son, but the two families, beyond this point of similarity, could not be more dissimilar. This mirror imaging is emphasized when Mrs Nugent informs Francie of his own mother's death (and that he has missed the funeral) (45). It is also emphasized when Francie breaks into the Nugent's home, dons Philip's English private school uniform, and admires himself in the mirror of Philip's bedroom, pretending to be his nemesis (63). The Nugent's pleasant middle-class home life, replete with "refinement, reserve, restraint, taste, and order" – "the stereotypical English traits on which the old Celt versus Saxon dichotomy depended, qualities that for centuries had presumably made the English eminently suited to govern the Irish"[53] – all contrast starkly with the Bradys' impoverished, uncouth, and acrimonious domestic life.

In contrast to the Nugent's kitchen, for example, which is "warm and glowing" and contains a table "set for breakfast in the morning," a "butter dish with a special knife," a "jug with matching cups," and "not a thing out of place" (47), the Brady kitchen is fly-covered and pilchard-strewn, an unkempt and dirty place where meals are prepared for Francie irregularly if at all. In contrast to Mr Nugent's "high-up" London job, steady sobriety, and well-groomed appearance – like an "ad on the television" (57) – Francie's father is the epitome of indolence, drunkenness, and sloth. The neglect and abuse doled out to Francie by his parents contrast sharply with the meticulous upbringing and private school education provided to Philip by his. Even Philip's comic books – which are "neatly filed away in shirt boxes not a crease or a dog-ear in sight" and which look as if "they had come straight out of the shop" (3) – seem to express the bourgeois order, pride, and respectability upheld by the family at large. All of this contributes to the opposition in Francie's (and in the reader's) mind between the Nugent abode of domestic order and harmony and the Brady one of domestic chaos and dysfunction.

In contrast to a statement that Francie imagines Philip to make, "I love my mother more than anything in the world and I'd never do anything in the world to hurt her. I love my parents and I love my happy home," Francie imagines that people think of him, "I hope he's proud of himself now, the pig, after what he did on his poor mother" (47). That the Bradys come to be "pigs" in the town's (and in his own) mind Francie blames directly on the Nugents. The label of "pigs" that attaches to the Bradys is also related in Francie's thinking to the disparity between the Nugent and Brady homes and to the fact that he both idealizes and demonizes the Nugents: that he wishes to be like them yet regards their evident superiority as a rebuke to Brady honor, and so comes to resent them deeply.

Francie blames Mrs Nugent for inaugurating the use of the expression "pigs" to describe his family. As Francie sees it, Mrs Nugent is the one who

> started on about the pigs. She said she knew the kind of us long before she went to England and she might have known not to let her son anywhere near the likes of me what else would you expect from a house where the father's never in, lying about the pubs from morning to night, he's no better than a pig. (4)

Most of the disparaging comments about the Bradys that Francie imagines Mrs Nugent to be making are revealed to be projections of Francie's own guilty fears about his family and the role he plays in its disintegration.

Francie's solution to his imagined sense of persecution at the hands of Mrs Nugent and Philip is to bait, harass, and violently assault them. His first hostile act is to institute a mock "pig toll tax" that he attempts to extract from Mrs Nugent and Philip as they pass him on the sidewalk. He ceases his harassment only when he perceives "a tear" in Mrs Nugent's eye (13). His next move is to invite Philip to play with him in his hideaway, a chicken house, where he assaults him violently. Philip is rescued by the fortuitous arrival of Joe. Later, Francie attempts to barge into the Nugent home, struggles with Mrs Nugent and Philip in the doorway, and agrees to leave only when Philip looks at Francie with "them sad eyes"[54] – a mirror of his own sad eyes.

Francie next visits the Nugent home when the family is away for the day. He breaks into the house, admires the polished floors and clean kitchen, helps himself to food, tries on Philip's English private school uniform, scrawls "PHILIP IS A PIG" in lipstick on the wallpaper (63–7), and, in a fantasy episode in which he imagines he is running a school for pigs aimed at helping Mrs Nugent and Philip become "good" pigs, he defecates as a pig would do on the carpet of Philip's bedroom ("pigs are poo animals," Francie explains; "I'm afraid and they simply will cover the place in it no matter what you do" [66]). Caught in this perverse act of vandalism, Francie is sent to an industrial school that he nicknames the "school for pigs" (73). During Francie's time in this school Joe and Philip become friends, a development that shakes Francie to the core and that exaggerates his feeling of persecution at the hands of the Nugents. After he is released from the school, Mrs. Nugent's brother, appropriately, threatens to "gut" Francie "like a pig" (118).

The novel's pig motif is further developed when Francie, in the mental asylum, hallucinates that he is a pig performing before Mrs Connolly and other women from the neighborhood. His parents, "Ma and Da Pig," are also present in this hallucination. The assembled women anticipate "the mother and father of a row" between Francie's parents while Francie Pig stands there "watching the flesh of the apple" that the women have given him "browning" in his hand (162). Mrs Connolly's appeal for a "row" between his parents (162) emphasizes the extent to which Francie self-ashamedly views Brady family freakishness to be a source of gossip and entertainment for the town. A passage in another contemporary novel, Zadie Smith's *White Teeth*, nicely addresses the variety of *schadenfreude* experienced by the townspeople at Francie's expense:

> [D]on't ever underestimate the pleasure [people] receive from viewing pain that is not their own, from delivering bad news, watching bombs fall on television, from listening to stifled sobs from the other end of a telephone line. Pain by itself is just Pain. But Pain + Distance can = entertainment, voyeurism, human interest . . . a raised eyebrow, disguised contempt.[55]

Francie both "loves and hates" Mrs Nugent;[56] he wants to be welcomed into the Nugent home as an honored guest yet abhors this home for the contrast it presents with his own. When he breaks into the Nugent house it is clear how strongly Francie fantasizes becoming Philip.

> I went round the house like Philip. I walked like him and everything. Mrs Nugent called up the stairs to me are you up there Philip? I said I was and she

told me to come down for my tea. Down I came and she had made me a big
feed of rashers [Francie imagines them to be eating bacon] and eggs and tea and
the whole lot . . . I felt good about all this. (63–4)

Francie even expresses an awareness of his own wish to be a Nugent by
imagining Philip to be accusing him of wanting "to be one of us. He wants
his name to be Francis Nugent. That's what he's wanted all along!" (64).
In another hallucination Francie fantasizes that Mr Nugent accuses him of
having asked Mrs Nugent "to be his mother" and of giving "anything not to
be a pig" (97). All of this indirectly leads to Francie's murder of Mrs Nugent.
As Elizabeth Butler Cullingford argues, "Mrs Nugent's kind of mothering"
stands "as a reproach to the fragile capacities of Mrs. Brady," and Francie kills
her "partly as a way of affirming his family loyalty."[57] Francie's murder of Mrs
Nugent, moreover, fleshes out Francie's complex identity as both "pig" and
"Butcher Boy."

Francie's defensive and hurt pride, as expressed by his mother's earlier
assertion that "We don't want to be like the Nugents" (19), unfolds in an
extended fantasy reversal in which the Bradys are indifferent to the Nugents
and the Nugents desperately wish to be like the Bradys. When Uncle Alo
arrives for the Christmas-time family reunion, for example, Francie thinks,
"Nugent has *nobody* like him": "I still couldn't stop looking at" Alo, "the gold
tiepin and his polished nails, the English voice. Nugent's was only half-
English. The more you thought it the harder it was to believe that Nugent had
ever been anything worth talking about" (28–9). Time and again Francie
fantasizes a scene in which he and Alo are

on the Diamond getting ready to set off once more down the street and Mrs
Nugent [tries] to attract our attention. Please Francie, I'll give you anything
she'd say. Sorry, I'd say, too late. Then I'd cut her off and say: what was that you
were saying Uncle Alo? (22)

Such fantasies of superiority over the anglicized Nugents of course only reveal
the extent to which the Irish Bradys have internalized the townspeople's sense
of their inferiority.

An important text that further fleshes out the trope of the Irish as pigs and
that serves as a commentary on McCabe's novel in other ways is the Irishman
Jonathan Swift's satiric "A modest proposal" (1729), which proposes a solution
"For preventing the Children of poor People in Ireland, from being a Burden
to their Parents or Country; and for making them beneficial to the Publick."[58]
Swift's satire of proposed infanticide and cannibalism – of killing two birds

with one stone by butchering Ireland's poor children as a means of ridding Ireland of its overpopulation and of feeding the hungry masses – is obviously relevant to McCabe's novel. Not only does Swift refer to the mother of such unwanted children as "Breeders," and to the children themselves as "Swine," but he accuses these children of resorting to "Stealing"[59] (just as an impoverished Francie often resorts to stealing). Swift's references to Irish people who are "every Day *dying*, and *rotting*, by *Cold* and *Famine*, and *Filth*, and *Vermin*"[60] directly recalls the decline and demise of Francie's poverty-ridden father. The following passage in "A modest proposal" addresses many of the themes and motifs found in *The Butcher Boy* and reveals the extent to which McCabe is writing within a rhetorical tradition that equates impoverished, dirty Irish people with subhuman animals, particularly pigs:

> As to our city of *Dublin*; Shambles [slaughterhouses] may be appointed for this Purpose, in the most convenient Parts of it; and Butchers we may be assured will not be wanting; although I rather recommend buying the Children alive, and dressing them hot from the Knife, as we do *roasting Pigs*.[61]

Although she does not single out Swift's satire, Donna Potts writes convincingly of "McCabe's evocation of stereotypical Irishness," which "is nowhere more evident than in his extensive reference to pigs, which have long been associated with Ireland."[62] Indeed, Potts writes, "one of the oldest epithets for Ireland is *Muck Inis*, or 'Pig Island'."[63] "By associating Francie Brady, and indeed the whole Brady family, with pigs, McCabe alludes to the long English tradition of drawing a distinction between England and Ireland in the form of John Bull and Paddy the Pig."[64] Elizabeth Butler Cullingford broadens Potts's focus by observing that in

> Embracing the negative ethnic stereotype that Mrs. Nugent has used to classify his family, Francie becomes the pig she says he is by trashing her perfectly kept house. Pigs are always on the receiving end of violence, whether literal, as in Leddy's slaughterhouse; metaphorical, as in Mrs. Nugent's class-based tirades; geographical, as in the invasion of the Bay of Pigs; or colonial, as in England's denigration and bestialization of the people it had dispossessed.[65]

Although he is repeatedly figured in negative, porcine terms, Francie eventually comes to wear his piggishness as "an identity, a badge of pride."[66]

The novel's title is of course a reference to Francie as a slaughterer both of pigs and of Mrs Nugent. Francie gets a job with Leddy, a piggish-looking man with "a big pink face and a scrunched-up snout" (122), who runs a slaughterhouse and butcher shop. In Leddy's slaughterhouse Francie reports smelling "piss and shit and dirty guts you never seen the like of it" and describes the place as "crawling with bluebottles" (130) – flies and smells that connect this bloody work with the Brady household and Francie's decomposing father. To make matters more complex still, Francie, as an employee of the slaughterhouse, takes on the identity of both pig and murderer of pigs.

The novel's fiery and violent climax occurs after Francie's unsuccessful trip to Joe's (and Philip's) boarding school in a failed bid to reclaim his lost friend. Unsurprisingly, Francie focuses blame for this failure on Mrs Nugent, and pursues her with violent intentions. Upon arriving at her home, Francie accuses her of doing "two bad things": making him "turn my back on my ma" and taking "Joe away from me" (209); he then assaults and kills her with Leddy's "captive bolt pistol" and "butcher's steel" and "knife" (207), after which he sticks his "hand in her stomach" and writes "PIGS all over the walls" of her home with her blood (209).

Francie's attempt to hide the corpse of Mrs Nugent, his ideal mother yet his anti-mother, using a cart supplied by Leddy, is juxtaposed with the town's ecstatic anticipation of a visit by its symbolic mother, the Blessed Virgin Mary.[67] In Martin McLoone's words, "The novel juxtaposes the townspeople's preparations for the end of the world, foretold by the appearance of the Virgin Mary [and coinciding with the Cuban missile crisis, appropriately called the "Bay of Pigs" crisis, with its threat of nuclear cataclysm], with Francie's execution of Mrs. Nugent."[68] The apocalypticism inherent in both Francie's thinking and the town's mood is palpable; after committing the murder, Francie says, "this must be the end of the world. I hope the Blessed Virgin comes along to save me!" (215) His family and Joe now dead to him, Francie's world does indeed seem to be in its death throes.

Once Francie's murder of Mrs Nugent is suspected, the novel juxtaposes the search for two mothers – the Virgin Mary and Mrs Nugent – who are no longer of this world.[69] Hysteria over the end of time, coupled with a "visit" from the "Mother of God" (207) (signs around town proclaim: "AVE MARIA WELCOME TO OUR TOWN" [207–8]), are depicted against the backdrop of Francie's suicide attempt, the literal end of his world. In a perception that can only be described as psychotically ironic, Francie now sees his as the "holiest" and "brightest, happiest town in the whole world" (208).

Francie is caught by the police, escapes, makes his way home, and, in a final suicidal-apocalyptic moment, sets alight his entire house, an emblem of Brady family worth and unity, attempting to make his own funeral pyre out of his and his parents' belongings. This all occurs against the backdrop of the playing of his mother's recording of "The Butcher Boy" on the family phonograph, with Francie weeping "because we were all together now" (223–4). The song's lyrics now apply to Francie himself, who dies "for love," or rather, for the lack of it. Ironically, Francie, after being rescued from the fire, is accused of committing a brutal murder for the "meanest and most contemptible of motives – for the purpose of robbery and plunder!" (228) Readers know, however, that Francie is motivated not by robbery at all but by vengeance, a far more powerful currency for him than material wealth could ever be. "The Butcher Boy," his mother's favorite song, is about "a woman hanging from a rope all because the butcher boy told her lies" (49), a theme that anticipates her own suicide. It points to Francie's guilt over her death and to his despair over the fact that she has "died for love" (in the words of the song). Although Francie does not grasp the meaning of the lyrics, he does seem to grasp the general tenor of the song.

Francie's imprisonment in a third "house of a hundred windows" (229) returns us to the novel's opening, retrospective frame. Our final image of him, "Twenty or thirty or forty years" after the main action of the novel (230)(Francie has no conception of time), reveals him to have gone a long way to go nowhere at all: he is hacking away "at the ice on the big puddle behind the kitchens" (230) with a fellow inmate and substitute Joe figure. While Francie is unlikely ever to leave this prison hospital, he does manage an escape of sorts: a nostalgic return in his imagination to an idealized age of familial harmony and acceptance, to "the best days" Francie "ever knew, before da and Nugent and all this started" (43), when he and Joe met "hacking at the ice" and became best friends (53).

Chapter 11

Graham Swift's
Last Orders (1996)

I

Awarded the Booker Prize in 1996 for *Last Orders*, his sixth novel, Graham
Swift is now regarded, in the judgment of Irish author John Banville, as "one
of England's finest living novelists."[4] *Last Orders* chronicles the journey of
four residents of Bermondsey, a working-class district of southeast London,
who travel to Margate on the southeast coast on 2 April 1990 in order to fulfill
the "last orders" of their friend Jack Dodds, master butcher, who has recently
died and been cremated: to deposit his ashes in the sea. Like other "circadian"
or one-day novels – most famously James Joyce's *Ulysses* (1922), Virginia

Woolf's *Mrs Dalloway* (1925), and Malcolm Lowry's *Under the Volcano* (1947) – the limited present of the novel serves as an opportunity for the characters to recount and explore events from their past lives. These memories and musings in turn illuminate and embellish the present of the narrative, which becomes considerably more resonant and complex in the process. A subtle, psychologically probing novel reminiscent in particular of Faulkner's *As I Lay Dying* and Woolf's *Mrs Dalloway*, *Last Orders* muses on death and dying, on complex familial relationships and memory, and on the potent and uncanny impact of the dead on the living. As Salman Rushdie puts it, *Last Orders* is "about the ritual of death, this last rite of passage."[5]

Born in south London in 1949, Graham Swift was the son of a civil servant who served as a naval pilot during the Second World War (perhaps unsurprisingly, many of Swift's novels take the war as their chronological point of departure and chief point of reference). Graham Swift studied English literature at Queen's College, Cambridge University, graduating in 1970, following which, in 1973, he completed a Master's degree at York University. At York Swift devoted increasing amounts of time to his creative writing (he claims at this time to have been "pretending to be a student" while in fact he was "teaching himself to write" fiction[6]), an avocation that he continued while teaching school in London (where he now lives) and Greece in the years that followed. The critical and popular success of his third novel, *Waterland* (1983), allowed Swift to abandon teaching and turn full-time to creative writing.

Although Swift has published well-regarded stories that appeared in his collection *Learning to Swim and Other Stories* (1982) and elsewhere, it is principally his novels – *The Sweet Shop Owner* (1980), *Shuttlecock* (1981), *Waterland* (1983), *Out of this World* (1988), *Ever After* (1992), *Last Orders* (1996), and *The Light of Day* (2003) – for which he is best known and most critically acclaimed.

Swift's breakthrough novel, as noted above, was his third, *Waterland* (1983), which attracted as much critical attention as the rest of his early novels combined, and which one critic deemed "as significant to the 1980s as *The French Lieutenant's Woman* was for the 1970s."[7] Simultaneously "a murder confession, a history of England's fen country, an indictment of the modern world for its ignorance of history, an essay on the life of the eel, a meditation on the shapes of time – in short, a grim intertwining of incest, suicide, and murder played against two hundred years of family history and an apocalyptic sense that time may be coming to an end,"[8] *Waterland*, which was shortlisted for the Booker Prize, did for the Fens in eastern England what *Great Expectations* did for the marshes of northeast Kent and *Wuthering Heights* did for the moors of West Yorkshire: it imaginatively recreated it, imbuing it with a distinctive dramatic character and almost mythic spirit of place.

For all of their obvious differences, Swift's novels tend to be of a piece. For one thing, all of them contain a series of mysteries about the characters that are only slowly revealed, characters for whom the traumatic events of World War II were a formative experience. As Peter Widdowson observes, "It is as though Swift 'dates' his modern world from the catastrophic events of the mass warfare of the Second World War – one which remains in their shadow and in which the destinies of ordinary lives, even in the 1980s and 1990s, are still determined by them."[9] For another thing, all of Swift's novels reveal the extent to which national history and personal history are only knowable, ultimately and most fully, in subjective terms, through memory and the imaginative recreation of the past. The fictions also tend to foreground water (consider, for example, the titles *Learning to Swim* and *Waterland*) – both the literal substance (which can both sustain life and end it) and its symbolic aspects (as a metaphor for protean subjectivity, memory, and history, and as an objective correlative for the nostalgic idealization of past life or for the end of life). In *Last Orders*, for example, the sea is both the terminus for the journey and the site of childhood family vacations. As one of the novel's characters puts it of coastal Margate, it "smells like something you remember, like the seaside you remember . . . It smells like memory itself" (287).

All of Swift's novels, moreover, may be said to explore the extraordinary within the quotidian, the miracle and enigma of the everyday. As Swift himself has pointed out, "I always . . . write about so-called ordinary people and ordinary things, if only because I believe there is no such thing as an ordinary person . . . everyone is unique . . . and so the challenge of writing about ordinary and common things is to show that."[10] *Last Orders*, even more than Swift's earlier novels, depicts "common" characters in "common" situations, though their collaborative story amounts to a narrative that easily transcends the commonplace.

In addition to receiving the Booker Prize and the James Tait Black Memorial Prize for *Last Orders*, Swift won the Geoffrey Faber Memorial Prize for *Shuttlecock* and *Waterland*, the *Guardian* Fiction Prize, Italy's *Premio Ginzane Cavour*, and the Winifred Holtby Memorial Prize for *Waterland*, and France's *Prix du Meilleur Livre Etranger* for *Ever After*. A Fellow of the Royal Society of Literature, Swift was awarded honorary degrees, by the Universities of East Anglia and York, in 1984. Three of Swift's novels have been adapted for the screen: *Shuttlecock* (1991), *Waterland* (which starred Jeremy Irons, 1992), and *Last Orders* (filmed by the Australian Fred Schepsi and starring Michael Caine and Bob Hoskins, 2002).

II

Although *Last Orders* represents a continuation of Swift's earlier novelistic agendas, it also "represents the most formally complicated experiment so far, with its multiple tellers all talking to themselves but also in some magical way to each other."[11] As Swift himself comments, *Last Orders* is "a novel in which six or seven characters collaboratively tell the story."[12] Indeed, like many modernist and postmodernist novels, *Last Orders* may be said to be as much about its own telling – about its intricate, interweaving, interlocking narrative yarns, with their poignant time-shifts and spatial and narrative digressions – as it is about anything else. As John Banville observes, "Swift carefully and seemingly effortlessly piles up the layers of narrative by means of a judicious accumulation of small revelations."[13]

The entire novel is narrated in the first person by seven different people in 75 unnumbered sections. The four men who accompany Jack's ashes – Vic, Vince, Lenny, and Ray – narrate the vast majority of the novel. Ray "Lucky" Johnson, who had met Jack in the British army in Africa in World War II, is an insurance clerk and inveterate gambler on horse-racing; Vic Tucker, whose funeral home is situated across the street from Jack's butcher shop, is an undertaker "and canny observer of human beings in their living and dead states";[14] Vince Dodds (né Pritchett), who owns a used car dealership and who supplies the Mercedes Benz for the day's outing, is Jack's adopted son; and Lenny Tate is a greengrocer and former prize boxer, whose daughter was seduced and left pregnant by Vince years earlier and who to this day nurses a grudge against him. In the present of the novel Vince is in his mid-forties; the other three major characters (who are contemporaries of Jack) are in their late sixties. While these four narrators dominate the novel, three other characters – the deceased Jack himself (like Addie Bundren in Faulkner's *As I Lay Dying*, he gets a few words); Amy, Jack's wife; and Mandy, Vince's wife – also narrate a few sections of the novel. Conspicuously (yet appropriately) absent is the voice of Amy's and Jack's retarded (and apparently mute) daughter June. (Instead of accompanying the others on their mission that day, Amy pays one final visit to her institutionalized daughter, whom she has been visiting twice weekly for the better part of five decades, but who has never once shown any sign of recognizing her mother.) Collectively, the novel's 75 first-person narrative episodes combine descriptions of past and unfolding events with interior monologues that probe and complicate the meaning of these events.

The narrative sections have titles that either identify the narrator or specify a place; those with place-names are all by Ray. The place-names sequentially trace the route of the London-to-Margate journey. The four set off from the "Coach and Horses" pub in Bermondsey (its name already suggests a journey) and drive to the town of Rochester (where they take lunch and drinks in a pub), to the outskirts of the town of Chatham (where they visit a British naval war memorial), to Wick's Farm in Kent (the sight of Amy's and Jack's meeting and June's conception), to Canterbury (to pay a visit to the famous cathedral), and finally to Margate pier (to dispose of Jack's ashes in accordance with his wishes).

In addition to being more complex than his earlier work from a narrative standpoint, *Last Orders* also represents a break from Swift's earlier fiction in that the narrators here are working class rather than college-educated or in any way intellectual (compare them, say, with Tom Crick in *Waterland* or Harry Beech in *Ever After*). As Swift himself notes, "Articulate [and] sophisticated language," as typically found in his earlier work, "has the problem of getting tangled up in itself. It's a system of protection, in a sense. If you take that away you do strip things bare. There's a sort of nakedness in [*Last Orders*] which I don't think I've achieved before."[15]

To a greater degree than his earlier novels, *Last Orders* is a literary-historical encomium; it is richly suffused with echoes of and allusions to prior literary texts, with what Pamela Cooper calls a "palimpsest layering of ancient and modern literary voices."[16] These texts include Chaucer's *The Canterbury Tales* (one critic views Swift's pilgrimage in the footsteps of Chaucer's story-tellers as invoking "the robust culture of *The Canterbury Tales*"[17]), T. S. Eliot's *The Waste Land* (1922) (both Swift's title and the "location of the final scene subtly evoke T. S. Eliot's *The Waste Land*, which mourns what is portrayed as last orders for European civilization . . . and expresses profound anxiety about the disruption of traditional class and gender boundaries"[18]), and Kazuo Ishiguro's *The Remains of the Day* (1988), the Booker Prize-winning novel by Swift's contemporary and friend. Both *The Remains of the Day* and *Last Orders* depict a journey of remembrance, loss, and, ultimately, recovery that ends at a "pleasure pier" at the English seaside (Weymouth and Margate, respectively). As Pamela Cooper observes, both Ishiguro's and Swift's novels depict "characters whose lives have been changed by the trauma of World War II, and who doubt their value as members of a postwar British society in which the power of empire has dwindled and the country's historical mission is profoundly unclear."[19]

Particularly strong echoes of two other modern novels resound in *Last Orders*: William Faulkner's *As I Lay Dying* (1930) and Virginia Woolf's *Mrs Dalloway* (1925). As to the connection with Faulkner's novel, Swift himself attests to "a little homage at work": "I admire Faulkner very much, and there are obvious similarities" between the two novels. Yet while "I have my jar of ashes, Faulkner has his rotting corpse, and the setting is clearly very different."[20] That said, for Swift the "funereal" emphasis, the story of "laying the dead to rest" and of "how the dead apply pressure on the living," is not so much a Faulknerian as a perennial, "primitive," "archetypal" concern. The fact that both novels feature a dead character whose remains are being transported and who narrates a small section of the text (Addie Bundren/Jack Dodds) has led one reviewer, John Frow, to accuse Swift of plagiarism.[21]

As for the echoes in *Last Orders* of *Mrs Dalloway*, these have been little commented on but are, if anything, still stronger than are the echoes of Faulkner. Both Woolf's and Swift's are circadian novels that view events through the eyes of numerous characters, whose flashbacks of events long ago explain and embellish their present lives. Both are keenly observant psychological novels that sport a web of interweaving, interior monologues that collectively reveal dramatic meaning; both resemble jigsaw puzzles that must be assembled by the reader in order for their "pictures" to become clear. Both explore the ways in which the past elucidates the present. Both depict a paradoxically run-of-the-mill yet extraordinary day: average in one sense, special in another (Swift's novel opens with Ray's comment, "It ain't like your regular sort of day" [1]). Both are fascinated with the passage of time and use clocks to mark the unfolding hours of the day (references to clocks first occur on the second page of Woolf's novel and on the first page of Swift's).

Equally important are the echoes to be found in Swift's novel of the BBC's popular British working-class television drama, *EastEnders*. Like many modernist and postmodernist novels (Joyce's *Ulysses* and Thomas Pynchon's *Gravity's Rainbow* are two examples) *Last Orders* conflates and blurs together elite and popular culture, "high" and demotic art. This is even hinted at in the two epigraphs to Swift's novel, the first from a Sir Thomas Browne poem and the second from a popular music-hall song. As David Malcolm remarks, *Last Orders* embraces both

> exalted literary and philosophical and demotic and workaday realms. It is both a complex meditation on grand, universal matters [and] is set in a lower-class world of nonstandard dialect, mundane work . . . and trips to the seaside. The title of the novel itself embodies this paradox. "Last Orders" are the final drinks one can obtain in a British pub before it closes [yet also] suggest last things, death, mortality, and the ineluctable passage of time.[22]

Indeed, in Swift's novel the very distinction between perennial/exalted and quotidian/mundane is undone.

III

Last Orders is comprised of a series of interlinked and inter-animating narratives through which the novel's mysteries and ironies and its keen psychological and philosophical insights are revealed and reverberate. Ray observes that "what a man does and how he lives in his head are two different things" (38), and that life is like "the sound of the Coach" – the group's regular pub-haunt – on a Friday night: "Rattling on, going nowhere" (191). And Lenny reckons that "every generation makes a fool of itself for the next one" (44); *Last Orders*, like an E. M. Forster novel, is full of such pithy observations. That said, the "meaning" of the novel, for Swift at least, is more than anything else "the story" itself.

> The story is the heart of the matter. However you talk about it, however you analyze it, it is this ultimately magical, marvelous, mysterious, wonderful thing. It's got to be there. That's what makes the reader read. Whatever else you're attempting, whatever else you're doing, it's the story that remains.[23]

Paradoxically, at the center of the story is the absent (deceased and cremated) yet omnipresent Jack Dodds, master butcher, who has just died of stomach cancer and who has left a letter, "To whom it may concern" (13), stating his last orders. As Pamela Cooper puts this paradox, Jack Dodds is "Dead on arrival in terms of the novel's plot," yet "he remains vividly alive at its core."[24] While Jack is of course a particular – and highly particularized – character, the novel also takes pains to universalize, to render common, his mortal condition. As one critic maintains, "Jack's name makes him an Everyman figure, 'Jack' being a representative name or form used to address an unknown person."[25] Vic, Jack's undertaker friend, makes this same point when ruminating on his friend's mortality. "Jack's not special, he's not special at all," Vic thinks.

> He's just one of the many now. In life there are differences, you make distinctions . . . But the dead are the dead, I've watched them, they're equal . . . It's what makes all men equal for ever and always. (143)

Jack's "absent presence" is also hinted at by his wife, Amy, who toward the end of the novel's long day muses on her deceased husband: "He's not anywhere. Or by now he'll be washed out to sea or mingling with Margate Sands" (278). Although Jack is now gone forever and literally insubstantial, she feels that he will never leave her: "I'll always see Jack's face, like a little photo in my head. Like a person never dies in the mind's eye" (267). And the novel's final words, thought by Ray, make the same universalizing gesture, likening the "ash" and "wind" to "Jack[,] what we're [all] made of" (295).

Last Orders is a visceral novel, and not only because it is an affliction of the stomach that does Jack in. As Pamela Cooper observes, "The novel is predicated upon the body of Jack Dodds – its propensities during life and its transformations in death. It is Jack's body that unites the group of travelers in a common purpose."[26] However, more than being a mere focal point of the novel, Jack's body, in both its dying/bleeding and its cremated ashes state, becomes a means for Swift to muse on the nature of human mortality and identity.

On the one hand, characters time and again depict each other in a grossly material way, as so much perishable meat: now living (and bleeding), later dead (and cooked). For example, Vince tellingly refers to Jack as "his own bleeding man all right" (25), and Lenny refers to people in general as "bleeders" (44). The hospitalized Jack likens himself, in an image appropriate to a butcher, to a lamb "to the slaughter" (152). Vince, visiting Jack on his deathbed, thinks, "He ain't Jack Dodds, no more than I'm Vince Dodds. Because nobody ain't nobody. Because nobody ain't more than just a body, than just their own body" (21). Ray, once Jack has been cremated, refers to him as "nothing" (210), and even wonders, referring to the urn, "Whether it's all Jack in there or Jack mixed up with bits of others, the ones who were done before and the ones who were done after" (4). Amy imagines Jack dying behind the counter of his butcher shop, "cleaver in his hand, and that's how he'd want it, another carcass to deal with" (229). Later, feeling Jack's cold forehead, she thinks: "They'll have fetched him out the fridge and they'll pop him back, like he used to do with his pork and beef" (275). As the above passages suggest, the novel develops the trope of cannibalism as a means of exploring the ways in which people devour each other, use each other up, figuratively speaking.

Occasionally this metaphor takes on a sexual connotation – Lenny, in an erotic reverie, muses that "You can't help flesh being flesh" (210) – but usually it is alimentary in nature. Edible meat and human corpses are conjoined at numerous places in the novel. For example, it strikes Ray as fitting that Jack's butcher shop and Vic's funeral home in Bermondsey are directly across the street from each other, "seeing as there was dead animals in the one and stiffs in the other" (5). Lenny too contemplates this coincidence with linguistic playfulness, merging their businesses in his mind as "Dodds and Tucker, steaks and stiffs" (131). And at numerous points Jack, his cremated remains placed in a jar for transporting, is likened to food. The jar containing Jack's ashes is thought to look like "a large instant-coffee jar" (3) and to be "about the same size as a pint glass" (10). For a large portion of the journey the jar is transported in a bag labeled "*Rochester Food Fayre*" (116), and Ray imagines Vic "holding the box" containing Jack's ashes as if "it might be his lunch" (21). In Margate Ray holds the open jar of ashes for the others to dispense, "like I'm holding out a tin of sweets or doling out rations" (293). The novel's meat metaphor even extends to the viscerally-depicted megalopolis itself. Amy remembers Jack's father, also a butcher, calling London's Smithfield district, with its meat market, the bleeding "heart of London," with the "red lines of the bus routes" being its "arteries, bleedin arteries, and veins" (230).

That the novel possesses a graphically materialist, visceral vision of things does not mean that it depicts humans as reducible to their bodies – bodies that exist and then cease to exist. Rather, *Last Orders* shows the dead as affecting the living as much as the living do themselves. Indeed, Jack's passing and the journey taken by Vince, Lenny, and Ray provide them with the opportunity to mend their ways with their daughters (from whom they are estranged) and with each other (this does not apply to Vic, whose personal affairs are in order and who instead has sons). In escorting Jack's ashes to the sea, in becoming Jack's "guard-of-honour," Ray imagines the four compatriots to be transformed: "We all straighten up, as if we've got to be different people, as if we're royalty and the people on the pavement ought to stop and wave" (22). Early in the trip Ray imagines that all four of them appreciate what "Jack has done for us [in organizing this journey], so as to make us feel special, so as to give us a treat. Like we're off on a jaunt, a spree, and the world looks good, it looks like it's there just for us" (18). Soon afterwards, during their lunchtime break in a Rochester pub, "getting slowly pickled and at peace with the world," Ray thinks,

Jack wouldn't have minded, it's even what he would've wanted for us, to get sweetly slewed on his account. *You carry on lads, don't you worry about me.* If he was here now he'd be recommending it, he'd be doing the same as us. *Forget them ashes, fellers.* (110–11)

Later, at Canterbury Cathedral, each of the four muses on the fact that it is Jack who has led them there – and not for him but for them. Lenny thinks, "It wasn't for *him*. Who's he going to tell, who's he going to brag about it to over a slow beer at the end of the day? My mates did me proud, they carried me round Canterbury Cathedral. It was for us, to put us back on our best behaviour, to clean up our acts" (210). Ray imagines the four of them having lived all their lives and never having "seen Canterbury Cathedral, [yet now] it's something Jack's put right" (193). As Swift himself comments of the journey, while its immediate purpose is "to do with death quite clearly, honouring the dead,"[27] it is ultimately more about providing a salutary experience for the living. In this connection, it is surely not coincidental that Ray likens the scattering of Jack's ashes in Margate to the "scattering of seed" (293), that Jack's death is figured in ultimately life-affirming terms.

Jack and the four major characters in Swift's novel are united not only by the crisscrossing paths their lives have taken but by the problematic husband–wife and father–daughter relationships (Vic excluded) in which they find themselves. Chief among the marital conflicts explored is that between Jack and Amy Dodd over their retarded daughter June, by now 50 years old, who proved to be an "accident" (97) in more ways than one. Jack rejects his daughter, never once visiting her in the decades in which she is institutionalized. Indeed, Amy remembers Jack saying to her decades ago, "Best thing we can do, Ame, is forget all about her" (253). Even on his deathbed, during a final conversation with his wife, Jack altogether neglects to mention June (267), to which Amy responds by not mentioning her love affair of many years earlier with Ray (268). By contrast, Amy has dutifully visited her daughter twice weekly over the decades – despite the fact that June never gives any indication that she recognizes her mother – a trip that Jack deems a "fool's errand" (15). In response to Jack's rejection of his daughter, Amy also determines to favor June over Jack, since Jack refuses to "choose what was his" (229).

Swift identifies Amy as "the strongest character" in the novel, the one with "the greatest power of decision in the book."[28] Perhaps the most important decision she makes in the present of the novel is to beg off joining the party that accompanies Jack's ashes, even though "you don't ever get a second chance to scatter your husband's ashes" (228). Instead, she visits June in order to tell her both that her father – the one "who never came to see you, who you never knew because he never wanted to know you" (278) – is dead and that she will now stop making these visits; "I've got to fend for myself now" (277), Amy reasons. Rehearsing exactly what she will tell her daughter as she rides the number 44 bus to the institution in which June lives, Amy explains, "You can blame me that you were born in the first place but you can't blame me now. . . . Fifty years is beyond the call, for bringing up baby" (277). Ray (through Amy's eyes) fleshes out the conflict between Jack and Amy over June:

> That was Jack's failing plain and simple . . . that he didn't want to know his own daughter. And [Amy's] failing . . . was just the opposite, that she'd kept on coming, two times a week all these years, and it made no difference, but she couldn't stop now, a mother was a mother. And if he'd only come himself just now and then, just once in a while, it might have balanced things out, she might have spared some of her visits for some of his, and they wouldn't have become the people they'd become, pulling opposite ways on the same rope. (171)

Amy imagines what their married life might have been like without June, had she been aborted, in an echo of the abortion that Lenny's daughter Sally has in response to her unwanted pregnancy: "So Jack and me would've been free to lead different lives, thanks to you having laid down yours" (275); "[I]t would've been better all along, wouldn't it, if we'd done what other couples do when a hot night in a hop-field [the site of June's conception] catches up with them?" (238) Amy also imagines apologizing to June for taking in a series of surrogate children, "second-stringers, VinceySallyMandy" (277), because of June's inadequacies as a daughter.

Ironically, the deceased Jack's single narrative section is given over entirely to his dead father's monologue, in a voice that Adrian Poole calls a "doubled ghost."[29] Jack, in quoting his father, only gets two words ("He said") to himself. His father's message is simple: the "whole art of butchery's in avoiding wastage" (285). This monologue is ironic in that Jack's success at avoiding wastage in the butcher business has not prevented him from wasting another perishable thing – his own life.

Another major conflict within the Dodds family through which Swift teases out questions of identity is that between Jack and Vince, father and adopted son. Born Vince Pritchett, he joins the Dodds family as a newborn, in 1944, after a "doodlebug" (103), a German flying bomb, lands on the Pritchett home in London, killing Vince's parents but sparing him. Amy, despite – or because of – having a child of her own who is retarded, adopts Vince while Jack is off fighting in the war. She does this in part as a strategy to bring Jack, who is alienated from his wife on account of June's condition, back into the fold. Vince reflects on how his introduction into the Dodds family must have originally struck Jack: "All he did was come home from winning the war and there I was – his welcome-home present – lying in that cot that was meant for June" (25).

Because of his origins and upbringing, Vince remains haunted by questions of identity, at one point thinking, "So if that bomb had killed me too, I'd never've known I'd been born, I'd never've known I'd died. So I might've been anyone" (189). Obsessing over his complex origins – "I aint who you think I am, I aint Vince Dodds" (158) – Vince wavers between identifying as a Dodds and as an outsider. At one point he imagines not really being Jack's "next-of-kin" (25) at all; at another he thinks of Amy, "She aint my mum" (188). These feelings of being an imposter date from his childhood, before he even knew where he came from, when Sally, Lenny's daughter, would accompany Vince and the Dodds to the seaside on weekends. While Sally would ride in the front of Jack's meat van, on Amy's lap, Vince would ride in the back of the van (62) because, in his imagining, "they preferred Sally to me" (63).

The most pronounced tension between Vince and his father, however, springs from their conflict over the question of whether he will join his father in the family butcher business. On this account Amy sums up the relationship between the two as tense, as typically "at daggers drawn, cleavers drawn" (240). Even as a boy Vince feels pressure to join the family business; he remembers thinking, "I ain't going to be a butcher never, it ain't what I'm going to be" (63). Just as Jack "never wanted to be a butcher in the first place, never. It was only because [his] old man wouldn't have it otherwise. Dodds and Son, family butcher since 1903" (27), so Vince wishes not to join his father in this work. Vince successfully dodges the family business by joining up for military service for five years, traveling to the Yemeni port city of Aden, "just to keep out of Jack's reach" (44) (his departure is also convenient because it allows him to flee Sally's pregnancy). As Lenny puts it of Vince, "I reckon a tour in the Middle East was a hard price to pay for not being a butcher's apprentice . . . Lad might even have had his arse shot off" (44). Vince explains, "Why d'you think I took off in the first place? Why d'you think I joined up? Because I wasn't going to be no Vince Dodds. I wasn't going to be no butcher's boy" (159). For Vince – indeed, for all of the major characters in the novel – one's identity and trade are intimately connected. Vince interprets Jack's gaze at him while on his deathbed "As if the least I owed him . . . was to have teamed up with him years ago and acted like it was a real case of flesh and blood. Except it wasn't flesh and blood, it was meat. Meat or motors. That was the choice" (24). Vince chooses "motors," becoming a used-car dealer, but laments that "you have to pick [a trade] and then you have to pretend for the rest of your life that that's what you *are*" (96).

Vince's wife Mandy further complicates his relationship with Jack and Amy. Years earlier, having run away from her native Lancashire and hitchhiked to London, Mandy meets Jack by chance in a cafeteria at Smithfield meat market (161). Jack offers her a job and a place to live, and she becomes yet another daughter substitute for Jack and Amy. Vince even tells Mandy, "you're supposed to be the sister I ain't got" (103). Vince also believes her to be bait, laid by Jack, to keep Vince at home and convince him to join the family firm. Mandy remembers summing up the situation in the Dodds household as "all the opposite of what it seemed: a son whose home it wasn't but it was, a daughter whose home it was but it wasn't because she had to be kept in a Home, a mum and dad who weren't really a mum and dad, except to me" (157). That Mandy's original father abandoned her (and her mother) links Mandy's story to many others in *Last Orders*: Vince is "abandoned" by his parents; June by Jack; Jack by Amy; and Ray by his wife Carol and his daughter Susie.

Abandonment seems also to be relevant to Mandy's and Vince's daughter, Kath, who in the novel's present is of marrying age and who is described by her mother as "a daughter on the hustle" (161). Just as Jack used Mandy to lure Vince, so Vince uses Kath to entice male buyers of his used cars (168). Specifically, Vince is depicted as pimping for his daughter; at one point he has Kath take a wealthy Arab would-be customer, Hussein, out for a spin in one of his cars, telling him, "You're in good hands with Kath" (167). Vince remembers Hussein looking at him "as though to say, Throw in the girl and I'll buy, and I look at him as though to say, Throw in an extra half-grand and she's yours" (167). Vince even imagines others thinking, "There goes Vince Dodds who sold his daughter to an Ayrab" (166). Now Hussein appears to be poised to dump Kath. As one critic puts the situation, not only does Vince "greatly resent" his dependence on Mr Hussein, "but he is especially distressed by the fact that his daughter Kath, whom he had dangled as bait before Mr. Hussein when the latter first appeared, has gone to live with Mr. Hussein and might soon be abandoned by him."[30]

As tense as things are between Vince and Kath, they are still tenser between Vince and Lenny. This tension dates from the 1960s, when Vince got Lenny's daughter Sally pregnant (the two had been childhood friends) and abandoned her to an abortion when he joined the military, just in time to be among "the last troops to clear out of Aden" (69). Vince having left Sally "a little leaving present," Lenny imagines Vince's motto to be, "Out of sight, out of mind" (49). Lenny at that time advised Sally to "get rid of it" (45) and found a doctor to "do the job" (abortion was legalized in Britain only later). And Ray, with his penchant for picking just the right horse at the racetrack, was asked by Lenny to pick a winner; this enabled Lenny to fund his daughter's expensive (because illegal) operation (204). Just five years later, Lenny notes ironically,

> we could've solved that little problem, no fuss, all above board and legal. Different time, different rules. Like one moment we're fighting over a whole heap of desert [as Jack and Ray do in North Africa], next we're pulling out of Aden snappy [as Vince does two decades later]. (204)

Similar to the way Vince treats Kath is the way Sally is viewed by her father, as something of a prostitute. On "the rebound from Big Boy," is how Lenny describes his daughter's situation; in the 1960s, Sally married Tommy Tyson, a "nutter" (132), who was subsequently convicted of "Four counts of larceny and one of assault" and who now serves time in Pentonville prison (69). Sally later started "taking on all-comers" (204), leading Amy to note that after

Sally's experience with her "Jailbird of a husband" she had "visitors of her own, paying guests. It's a living, you can see what drives a woman to it" (276). Lenny, in an echo of the Jack–June relationship, then washes his hands altogether of his daughter. Lenny comes to feel that Sally "should've stuck with [Tyson], it'll be worse when he gets out [of prison], she should've kept going to see him. Like Amy sees June"; that "It's a question of paying your dues."

> It's like Ray should patch things up with Susie, like Carol should never've run out on Ray. There shouldn't ever be no running off, deserting . . . And Jack shouldn't ever've given up on his own. (132)

At Wick's Farm in Kent Vince and Lenny actually come to blows (148).

The diminutive and lonely Ray "Lucky" Johnson, who narrates approximately half of the novel, remains superficially outside of the above entanglements and conflicts yet on a deeper level is thoroughly enmeshed in them. Lenny articulates Ray's craftiness and stealth this way: "you have to watch out for Raysy. Just when you think he aint got no advantage he pops up and surprises you, he pops out and does something canny. It's like he hides behind being small" (138).

Years ago abandoned by his wife Carol, who leaves him for another man, and half a year earlier by his daughter Susie, who moves to Australia with her boyfriend, Ray thinks, "First my daughter buggers off to Sydney and stops writing, now my wife goes and bunks it. And they call me Lucky" (100). Lucky with horses – he wins thirty-thousand pounds on the horse "Miracle Worker," for example – Ray is unlucky in love. The one bright spot in his lackluster love life was his brief affair with Amy two decades earlier (only Vic learns of the affair), in the mid-1960s, when Amy was in her mid-forties; it ended just before Vince's return from military service. The affair began with Ray's offer to join Amy during her visits to June at the "home," an obligation that Jack did not accept. While Amy seems to prize Ray's kindness above his sex-appeal – "Oh Ray, you're a lovely man, you're a lucky man, you're a little ray of sunshine, you're a little ray of hope" (284), she tells him – Ray has harbored romantic feelings for Amy dating from the time, in North Africa during World War II, that Jack showed him his wife's photograph, apparently snapped in Margate (89).

On his deathbed Jack asks Ray to secure funds by betting on the horses so that Jack can pay back his significant debt and set up Amy for the rest of her life. Ray takes Jack's request as a "sign" and "permit" and "blessing" for Ray to become re-involved with Amy, "to carry on where we left off" (283). Ray surmises that Jack knew about their affair of long ago all along and now is thinking, "These are my shoes, Raysy, go on, step in 'em, wear 'em. You always should've worn them, if there was anything other than the rule of blind chance in this world" (283). "Miracle Worker" having come in and Jack having died before he could learn of Ray's successful gamble, Ray is faced with the choice of pocketing the winnings from "Miracle Worker" (as only the deceased Jack certainly knew of the bet), or of giving the winnings outright to Amy, or of using the winnings, "thirty thousand smackers in my wallet" (283), to take himself and Amy on a holiday to Australia to see Susie. Ray feels guilty even contemplating the former course (he imagines Vic, Vince, and Lenny being able to see "that Raysy's got a lot of something that aint his" [225]), yet this does not stop him from entertaining it as a possibility. Ray also feels profound guilt for not writing his daughter for decades because of the shame he felt when his wife left him for another man. The present of *Last Orders* is limited to one long day; we never learn what Ray chooses to do with the money he won in order to buy Jack out of his crippling debt and subsidize Amy's life, or what happens between Ray and Amy or between Ray and Susie. That said, the trajectory of the novel's action is toward connection, reconciliation, integration, making amends.

Last Orders is a novel that yearns for closure, summing up, finality, reclaiming origins, while at the same time it rejects the possibility of achieving such things. Margate plays an important role in this yearning: it is a nostalgic site of weekend vacations in the past; the place where Jack hoped to retire with Amy (but not with June) after giving up his (by then failing) butcher business; and a terminus point for Vic's, Vince's, Lenny's, and Ray's journey (and the place where Jack's ashes will be committed to the sea). Margate is also a means for the novel to probe the tension between nostalgic ideals and quotidian realities, between life as the characters wish it to be and life as it is in fact lived.

Toward the end of Jack's life Margate was both the site of the distant, idealized past and of the prospective future. A destination for family weekend excursions, the pleasure pier at Margate was also the place that Jack and Amy visited years earlier, after June's birth. The gap then, between what the two were supposed to feel at the funfair of "Dreamland" and what they in fact felt, yawned wide. While the pleasure pier atmosphere was meant to encourage joviality and hopefulness, Jack and Amy were anything but happy. Jack won Amy a teddy bear in the duck-shooting gallery, but ended up throwing the stuffed animal, a figuration of June, over the side of the pier, just as Jack's ashes were to be thrown years later by his cronies. In this remembered episode Amy thinks of Margate, "This [funfair] isn't true, it's only a picture, a seaside postcard" (254); and we learn that she even contemplated leaving Jack altogether (254–5). Jack's dream, years later, of escaping London with Amy (but not with June) to retire in Margate, is used to explore the a gap between the attempt to rewrite history and the impossibility of doing so. Amy recalls Jack saying, "'Margate. How about Margate?' As if we could put the clock back and start off again where it all stopped. Second honeymoon. As if Margate was another word for magic" (229).

In the present of the novel, as his friends prepare to dispense Jack's ashes, Margate once again functions to explore the yawning gap between the nostalgic ideal and the all-too-real. The seedy appearance of the pleasure pier on this day of severe weather, Ray thinks, makes Margate an unlikely candidate for a "journey's end" and a "final resting-place, where you'd want to come to finish your days and find peace and contentment for ever and ever" (269). For Ray, Margate, after all the anticipation, "aint much to write home about" (281), with its decayed pier resembling "a dump" (289), and with its shuttered arcades save for "one or two . . . all flickering and winking" (269). "It's a poor dream," Ray thinks of the "Dreamland" funfair, "Except all dreams are poor" (281). Like the four travelers themselves, the pleasure pier looks haggard, faded, and aged; like them, it does not live up to its ideal. As in Ishiguro's *The Remains of the Day*, the final scene of *Last Orders*, also on a pleasure pier, exudes disappointment while probing life's boundaries: "One way there's Margate and Dreamland, the other there's the open sea," Ray reflects; "We are at the end" (292). Margate, according to Ray,

> doesn't look like the end of the road, it doesn't look like what you'd aim for and work for. It looks like it's trying to keep going all year round something that only happened once one whoopsy weekend. So this is what you get, this is where you come. I reckon it's all about wanting to be a kid again, bucket and spade and a gob full of ice cream. Or it's all about being on the edge, which you are, other sense, and you know it. Not where the road's going, just where it don't go no further . . . End of the road, end of the pier. Splash. (272–73)

The friends become "soaked" (291) in the blinding rainstorm that finally comes. Tellingly, the four cannot prevent Jack's ashes from sticking to them (293) as they attempt to grab handfuls of it from the urn and scatter it into the sea. Like it or not, living or dead, Jack literally and figuratively rubs off on them all.

While Swift's novel exhibits many recognizably postmodern features – narrative self-reflexivity, the use of pastiche, the inter-animation of past and present times, a blurring of elite and demotic, "high" and "low" art forms, and the fragmentation of unified subjectivity[31] – it nevertheless "hesitates between a postmodern subversion of identity and a commitment to identity politics."[32] Indeed, many readers have noted that Swift's postmodern orientation is coupled with a more backward-looking view. David Leon Higdon, for example, writes of Swift's ability to "create a type of closure which successfully combines the postmodern sense of the human being perpetually *en passant* with the aesthetic demands for some type of boundary";[33] while Pamela Cooper wonders whether it is perhaps more appropriate to see Swift as "a neo-modernist rather than a postmodernist."[34] In this respect *Last Orders* is paradoxical, yearning for yet also severely ironizing the possibility of stable identity, interpretive closure, fixed meanings, and objective history. What Lenny thinks of Vince's grasp of the meaning of Canterbury Cathedral as reducible to what he reads in his guidebook, for example – "He's studying that guidebook like it's got all the answers" (203) – is germane to the novel's warning about how *not* to read it. Swift's work does not contain "all the answers" to the questions and problems that it poses, any more than Ray possesses an objective view of the scene containing Jack's "guard of honour" and the local sheep at Wick's Farm:

> The sheep are still staring at us. I reckon we must look as daft to them as they do to us, and I reckon anyone looking up from down below at the four of us on the top of this hill must think we're stranger-looking than the sheep. (150)

Like most if not all of the novels explored in this volume, *Last Orders* emphasizes the great extent to which perspective determines knowledge and "truth," and to which narrative meaning is multivalent and endlessly open to reinterpretation. It is perhaps these emphases, above all, that give the novel of 1950–2000 its special character and force.

Notes

Preface

1 Arthur Marwick, *British Society since 1945*, 3rd edn. (Harmondsworth: Penguin Books, 1996), p. 7.
2 John Brannigan, *Orwell to the Present: Literature in England, 1945–2000* (Basingstoke: Palgrave Macmillan, 2003), p. 9.

1 Introduction: Contexts and Concepts

1 A. S. Byatt, "People in paper houses: attitudes to 'realism' and 'experiment' in English post-war fiction," in *Passions of the Mind: Selected Writings* (New York: Turtle Bay Books, 1992), p. 147.
2 Malcolm Bradbury, *The Modern World: Ten Great Writers* (Harmondsworth: Penguin Books, 1990), p. 3.
3 Pound quoted in Herbert Schneidau, *Waking Giants: The Presence of the Past in Modernism* (New York and Oxford: Oxford University Press, 1991), p. 137. I am indebted to Schneidau's articulation of the problem of "mortmain" in modernist literature.
4 Quoted in Bradbury, *Modern World*, p. 10.
5 George Bernard Shaw, *Major Barbara* [1905] (Harmondsworth: Penguin Books, 1960), pp. 140–1.
6 George Orwell, "Inside the whale," in *A Collection of Essays by George Orwell* (San Diego: Harcourt Brace Jovanovich, 1954), pp. 228–9.
7 Orwell, "Inside the whale," p. 245.
8 T. S. Eliot, "The metaphysical poets," in *Selected Prose* (New York: Harcourt Brace Jovanovich and Farrar, Straus, and Giroux, 1975), p. 65.
9 Matthew Arnold, "Dover Beach," in *The Norton Anthology of English Literature*, 7th edn., vol. 2, ed. M. H. Abrams (New York: W. W. Norton, 2000), p. 1492.

10   W. B. Yeats, "The Second Coming," in *Collected Poems* (New York: Macmillan, 1956), p. 184.

11   Karl Marx, "Contribution to the critique of Hegel's *Philosophy of Right*: Introduction," in *The Marx–Engels Reader*, 2nd edn., ed. Robert C. Tucker (New York: W. W. Norton, 1978), p. 54.

12   Friedrich Nietzsche, *The Gay Science* (New York: Vintage Books, 1974), p. 181.

13   Sigmund Freud, *Future of an Illusion* (New York: W. W. Norton, 1961), pp. 53, 49.

14   Orwell, "Inside the whale," p. 228.

15   For more on this see Sigmund Freud, *Five Lectures on Psycho-Analysis* (New York: W. W. Norton, 1961), pp. 18–27.

16   Kenneth Graham, "Conrad and modernism," in *Cambridge Companion to Joseph Conrad*, ed. J. H. Stape (Cambridge: Cambridge University Press, 1996), p. 211.

17   Malcolm Bradbury, *The Modern British Novel* (Harmondsworth: Penguin Books, 1994), p. 268.

18   Gerald Graff, "The myth of the postmodernist breakthrough," in *The Novel Today: Contemporary Writers on Modern Fiction*, ed. Malcolm Bradbury (Manchester: Manchester University Press and Rowman & Littlefield, 1977), p. 219.

19   John Barth, "The literature of replenishment," in *Essentials of the Theory of Fiction*, ed. Michael Hoffman and Patrick Murphy (Durham and London: Duke University Press, 1988), p. 430.

20   John Wain, quoted in Rubin Rabinovitz, *The Reaction Against Experiment in the English Novel, 1950–1960* (New York and London: Columbia University Press, 1967), p. 8.

21   C. P. Snow, quoted in Randall Stevenson, *A Reader's Guide to the Twentieth-Century Novel in Britain* (Lexington: University Press of Kentucky, 1993), p. 96.

22   C. P. Snow, quoted in Frank Kermode, "The house of fiction: interviews with seven novelists," in Bradbury, *The Novel Today*, p. 129.

23   Kingsley Amis, quoted in Michael Barber, "The art of fiction LIX, Kingsley Amis" (interview), *Paris Review* 64 (1975), p. 46.

24   Quoted in Rabinovitz, *Reaction Against Experiment*, pp. 40–1.

25   David Lodge, *The Novelist at the Crossroads and Other Essays on Fiction and Criticism* (Ithaca, NY: Cornell University Press, 1971), p. 19.

26   David Lodge, *Modernism, Antimodernism and Postmodernism* (published lecture) (Birmingham: University of Birmingham, 1977), p. 10.

27   B. S. Johnson, "Introduction to *Aren't You Rather Young to be Writing Your Memoirs?*," in Bradbury, *The Novel Today*, p. 152.

28   Ibid.

29   Ibid., p. 155.

30   Ibid., p. 167.

31   John Fowles, "Notes on an unfinished novel," in Bradbury, *The Novel Today*, p. 147.

32   Malcolm Bradbury, *Modern British Novel*, p. 408.

33 Hans Bertens, *The Idea of the Postmodern: A History* (London and New York: Routledge, 1995), p. 3.

34 Ibid., pp. 10–11.

35 Jean-François Lyotard, *The Postmodern Condition: A Report on Knowledge* (Minneapolis: University of Minnesota Press, 1984), p. xiv.

36 Han Bertens, "Jean-François Lyotard," in *Postmodernism: The Key Figures*, ed. Hans Bertens and Joseph Natoli (Oxford: Blackwell Publishing, 2002), p. 247.

37 Douglas Kellner, "Jean Baudrillard," in Bertens and Natoli, *Postmodernism*, p. 52.

38 Ibid., p. 53.

39 Jean Baudrillard, *Simulacra and Simulation* (Ann Arbor: University of Michigan Press, 1994), p. 1.

40 Steven Best and Douglass Kellner, *The Postmodern Turn* (New York and London: Guilford Press, 1997), pp. 132, 130.

41 Ibid., p. 130.

42 Ibid.

43 Ibid., p. 131.

44 Ibid., p. 132.

45 Andrei Codrescu, quoted in R. B. Kershner, *The Twentieth-Century Novel: An Introduction* (Boston: Bedford Books, 1997), p. 76.

46 Virginia Woolf, "Modern fiction," in *The English Modernist Reader, 1910–1930*, ed. Peter Faulkner (Iowa City: University of Iowa Press, 1986), pp. 108–9.

47 Douwe W. Fokkema, *Literary History, Modernism, and Postmodernism* (Amsterdam and Philadelphia: John Benjamins, 1984), p. 40.

48 John Carey, *The Intellectuals and the Masses: Pride and Prejudice Among the Literary Intelligensia, 1880–1939* (New York: St Martin's Press, 1992), p. vii.

49 D. H. Lawrence, "Why the novel matters," in Faulkner, *English Modernist Reader*, p. 145.

50 George Orwell, "England your England," in *Collection of Essays*, p. 252.

51 Bradbury, *Modern British Novel*, p. 264.

52 Iris Murdoch, "Against dryness," in *Existentialists and Mystics: Writings on Philosophy and Literature* (New York: Allen Lane/The Penguin Press, 1998), p. 287.

53 George Steiner, *Language and Silence: Essays on Language, Literature, and the Inhuman* (New York: Atheneum, 1967), p. ix.

54 Ibid., pp. viii–ix.

55 H. Rider Haggard, *She, King Solomon's Mines, Allan Quatermain: Three Novels* (New York: Dover, 1951), p. 420.

56 Joseph Conrad, *Heart of Darkness* and *The Secret Sharer* (New York: New American Library, 1950), p. 83.

57 Zygmunt Bauman, *Modernity and the Holocaust* (Ithaca, NY: Cornell University Press, 1989), p. 98.

58 Ibid., p. 101.

59 Ibid., p. 102.

60 Ibid.

61 Ibid.

62 Ibid., p. 103.

63 Ibid., p. 104.

64 Muriel Spark, *The Prime of Miss Jean Brodie* (New York: HarperPerennial, 1994), p. 45.

65 Kazuo Ishiguro, *The Remains of the Day* (New York: Vintage Books, 1989), p. 146.

    First awarded in 1969, the Booker Prize has come to be recognized, for better or worse, as Britain's most prestigious and influential literary prize. The increasingly generous award and publicity are career-changing for the winner, although the judging – by a different panel each year – is inevitably that of the moment rather than of history. For its first 35 years the prize went to the author whose novel published in the previous year was judged the best of those submitted from Britain, the Commonwealth and the Republic of Ireland. Since then its terms of entry have widened, and it is now called the Man Booker Prize for Fiction. For more on this prize and on other British literary awards, see James F. English, "The literary prize phenomenon in context," in *A Companion to the British and Irish Novel 1945–2000*, ed. Brian W. Shaffer (Oxford: Blackwell Publishing, 2005).

66 Erich Fromm, *Escape from Freedom* (New York: Avon Books, 1965), p. 163.

67 William Golding, "Fable," in *The Hot Gates and Other Occasional Pieces* (New York: Harcourt, Brace and World, 1966), pp. 86–7.

68 Caryl Phillips, *A New World Order: Essays* (New York: Vintage Books, 2002), p. 242.

69 Linda Richards, "January interview with Kazuo Ishiguro," www.januarymagazine.com/profiles/ishiguro

70 Salman Rushdie, *Imaginary Homelands: Essays and Criticism 1981–1991* (London: Granta Books, 1991), p. 20.

71 Emma Tennant, quoted in Stevenson, *Reader's Guide*, p. 131.

72 Feroza Jussawalla and Reed Way Dasenbrock, "Introduction," in *Interviews with Writers of the Post-Colonial World* (Jackson and London: University Press of Mississippi, 1992), p. 3.

73 Stevenson, *Reader's Guide*, p. 126.

74 Jussawalla and Dasenbrock, "Introduction," p. 4.

75 Rushdie, *Imaginary Homelands*, pp. 64, 70.

76 Raymond Williams, *Keywords: A Vocabulary of Culture and Society* (New York: Oxford University Press, 1976), pp. 131–2.

77 Bill Ashcroft, Gareth Griffiths, and Helen Tiffin, *The Empire Writes Back: Theory and Practice in Post-Colonial Literatures* (London and New York: Routledge, 1989), p. 195.

78 Jussawalla and Dasenbrock, "Introduction," p. 6.

79 Ibid., p. 13.

80 Ibid., p. 14.

81 Simon Gikandi, *Maps of Englishness: Writing Identity in the Culture of Colonialism* (New York: Columbia University Press, 1996), p. xi.

82 O'Brien has even authored a short biography of James Joyce.

83 Another internationally celebrated Canadian prose writer, Alice Munro, is known mainly for her short fiction.

84 Rushdie, *Imaginary Homelands*, p. 64.

85 Jussawalla and Dasenbrock, "Introduction," p. 4.

86 Chinua Achebe, "African literature as restoration of celebration," in *Chinua Achebe: A Celebration*, ed. Kirsten Holst Peterson and Anna Rutherford (Oxford: Heinemann, 1990), pp. 7–8.

87 Chinua Achebe, "Role of the writer in a new nation," in *African Writers on African Writing*, ed. G. D. Killam (Evanston, IL: Northwestern University Press, 1973), p. 12.

88 Rushdie, *Imaginary Homelands*, p. 17.

89 Phillips, *New World Order*, p. 192.

90 Ibid., p. 130.

91 Jean Rhys, *Letters 1931–1966* (Harmondsworth: Penguin Books, 1985), p. 24.

92 Rushdie, *Imaginary Homelands*, p. 19.

93 Phillips, *New World Order*, p. 294.

94 Rushdie, *Imaginary Homelands*, p. 19.

95 Ibid., pp. 124–5.

96 Dominic Head, *Cambridge Introduction to Modern British Fiction, 1950–2000* (Cambridge: Cambridge University Press, 2002), p. 164.

97 Phillips, *New World Order*, pp. 1, 2, 3, 4.

98 Ibid., p. 283.

99 Ibid., p. 286.

100 Head, *Cambridge Introduction*, p. 180.

101 Rushdie, *Imaginary Homelands*, p. 136.

102 Ibid., p. 134.

103 Ibid., p. 130.

104 Phillips, *New World Order*, p. 296.

105 Allan Vorda and Kim Herzinger, "An interview with Kazuo Ishiguro," *Mississippi Review* 20 (1991), pp. 139–40. For an insightful full-length study of the "black British" novel, see Bruce King, *The Internationalization of English Literature*, Oxford English Literary History, vol. 13: 1948–2000 (Oxford: Oxford University Press, 2004).

106 John Fowles, "Notes on an unfinished novel," p. 138.

107 M. M. Bakhtin, *The Dialogic Imagination: Four Essays* (Austin: University of Texas Press, 1981), p. 331.

108 For more on the history and origins of the novel in English, see Ian Watt's *The Rise of the Novel* and Michael McKeon's *The Origins of the English Novel, 1600–1740*.

109 Forster, quoted in David K. Danow, *The Thought of Mikhail Bakhtin: From Word to Culture* (New York: St Martin's Press, 1991), p. 43.

110 T. S. Eliot, "*Ulysses*, order, and myth," in *Selected Prose*, p. 177.

111 Danow, *Thought of Mikhail Bakhtin*, pp. 50, 43.

112 Bakhtin, *Dialogic Imagination*, p. 47.

113 Ibid., pp. 17, 39, 11.

114 Frank Kermode, *The Sense of an Ending: Studies in the Theory of Fiction* (London: Oxford University Press, 1967), p. 39.

115 Rushdie, *Imaginary Homelands*, p. 14.

116 Orwell, "Inside the whale," p. 241.

117 Rushdie, *Imaginary Homelands*, p. 100.

118 Ibid., p. 15.

119 John Barth, "Literature of replenishment," p. 432.

120 M. M. Bakhtin, *Speech Genres and Other Late Essays* (Austin: University of Texas Press, 1986), p. 7.

121 Ibid., p. 162.

2 Kingsley Amis's *Lucky Jim* (1954)

1 Kingsley Amis, *Lucky Jim* [1954] (Harmondsworth: Penguin Books, 1992), p. 204. Further references are noted parenthetically in the text.

2 Malcolm Bradbury, *The Modern British Novel* (Harmondsworth: Penguin Books, 1993), p. 324.

3 David Lodge, "Introduction" to Kingsley Amis, *Lucky Jim* (Harmondsworth: Penguin Books, 1992), p. v.

4 Merritt Moseley, *Understanding Kingsley Amis* (Columbia: University of South Carolina Press, 1993), pp. 18–19.

5 Bradbury, *Modern British Novel*, p. 320.

6 Malcolm Bradbury, *No, Not Bloomsbury* (New York: Columbia University Press, 1988), pp. 207, 204.

7 William Van O'Connor, *The New University Wits and the End of Modernism* (Carbondale: Southern Illinois University Press, 1963), p. 78.

8 Dale Salwak, "An interview with Kingsley Amis," *Contemporary Literature* 16 (1975), p. 18.

9 Moseley, *Understanding Kingsley Amis*, p. 1.

10 Lodge, "Introduction," p. vii.

11 Ibid., pp. vii–viii. See also Christian Gutleben, "English academic satire from the Middle Ages to postmodernism: distinguishing the comic from the satiric," in *Theorizing Satire: Essays in Literary Criticism*, ed. Brian A. Connery and Kirk Combe (New York: St Martin's Press, 1995).

12 Amis quoted in Elaine Showalter, "Ladlit.," in *On Modern British Fiction*, ed. Zachary Leader (Oxford: Oxford University Press, 2002), p. 62.

13 Janice Rossen, "Philip Larkin and *Lucky Jim*," *Journal of Modern Literature* 22 (1998), p. 147.

14 Kingsley Amis, *Memoirs* (New York: Summit Books, 1991), p. 56.

15 Amis writes: "In 1950 or so I sent [Larkin] my sprawling first draft and got back what amounted to a synopsis of the first third of the structure and other things

besides. He decimated the characters that, in carried-away style, I had poured into the tale without care for the plot . . . He helped me to make a proper start" (*Memoirs*, p. 57).

16 Lodge, "Introduction," p. ix.

17 Peter Kalliney, "Cities of affluence: masculinity, class, and the Angry Young Men," *Modern Fiction Studies* 47 (2001), p. 93.

18 Harry Blamires, *Twentieth-Century English Literature* (New York: Schocken Books, 1982), p. 222. Sir William Beveridge's 1942 *Social Insurance and Allied Services* became a best-selling blueprint for postwar British social policy. As Dominic Head observes, "Beveridge's plan was for a comprehensive welfare programme, premised on the expectation of full employment, and involving a universal national insurance scheme, and a national health service. It was a social vision that caught the public mood" (Dominic Head, *Cambridge Introduction to Modern British Fiction, 1950–2000* [Cambridge: Cambridge University Press, 2002], pp. 13–14).

19 Salwak, "Interview," pp. 2–3.

20 Michael Barber, "The art of fiction LIX, Kingsley Amis" (interview), *Paris Review* 64 (1975), p. 46.

21 Kingsley Amis, "Myths about "The Angry Young Men," *Encounter* 31/5 (1968), p. 95. Amis went so far as to assert, in a letter to Larkin, "Well, what a load of bullshit all that was in the *Spr* about the new movt. Etc." (quoted in Christopher Hitchens, "The man of feeling," *Atlantic Monthly* [May 2002], p. 106).

22 Bradbury, *Modern British Novel*, p. 318. For example, Iris Murdoch, who had just published her first novel *Under the Net* (1954), also was included in this "movement" by many contemporary critics.

"The Angry Young Men" authors also overlapped socially and intellectually with a group of poets loosely termed "The Movement," which included Amis himself, John Wain, Thom Gunn, Donald Davie, D. J. Enright, Robert Conquest, and of course their mentor Philip Larkin. As David Lodge explains, these poets consciously set out "to displace the declamatory, surrealistic, densely metaphorical poetry of Dylan Thomas and his associates with verse that was well-formed, comprehensible, dry, witty, colloquial and down-to-earth" (Lodge, "Introduction," pp. viii–ix). These poets first appeared together in 1956 in two important volumes: Robert Conquest's *New Lines* and G. S. Fraser's *Poetry Now*. Members of "The Movement" rejected Romanticism as well as its stepchild, modernism. J. D. Scott, writing in the *Spectator* in 1954, summarized the poets in this group as being "bored by the despair of the Forties, not much interested in suffering, and extremely impatient of poetic sensibility, especially poetic sensibility about 'the writer and society'" (quoted in Hitchens, "Man of feeling," p. 106). The poetry of Philip Larkin in particular exemplified the new voice – "plain-speaking, exact, observant, pessimistic, anti-romantic" (Bradbury, *No, Not Bloomsbury*, p. 207) – of this rebellious group. Dominic Head believes that it may be more appropriate "to read *Lucky Jim* as embodying the sensibility of the Movement primarily," rather than that of the Angries (*Cambridge Introduction*, p. 50).

23 Salwak, "Interview," p. 2.

24 John Osborne, *Look Back in Anger* (Harmondsworth: Penguin Books, 1957), p. 84.

25 Lodge, "Introduction," p. xi.

26 Leslie Paul, "The Angry Young Men revisited," *Kenyon Review* 27 (1965), p. 345.

27 Kingsley Amis, "Why Lucky Jim turned right," in *What Became of Jane Austen? And Other Questions* (New York: Harcourt Brace Jovanovich, 1970), p. 201.

28 Bradbury, *No, Not Bloomsbury*, p. 204. The Fabians were a moderate Socialist order with which Bernard Shaw earlier had been associated.

29 Bradbury, *No, Not Bloomsbury*, p. 205. Amis himself notes that in 1956 he "let it be known" that he "had always voted Labour" and probably "always would," yet in 1964 "voted Labour for the last time" (Amis, "Why Lucky Jim turned right," p. 200).

30 Rubin Rabinovitz, *The Reaction Against Experiment in the English Novel, 1950–1960* (New York: Columbia University Press, 1967), p. 61.

31 O'Connor, *New University Wits*, p. 98.

32 Quoted in Moseley, *Understanding Kingsley Amis*, p. 3.

33 Ibid., p. 3.

34 Quoted in Edmund Wilson, *The Bit Between My Teeth: A Literary Chronicle of 1950–1965* (New York: Farrar, Straus, and Giroux, 1966), p. 276.

35 Bradbury, *No, Not Bloomsbury*, p. 207.

36 Barber, "Art of fiction," p. 46. Amis is known to have deemed Joyce "a waste of time" (quoted in Richard Fallis, "*Lucky Jim* and academic wishful thinking," *Studies in the Novel* 9 [1977], p. 66). Similarly, the novelist C. P. Snow in 1958 remarked that many authors viewed "Joyce's way" as "at best a cul-de-sac" (quoted in Randall Stevenson, *A Reader's Guide to The Twentieth-Century Novel in Britain* [Lexington: University Press of Kentucky, 1993], p. 96).

37 Bradbury, *No, Not Bloomsbury*, p. 207.

38 Gilbert Phelps, "The post-war English novel," in *The New Pelican Guide to English Literature*, vol. 8: *The Present*, ed. Boris Ford (Harmondsworth: Penguin Books, 1983), p. 431.

39 Barber, "Art of fiction," p. 47.

40 Quoted in Rabinovitz, *Reaction Against Experiment*, p. 39.

41 Quoted in ibid., pp. 40–1.

42 Bradbury, *Modern British Novel*, p. 321.

43 Amis's friend Robert Conquest published an essay, "Christian symbolism in 'Lucky Jim'," written as a joke but widely read in earnest, which parodied academic literary criticism for being arcane, obscure, and pretentious.

44 Lodge, "Introduction," p. vi.

45 Bradbury, *No, Not Bloomsbury*, p. 206.

46 Quoted in Bradbury, *Modern British Novel*, p. 322.

47 In his prefatory essay to *Joseph Andrews* Fielding makes an observation that is of obvious relevance to *Lucky Jim*: "the only source of the true Ridiculous is affectation, which has two aspects: vanity and hypocrisy" (quoted in David Lodge,

Language of Fiction: Essays in Criticism and Verbal Analysis of the English Novel [London: Routledge and Kegan Paul, 1966], p. 250).

48 Walter Allen, *Tradition and Dream: The English and American Novel from the Twenties to Our Time* (London: Phoenix Books, 1964), pp. 281–2.

49 Quoted in Moseley, *Understanding Kingsley Amis*, p. 12.

50 Barber, "Art of fiction," p. 49.

51 Kingsley Amis, "Laughter's to be taken seriously," *The New York Times Book Review*, July 7, 1957, p. 1.

52 Salwak, "Interview," p. 7.

53 O'Connor, *New University Wits*, p. 85.

54 Moseley, *Understanding Kingsley Amis*, p. 22.

55 David Lodge notes that "Several critics have perceived a fairy-tale buried in the deep structure of *Lucky Jim*, in which Jim is the Frog Prince, Christine the Princess, Gore-Urquhart the Fairy Godmother, and Margaret the Witch" ("Introduction," p. xiii).

56 Bradbury, *Modern British Novel*, p. 321.

57 "He'd been drawn into the Margaret business," Jim reasons, "by a combination of virtues he hadn't known he possessed: politeness, friendly interest, ordinary concern, a good-natured willingness to be imposed upon, a desire for unequivocal friendship" (10). Jim's "passably decent treatment" of her is attributed to his "temporary victory of fear over irritation and/or pity over boredom" (111).

58 Amis has called Margaret "a sort of sexual bore" (Barber, "Art of fiction," p. 50) and "a neurotic person who brings pressure to bear by being neurotic" (Salwak, "Interview," p. 7).

59 The distinction in E. M. Forster's 1908 novel *A Room with a View* between (English) gentility, decorum, and civility and (Italian) passion, feeling, and emotion is relevant here.

60 For example, compare the Jim–Margaret and the Jim–Christine romance scenes (p. 58 and p. 151).

61 This anxiety and repression dominate Jim's experience; he is made uncomfortable by lust – his own or another's – and by the sight of an attractive female.

62 Salwak, "Interview," p. 8.

63 James Gindin, *Postwar British Fiction: New Accents and Attitudes* (Berkeley: University of California Press, 1962), p. 49.

64 Jim wins over Gore-Urquhart because of his lecture and because of his reference to himself as a "boredom-detector . . . a finely-tuned instrument," who would be of great use to any millionaire who hires him. "Like a canary down a mine," Dixon could be sent into "dinners and cocktail parties and night-clubs" in advance of his employer, would could then read his "boredom-coefficient" and determine "whether it was worth going in himself or not" (215).

65 Fallis, "*Lucky Jim*", p. 68.

66 Ibid.

67 Lodge adds, "The longest and most important piece of continuous action in the novel, extending over six chapters and some fifty pages, centres on a ball, a device

for bringing characters together that goes back as far as the eighteenth-century novel" ("Introduction," p. viii).

68 Lodge, "Introduction," p. xiii.

69 Ibid., pp. xv–xvi. Again like Forster in *A Room with a View*, Amis in *Lucky Jim* teases us with false engagements (Bertrand and Christine, Dixon and Margaret) that never materialize, and brings hero and heroine together despite the numerous foils (Margaret and the Welch family) that labor tirelessly to keep them apart.

70 Quoted in Ted E. Boyle and Terence Brown, "The serious side of Kingsley Amis's *Lucky Jim*," *Critique: Studies in Modern Fiction* 9 (1966), p. 100.

71 C. Hugh Holman, *A Handbook to Literature*, 3rd edn. (Indianapolis: Bobbs-Merrill, 1972), p. 473.

72 Barber, "Art of fiction," p. 45.

73 Amis, "Laughter's to be taken seriously," p. 1.
   Amis distinguishes between the satirist and the "social" novelist and aligns himself with the former camp while eschewing any association with the latter. "I have ideas about society, naturally," Amis writes, "but human behaviour is what I see myself writing about" (quoted in O'Connor, *New University Wits*, p. 76).

74 For more on this see Gutleben, "English academic satire," p. 134.

75 Lodge, "Introduction," p. viii.

76 Stevenson, *Reader's Guide*, p. 121.

77 Phelps, "Post-war English novel," p. 430.

78 As Bradbury points out, "A redbrick university was an ideal location for Jim Dixon's story, since here the manners of other places – the traditions and snobberies of privileged Oxbridge colleges, the mannered eccentricities of upper-middle-class donnish style, the constant appeal beyond the here-and-now to an imaginary Merrie England – prevailed in a world which gave them no support" (*No, Not Bloomsbury*, p. 209).

79 Lodge, "Introduction," p. viii.

80 Ibid., p. xi.

81 At the musicale Jim "tried to listen to Welch's song, to marvel at its matchless predictability, its austere, unswerving devotion to tedium" (64). The combined voices at song strike Jim as so much "soporific droning" (36).

82 Bradbury, *No, Not Bloomsbury*, p. 208.

83 Fallis, "*Lucky Jim*", p. 65.

84 In this connection, Jim disparages the modern world ("The hydrogen bomb, the South African Government, Chiang Kai-shek, Senator McCarthy" [87]) as much as he does the medieval one, avoiding both left-wing progressivism and right-wing antiquarianism.

85 Salwak, "Interview," p. 8.

86 Lodge, "Introduction," p. xi.

87 Hitchens, "Man of feeling," p. 105. Beesley, a colleague of Jim's in the English Department, maligns recent educational reforms in general and the "Education Authority grants" in particular, which in his view lower the aggregate academic level of students, increase their numbers, and have implications for education

hiring, particularly in the "provincial universities" (170). For him (and one imagines for Amis), overall educational quality diminishes in Britain as overall student numbers increase.

88 Lodge, "Introduction," p. vi.
89 Lodge, *Language of Fiction*, p. 251.
90 Ibid., p. 252.
91 For example, Jim "looked at his face now in the mirror: it looked back at him, humourless and self-pitying" (164); Jim's reflection in the mirror "looked healthy and, he hoped, honest and kindly. He'd have to be content with that" (65).
92 Lodge, *Language of Fiction*, pp. 254–5.
93 Ibid., p. 255.
94 Ibid.

3 William Golding's *Lord of the Flies* (1954)

1 William Golding, "Fable," in *The Hot Gates and Other Occasional Pieces* (New York: Harcourt, Brace & World, 1966), pp. 86–7.
2 William Golding quoted in Jack I. Biles (ed.) *Talk: Conversations with William Golding* (New York: Harcourt, Brace, Jovanovich, 1970), p. 3.
3 E. M. Forster, "Introduction," in *William Golding's "Lord of the Flies": Casebook Edition; Text, Notes & Criticism*, ed. James R. Baker and Arthur P. Ziegler (New York: G. P. Putnam's Sons, 1964), p. 207.
4 Bernard F. Dick quoted in Kathleen Woodward, "On aggression: William Golding's *Lord of the Flies*," in *No Place Else: Explorations in Utopian and Dystopian Fiction*, ed. Eric S. Rabkin, Martin H. Greenberg, and Joseph D. Olander (Carbondale: Southern Illinois University Press, 1983), p. 205.
5 Golding's novel is reminiscent of certain works of Joseph Conrad and of Euripides. As for the Conrad connection, although Golding in 1962 claims not to have read *Heart of Darkness* (see James Keating, "Interview with William Golding," in *William Golding: Casebook Edition*, p. 194), E. L. Epstein notes an allusion to Conrad's novella in *Lord of the Flies* and says that "Golding seems very close to Conrad, both in basic principles and in artistic method" (E. L. Epstein, "Notes on *Lord of the Flies*," in *William Golding: Casebook Edition*, p. 281). And Frederick R. Karl maintains that, "Ideologically, *Lord of the Flies* and *Heart of Darkness* are analogous," and that "throughout his entire canon" Golding "is treading on Conrad's territory" (Frederick R. Karl, "Assessing *Lord of the Flies*," in *Readings on "Lord of the Flies"*, ed. Clarice Swisher [San Diego: Greenhaven Press, 1997], p. 157). For Golding's connection with Euripides' *Bacchae*, see James R. Baker, "The decline of *Lord of the Flies*," *South Atlantic Quarterly* 69 (1970), p. 455, and Bernard F. Dick, *William Golding*, rev. edn. (Boston: Twayne Publishers, 1987), pp. 9–13.
6 Malcolm Bradbury, *No, Not Bloomsbury* (New York: Columbia University Press, 1988), p. 341.

7 The *Time* magazine essay, "Lord of the campus," is reprinted in *William Golding: Casebook Edition*, pp. 283–5.

8 See William Golding, *A Moving Target* (New York: Farrar, Straus, and Giroux, 1982), p. 171.

9 See, for example, the essays collected in *William Golding: Casebook Edition*; in *William Golding's "Lord of the Flies": Bloom's Notes*, ed. Harold Bloom (Broomall, PA: Chelsea House Publishers, 1996); and in Swisher, *Readings on "Lord of the Flies"*.

10 James R. Baker, *William Golding: A Critical Study* (New York: St Martin's Press, 1965), pp. 15–16.

11 Baker, *William Golding*, p. 16.

12 Forster, "Introduction," pp. 209–10. And Arthur P. Ziegler, in his forward to *William Golding: Casebook Edition*, observes that Golding's view is not "traditionally Christian" (p. x).

13 Baker, *William Golding*, p. 15.

14 Among other differences, according to "angry" novelist John Wain, Golding "is not a novelist" at all but "an allegorist" (quoted in Randall Stevenson, *The British Novel since the Thirties: An Introduction* [Athens: University of Georgia Press, 1986], p. 171). Kingsley Amis says something similar in a review of Golding's third novel, *Pincher Martin*: "I hope Mr. Golding will forgive me if I ask him to turn his gifts of originality, of intransigence, and above all of passion, to the world where we have to live" (quoted in L. L. Dickson, *The Modern Allegories of William Golding* [Tampa: University of South Florida Press, 1990], p. 11).

15 Randall Stevenson, *A Reader's Guide to The Twentieth-Century Novel in Britain* (Lexington: University Press of Kentucky, 1993), p. 99. Novelist John Fowles stresses Golding's distance not only from the "Angries" but from all literary groups when he calls him "his own writer, his own school of one" (quoted in the Introduction to Swisher, *Readings on "Lord of the Flies"*, p. 11).

16 Baker, *William Golding*, p. xiii.

17 Golding comments that the war had the overall effect of having his "nose rubbed in the human condition" (quoted in Biles, *Talk*, p. 33).

18 Forster, "Introduction," p. 208.

19 Bradbury, *No, Not Bloomsbury*, p. 341.

20 Walter Allen, *Tradition and Dream: The English and American Novel from the Twenties to Our Time* (London: Phoenix House, 1964), p. 289.

21 Ian McEwan, "Golding portrays young boys accurately," in Swisher, *Readings on "Lord of the Flies"*, p. 106.

22 Golding quoted in Biles, *Talk*, p. 41.

23 Malcolm Bradbury, *The Modern British Novel* (Harmondsworth: Penguin Books, 1993), p. 328.

24 Ibid.

25 Baker, "Decline," p. 454.

26 For more on this see Dickson, *Modern Allegories*.

27 Baker, "Decline," p. 446.

28 See, for example, Baker, "Decline," p. 448; and Dick, *William Golding*, pp. 19–20. Dick argues that "Golding's island is a dystopia in which the classes do not cooperate for the common good" (p. 20).

29 Woodward, "On aggression," pp. 203, 202.

30 McEwan, "Golding portrays young boys," p. 105.

31 Quoted in Biles, *Talk*, pp. 7–8.

32 Minnie Singh, "The government of boys: Golding's *Lord of the Flies* and Ballantyne's *Coral Island*," *Children's Literature* 25 (1997), p. 206.

33 Ibid.

34 "The meaning of it all" (transcript of a radio broadcast of William Golding speaking with Frank Kermode), in *William Golding: Casebook Edition*, p. 201.

35 Golding, "Fable," p. 89.

36 Baker, *William Golding*, p. 14.

37 An "atom bomb" is referenced on p. 14. William Golding, *Lord of the Flies* (New York: Perigee, 1954). Further references are noted parenthetically in the text.

38 For more on the Golding–Ballantyne connection see Singh, "Government of boys," and see Carl Niemeyer, "The Coral Island revisited," in *William Golding: Casebook Edition*.

39 Bradbury, *Modern British Novel*, p. 327.

40 Baker, "Decline," p. 453.

41 Ibid., p. 452.

42 Baker, *William Golding*, p. 4.

43 Woodward, "On aggression," p. 200.

44 Singh, "Government of boys," p. 207.

45 Golding quoted in "The meaning of it all," p. 201. For Niemeyer, Golding "regards Ballantyne's book as a badly falsified map of reality" (Niemeyer, "Coral Island revisited," p. 219).

46 Singh, "Government of boys," p. 210.

47 Golding's boys, according to the author, "are innocent of their own natures"; because they do not possess self-knowledge when they reach the island, "they can look forward to a bright future, because they don't understand the things that threaten it" (quoted in James Keating, "Interview with William Golding," p. 190). One critic goes even farther: Golding's "entire fable" suggests "a grim parallel with the prophecies of the Biblical Apocalypse" (Baker, *William Golding*, p. 16).

48 Woodward, "On aggression," p. 200.

49 At one point, for example, we read that Ralph "excitedly" boasts hitting the pig: "'The spear stuck in. I wounded him!' He sunned himself in their new respect and felt that hunting was good after all" (113).

50 For example, we read that Ralph becomes "conscious of the weight of [his] clothes" (10).

51 Samuel Hynes, in "Several interpretations of *Lord of the Flies*," in Swisher, *Readings on "Lord of the Flies"*, p. 59, sees echoes of Cain and Abel in the Jack–Ralph relationship.

52 When Jack lets the fire go out, possibly costing the boys a much earlier rescue, Ralph remarks, "I'd like to put on war-paint and be a savage [too]. But we must keep the fire burning" (142).

53 Forster, "Introduction," p. 208.

54 Baker, *William Golding*, p. 11.

55 Golding quoted in Biles, *Talk*, pp. 13, 12.

56 Sigmund Freud, *Civilization and Its Discontents* (New York: W. W. Norton, 1961), p. 61.

57 Dick, *William Golding*, p. 21.

58 Ibid., p. 17.

59 Ibid., p. 21. In "Fable" Golding makes reference to "the objectivizing of our own inadequacies so as to make a scapegoat," p. 94.

60 Golding quoted in Biles, *Talk*, p. 14.

61 At one point, for example, he turns away from the boys and goes "where the just perceptible path led him" until the "high jungle closed in" (56). At another he "retired and sat as far away from the others as possible" (129).

62 Baker, *William Golding*, p. 11.

63 Golding quoted in Keating, "Interview with William Golding," p. 190.

64 Ralph says, "I'm frightened. Of us" (157); and Piggy remarks that there is nothing to fear "Unless we get frightened of people" (84).

65 Even Jack gets the sense, when hunting, that he is "being hunted, as if something's behind you all the time in the jungle" (48).

66 Golding, "Fable," pp. 97–8.

67 Golding quoted in Keating, "Interview with William Golding," p. 192. For Simon "The beast was harmless and horrible; and the news must reach the others as soon as possible" (134).

68 Dick, *William Golding*, p. 26.

69 Baker, *William Golding*, p. 13.

70 Jean-Paul Sartre, *No Exit and Three Other Plays* (New York: Vintage International, 1989), p. 45.

71 For more on Simon, see Donald R. Spangler, "Simon," in *William Golding: Casebook Edition*.

72 Dick, *William Golding*, p. 24.

73 Also, and tellingly, a pecking order by physical size is established among the boys, from Ralph at the top, who is "big enough to be a link with the adult world of authority," to the powerless 6-year-old "littluns" (59) at the bottom.

74 And Ralph's fantasy of a "tamed [English] town where savagery could not set foot" (164) must strike the reader as ironic: there is no such "town" in the world, Golding's novel seems to suggest, that is immune from such barbaric social pressures.

75 Golding, "Fable," p. 89. Erich Fromm, in *Escape From Freedom* [1941] (New York: Avon Books, 1965), says something similar: "the crisis of democracy is not a peculiarly Italian or German problem, but one confronting every modern state" (p. 19).

76 Dick, *William Golding*, p. 21.
77 As Dick writes, "excrement is ubiquitous on the island. Eating fruit causes diarrhea, and the island is dotted with feces" (*William Golding*, p. 27).
78 Baker, in "Decline," p. 459, notes that Fromm, no less than Golding, laments "the collapse of individualism in alienation and mass insanity."
79 Fromm, *Escape from Freedom*, pp. 266, 18, 17, 265–6.
80 Ibid., p. 20.
81 Ibid., p. 24.
82 Ibid., p. 163.
83 Ibid., p. 36.
84 Ibid., pp. 34–5.
85 Ibid., p. 38.
86 Ibid., pp. 177–8.
87 Ibid., p. 209.
88 Ibid., pp. 174, 180.
89 Golding, "Fable," pp. 94–5.
90 Ibid., p. 202.
91 Singh, "Government of boys," p. 209.
92 Fromm, *Escape from Freedom*, p. 173.
93 Ibid., p. 166.
94 Ibid.
95 Ibid., p. 191.
96 Ibid., p. 193.
97 Dick, *William Golding*, p. 12.
98 Hynes, "Several interpretations," p. 64.
99 Baker, "Decline," p. 450.
100 Golding quoted in Baker, *William Golding*, p. xix.

4 Chinua Achebe's *Things Fall Apart* (1958)

1 Chinua Achebe, "The novelist as teacher," in *Hopes and Impediments: Selected Essays* (New York: Doubleday, 1989), p. 45.
2 Jules Chametzky, *Our Decentralized Literature: Cultural Mediations in Selected Jewish and Southern Writers* (Amherst: University of Massachusetts Press, 1986), p. 3.
3 Abdul R. JanMohamed puts the balance struck by the novel's representation of African tribal history this way: Although Achebe's fiction "eschews a perfect utopia, a lost golden age, it does nevertheless manifest a powerful . . . nostalgia for the past" (*Manichean Aesthetics: The Politics of Literature in Colonial Africa* [Amherst: University of Massachusetts Press, 1983], p. 181).
4 JanMohamed, *Manichean Aesthetics*, p. 11. See C. L. Innes, *Chinua Achebe* (Cambridge: Cambridge University Press, 1990), ch. 2, for a reading of *Things Fall Apart* as a retelling of Cary's *Mr Johnson*.

5   See Achebe's powerful, influential, yet controversial "An image of Africa: racism in Conrad's *Heart of Darkness*," in *Hopes and Impediments*, for his critique of Conrad's representation of Africa. Also see Hunt Hawkins, "*Things Fall Apart* and the literature of empire," in *Approaches to Teaching Achebe's "Things Fall Apart"*, ed. Bernth Lindfors (New York: Modern Language Association of America, 1991), and P. J. M. Robertson, "*Things Fall Apart* and *Heart of Darkness*: a creative dialogue" (*International Fiction Review* 7, 1980) for two assessments of Achebe's debt to Conrad.

6   Gilbert Phelps, "Two Nigerian novelists: Chinua Achebe and Wole Soyinka," in *The New Pelican Guide to English Literature*, vol. 8: *The Present*, ed. Boris Ford (Harmondsworth: Penguin Books, 1983), p. 331.

7   Ashton Nichols, "The politics of point of view: teaching *Things Fall Apart*," in Lindfors, *Teaching Achebe's "Things Fall Apart"*, p. 55.

8   Robert M. Wren, "*Things Fall Apart* in its time and place," in Lindfors, *Teaching Achebe's "Things Fall Apart"*, p. 38.

9   Ibid., p. 39.

10   Ibid.

11   Chinua Achebe, *Home and Exile* (Oxford: Oxford University Press, 2000), pp. 3–4, 6.

12   Feroza Jussawalla and Reed Way Dasenbrock (eds.), *Interviews with Writers of the Post-Colonial World* (Jackson: University of Mississippi Press, 1992), p. 12. David Carroll in *Chinua Achebe*, 2nd edn. (New York: St Martin's Press, 1980), p. 22, notes that "Casualties in the fighting were heavy, and the number of deaths by starvation among the Igbo population were by all reports high."

13   Chinua Achebe, "Named for Victoria, Queen of England," in *Hopes and Impediments*, p. 33.

14   Achebe, "Named for Victoria," p. 38.

15   Innes, *Chinua Achebe*, p. 2.

16   Achebe, "Named for Victoria," p. 34.

17   Abdul JanMohamed, "Sophisticated primitivism: the syncretism of oral and literate modes in Achebe's *Things Fall Apart*," *Ariel* 15/4 (1984), p. 19.

18   JanMohamed, "Sophisticated primitivism," p. 38.

19   Ibid., pp. 20–1.

20   Innes, *Chinua Achebe*, p. 35.

21   In this connection, the Nigerian critic Chinweizu has attacked Nigerian Nobel Prize winner Wole Soyinka for writing in English and for his "Eurocentrism." Chinweizu argues that Soyinka's plays, while ostensibly African, remain "in thrall to European forms" (Jussawalla and Dasenbrock, *Interviews*, p. 9). By contrast, Chinweizu defends Achebe's art for its "simplicity, directness, and relation to oral [African] traditions" (quoted in Bill Ashcroft, Gareth Griffiths, and Helen Tiffin, *The Empire Writes Back: Theory and Practice in Post-Colonial Literatures* [London: Routledge, 1989], p. 128).

22   Chinua Achebe, "African literature as restoration of celebration," in *Chinua Achebe: A Celebration*, ed. Kirsten Holst Petersen and Anna Rutherford (Oxford: Heinemann, 1990), pp. 7–8.

23 Phelps, "Two Nigerian novelists," pp. 328–9.

24 Achebe, "Named for Victoria," p. 38.

25 Zoreh T. Sullivan, "The postcolonial African novel and the dialogic imagination," in Lindfors, *Teaching Achebe's "Things Fall Apart,"* p. 101.

26 Ibid., p. 102.

27 Chinua Achebe, "Role of the writer in a new nation," in *African Writers on African Writing*, ed. G. D. Killam (Evanston, IL: Northwestern University Press, 1973), p. 12.

28 Phelps, "Two Nigerian novelists," p. 335. Achebe writes that no one should "be fooled by the fact that [he and fellow Nigerians] write in English, for we intend to do unheard things with it" (Chinua Achebe, "Colonialist criticism," in *Hopes and Impediments*, p. 74). For JanMohamed, Achebe in *Things Fall Apart* successfully "pushes the English language to its limits"; he "is able to expand the English language through the transfusion of Igbo material." "Achebe," this critic concludes, "takes the English language and the novelistic form and creates a unique African form with them" ("Sophisticated primitivism," pp. 37, 38).

29 Jussawalla and Dasenbrock go even further: Achebe is for them both African and European: his formative, cultural contexts are Igbo, Nigerian, and British (*Interviews*, pp. 12–13). Yet this hybrid identity is to be expected and even celebrated in postcolonial culture, which has been described as "inevitably a hybridized phenomenon involving a dialectical relationship between the 'grafted' European cultural systems and an indigenous ontology, with its impulse to create or recreate an independent local identity. Such construction or reconstruction only occurs as a dynamic interaction between European hegemonic systems and 'peripheral' subversions of them" (Ashcroft et al., *The Empire Writes Back*, p. 195).

30 Achebe, "Named for Victoria," p. 38.

31 For more on the British *Bildungsroman* tradition, see Jerome Hamilton Buckley, *Season of Youth: The Bildungsroman from Dickens to Golding* (Cambridge, MA: Harvard University Press, 1974).

32 Although Achebe denies "responding to that particular format," he also remarks: "If we are to believe what we are hearing these days, the Greeks did not drop from the sky. They evolved in a certain place which was very close to Africa . . . I think a lot of what Aristotle says makes sense" (Achebe, in Charles H. Rowell, "An interview with Chinua Achebe," *Callaloo* 13 [1990], p. 78).

33 Raman Selden, Peter Widdowson, and Peter Brooker, *A Reader's Guide to Contemporary Literary Theory*, 4th edn. (London: Prentice Hall, 1997), p. 226.

34 Chinua Achebe, *Things Fall Apart* [1959] (New York: Doubleday, 1994), p. 3. Further references are noted parenthetically in the text.

35 "[T]he Igbo postulate an unprecedented uniqueness for the individual by making him or her the sole creation and purpose of a unique god-agent, *chi*," Achebe explains; "No two persons, not even blood brothers, are created and accompanied by the same *chi*" (Chinua Achebe, "The writer and his community," in *Hopes and Impediments*, pp. 57–8). For more on the Igbo conception of *chi*, see Chinua Achebe, "Chi in Igbo cosmology," in *Morning Yet on Creation Day: Essays* (New

York: Doubleday, 1975), p. 160, in which the author asserts: "Without an understanding of the nature of chi one could not begin to make sense of the Igbo world-view."

36 JanMohamed, *Manichean Aesthetics*, p. 181.
37 Western readers today will be struck by Okonkwo's flagrant misogyny, which is everywhere apparent in the novel: Okonkwo "trembled with the desire to conquer and subdue. It was like the desire for women" (42); "No matter how prosperous a man was, if he was unable to rule his women and his children (and especially his women) he was not a real man" (53); Okonkwo likes "masculine stories of violence and bloodshed" (53) and dislikes women's "silly" stories (75). Okonkwo's "sexism" clearly reflects that of his culture at large. For example, we read that Igbo women stand on the "fringe" of an all-male village ceremony like "outsiders": "These women never saw the inside of the hut. No woman ever did. They scrubbed and painted the outside walls under the supervision of men" (87–8). This hierarchy prevails in British colonial culture as well, however ("Mr. Kiaga had asked the women to bring red earth and white chalk and water to scrub the church for Christmas" [159]): both Igbo and British cultures, according to Achebe's novel, take for granted the lower social status of females. For a critique of the novel's representation of women, see Rhonda Cobham, "Making men and history: Achebe and the politics of revisionism," in Lindfors, *Teaching Achebe's "Things Fall Apart"*. Also see Innes, *Chinua Achebe*, ch. 2, for a discussion of Okonkwo's masculinist values.
38 Jeffrey Meyers, "Culture and history in *Things Fall Apart*," *Critique: Studies in Modern Fiction* 11 (1969), p. 29.
39 Innes, *Chinua Achebe*, p. 29.
40 JanMohamed, *Manichean Aesthetics*, p. 181.
41 Arlene A. Elder, "The paradoxical characterization of Okonkwo," in Lindfors, *Teaching Achebe's "Things Fall Apart"*, pp. 62–3.
42 Raymond Williams, *The Country and the City* (New York: Oxford University Press, 1973), p. 286.
43 Chinua Achebe, "The African writer and the Biafran cause," in *Morning Yet on Creation Day*, p. 138.
44 Achebe's third novel, *Arrow of God*, is set in the 1920s, in between the time periods of *Things Fall Apart* and *No Longer at Ease*, which is set in the 1950s.
45 Achebe, *Home and Exile*, p. 12.
46 Later, the narrator remarks: "But apart from the church, the white men had also brought a government. They had built a court where the District Commissioner judged cases in ignorance" (174).
47 Wren, "*Things Fall Apart*," p. 42.
48 Ibid., p. 41.
49 Frantz Fanon, *The Wretched of the Earth* (New York: Grove Press, 1968), pp. 210–11.
50 E. M. Forster, *A Passage to India* (San Diego: Harcourt Brace Jovanovich, 1924), p. 343.

51 Achebe, "Colonialist criticism," p. 71.

52 Wren, "*Things Fall Apart*," p. 41.

53 Achebe, "Named for Victoria," p. 32.

54 Nichols, "Politics of point of view," p. 55.

55 Chinweizu, Onwuchekwa Jemie, and Ihechukwu Madubuike, "Decolonizing African literature," in *Literature in the Modern World: Critical Essays and Documents*, ed. Dennis Walder (Oxford: Oxford University Press, 1990), p. 286.

56 Achebe, "Named for Victoria," p. 31.

57 JanMohamed, *Manichean Aesthetics*, p. 181.

58 Chametzky, *Our Decentralized Literature*, p. 3.

59 Achebe, "The role of the writer in a new nation," p. 8. The Igbo's frequent use of richly metaphorical proverbs is a case in point. These proverbs employ animals and animal life in order to shed light on human affairs – human psychology, human social interaction, and the like – and on natural and divine processes. In addition to celebrating the Igbo's teleological and moral approach to reality, the novel uses these proverbs implicitly to challenge the modern western scientific episteme, which construes cosmic processes neither in teleological nor in moral terms. For example, while for modern westerners there is no cosmic "meaning" to weather patterns, in Umuofia the weather is "read" as an expression of cosmic purpose, with unpredictable weather signifying that "the world had gone mad" (23), or that Ani, the "earth-goddess," the "source of all fertility" and the "ultimate judge of morality and conduct" (36), is in some way displeased.

60 Meyers, "Culture and history," p. 26.

61 Sigmund Freud, *Civilization and Its Discontents* (New York: Norton, 1961), p. 61.

62 Achebe has remarked that Obierika is "more subtle and more in tune with the danger, the impending betrayal by the culture" than is Okonkwo (Biodun Jeyifo, "For Chinua Achebe: the resilience and the predicament of Obierika," in Petersen and Rutherford, *Chinua Achebe: A Celebration*, p. 57).

63 Nichols, "Politics of point of view," p. 55.

64 One of Okonkwo's tribesman explains to the British District Commissioner: "It is an abomination for a man to take his own life. It is an offense against the Earth, and a man who commits it will not be buried by his clansmen. His body is evil, and only strangers may touch it" (208). Obierika adds that Okonkwo "was one of the greatest men in Umuofia. You [British] drove him to kill himself; and now he will be buried like a dog" (209).

65 Wren notes that "The 'pacification,' as it is ironically identified at the end of the novel, occurred between 1900 and 1920, a time span that roughly indicates the period from the start of the action of *Things Fall Apart* to the beginning of Achebe's third novel, *Arrow of God*" (p. 39). The District Commissioner's book-title alludes to works, such as Frederick Lugard's *Report on the Amalgamation of Northern and Southern Nigeria, 1912–1919*, that actually existed. Amazingly, Lugard's report includes the following sentence: "The southern Provinces were [mostly] populated by tribes in the lowest stage of primitive savagery, without

any central organisation" (Dan Izevbaye, "The Igbo as exceptional colonial subjects: fictionalizing an abnormal historical situation," in Lindfors, *Teaching Achebe's "Things Fall Apart"*, p. 46).

66 This final paragraph also stands as a pessimistic allusion to the end of E. M. Forster's *A Passage to India*, in which British and Indian cultures cannot be successfully bridged; and to the genocidal postscript to Kurtz's peroration, "Exterminate all the brutes!" (p. 51), in Joseph Conrad's *Heart of Darkness*, ed. Robert Kimbrough (New York: Norton Critical Edition, 3rd edn., 1988).

67 James Smead, "European pedigrees/African contagions: nationality, narrative, and communality in Tutuola, Achebe, and Reed," in *Nation and Narration*, ed. Homi K. Bhabha (London: Routledge, 1990), p. 242.

68 Phelps, "Two Nigerian novelists," p. 330.

69 Chinua Achebe, "The truth of fiction," in *Hopes and Impediments*, p. 149.

5 Muriel Spark's *The Prime of Miss Jean Brodie* (1961)

1 Muriel Spark and Derek Stanford, *Emily Brontë: Her Life and Work* (quoted in Norman Page, *Muriel Spark* [New York: St Martin's Press, 1990], p. 4).

2 Muriel Spark, *The Prime of Miss Jean Brodie* [1961] (New York: Perennial Classics, 1999), p. 103. Further references are noted parenthetically in the text.

3 Anne L. Bower, "The narrative structure of Muriel Spark's *The Prime of Miss Jean Brodie*," *Midwest Quarterly* 31 (1990), p. 496.

4 Frank Kermode quoted in Page, *Muriel Spark*, p. 119.

5 Page, *Muriel Spark*, p. 41.

6 Ibid., p. 39.

7 Ibid.

8 Ibid., pp. 4–5.

9 David Lodge, "The uses and abuses of omniscience: method and meaning in Muriel Spark's *The Prime of Miss Jean Brodie*," *The Novelist at the Crossroads and Other Essays on Fiction and Criticism* (Ithaca, NY: Cornell University Press, 1971), pp. 125–6.

10 Allan Massie, "Calvinism and Catholicism in Muriel Spark," in *Muriel Spark: An Odd Capacity for Vision*, ed. Alan Bold (London and New York: Vision and Barnes and Noble, 1984), p. 97.

11 Massie, "Calvinism and Catholicism," pp. 95–6.

12 Spark, *Curriculum Vitae* (Boston and New York: Houghton Mifflin, 1992), pp. 102, 206.

13 Alan Bold, "Introduction," in *Muriel Spark: An Odd Capacity for Vision*, p. 9.

14 Lodge, "Uses and abuses of omniscience," pp. 124–5.

15 Mary W. Schneider, "The double life in Muriel Spark's *The Prime of Miss Jean Brodie*," *Midwest Quarterly* 18 (1977), p. 418.

16 Bower, "Narrative structure," p. 488.

17 Lodge, "Uses and abuses of omniscience," p. 126.

18 See Lodge "Uses and abuses of omniscience," p. 132, for a fascinating treatment of *Brodie*'s resemblance to *Jane Eyre*.
19 Ibid., p. 133.
20 Bryan Cheyette, *Muriel Spark* (Tavistock: Northcote House, in association with the British Council, 2000), p. 56
21 Lodge, "Uses and abuses of omniscience," p. 127.
22 Massie, "Calvinism and Catholicism," p. 102.
23 Page, *Muriel Spark*, p. 43.
24 Lodge, "Uses and abuses of omniscience," p. 127.
25 Ibid., p. 126.
26 Spark quoted in Trevor Royle, "Spark and Scotland," in Bold, *Muriel Spark: An Odd Capacity for Vision*, p. 151.
27 Royle, "Spark and Scotland," pp. 159–60.
28 Bold, "Introduction," in *Muriel Spark: An Odd Capacity for Vision*, p. 14. As one critic puts it, "Jean Brodie herself functions as a personification of certain attitudes common to the citizens of Edinburgh, attitudes that are basically religious or theological in nature" (Philip E. Ray, "Jean Brodie and Edinburgh: personality and place in Muriel Spark's *The Prime of Miss Jean Brodie*," *Studies in Scottish Literature* 13 [1978], p. 24). For more on Edinburgh's peculiar spirit of place see Robert Louis Stevenson's evocative *Edinburgh: Picturesque Notes* [1879] (London: Pallas Athene, 2001).
29 Spark, *Curriculum Vitae*, p. 56.
30 Stevenson quoted in Ray, "Jean Brodie and Edinburgh," p. 27.
31 Ray, "Jean Brodie and Edinburgh," p. 29.
32 Royle, "Spark and Scotland," p. 162.
33 Ray observes "certain similarities between the plots of the Spark novel and the Stevenson–Henley melodrama" (Stevenson collaborated with W. E. Henley on the 1880 play *Deacon Brodie* [Ray, "Jean Brodie and Edinburgh," p. 29]); and Page argues that, "In her bid to secure for ever a girl's mind and soul, Miss Brodie recalls [the] Satanic figure in James Hogg's novel" (Page, *Muriel Spark*, p. 40).
34 Royle, "Spark and Scotland," pp. 155–6.
35 Lodge, "Uses and abuses of omniscience," p. 131.
36 Spark, *Curriculum Vitae*, p. 57.
37 Ibid., p. 61. Brodie is described as among the "war-bereaved spinsterhood" of Edinburgh who undertook "voyages of discovery into new ideas and energetic practices in art or social welfare, education or religion" (43).
38 Ibid., pp. 58, 56.
39 Ibid., p. 58.
40 Miss Mackay is also described with subtle irony at many points in the novel. For example, she greets her girls at the start of a new academic term: "I hope you all had a splendid summer holiday and I look forward to seeing your splendid essays on how you spent them" (10).
41 Lodge, "Uses and abuses of omniscience," p. 132.
42 Massie, "Calvinism and Catholicism," p. 102.

43 Lodge, "Uses and abuses of omniscience," p. 130.

44 Ibid., pp. 127, 135.

45 Ibid., p. 135.

46 Ibid.

47 Ibid., p. 138.

48 Ibid., p. 139.

49 Cairns Craig, *The Modern Scottish Novel: Narrative and the National Imagination* (Edinburgh: Edinburgh University Press, 1999), p. 204.

50 Bold, "Introduction," in *Muriel Spark: An Odd Capacity for Vision*, p. 14.

51 As Lodge explains, "Sandy's diagnosis of Miss Brodie's instability as a private and distorted form of Calvinism is followed by her own conversion to Roman Catholicism, the theological antithesis of Calvinism" ("Uses and abuses of omniscience," p. 142).

52 Cheyette, *Muriel Spark*, p. 57.

53 Ibid., pp. 54–5, 57.

54 Norman Page does not equivocate on this matter: Brodie is for him "guilty of the sin of presumption: her motive in appropriating a group of girls as 'the Brodie set' is not a quasi-maternal or pedagogical concern for their welfare or their intellectual development . . . but a craving to usurp the role of God . . . by determining the future lives of 'her' girls" (*Muriel Spark*, p. 39). In *Curriculum Vitae* Spark reports being "absorbed," in 1953, by the "theological writings of John Henry Newman through whose influence I finally became a Roman Catholic" (p. 202).

55 Bower, "Narrative structure," p. 497.

56 Francis Russell Hart quoted in Page, *Muriel Spark*, p. 39.

57 Bold, "Introduction," in *Muriel Spark: An Odd Capacity for Vision*, p. 13.

58 Lodge, "Uses and abuses of omniscience," p. 133.

59 As early as the novel's second page, Mussolini is referenced.

60 Brodie's monomania is also suggested in the fact that, when she speaks admiringly of another, she seems usually to be thinking of herself. When Brodie describes "the great Anna Pavlova," for example, "a dedicated woman who, when she appears on the stage, makes the other dancers look like elephants" (65), she seems to be comparing herself with the other teachers at the school. The reference to Brodie's time at the school being "filled with legends of Pavlova and her dedicated habits, her wild fits of temperament and her intolerance of the second-rate" (65), strongly recalls Brodie's own habits, fits of temperament, and intolerance of the second-rate. Brodie also seems to have herself in mind when she speaks of Rose, the girl in her set who is famous for her sex: she only needed "to realize the power she had within her, it was a gift and she an exception to all the rules" (117).

61 And in the summer of 1938 she travels to Germany and Austria, which are "now magnificently organized" (130, 131).

62 The references (57, 61) to *Jane Eyre*, the novel that Brodie is reading to her class, are relevant: Rochester, like Lloyd, is already married and both Lloyd and Rochester possess "artistic" natures that set them apart.

63 Another version of Brodie's projection/displacement occurs when she turns her former fiancé (and now deceased) Hugh into a singer and a painter, "newly" embroidering her "old love story" (75): Sandy recognizes that "Miss Brodie was making her new love story fit the old . . . Sandy was fascinated by this method of making patterns with facts (76). While not articulating the idea, Sandy envisions Brodie as an artist. This is appropriate in the light of Spark's citing of John Steinbeck's words on great teachers to explain her teacher Christina Kay: "a great teacher is a great artist" (quoted in *Curriculum Vitae*, p. 67), as these words apply perfectly to Jean Brodie as well, at least in her own mind.
64 Cheyette, *Muriel Spark*, p. 58.
65 Lodge, "Uses and abuses of omniscience," p. 139.
66 Schneider, "Double life," p. 424.
67 Cheyette, *Muriel Spark*, p. 59.

6 Jean Rhys's *Wide Sargasso Sea* (1966)

1 Adrienne Rich, "When we dead awaken: writing as re-vision," in *On Lies, Secrets, and Silence: Selected Prose, 1966–1978* (New York: W. W. Norton, 1979), p. 35.
2 Jean Rhys, "Selected letters," in *Norton Critical Edition of Jean Rhys's "Wide Sargasso Sea*," ed. Judith L. Raiskin (New York: W. W. Norton, 1999), p. 173.
3 Raiskin, *Norton Critical Edition of Jean Rhys's "Wide Sargasso Sea*", p. 77. Further references are noted parenthetically in the text.
4 Ellen G. Friedman, "Breaking the master narrative: Jean Rhys's *Wide Sargasso Sea*," in *Breaking the Sequence: Women's Experimental Fiction*, ed. Ellen G. Friedman and Miriam Fuchs (Princeton: Princeton University Press, 1989), p. 117.
5 Friedman, "Breaking the master narrative," p. 119.
6 Caroline Rody, "Burning down the house: the revisionary paradigm of Jean Rhys's *Wide Sargasso Sea*," in Raiskin, *Norton Critical Edition*, p. 217.
7 Friedman, "Breaking the master narrative," p. 119. Thomas F. Staley puts it this way: "To re-read *Jane Eyre* after reading *Wide Sargasso Sea* is a startling experience . . . The text of [the first novel] is expanded by the reader's participation in [the second], and the aesthetic awareness is widened. Surely when we re-read *Jane Eyre* after reading *Wide Sargasso Sea* our participation in that experience is transformed; our considerations of Rochester and Bertha are more deeply engaged" (*Jean Rhys: A Critical Study* [Austin: University of Texas Press, 1979], p. 119).
8 Although *Wide Sargasso Sea* is not, chronologically speaking, a high modernist novel, its author began her novelistic career in the 1930s, and Rhys herself came to be regarded by many "as second only to [Virginia] Woolf as the most significant woman novelist of the high modernist period" (Sanford Sternlicht, *Jean Rhys* [New York: Twayne Publishers, 1997], p. 136).
9 Joyce Carol Oates, "Romance and anti-romance: from Brontë's *Jane Eyre* to Rhys's *Wide Sargasso Sea*," *Virginia Quarterly Review* 61 (1985), p. 44.

10   V. S. Naipaul, "Without a dog's chance," in *Critical Perspectives on Jean Rhys*, ed. Pierette Frickey (Washington: Three Continents, 1990), p. 58.

11   M. Keith Booker and Dubravka Juraga, *The Caribbean Novel in English: An Introduction* (Portmouth, NH: Heinemann, 2001), p. 165.

12   "Creole," one of Rhys's working titles for the novel, was dropped because she felt that its other meaning, designating a person of mixed race, would confuse readers.

13   Joy Castro, "Jean Rhys," *Review of Contemporary Fiction* 20 (2000), p. 13.

14   Mary Lou Emery, "Modernist crosscurrents," in Raiskin, *Norton Critical Edition*, p. 161.

15   Oates, "Romance and anti-romance," p. 54.

16   Ibid., p. 58.

17   Walter Allen quoted in Helen Nebeker, *Jean Rhys: Woman in Passage* (Montreal: Eden Press, 1981), p. 123.

18   Francis Wyndham, "Introduction," in Raiskin, *Norton Critical Edition*, p. 6.

19   Staley, *Jean Rhys*, p. 101.

20   Sandra Drake, "Race and Caribbean culture as thematics of liberation in Jean Rhys's *Wide Sargasso Sea*," in Raiskin, *Norton Critical Edition*, p. 194.

21   Molly Hite, "Writing in the margins: Jean Rhys," in *The Other Side of the Story: Structures and Strategies of Contemporary Feminist Narrative* (Ithaca, NY: Cornell University Press, 1989), p. 32.

22   Judith Kegan Gardiner, *Rhys, Stead, Lessing, and the Politics of Empathy* (Bloomington: Indiana University Press, 1989), p. 133.

23   Carmen Wickramagamage, "An/other side to Antoinette/Bertha: reading 'race' into *Wide Sargasso Sea*," *Journal of Commonwealth Literature* 35 (2000), p. 28.

24   Friedman, "Breaking the master narrative," p. 124. For differing accounts of this textual relationship, see Robert Kendrick, "Edward Rochester and the margins of masculinity in *Jane Eyre* and *Wide Sargasso Sea*," *Papers on Language and Literature* 30 (1994), pp. 235–56; Nicola Nixon, "*Wide Sargasso Sea* and Jean Rhys's interrogation of the 'nature wholly alien' in *Jane Eyre*," *Essays in Literature* 21 (1994), pp. 267–84; Rody, "Burning down the house," pp. 217–25; and Michael Thorpe, " 'The other Side': *Wide Sargasso Sea* and *Jane Eyre*," in Raiskin, *Norton Critical Edition*, pp. 173–81.

25   Gardiner, *Rhys, Stead, Lessing*, p. 125. For a comparison of Jane's development in *Jane Eyre* and Antoinette's development in *Wide Sargasso Sea*, see Thorpe, " 'The other side'," p. 176, and Nixon, "*Wide Sargasso Sea*," p. 276.

26   Rhys, "Selected letters," p. 136.

27   See ibid., pp. 137, 139, 144.

28   Ibid., pp. 139, 136.

29   Ibid., pp. 136–7.

30   Caroline Rody, for example, views Rhys's novel as a "text about a rewriting of a text." For her, "The postmodern aspects of this rewriting are evident in its subversion of the authority of authorship, its inscription of the adventure of the reader, and its delight in the empowering possibility of shared knowledge of a literary tradition" ("Burning down the house," pp. 221–2).

31 Rody's above comments, in any case, are equally attributable, say, to Joyce's *Ulysses* and Eliot's *Waste Land*, two watershed works of literary modernism's high tide of 1922.

32 Sylvie Maurel, *Jean Rhys* (New York: St Martin's Press, 1998), p. 6. Staley too views this novel as possessing aspects and themes that are "characteristic of literary modernism" (*Jean Rhys*, p. 101).

33 Maurel, *Jean Rhys*, p. 129.

34 Oates, "Romance and anti-romance," p. 55.

35 Ibid., p. 52.

36 Virginia Woolf quoted in Peter Faulkner, *The English Modernist Reader, 1910–1930* (Iowa City: University of Iowa Press, 1986), pp. 108–9.

37 Rhys, "Selected letters," p. 138.

38 Ibid., p. 144.

39 Booker and Juraga, *Caribbean Novel*, p. 167.

40 Ibid., p. 169.

41 O. Mannoni, *Prospero and Caliban: The Psychology of Colonization* [1956], 2nd edn. (New York: Praeger, 1964), p. 19.

42 Nicola Nixon points to this link between Rochester's colonial and patriarchal agendas when she comments, "Brontë depicts the West Indies as the place where the young English gentleman can sow his wild oats and gain economic independence through the exploitation of rich foreign heiresses" (p. 273).

43 One important debate in postcolonial theory centers on Rhys's novel: that between Benita Parry and Gayatri Spivak over the question of the representation of racial otherness. Parry argues that Rhys's Christophine, an example of a historically repressed subject and the speaking position of the subaltern, provides a potent counter or oppositional discourse to the dominant colonialist discourse of Brontë's Rochester. Spivak, by contrast, argues that the very attempt to resuscitate the racially other's voice "reproduces the 'epistemic violence' of imperialism: it imposes on the subaltern Western assumptions of embodied subjectivity and fails to acknowledge that the other has always already been constructed according to the colonizer's self-image and can therefore not simply be given back his/her voice" (Carine M. Mardorossian, "Shutting up the subaltern: silences, stereotypes, and double-entendre in Jean Rhys's *Wide Sargasso Sea*," *Callaloo* 22 [1999], p. 1071). "Christophine," Spivak argues, is "tangential" to Antoinette's narrative and cannot be "contained by a novel which rewrites a canonical English text within the European novelistic tradition in the interest of the white Creole rather than the native. No perspective *critical* of imperialism can turn the Other into a self, because the project of imperialism has always already historically refracted what might have been the absolutely Other into a domesticated Other that consolidates the imperialist self" (Gayatri Spivak, "*Wide Sargasso Sea* and a critique of imperialism," in Raiskin, *Norton Critical Edition*, p. 246). Put simply, when we look at another, according to Spivak, all we can ever see is our self. (For more on this debate, see Spivak's essay in full, and Parry's "Two native voices in *Wide Sargasso Sea*," in Raiskin, *Norton Critical Edition*, pp. 240–50.)

For other provocative postcolonial readings of *Wide Sargasso Sea*, see Laura E. Ciolkowski, "Navigating the *Wide Sargasso Sea*: colonial history, English fiction, and British Empire," *Twentieth Century Literature* 43 (1997), pp. 339–59; Drake, "Race and Caribbean culture"; Lee Erwin, "History and narrative in *Wide Sargasso Sea*," in Raiskin, *Norton Critical Edition*, pp. 207–16; Moira Ferguson, "Sending the younger son across the *Wide Sargasso Sea*: the new colonizer arrives," in *Postcolonial Discourses: An Anthology*, ed. Gregory Castle (Oxford: Blackwell Publishing, 2001), pp. 310–27; Mardorossian, "Shutting up the subaltern"; Hilda van Neck-Yoder, "Colonial desires, silence, and metonymy: 'all things considered' in *Wide Sargasso Sea*," *Texas Studies in Literature and Language* 40 (1998), pp. 184–208; and Wickramagamage, "An/other side to Antoinette/Bertha."

44 If Brontë suggests that Bertha and Jane are doubles of each other, Rhys suggests that Antoinette's husband and Antoinette exist in this relationship.

45 Hite, "Waiting in the margins," p. 23.

46 Rhys, "Selected letters," p. 137.

47 Hite, "Waiting in the margins," p. 32.

48 The novel's myriad allusions to Shakespeare's *Othello* (see p. 55, for example) make sense in this connection: the Rochester figure's paranoia, like that of Shakespeare's Moor, is also linked with racial prejudice and sexual jealousy. Othello murders his wife Desdemona for her alleged infidelity; this is what the Rochester figure does, at least figuratively, to Antoinette. Daniel Cosway's letter to the Rochester figure (56–9), which plays upon the latter's sexual jealousy, attempts to convince him of his wife's nymphomania and inconstancy. This letter plants the seed of doubt in the husband's mind: a seed of doubt that eventually leads to his hostile actions, which in turn lead to Antoinette's death. In this sense Daniel plays the role of Iago to the Rochester figure's Othello. Like Iago, Daniel encourages the jealous male to see what he is looking for, not what is there: "I felt no surprise," he comments at receiving Daniel's letter; "It was as if I'd expected it, been waiting for it" (59). Moreover, when Christophine threatens the Rochester figure with the possibility that Antoinette will leave him and marry another, he admits to "A pang of rage and jealousy" shooting through him (95). "Vain, silly creature," he shortly later thinks of Antoinette; "Made for loving? Yes, but she'll have no lover, for I don't want her and she'll see no other" (99).

49 Editor's Note in Raiskin, *Norton Critical Edition*, p. 1.

50 Rachel L. Carson, "The Sargasso Sea," in Raiskin, *Norton Critical Edition*, p. 119.

51 Ezra Pound quoted in Sternlicht, *Jean Rhys*, p. 104.

7 J. M. Coetzee's *Waiting for the Barbarians* (1980)

1 Leonard Woolf, *Barbarians Within and Without* (New York: Harcourt Brace, 1939), pp. 65–6.

2 J. M. Coetzee, *Waiting for the Barbarians* [1980] (New York: Penguin Books, 1982), p. 68. Further references are noted parenthetically in the text.

3 Sigmund Freud, *Civilization and Its Discontents* (New York: W. W. Norton, 1961), p. 61.

4 Simone de Beauvoir, "Woman and the Other," *Literature and the Modern World*, ed. Dennis Walder (Oxford: Oxford University Press, 1990), pp. 307–8.

5 Ian Glenn, "Nadine Gordimer, J. M. Coetzee, and the politics of interpretation," *South Atlantic Quarterly* 93 (1994), p. 23.

6 Cited in Dominic Head, *J. M. Coetzee* (Cambridge: Cambridge University Press, 1997), p. 25.

7 J. M. Coetzee, *Doubling the Point: Essays and Interviews*, ed. David Attwell (Cambridge, MA: Harvard University Press, 1992), p. 1.

8 Head, *J. M. Coetzee*, p. 1.

9 Attwell, *Doubling the Point*, p. 3.

10 Derek Attridge, "Literary form and the demands of politics: otherness in J. M. Coetzee's *Age of Iron*," in *Aesthetics and Ideology*, ed. George Levine (New Brunswick: Rutgers University Press, 1994), p. 244.

11 Cited in Randall Stevenson, *A Reader's Guide to the Twentieth-Century Novel in Britain* (Lexington: University Press of Kentucky, 1993), p. 116.

12 Tony Morphet, "Two interviews with J. M. Coetzee, 1983 and 1987," *Triquarterly* 69 (1987), p. 455.

13 These are the assessments of Attwell, *Doubling the Point*, p. 10, and Head, *J. M. Coetzee*, p. 4, respectively.

14 Attwell, *Doubling the Point*, p. 10.

15 Daphne Merkin, "A new man: the force of grace in South Africa," *New Yorker*, November 15, 1999, p. 112.

16 Attridge, "Literary form," pp. 243–4.

17 James Wood, Review of *Disgrace*, *New Republic*, December 20, 1999, p. 42.

18 Graham Huggan and Stephen Watson (eds.), *Critical Perspectives on J. M. Coetzee* (New York: St Martin's Press, 1996), p. 1.

19 Michael Valdez Moses, "The mark of empire: writing, history, and torture in Coetzee's *Waiting for the Barbarians*," *Kenyon Review* 15 (1993), p. 115.

20 Attridge, "Literary form," p. 244.

21 Cited in Attwell, *Doubling the Point*, p. 298.

22 Head, *J. M. Coetzee*, p. 8.

23 Moses, "Mark of empire," p. 115.

24 Coetzee, "The novel today," cited in Moses, "Mark of empire," p. 126.

25 Caryl Phillips, Review of *Boyhood: Scenes from Provincial Life* by J. M. Coetzee, *New Republic*, February 9, 1998, p. 37.

26 Moses, "Mark of empire," p. 116. See Teresa Dovey, "*Waiting for the Barbarians*: allegory of allegories" (in Huggan and Watson, *Critical Perspectives*, pp. 138–51), for the most comprehensive and compelling exploration of allegory in Coetzee's novel. Also see Benita Parry, "Speech and silence in the fictions of J. M. Coetzee," in *Writing South Africa: Literature, Apartheid, and Democracy, 1970–1995*, ed. Derek Attridge and Rosemary Jolly (Cambridge: Cambridge University Press, 1998), pp. 149–65.

27 Richard Begam, "An interview with J. M. Coetzee," *Contemporary Literature* 33 (1992), p. 424. This insight would make sense of the echo of "Third Reich" in "Third Bureau."

28 Coetzee cited in Attwell, *Doubling the Point*, p. 142.

29 Attwell, *Doubling the Point*, p. 98.

30 Coetzee has remarked that the concentration on imprisonment, regimentation, and torture in *Waiting for the Barbarians* "was a response – I emphasize, a pathological response – to the ban on representing what went on in police cells in this country" (Attwell, *Doubling the Point*, p. 300).

31 Barbara Eckstein, "The body, the word, and the state: J. M. Coetzee's *Waiting for the Barbarians*," *Novel: A Forum on Fiction* 22 (1989), p. 186.

32 Eckstein, "The body," p. 191. That the Empire labels such torture sessions "investigations" (9) – using language to obscure, not to reveal, its true work – and that it executes this work with such bureaucratic flair are reminiscent of events in Conrad's *Heart of Darkness*. In that work the European colonists employ language to hide, not to describe, their murderous treatment of the African slaves. The native Congolese prisoners are called "enemies," "rebels," "transgressors," and "criminals," yet it is Europeans, not Africans, who best fit these descriptors (cited in Brian W. Shaffer, *The Blinding Torch: Modern British Fiction and the Discourse of Civilization* [Amherst: University of Massachusetts Press, 1993], pp. 69–70. For a fuller discussion of Conrad's understanding of language in *Heart of Darkness*, see ch. 3 of that work).

And Coetzee's novel also correlates bureaucratic rigor and barbaric activity, suggesting that clerical neatness comports with simplistic binary thinking – and with murder. When Mandel takes over for the magistrate, for example, the latter notes "The careful reorganization of my office from clutter and dustiness to this vacuous neatness" (82). This episode is reminiscent of Marlow's encounter with the outer station chief, who is connected to the enslavement and murder of the Congolese yet whose books are "in apple-pie order." He is seen by Marlow "bent over his books" in order to make "correct entries of perfectly correct transactions" (Joseph Conrad, *Heart of Darkness*, Norton Critical Edition, 3rd edn., ed. Robert Kimbrough [New York: W. W. Norton, 1988], pp. 21–2). In Coetzee's novel torture occurs while the magistrate, nearby, works on "the ledgers in my office" (81). Moses refers to the magistrate as an "inverted version of Conrad's Kurtz" for intending "to represent for posterity both the enlightened hope at which his civilization aimed and its failure to fulfill those hopes" (p. 119); but this better describes Marlow.

33 The novel thus gestures toward circularity – to life cycles and to the seasons – which undercuts the imperial view of history, as understood by the magistrate: "Empire has located its existence not in the smooth recurrent spinning time of the cycle of the seasons but in the jagged time of rise and fall, of beginning and end, of catastrophe. Empire dooms itself to live in history and plot against history. One thought alone preoccupies the submerged mind of Empire: how not to end, how not to die, how to prolong its era" (133).

34 James Phelan, "Present tense narration, mimesis, the narrative norm, and the positioning of the reader in *Waiting for the Barbarians*," in *Understanding Narrative*, ed. James Phelan and Peter J. Rabinowitz (Columbus: Ohio State University Press, 1994), p. 222. In this essay Phelan writes persuasively on the nature and implications, for readers, of Coetzee's choice of "homodiegetic simultaneous present" narration, in which the magistrate tells his story in the present tense as the events themselves unfold. This narrative strategy, for Phelan,

> Places the reader in a very different relationship to the magistrate and to the events of the narrative than would any kind of retrospective account. The strategy takes teleology away from the magistrate's narrative acts: since he does not know how events will turn out, he cannot be shaping the narrative according to his knowledge of the end. Consequently, we cannot read with our usual tacit assumptions that the narrator, however unself-conscious, has some direction in mind for his tale. Instead, as we read any one moment of the narrative we must assume that the future is always – and radically – wide open: the narrator's guess about what will happen next is really no better than our own. (p. 223)

35 James Wood, Review of *Disgrace*, p. 42.
36 For more on the "In the penal colony"/*Waiting for the Barbarians* connection, see Head, *J. M. Coetzee*, pp. 76–7, and Moses, "Mark of empire," p. 121.
37 Moses, "Mark of empire," p. 121.
38 Ibid., p. 115. Coetzee (in Begam, "Interview," p. 421) has called Kafka and Beckett "writers of the ordinary – of the experience of being alive, of intimations of death and the hereafter."
39 Quoted in Attwell, *Doubling the Point*, p. 20.
40 Merkin, "New man," p. 112.
41 C. P. Cavafy, "Waiting for the Barbarians," in *Collected Poems*, ed. George Savidis, trans. Edmund Keeley and Philip Sherrard (Princeton: Princeton University Press, 1975), p. 33.
42 Moses, "Mark of empire," p. 116. See the Leonard Woolf epigraph to this chapter. Also see ch. 1 of Shaffer, *The Blinding Torch*.
43 Eckstein, "The body," p. 185.
44 W. J. B. Wood, "*Waiting for the Barbarians*: two sides of imperial rule and some related considerations," in *Momentum: On Recent South African Writing*, ed. M. J. Daymond, J. U. Jacobs, and Margaret Lenta (Pietermaritzburg: University of Natal Press, 1984), p. 129.
45 Ibid., p. 131.
46 Ibid., p. 132.
47 O. Mannoni, *Prospero and Caliban: The Psychology of Colonization* (New York and Washington: Praeger, 1964), p. 19.
48 Bill Ashcroft, Gareth Griffiths, and Helen Tiffin, *The Empire Writes Back: Theory and Practice in Post-Colonial Literatures* (London: Routledge, 1989), p. 103.

49 See the second epigraph for this chapter.
50 Fredric Jameson, in *The Political Unconscious: Narrative as a Socially Symbolic Act* (Ithaca, NY: Cornell University Press, 1981), p. 115, makes a point of relevance to Coetzee's novel: we deem others "evil" not necessarily because they threaten us but because we fear their difference from us. "So from the earliest times, the stranger from another tribe, the 'barbarian' who speaks an incomprehensible language and follows 'outlandish' customs [and] behind whose apparently human features a malignant and preternatural intelligence is thought to lurk [has been one] of the archetypal figures of the Other, about whom the essential point to be made is not . . . that he is feared because he is evil; rather, he is evil *because* he is Other, alien, different, strange, unclean, and unfamiliar."
51 And the more imperial, too. As the magistrate has observed, "One thought alone preoccupies the submerged mind of Empire: how not to end, how not to die, how to prolong its era. By day it pursues its enemies. It is cunning and ruthless, it sends its bloodhounds everywhere. By night it feeds on images of disaster: the sack of cities, the rape of populations, pyramids of bones, acres of desolation" (133).
52 Attwell, *Doubling the Point*, p. 143.
53 Phillips, Review of *Boyhood*, p. 39.
54 Attwell, *Doubling the Point*, p. 243.
55 W. J. B. Wood, "*Waiting for the Barbarians*," p. 134.
56 The magistrate, like Lady Macbeth in Shakespeare's play, is nevertheless complicitous both in an act of murder and in an attempt to avoid the recognition of it. He attempts to put out of mind by putting out of sight his guilt at the atrocities being committed by representatives of the Empire by having the dead body of a tortured man sewn up in a shroud. "I know somewhat too much [about the torture]; and from this knowledge, once one has been infected, there seems to be no recovering. I ought never to have taken my lantern to see what was going on in the hut by the granary" (21). His response, again like Lady Macbeth's, is to attempt to wash away his knowledge of the crime (and therefore his guilt) by ordering his men to "clean" everything up: "Soap and water! I want everything as it was before!" (24).
57 Moses, "Mark of empire," p. 122.
58 The magistrate does not celebrate "barbarian" ways even if he remains skeptical about "civilized" ones. He is critical of the native peoples' "intellectual torpor, slovenliness, [and] tolerance of disease and death." "If we were to disappear," he ironically asks, "would the barbarians spend their afternoons excavating our ruins?" (52). "Seduced utterly by the free and plentiful food, above all by the bread, they relax, smile at everyone, move about the barracks yard from one patch of shade to another, doze and wake, grow excited as mealtimes approach" (19). "Above all I do not want to see a parasite settlement grow up on the fringes of the town populated with beggars and vagrants enslaved to strong drink," confirming "thereby the settlers' litany of prejudice: that barbarians are lazy, immoral, filthy, stupid" (38).

59 J. M. Coetzee, *White Writing: On the Culture of Letters in South Africa* (New Haven: Yale University Press, 1988), p. 81.

60 W. J. B. Wood, *"Waiting for the Barbarians,"* p. 135.

61 Mikhail Bakhtin, *Problems in Dostoevsky's Poetics* (Minneapolis: University of Minnesota Press, 1984), p. 287.

62 Giles Gunn, *The Culture of Criticism and the Criticism of Culture* (New York: Oxford University Press, 1987), pp. 145–6.

63 M. M. Bakhtin, *Speech Genres and Other Late Essays* (Austin: University of Texas Press, 1986), p. 7.

64 Cited in Tzvetan Todorov, *Mikhail Bakhtin: The Dialogical Principle* (Minneapolis: University of Minnesota Press, 1984), p. 97.

65 For Bakhtin, in other words, meaning is "created in dialogue, on the borders where two consciousnesses meet . . . Truth, in other words, belongs to no one; it is realized, rather, in the realm of dialogue, where the linked utterances of the self and other interpenetrate, yielding a truth which is fluid, ephemeral, and evanescent. Not only does it not reside with *anyone*, but it is itself contextual, depending upon its temporal and spatial configuration, on the interlacing of the dialogic word of the self and other" (David K. Danow, *The Thought of Mikhail Bakhtin: From Word to Culture* [New York: St Martin's Press, 1991], pp. 64–5).

66 The magistrate is also concerned with his own "body that is slowly cooling and dying" (46), with his withering "erotic impulse": "with surprise I see myself clutched to this stolid girl, unable to remember what I ever desired in her, angry with myself for wanting and not wanting her . . . I have not entered her. From the beginning my desire has not taken on that direction, that directedness. Lodging my dry old man's member in that blood-hot sheath makes me think of acid in milk, ashes in honey, chalk in bread" (33–4).

67 Taken together, the Empire–barbarian and magistrate–girl relationships allow Coetzee to explore a series of dichotomies: male/female, civilization/savage, white/black, master/servant, good/evil, subject/object, sighted/blind, each of which is expressive of the Empire's sociopolitical hierarchy.

68 Eckstein, "The body," p. 192. Michael Valdez Moses puts it this way: "Although the magistrate regards his behavior as benevolent, paternal, and humane, his solicitous attention to the *Other* cannot be separated from the sinister apparatus of torture that the Empire employs ("Mark of empire," p. 121).

69 Eckstein links the magistrate's "pursuit of the girl's secrets" and his "sexual desire" ("The body,", p. 188).

70 This imperialism-as-rape trope is deployed throughout Coetzee's novel. For example, the magistrate uses the term "raped" to describe what the civilized have done to the barbarian lands (108); the barbarian girl admits to having had sex with soldiers in town, explaining, "I did not have a choice. That was how it had to be" (54).

71 Eckstein, "The body," p. 193.

72 Ashcroft et al., *Empire Writes Back*, p. 172.

73 W. J. B. Wood, *"Waiting for the Barbarians,"* p. 134.

74 Danow, *Thought of Mikhail Bakhtin*, p. 64.

75 Even the magistrate's sleep – which alternates between dreamless sleep that resembles "an oblivion, a nightly brush with annihilation" (21) and dreams that express his fears and desires and therefore serve to comment on his unfolding psychological saga – fails to offer him a respite from his failures of alterity. For more on this see the dream episodes in the novel.

76 Head, *J. M. Coetzee*, p. 75. If it is true, as James Phelan argues of the novel's end, that "we reach a complex judgment of the magistrate that combines resistance to his resumed complicity with an understanding of its inescapability," then we must be "wary of adopting any stance based on our moral superiority to others whom we might consider complicit in the perpetuation of racism, sexism, or other dehumanizing ideologies." Like the magistrate, we should examine our lives for "evidence" of our "complicity in the perpetuation of oppression and then do something about it . . . To do anything else is, in effect, to be complicit with complicity" (Phelan, "Present tense narration," p. 242).

77 Abdul R. JanMohamed, "The economy of Manichean allegory: the function of racial difference in colonialist literature," in *"Race," Writing, and Difference*, ed. Henry Louis Gates, Jr. (Chicago: University of Chicago Press, 1986), p. 92.

78 Ibid.

8 Margaret Atwood's *The Handmaid's Tale* (1985)

1 Margaret Atwood, *The Handmaid's Tale* [1986] (New York: Anchor Books, 1998), p. 143. Further references are noted parenthetically in the text.

2 It is probably no coincidence that 33 is also the age at which Jesus was crucified.

3 · Michael Foley quoted in David S. Hogsette, "Margaret Atwood's rhetorical epilogue in *The Handmaid's Tale*: the reader's role in empowering Offred's speech act," *Critique: Studies in Contemporary Fiction* 38 (1997), p. 273.

4 Karen Stein, "Margaret Atwood's modest proposal: *The Handmaid's Tale*," *Canadian Literature* 148 (1996), p. 59.

5 Erika Gottlieb, *Dystopian Fiction East and West: Universe of Terror and Trial* (Montreal and Kingston: McGill-Queen's University Press, 2001), p. 15.

6 Atwood quoted in Lucy M. Freibert, "Control and creativity: the politics of risk in Margaret Atwood's *The Handmaid's Tale*," in *Critical Essays on Margaret Atwood*, ed. Judith McCombs (Boston: G. K. Hall, 1988), p. 284.

7 Atwood quoted in J. Brooks Bouson, *Brutal Choreographies: Oppositional Strategies and Narrative Design in the Novels of Margaret Atwood* (Amherst: University of Massachusetts Press, 1993), p. 136.

8 Hogsette, "Margaret Atwood's rhetorical epilogue," p. 271. In Atwood's words, "A new regime would never say, 'we're socialist; we're fascist.' They would say that they were serving God" (Atwood quoted in Linda Kauffman, "Special delivery: twenty-first-century epistolarity in *The Handmaid's Tale*," in *Writing the Female*

Voice: Essays on Epistolary Literature, ed. Elizabeth C. Goldsmith (Boston: Northeastern University Press, 1989), p. 233.

9 Gottlieb, *Dystopian Fiction*, p. 12.

10 David Coad, "Hymens, lips and masks: the veil in Margaret Atwood's *The Handmaid's Tale*," *Literature and Psychology* 47 (2001), p. 54.

11 Amin Malak, "Margaret Atwood's 'The Handmaid's Tale' and the dystopian tradition," *Canadian Literature* 112 (1987), pp. 11–12.

12 Bouson, *Brutal Choreographies*, p. 138.

13 Quoted in Lois Feuer, "The calculus of love and nightmare: *The Handmaid's Tale* and the dystopian tradition," *Critique: Studies in Contemporary Fiction* 38 (1997), p. 83.

14 *Approaches to Teaching Atwood's "The Handmaid's Tale" and Other Works*, ed. Sharon R. Wilson, Thomas B. Friedman, and Shannon Hengen (New York: Modern Language Association, 1996), p. 7.

15 Glenn Deer, "Rhetorical strategies in *The Handmaid's Tale*: dystopia and the paradoxes of power," *English Studies in Canada* 18 (1992), p. 215.

16 Stein, "Margaret Atwood's modest proposal," p. 59.

17 These three epigraphs are highly relevant to the implications in Atwood's novel. The first, Genesis 30: 1–3, the account of Rachel offering Jacob her maid Bilhah, obviously "justifies" Gilead's mandating of Offred's monthly intercourse with her Commander, who is married to a woman who cannot conceive. The second epigraph, from Jonathan Swift's *A Modest Proposal*, calls attention to Atwood's satiric intent and addresses, like Atwood's novel, the question of population control. Yet while Swift is concerned with Irish *over*population, "the rulers of Gilead are obsessed with resolving their crisis of underpopulation . . . In each case, the measures taken to rectify the population are draconian" (Stein, "Margaret Atwood's modest proposal," p. 64). The third epigraph, the Sufi proverb, "In the desert there is no sign that says, Thou shalt not eat stones," challenges Gilead's gratuitous "social control" and implies "that on the most basic level of survival human beings instinctively know what to do and what to avoid; it suggests the corollary that authorities should avoid unnecessary regulation. Sufi simplicity counterpoints the outrageous legalism of Gilead's political structure and pleads for human freedom and survival" (Freibert, "Control and creativity," p. 285).

18 Arnold E. Davidson, "Future tense: making history in *The Handmaid's Tale*," in *Margaret Atwood: Vision and Form*, ed. Kathryn VanSpanckeren and Jan Garden Castro (Carbondale: Southern Illinois University Press, 1988), p. 120.

19 Bouson, *Brutal Choreographies*, p. 136.

20 Note, for example, Gilead's breeding practices and its reliance on computers, its "Compuchek" (21), "Compudoc" (59), "Compucount" (85), "Computalk" (137), "Compuphone" (167), and "Compubite" (26).

21 Jocelyn Harris, "*The Handmaid's Tale* as a re-visioning of *1984*," in *Transformations of Utopia: Changing Views of the Perfect Society*, ed. George Slusser et al. (New York: AMS Press, 1999), p. 268.

22 George Orwell, *Nineteen Eighty-Four* [1949] (New York: Plume Books, 1983), p. 5.

23 Ibid., pp. 246–56.

24 Ibid., p. 32.

25 Harris, "*The Handmaid's Tale*," p. 269.

26 Orwell, *Nineteen Eighty-Four*, p. 245.

27 Ruud Teeuwen, "Dystopia's point of no return: a team-taught utopia class," in Wilson et al., *Approaches to Teaching Atwood's "The Handmaid's Tale,"* p. 117.

28 Ibid.

29 Feuer, "Calculus of love and nightmare," p. 83.

30 For more on *The Handmaid's Tale* as satire and dystopia, see M. Keith Booker, *The Dystopian Impulse in Modern Literature* (Westport: Greenwood Press, 1994); Deer, "Rhetorical strategies"; Feuer, "Calculus of love and nightmare"; Gottlieb, *Dystopian Fiction*; Stephanie Barbe Hammer, "The World as it will be? Female satire and the technology of power in *The Handmaid's Tale*," *Modern Language Studies* 20 (1990); Harris, "*The Handmaid's Tale*"; Earl Ingersoll, "Margaret Atwood's 'The Handmaid's Tale': echoes of Orwell," *Journal of the Fantastic in the Arts* 5 (1993); Krishan Kumar, *Utopianism* (Minneapolis: University of Minnesota Press, 1991); Malak, "Margaret Atwood's 'The Handmaid's Tale'"; and Teeuwen, "Dystopia's point of no return."

31 Hammer, "The World," p. 46.

32 One other social dystopia is referenced directly in *The Handmaid's Tale*: Charles Dickens's *Hard Times*, a novel about the commodification and dehumanization of people in mid-nineteenth-century industrial England, which, like all novels, has become "illicit reading" material in Gilead (184). This novel of bodily exploitation sheds light, however obliquely, on Atwood's narrative. In its concern with bodily torture and the female Other, *The Handmaid's Tale* also alludes to Coetzee's *Waiting for the Barbarians*, published six years earlier. For example, the tortured feet of Offred's friend Moira, like the feet of Coetzee's "barbarian" woman, did not "look like feet at all. They looked like drowned feet, swollen and boneless, except for the color. They looked like lungs" (91). Offred's stark descriptions of her body remind one of those of Coetzee's magistrate: "I am dry and white, hard, granular; it's like running my hand over a plateful of dried rice; it's like snow. There's something dead about it, something deserted" (104). Like the magistrate studying an earlier and foreign culture, Offred considers the society of her childhood as something of a foreign land: "These habits of former times appear to me now lavish, decadent almost; immoral, like the orgies of barbarian regimes. *M. loves G. 1972.* This carving, done with a pencil dug many times into the worn varnish of the desk, has the pathos of all vanished civilizations" (113). Finally, a reference in Atwood's novel to "a road that turns out to lead nowhere" (204) echoes Coetzee's closing line, in which the magistrate envisions "a road that may lead nowhere."

33 Deer, "Rhetorical strategies," p. 215.

34 Freibert, "Control and creativity," pp. 283–4.

35 Ibid., p. 282.
36 Kauffman, "Special delivery," p. 232.
37 According to the author, the Wall in *The Handmaid's Tale* "is the wall around Harvard yard" (Atwood quoted in Sandra Tomc, "'The missionary position': feminism and nationalism in Margaret Atwood's *The Handmaid's Tale*," *Canadian Literature* 138–9 (1993), p. 79.
38 Kauffman, "Special delivery," pp. 233–4.
39 Kauffman adds, "This emphasis on the collusion of women with their oppressors is significant; one of the regime's strokes of genius is their discovery that the least expensive way to enforce its policies is by using women against each other" ("Special delivery," p. 234).
40 Ibid., p. 236.
41 Offred's separation from her family and adoption by the Commander are explained in the novel's historical epilogue: "The [Gilead] regime created an instant pool of [Handmaids] by the simple tactic of declaring all second marriages and nonmarital liaisons adulterous, arresting the female partners, and, on the grounds that they were morally unfit, confiscating the children they already had, who were adopted by childless couples of the upper echelons who were eager for progeny by any means . . . Men highly placed in the regime were thus able to pick and choose among women who had demonstrated their reproductive fitness by having produced one or more healthy children (304).
42 Hilde Staels, "Margaret Atwood's *The Handmaid's Tale*: resistance through narrating," *English Studies* 78 (1995), p. 455.
43 Kauffman, "Special delivery," p. 237.
44 Ibid.
45 Orwell, *Nineteen Eighty-Four*, p. 105.
46 Celia Floren, "A reading of Margaret Atwood's dystopia, *The Handmaid's Tale*," in *Postmodern Studies 16: Gender, I-deology: Essays on Theory, Fiction, and Film*, ed. Chantal Cornut-Gentille D'Arcy and Jose Angel Garcia Landa (Amsterdam: Rodopi, 1996), pp. 254–5.
47 Hogsette, "Margaret Atwood's rhetorical epilogue," pp. 265, 263.
48 Margaret Atwood, *Negotiating with the Dead: A Writer on Writing* (Cambridge: Cambridge University Press, 2002).
49 For more on this see Earl G. Ingersoll, "Margaret Atwood's *The Handmaid's Tale* as a self-subverting text," in *Cultural Identities in Canadian Literature*, ed. Benedicte Mauguiere (New York: Peter Lang, 1998), pp. 103–4.
50 Ingersoll, "Self-subverting text," p. 104. And Kauffman remarks that "Postmodernism" is indelibly stamped on Atwood's text ("Special delivery," p. 222).
51 Kauffman believes that Atwood's text "articulates the problems of transmission and reception" ("Special delivery," p. 223).
52 Ibid., p. 240.
53 Floren, "A reading," p. 253.
54 Hogsette, "Margaret Atwood's rhetorical epilogue," p. 265.
55 Davidson, "Future tense," p. 114.

56 Ibid., p. 120.

57 Debrah Raschke, "Margaret Atwood's *The Handmaid's Tale*: false borders and subtle subversions," *Literature, Interpretation, Theory* 6 (1995), p. 257. Staels makes a similar point to Raschke: "The desire of the scholars for univocal, transparent meaning ironically mirrors the authoritative word of Gilead" ("Resistance through narrating," p. 465).

58 Deer, "Rhetorical strategies," pp. 226–7.

59 Kauffman, "Special delivery," p. 240.

60 Malak, "Margaret Atwood's 'The Handmaid's Tale'," p. 15.

61 Hogsette, "Margaret Atwood's rhetorical epilogue," p. 263.

62 Feuer, "Calculus of love and nightmare," p. 91.

63 Freibert, "Control and creativity," p. 281.

64 Stein, "Margaret Atwood's modest proposal," p. 59. Offred senses the power of written expression that is forbidden to women but available to men when she is given a pen by the Commander during one of their illicit meetings in his office and reports: "The pen between my fingers is sensuous, alive almost, I can feel its power, the power of the words it contains. Pen Is Envy," she then puns (186).

65 Stein, "Margaret Atwood's modest proposal," p. 62.

9 Kazuo Ishiguro's *The Remains of the Day* (1989)

1   Kazuo Ishiguro, *The Remains of the Day* [1989] (New York: Vintage, 1993), pp. 42–3. Further references are noted parenthetically in the text.

2   Sigmund Freud, *Five Lectures on Psychoanalysis* (New York: W. W. Norton, 1961), p. 43.

3   Mark Kamine, "A servant of self-deceit," *The New Leader*, November 13, 1989, p. 22.

4   Salman Rushdie, "What the butler didn't see," *The Observer*, May 21, 1989, p. 53.

5   Graham Swift, "Kazuo Ishiguro," *Bomb*, Fall 1989, p. 23.

6   For more on the context for *The Remains of the Day*, see Brian W. Shaffer, *Understanding Kazuo Ishiguro* (Columbia: University of South Carolina Press, 1998), and Brian W. Shaffer, "An interview with Kazuo Ishiguro," *Contemporary Literature* 42 (2001).

7   Allan Vorda and Kim Herzinger, "An interview with Kazuo Ishiguro," *Mississippi Review* 20 (1991), p. 139.

8   Dylan Otto Krider, "Rooted in a small space: an interview with Kazuo Ishiguro," *Kenyon Review* 20 (1998), pp. 149–50.

9   Vorda and Herzinger, "An interview," p. 142.

10 Gregory Mason, "An interview with Kazuo Ishiguro," *Contemporary Literature* 30 (1989), p. 347.

11 Swift, "Kazuo Ishiguro," p. 23.

12 John Kucich, *Repression in Victorian Literature: Charlotte Brontë, George Eliot, and Charles Dickens* (Berkeley: University of California Press, 1987), p. 2.

13 Freud, *Five Lectures*, p. 43.

14 Kathleen Wall astutely observes that nothing can "tear the fabric" that Stevens "has erected between his private and his professional selves" and that "Threatening moments . . . are shrouded by Stevens in layers of more comfortable memory" (Kathleen Wall, "*The Remains of the Day* and its challenges to theories of unreliable narration," *Journal of Narrative Technique* 24 [1994], pp. 28–9).

15 Marshall Berman, *All That is Solid Melts into Air* (New York: Simon and Schuster, 1982), p. 106. I am indebted to Caroline Patey, "When Ishiguro visits the West Country," *Acme* 44 (1991), p. 151, for making the Ishiguro–Berman connection.

16 Quoted in Berman, *All That is Solid*, pp. 108–9.

17 Frank E. Huggett, *Life Below Stairs: Domestic Servants in England from Victorian Times* (New York: Charles Scribner's Sons, 1977), p. 35.

18 Huggett, *Life Below Stairs*, p. 46.

19 Rushdie, "What the butler didn't see," p. 53.

20 Ihab Hassan, "An extravagant reticence," *The World and I* 5/2 (February 1990), p. 374.

21 Kucich, *Repression*, p. 1.

22 Freud, *Five Lectures*, pp. 21–2.

23 Ibid., p. 22.

24 Sigmund Freud, "Repression," in vol. 14, *The Standard Edition of the Complete Psychological Works of Sigmund Freud* (London: Hogarth Press and the Institute of Psychoanalysis, 1957), p. 147.

25 Galen Strawson calls *Remains* a "finely nuanced and at times humorous study of repression" ("Tragically disciplined and dignified," *Times Literary Supplement*, May 19–25, 1989, p. 535).

26 Compare this statement with Freud's claim that the "motive and purpose of repression" is "nothing else than the avoidance of unpleasure," in "Repression," p. 153.

27 Kazuo Ishiguro, "Getting poisoned," in *Introduction 7: Stories by New Writers* (London: Faber and Faber, 1981), p. 51.

28 Patey, "When Ishiguro visits the West Country," p. 150.

29 In a rare honest moment, Stevens responds to the question, "Have you had much to do with politics yourself," by answering, "Not directly as such" (187).

30 David Gurewich, "Upstairs, downstairs," *The New Criterion*, December 1989, p. 78.

31 Vorda and Herzinger, "An interview," p. 153.

32 Cynthia F. Wong, "The shame of memory: Blanchot's self-dispossession in Ishiguro's *A Pale View of Hills*," *CLIO* 24 (1995), p. 130.

33 Hassan, "Extravagant reticence," p. 370.

34 Kamine, "Servant of self-deceit," p. 22.

35 Kathleen Wall is correct to argue that "Stevens has attempted to avoid, in his life as well as in his narrative, the voices and needs of the feeling self" ("Theories of unreliable narration," p. 26).

36 Kathleen Wall puts it well: "Stevens has truncated his life to fit a professional mold"; the word "professional," which arises in inappropriate contexts, "becomes

either a disguise for other, more emotional motives or a defense for his strangely unemotional behavior" (ibid., pp. 23–4).

37 Swift, "Kazuo Ishiguro," p. 22.

38 Gurewich, "Upstairs, downstairs," p. 78.

39 Lord Darlington may be the namesake of the character in Oscar Wilde's *Lady Windermere's Fan*.

Interestingly, the servant-class inhabitants of Ishiguro's novel, Smith, Kenton, Benn, and Stevens have common-sounding names, while the aristocrats, Cardinal and Darlington, have more elaborate and elegant ones. In any case, Darlington should not be viewed as aligned with Hitler so much as seduced by him. What George Orwell argues of Chamberlain applies equally well to Stevens's employer: "His opponents professed to see in him a dark and wily schemer, plotting to sell England to Hitler, but it is far likelier that he was merely a stupid old man doing his best according to his very dim lights" (*A Collection of Essays* [San Diego: Harcourt Brace Jovanovich, 1954], p. 265).

40 Joseph Conrad, *The Collected Letters of Joseph Conrad*, vol. 2, ed. Frederick R. Karl and Laurence Davies (Cambridge: Cambridge University Press, 1986), p. 108.

41 Vorda and Herzinger, "An interview," pp. 135–6.

42 Swift, "Kazuo Ishiguro," p. 23.

43 Patey, "When Ishiguro vists the West Country," p. 147.

44 Wall, "Theories of unreliable narration," p. 24.

45 And in those few moments when Stevens actually addresses his own feelings, he substitutes a vague adjective for a precise one in order to avoid revealing himself. For example, he claims to be "tired" (105, 220, 242–3) when he really means "sad," "disappointed," or "defeated."

46 As an example of the first instance: "one should not be looking back to the past so much . . . It is essential . . . to keep one's attention focused on the present; to guard against any complacency creeping in on account of what one may have achieved in the past" (139). As an example of the second instance: "But I see I have become somewhat lost in these old memories. This had never been my intention, but then it is probably no bad thing if in doing so I have at least avoided becoming unduly preoccupied with the events of this evening" (159).

47 Perhaps for this reason Hassan calls the novel a "mental journey, a grudging access to Stevens' past" ("Extravagant reticence," p. 373).

48 Gurewich, "Upstairs, downstairs," p. 80.

49 Vorda and Herzinger, "An interview," p. 142.

50 Hassan, "Extravagant reticence," p. 374.

51 Meera Tamaya, "Ishiguro's *Remains of the Day*: the Empire strikes back," *Modern Language Studies* 22 (1992), p. 54.

52 He notes a "sharp decline in professional standards" of late (7); observes that the staff at Darlington Hall has dwindled from 28 to four persons over the years; and points out that when he takes his excursion "Darlington Hall would probably stand empty for the first time this century" (23).

53   Stevens notes that Darlington Hall has been purchased by Americans after "two centuries" in "the hands of the Darlington family" (6); observes that Americans are "the only ones that can afford" grand old English homes (242); and takes his excursion in Farraday's American Ford.
54   Gurewich, "Upstairs, downstairs," pp. 78–9.
55   Hassan, "Extravagant reticence," pp. 372–3.
56   Vorda and Herzinger, "An interview," pp. 139–40.

10 Patrick McCabe's *The Butcher Boy* (1992)

1   Jonathan Swift, "A modest proposal" [1729], in *The Writings of Jonathan Swift*, ed. Robert A. Greenberg and William B. Piper (New York: W. W. Norton, 1973), p. 505.
2   James Joyce, *A Portrait of the Artist as a Young Man* [1916] (New York: Penguin Books, 1956), p. 203.
3   Patrick McCabe, *The Butcher Boy* (New York: Delta Books, 1992), p. 20. Further references are noted parenthetically in the text.
4   Donna Potts, "From Tir na nOg to Tir na Muck: Patrick McCabe's *The Butcher Boy*," *New Hibernia Review/Iris Eireannach Nua: A Quarterly Record of Irish Studies* 3 (1999), p. 93.
5   Ibid., p. 95.
6   "I wrote *The Butcher Boy* in about a month and a half and then thought absolutely nobody would read it," McCabe reports. "I thought, 'Here's a book written in a ska kind of style, in run-on dialogue, in a small inland town – who the hell's going to read this?' And it still amazes me [that] that book took off..." (Christopher FitzSimon [Patrick McCabe interviewed], "St Macartan, Minnie the Minx and Mondo Movies: elliptical peregrinations through the subconscious of a Monaghan writer traumatized by cows and the brilliance of James Joyce," *Irish University Review* 28 [1998], p. 181).
7   I am indebted to Anna Teekell for this observation and for her insightful comments on this chapter generally.
8   McCabe has commented that he "used to pass an abattoir every day" on the way to school; "So you encounter brutality at a very early age, anybody growing up in a small town does. I particularly did because the abattoir was beside the house" (FitzSimon, "Peregrinations," p. 184).
9   Ibid., p. 177.
10   Ibid., p. 188.
11   Ibid., p. 185.
12   To identify merely a few of *The Butcher Boy*'s myriad allusions to *Dubliners*: Francie notes, during his excursion to Dublin, the Gresham Hotel (41) and the statue of Daniel O'Connell (40), both of which figure prominently in Joyce's "The dead." Another time Francie "sat at the window. The lane outside was deserted. There was no sign of the children . . ." (53), in a scene that recalls Joyce's Eveline

at the beginning of her eponymous story. Elsewhere, Father Sullivan, a homo-
sexual pederast who sexually abuses Francie and who is said to be looked after by
his sister (101), recalls Father Flynn in Joyce's "The sisters." And Francie's Indian
cry uttered when playing with his friend Joe, "Yamma yamma yamma! Yama
yamma yamma!" (201), recalls Joe Dillon's American Wild West-inspired war
games and Indian "war dance of victory" yell, "Ya! Yaka, yaka, yaka!," in Joyce's
"An encounter." See Alan Forrest Hickman, "Growing up Irish: an update on
Stephen Dedalus," *Publications of the Arkansas Philological Association* 22 (1996),
pp. 9–18, for a treatment of *The Butcher Boy* as a latter-day *A Portrait of the Artist
as a Young Man.*

13 FitzSimon, "Peregrinations," p. 177.
14 Ibid., pp. 182–3.
15 Ibid., p. 186.
16 John Scaggs, "Who is Francie Pig? Self-identity and narrative reliability in *The
Butcher Boy*," *Irish University Review: A Journal of Irish Studies* 30 (2000), p. 51.
17 Wayne Booth, *The Rhetoric of Fiction*, 2nd edn. (Chicago: University of Chicago
Press, 1983), pp. 158–9.
18 Tom Herron, "ContamiNation: Patrick McCabe and Colm Tóibín's pathographies
of the Republic," in *Contemporary Irish Fiction: Themes, Tropes, Theories*, ed.
Liam Harte and Michael Parker (New York: St Martin's Press, 2000), p. 169.
19 David Goldknopf, *The Life of the Novel* (Chicago: University of Chicago Press,
1972), p. 41.
20 "Repression" is understood in the Freudian sense as "forgotten material" that
originates in a "wishful impulse" that is "in sharp contrast to the subject's other
wishes" and that proves "incompatible with the ethical and aesthetic standards of
his personality." See Sigmund Freud, *Five Lectures on Psycho-Analysis* (New York:
W. W. Norton, 1977), p. 22.
21 Potts, "From Tir na nOg," p. 83.
22 Martin McLoone, "The abused child of history: Neil Jordan's *The Butcher Boy*,"
Cineaste 23 (1998), p. 33.
23 FitzSimon, "Peregrinations," p. 181.
24 De Valera, quoted in Herron, "ContamiNation," p. 175. In 1962, during the
novel's main action, De Valera is President of the Irish Republic.
25 Herron, "ContamiNation," p. 177.
26 Ibid., p. 176.
27 Francie paints a similar portrait of Mary, a neighbor of the Bradys who is in love
with Benny's married brother Alo. She has "the same face as ma used to have
sitting staring into the ashes it was funny that face it slowly grew over the other
one until one day you looked and the person you knew was gone" (212).
28 Francie's imagined relationship with the Blessed Virgin Mary can be understood
as his attempt to regain his lost mother. Another failed mother figure for Francie
is Queen Victoria, for whom a fountain in the town's Diamond was built (in
honor of her Jubilee). Victoria apparently failed attend the fountain's inaugura-
tion, leading Francie to ask, "where the fuck is she?" (110). This anecdote adds a

colonial dimension to the novel's neglectful mother motif, with the Empire (and the Church) neglecting Ireland just as Annie Brady neglects Francie.

29 The Tower Bar also recalls W. B. Yeats's *The Tower*, with its impotence-related imagery. In this volume of poems Yeats employs the tower as a crumbling, failed phallic symbol for the poet as well as for Ireland, which is of relevance for Francie's father, who seeks solace from his musical and personal "impotence." Thanks to Anna Teekell for making this connection.

30 Potts, "From Tir na nOg," p. 85.

31 As Tim Gauthier writes, in the Ireland of this time "There is no sense of the possibility of upward mobility within the community; such prestige can only be derived by realigning oneself with the colonizing power" (Tim Gauthier, "Identity, self-loathing and the neocolonial condition in Patrick McCabe's *The Butcher Boy*," *Critique* 44 [2003], p. 203).

32 FitzSimon, "Peregrinations," p. 178.

33 Ibid., pp. 178–9.

34 James M. Smith, "Remembering Ireland's architecture of containment: 'telling' stories in *The Butcher Boy* and *States of Fear*," *Eire-Ireland: A Journal of Irish Studies* 36 (2001), p. 126.

35 William Faulkner, "A rose for Emily," in *Collected Stories* (New York: Vintage Books, 1977), p. 124.

36 Smith, "Remembering Ireland's architecture," p. 126.

37 Ibid.

38 Ibid., p. 127.

39 Ibid., p. 125.

40 Ibid., p. 128.

41 Herron, "ContamiNation," p. 177.

42 Ibid., p. 175.

43 Smith, "Remembering Ireland's architecture," p. 127.

44 Herron, "ContamiNation," p. 177.

45 Elizabeth Butler Cullingford, "Virgins and mothers: Sinead O'Connor, Neil Jordan, and *The Butcher Boy*," *Yale Journal of Criticism* 15 (2002), p. 201.

46 Smith, "Remembering Ireland's architecture," p. 126.

47 McLoone, "Abused child," p. 36.

48 Smith, "Remembering Ireland's architecture," p. 127.

49 Ibid.

50 Herron, "ContamiNation," p. 174.

51 Ibid. Tim Gauthier takes the novel's neocolonial context further by arguing that "Francie's ambivalent relationship with the community, his search for identity, his lack of a sense of history combined with an idealization of the past, his fascination with the life led by the Nugents as adopters and representatives of dominant culture values, and finally his own self-loathing all mirror the country's neocolonial condition" ("Identity, self-loathing," p. 196).

52 Ibid.

53 Potts, "From Tir na nOg," p. 84.

54 Interestingly, for all of his savagery, Francie responds strongly to the pain and despair of others, as expressed in the sympathetic reaction he has to the "tears" and "sad eyes" of others. He also sympathizes with non-human objects around him, from the houses in derelict Bundoran, which "were grey and blue and wet and in a sulk for the winter. Boo hoo nobody comes to stay in us any more" (185), to "the sniffer dogs woof woof" (220), to the "river hiss hiss" (221), to the pictures on the wall: "What about us said the pictures on the walls" (221–2). The novel even ends with "the tears streaming down" Francie's face (231).

55 Zadie Smith, *White Teeth* (New York: Vintage Books, 2000), p. 177.

56 Herron, "ContamiNation," p. 174.

57 Cullingford, "Virgins and mothers," p. 206.

58 Swift, "Modest proposal," p. 502.

59 Ibid., pp. 503–4.

60 Ibid., p. 506.

61 Ibid., p. 505.

62 Potts, "From Tir na nOg," p. 86.

63 Ibid.

64 Ibid., p. 87.

65 Cullingford, "Virgins and mothers," p. 199.

66 Potts, "From Tir na nOg," p. 86.

67 This also echoes the town's disappointed anticipation of a visit by Queen Victoria, for her Diamond Jubilee, in 1897.

68 McLoone, "Abused child," p. 128.

69 As Elizabeth Butler Cullingford puts it, instead of encountering "the Mother of God" the townspeople encounter "the blood of a murdered mother" (p. 205).

11 Graham Swift's *Last Orders* (1996)

1 T. S. Eliot, *The Complete Poems and Plays, 1909–1950* (New York: Harcourt, Brace & World, 1952), p. 46.

2 Graham Swift, *Last Orders* (New York: Vintage Books, 1996), pp. 193–4. Further references are noted parenthetically in the text.

3 Bettina Gossmann, Roman Haak, Melanie Romberg, and Saskia Spindler, "Graham Swift in interview on *Last Orders*," *Anglistik: Mitteilungen des Verbandes deutscher Anglisten* 8 (1997), p. 160.

4 John Banville, "That's life" (Review of *Last Orders*), *New York Review of Books*, April 4, 1996, p. 8.

5 http://archive.salon.com/weekly/swift960506.html, p. 2. This website is henceforth referred to as "Salon."

6 Gossmann et al., "Graham Swift in interview," pp. 157–8.

7 David Leon Higdon, "Double closures in postmodern British fiction: the example of Graham Swift," *Critical Survey* 3 (1991), p. 90.

8 Ibid.

9 Peter Widdowson, "The novels of Graham Swift," *Literature in Context*, ed. Rick Rylance (Basingstoke: Palgrave, 2001), p. 214.

10 Gossmann et al., "Graham Swift in interview," p. 155.

11 Adrian Poole, "Graham Swift and the mourning after," *An Introduction to Contemporary Fiction*, ed. Rod Mengham (Cambridge: Polity Press, 1999), p. 153.

12 Salon, p. 3.

13 Banville, "That's life," p. 9.

14 Ibid., p. 8.

15 Salon, p. 4.

16 Pamela Cooper, *Graham Swift's "Last Orders": A Reader's Guide* (New York: Continuum, 2002), p. 37.

17 Widdowson, "Novels of Graham Swift," p. 218.

18 Emma Parker, "No man's land: masculinity and Englishness in Graham Swift's *Last Orders*," *Posting the Male: Masculinities in Post-War and Contemporary British Literature*, ed. Daniel Lea and Berthold Schoene (Amsterdam: Rodopi, 2003), p. 99.

19 Cooper, *Graham Swift's "Last Orders"*, p. 19. Indeed, in both novels England is reduced to the status of a museum for tourists and for its own citizens. In Ishiguro's novel Darlington Hall, after World War II, is purchased by an American; in Swift's novel Rochester's High Street "looks like a high street in a picture book" (108) and the English characters are portrayed as consumers of a burgeoning English heritage industry. As Vic puts it of Vince, who clutches his *Wonders of Canterbury Cathedral* guidebook while touring Canterbury Cathedral, "He stands, flicking through, as if he doesn't want to look at the cathedral, just the guidebook, giving us snippets, as if we can't make a move till we've had the lecture" (196).

20 Salon, p. 4.

21 *Independent on Sunday*, March 9, 1997.

22 David Malcolm, *Understanding Graham Swift* (Columbia: University of South Carolina Press, 2003), p. 158.

23 Catherine Bernard, "An interview with Graham Swift," *Contemporary Literature* 38 (1997), pp. 230–1.

24 Cooper, *Graham Swift's "Last Orders"*, p. 24.

25 Parker, "No man's land," p. 90.

26 Cooper, *Graham Swift's "Last Orders"*, p. 39.

27 Gossmann et al., "Graham Swift in interview," p. 156.

28 Ibid., pp. 155–6.

29 Poole, "Graham Swift and the mourning after," p. 163.

30 Stef Craps, "'All the same underneath'? Alterity and ethics in Graham Swift's *Last Orders*," *Critique* 44 (2003), p. 413.

31 For more on this see Wendy Wheeler, "Graham Swift," in *Postmodernism: The Key Figures*, ed. Hans Bertens and Joseph Natoli (Oxford: Blackwell Publishing, 2002).

32 Parker, "No man's land," p. 103.

33 Higdon, "Double closures," p. 90.

34 Cooper, *Graham Swift's "Last Orders"*, p. 18.

Index

Barnes, Julian: *Flaubert's Parrot*, 5, 7
Barth, John, 5, 33, 123
Baudrillard, Jean, 7–8; *Simulacra and Simulation*, 8
Bauman, Zygmunt: *Modernity and the Holocaust*, 12
beast (within), the, 62, 65–6, 70–1
Beauvoir, Simone de, 122
Beckett, Samuel, 6, 40, 122, 123, 127, 240 n. 38; *Waiting for Godot*, 128
Behan, Brendan: *Borstal Boy*, 18
Behr, Mark, 11, 24–5
Bellow, Saul, 123
Berman, Marshall, 162
Bertens, Hans, 7
Best, Steven, 8–9
Beveridge Report (Great Britain), 38, 218 n. 18
Biafran revolt (Nigeria), 74
Bible, the, 139, 147; Genesis, 79, 139, 142, 224 n. 51, 244 n. 17; Revelation (Apocalypse), 224 n. 47
"black British" literature, 15, 17–18, 27–31
blindness: metaphor in *Lord of the Flies*, 64
Bloomsbury, 40, 41; *see also* Woolf, Virginia
Bold, Alan, 90, 94
Bolger, Dermot, 18
Booker, M. Keith, 113
Booker Prize, 19, 20, 21, 25, 215 n. 65
Booth, Wayne, 178
Borges, Jorge Luis, 123
Bower, Anne L., 100
Bradbury, Malcolm, 36, 158; on Amis (K.) and *Lucky Jim*, 35, 41, 49, 221 n. 78; on the "Angry Young Men," 38; on antimodernism, 4, 40; on Golding and *Lord of the Flies*, 55, 56, 57–8, 59; on postmodernism, 7; on Pound, 2; on World War II, 10
Braine, John, 5, 40; *Room at the Top*, 38
Brannigan, John, ix

British Empire, demise of, 15–17, 174; *see also* "black British" literature; postcolonialism
Brodie, Deacon William, 94
Brontë, Charlotte, 158, 236 n. 42–3; *Jane Eyre*, 23, 105–6, 108, 109–13, 117–18, 143, 233 n. 62, 234 n. 7, 237 n. 44
Brontë, Emily, 87, 89; *Wuthering Heights*, 196–7
Brookner, Anita, 4
Brown, George Mackay: *Beside the Ocean of Time*, 20
Browne, Sir Thomas, 200
bureaucracy: and dehumanization, 12, 239 n. 32
Burgess, Anthony: *A Clockwork Orange*, 14
Butcher Boy, The (McCabe), 7, 175–94, 250 n. 6; characterization, 181–3, 185, 188–9, 190–1; *Dubliners* (Joyce) allusions, 250–1 n. 12; film version, 175; language, 177; narrative voice, 178; plot, 181–5, 186–94
Byatt, A. S., 1, 5; *Possession*, 7, 9

caged animals/birds: metaphors for kept women, 116, 149
Calvinism: in *The Prime of Miss Jean Brodie*, 97–9, 100, 233 n. 51
Canada, 20; *see also* Atwood, Margaret; *Handmaid's Tale, The*
cannibalism: trope, 202
Carey, John, 10
Carey, Peter, 20, 21
Caribbean: Brontë (C.) and, 106, 236 n. 42; history, 16, 108–9; novelists, 26–7; *see also* "black British" literature; Creoles; Rhys, Jean; *Wide Sargasso Sea*
Carroll, David, 227 n. 12
Carter, Angela, 5, 7
Cary, Joyce: *Mr Johnson*, 22, 72
Catholic Church, 186–7